# Themes in Economics

## Theory, Empirics, and Policy

The main objective of the series is to publish volumes dealing with topics in economic theory and empirics with important policy implications. The series aims to publish monographs, both theoretical and empirical, on topics of contemporary interest. While topics that are important from a policy perspective are preferable, volumes in this series are one of the following types: (i) Research dealing with important economic theory topics; (ii) Rigourous empirical work on issues of contemporary importance; and (iii) Edited volumes of selected papers, either of individual authors, or those presented in Economic Theory and Policy conferences which will be conducted annually.

Some of the topics that explored in this series are: poverty, income inequality, eminent domain (land acquisition in particular), some theoretical aspects of the functioning of the market mechanism, economic and social implications of affirmative action.

More information about this series at http://www.springer.com/series/15590

Satya R. Chakravarty
Editor

# Poverty, Social Exclusion and Stochastic Dominance

Springer

*Editor*
Satya R. Chakravarty
Economic Research Unit
Indian Statistical Institute
Kolkata, India

Themes in Economics
ISBN 978-981-13-3431-3 ISBN 978-981-13-3432-0 (eBook)
https://doi.org/10.1007/978-981-13-3432-0



This Springer imprint is published by the registered company Springer Nature Singapore Pte Ltd.
The registered company address is: 152 Beach Road, #21-01/04 Gateway East, Singapore 189721, Singapore

# Contents

# About the Editor

**Satya R. Chakravarty** is Professor of Economics at the Indian Statistical Institute, Kolkata, India. He has served as Visiting Professor at the University of British Columbia, Vancouver, Canada; University of Karlsruhe, Germany; Paris School of Economics, Paris, France; Bocconi University, Milan, Italy; Yokohama National University, Yokohama, Japan; Kagawa University, Takamatsu, Japan; Bar-Ilan University, Israel, Chinese University of Hong Kong and University of International Business and Economics, Beijing, China. His areas of research interest are welfare issues, cooperative game theory, industrial organization, and mathematical finance. His research works have been published in leading theoretical and applied journals such as *Journal of Economic Theory*, *Games and Economic Behavior*, *Econometrica*, *Economic Theory*, *Journal of Development Economics*, *Social Choice and Welfare*, *International Economic Review*, *Canadian Journal of Economics*, *Mathematical Social Sciences*, *Theory and Decision*, *Economics Letters*, *European Journal of Operational Research*, *Journal of Economic Inequality*, *Health Economics*, and *Review of Income and Wealth*. He has published books with several leading publishers in varied areas encompassing welfare issues, game theory, industrial organization, mathematical finance and microeconomics. He currently serves on editorial boards of *Social Choice and Welfare, Journal of Economic Inequality and Review of Income and Wealth*. He worked as a consultant to the Asian Development Bank; as an advisor to the National Council of Social Policy Evaluation, Mexico; and has been associated in various capacities with the World Bank, the UN Environment Program and the UNDP. He was awarded the Mahalanobis memorial prize by the Indian Econometric Society in 1994 and is a fellow of the Human Development and Capability Association.

# About the Editor

# Introduction

**Satya R. Chakravarty**

Tony Atkinson has been and forever will remain an eminent figure in the field of economics. He had devoted his entire life to rigorous study of income inequality, poverty, and redistribution, with major contributions in every possible dimension like models, data, policies, etc. Every single work of his is marked with unparalleled clarity and depth leaving an impression on economists from around the globe. This collection of 13 articles has been influenced heavily by some of Atkinson's innovative ideas directly or indirectly.

The first essay, published in the Canadian Journal of Economics, 1983, considers general ethically flexible relative and absolute indicators of poverty. The framework we consider is axiomatic, which relies on Sen (1976). The relative index is a reasonably natural change-over of the Atkinson (1970)-Kolm (1969)-Sen (1973) relative inequality index of a censored income distribution, a distribution obtained by replacing all incomes above the poverty threshold limit by the threshold limit itself, into a relative poverty index. The poverty threshold limit or poverty line represents an income level necessary to maintain a subsistence standard of living. The Atkinson–Kolm–Sen index is the relative shortfall of the equally distributed equivalent or representative income of the society from its mean income. The representative income associated with a distribution of income is that level of income which, if enjoyed by everybody, makes the existing distribution socially welfare indifferent. It is a relative index in the sense that it remains invariant under equi-proportionate changes in all incomes. From policy perspective, it determines the fraction of total income that could be saved if society distributed incomes equally without any welfare loss. It also indicates size of proportionate welfare loss resulting from presence of inequality. Analogously, the relative poverty index, which remains unaltered under equi-proportionate variations in all incomes and the threshold limit, gives the magnitude of similar welfare loss because of existence of poverty. Pyatt (1987) studied this relative ethical poverty aggregator using the notion of affluence and basic incomes

S. R. Chakravarty (✉)
Indian Statistical Institute, Kolkata 700108, India
e-mail: satyarchakravarty@gmail.com



S. R. Chakravarty (ed.), *Poverty, Social Exclusion and Stochastic Dominance*, Themes in Economics, https://doi.org/10.1007/978-981-13-3432-0_1

and examined the implications when the population representative income is the sum of representative income of affluence and the representative basic income.

The absolute poverty index proposed in the essay turns out to be a fairly natural conversion of the Blackorby–Donaldson (1980a) absolute inequality index, when applied to a censored income profile, into an absolute poverty index. While an absolute inequality index is insensitive to an equal absolute addition to all incomes, its poverty sister fulfils this insensitivity property when along with incomes we also translate the threshold limit by the same absolute amount. From policy point of view the absolute poverty index ascertains the per capita cost of poverty. If in a censored income distribution each individual were given the amount of money, as measured by the value of the poverty index, then the index would be zero.

The ethical approach we adopt in the next essay of the collection, published in Econometrica, has a similarity with the Blackorby-Donaldson (1980b) proposal. Blackorby and Donaldson (1980b) showed that if social evaluation is done with respect to the Gini welfare function of the poor, then their general ethical relative poverty index, defined on the income distributions of the poor, coincides with the Sen (1976) index of poverty. Unfortunately, as shown in the first essay, the Blackorby–Donaldson (and hence the Sen) indices violate continuity and the transfer axiom, a postulate that requires poverty to increase from a poor person to any one richer, in a specific situation. Shorrocks (1995) suggested a modification of the Sen index that avoids this shortcoming. It is rigorously demonstrated in the second essay that this modification coincides with the general functional form for relative indices proposed in Essay 1, if social evaluation is done with respect to the Gini social welfare function defined on the censored income distributions.

The third essay, published in Mathematical Social Sciences, characterizes a subgroup decomposable index of poverty, using the symmetric utilitarian social welfare function. The symmetric utilitarian social welfare function is given by the sum of identical individual utility functions. In his pioneering contribution, Atkinson (1970) made use of this form of welfare function for characterizing his inequality index. He has also demonstrated that of two income distributions of a given total if one has higher welfare value than the other for the symmetric utilitarian form welfare function where the utility function is strictly concave, then the Lorenz curve of the former lies nowhere below that of the latter and strictly inside at some places. The converse is true as well. These two statements are equivalent to the condition that the former can be obtained from the latter by a sequence of rank-preserving transfers transferring incomes from persons with high incomes to persons with lower incomes. These results have been generalized substantially from different perspectives, among others, by Dasgupta et al. (1973) and Rothschild and Stiglitz (1970, 1973).

The subgroup decomposable index characterized in the third essay can be regarded as a normalized sum of the utility shortfalls of the incomes of the poor from the income situation when all the poor persons are at the poverty line. In the words of Zheng (1997, p. 150), "following Sen's axiomatic approach, Chakravarty (1983) proposed a decomposable measure. This was among the first distribution-sensitive measures possessing this property. Unlike the approach of Sen (1976), Chakravarty derived his measure by solving a functional equation, which directly takes the three basic axioms into account". The three basic axioms employed in the characterization are transfer, monotonicity and normalization. While the monotonicity axiom demands that a reduction in the income of a poor should increase poverty, the normalization axiom requires the poverty index to take on the value one when all the incomes are zero. According to subgroup decomposability, for any partitioning of the population into two or more subgroups with respect to some homogenous characteristic, such as age, sex, region, and ethnic classes; overall poverty is given by the population share weighted average of subgroup poverty levels. This property enables us to identify those subgroups that are characterized by low population proportions but high poverty values. Evidently, from poverty reduction policy perspective such subgroups should be given priority by policy analysts. The index, thus, has a straightforward policy application. Foster and Jin (1998) developed a poverty ordering using this index. Several multidimensional extensions of the index have been suggested in the literature from different perspectives (see Chapter "Multidimensional Indicators of Inequality and Poverty" of this volume).

Apart from its extensive applications for poverty evaluation, this decomposable index has been applied to many other situations, including vulnerability to poverty and dynamic and forward-plooking poverty analysis because of its simple analytical formulation. In a situation of vulnerability, it has been noted that "Calvo and Dercon's measure is the expected Chakravarty index" (Dutta et al. 2011, p. 645) (see also Calvo and Dercon 2013). In their analysis of forward-looking and dynamic metric of poverty, Calvo and Dercon (2009, p. 57) argued that "one of the contributions of this paper is to identify the Chakravarty poverty index as the best choice if the poverty analysis moves from static poverty on to vulnerability".

In many recent contributions, measurement of richness at the top of an income distribution as a complement to poverty at the bottom of the profile has become a cornerstone of analysis (see Piketty and Saez 2006; Atkinson 2007; Atkinson et al. 2017). The poverty measure presented in the third essay has been suitably transformed into an index of richness for investigation of the extent of affluence in a society (see Peichl et al. 2010).

A recent trend in the poverty literature is to consider an endogenous poverty threshold, a poverty cut-off limit that is responsive to the actual distribution of income. In fact, this is a well-accepted phenomenon in many developed countries. In many OECD countries, there is a practice of using a constant fraction of the mean or median income of a country as the poverty threshold of the respective country. Consequently, any change in the income distribution of the country will change its poverty cut-off limit also. In contrast, an absolute poverty threshold is independent of the actual distribution of income and given exogenously. Chapter 4 of the volume, written jointly with Nachiketa Cattopadhyay, Joseph Deutsch, Zoya Nissanov and Jacques Silber, published in Research in Economic Inequality, 2016, develops an axiomatic characterization of an amalgam poverty line, a poverty line expressed as a mixture of an absolute poverty line and a reference income (e.g., the mean or median income). Some of the existing suggestion, for instance, those put forward by Atkinson and Bourguignon (2001) and EU standard for basing the poverty threshold on the actual distributions of income, become polar cases of our general formulation.

Analysis of poverty based on a single period data does not give us a true picture of the extent of deprivation of the poor people of a society. There are many reasons for not regarding poverty as a timeless concept, instead to regard it as an inter-temporal issue. There are studies that demonstrate that consecutive periods of poverty are worse than scattered poverty occurrences over time (Rodgers and Rodgers 1993; Jenkins 2000). A person afflicted by long duration of poverty may become deprived from attainment of "minimally acceptable levels" of one or more basic dimensions of human well-being (Sen 1992, p. 139). The fifth chapter of the volume, written jointly with Bossert and D'Ambrosio, published in Journal of Economic Inequality, 2012, addresses this issue in an axiomatic framework. It examines the measurement of individual and global poverty in an inter-temporal context using subgroup decomposability. Consequently, duration of poverty spells plays a significant role in the analysis, which involves counting of the number of periods in poverty and number of periods out of poverty. (See Atkinson 2003, for a counting based approach in a static framework.) Importance of persistence of poverty in a state of poverty is focused.

Multidimensionality of human welfare is a well-accepted phenomenon now. As a result, in welfare economics research there has been a shift of emphasis from single dimensional to multidimensional framework in recent years. This is because often income alone cannot be sufficient to represent the well-being of a population. For instance, insufficient supply of a public good, say, inadequacy of a malaria prevention program in a society cannot be traded off by a rich person's high income. Prices of many dimensions of well-being, such as pollution control program may not exist. Consequently, an attempt to use prices as weights for dimensions to derive a single indicator of well-being may not be worthwhile. It is, therefore, quite reasonable to use dimension-by-dimension achievements of different individuals to design an overall indicator of well-being of a population. An achievement matrix gives us achievements of the persons in a society in different dimensions, when represented in a matrix form. It is also referred to as a social distribution, or a social/distribution matrix. (See Chakravarty 2018, for a detailed discussion.)

The sixth chapter of the collection presents the well-known Bourguignon–Chakravarty family of multidimensional relative poverty indices (Journal of Economic Inequality, 2003). This 'is an early seminal conceptual paper on this topic' (Klasen 2018, p. xiv). For each dimension, a threshold limit indicating minimally acceptable level of the dimension, required for a subsistence standard of living, is specified. A multidimensional relative poverty index is an indicator of global deprivation that satisfies ratio scale invariance, that is, it is one whose value does not change when achievements in a dimension and the associated poverty cutoff limit are scaled up/down by the same positive quantity, where the scaling factor may change from dimension to dimension. For instance, we can change income unit from euro to dollar and calorie intake unit from calorie to joule. (The value of a multidimensional absolute poverty index is insensitive to equal absolute changes in dimensional achievements and threshold quantities. Equivalently, it fulfills the translation invariance property.)

In this chapter, implications of postulates for a general multidimensional poverty index are investigated, particularly, in terms of tradeoffs between dimensional achievements above and below threshold limits, and shapes of iso-poverty contours are studied. Shapes of iso-poverty contours when the elasticity of substitution between dimensional deprivations, gaps between threshold limits and corresponding dimensional achievements, depends on the poverty levels are examined as well. The paper directly employs the notion of inter-dimensional association, suggested in Atkinson and Bourguignon (Review of Economic Studies, 1982), to judge how poverty changes under a correlation increasing switch between two individuals' achievements. While most of the axioms for a single dimensional poverty index can be generalized to a multidimensional framework, axioms relating to inter-dimensional association do not have any single dimensional counterpart. Detailed investigations are made on the analytical properties of the Bourguignon–Chakravarty complements, substitutes and Leontief indices (Vélez and Robles 2008). [For additional discussions and excellent characterizations of the Bourguignon-Chakravarty family see Lasso de la Vega et al. (2009) and Lasso de la Vega and Urrutia (2011).]

The seventh chapter, prepared jointly with Conchita D'Ambrosio, published in a Springer Volume edited by Berenger and Bresson (2012), deals with a family of unit consistent multidimensional poverty indices. Unit consistency of a multidimensional poverty index demands that when the individual achievements in a dimension and the corresponding threshold limit are equi-proportionally changed, where the proportionality factor need not be the same across dimensions, then the poverty ranking of two social distributions should not alter. Evidently, all relative indices are unit consistent, but the converse is not true. No member of the family can be regarded as an absolute index. Axioms relating to the Atkinson–Bourguignon (1982) notion of inter-dimensional association play a significant role in making clear distinction between members of the family in terms of parametric restrictions.

When complete information on dimensional achievements of different individuals are available, it is possible to dichotomize their positions with respect to deprivations, that is, whether a person is deprived or non-deprived in a dimension. However, often complete information on dimensional achievements becomes unavailable. For instance, some people may be reluctant to reveal correct information on income or expenditure data. Often it becomes difficult to judge exact literacy position of a person. There may exist a wide range of cutoff limits that becomes acceptable to a social planner. Consequently, it may become difficult to judge whether a person is deprived or not in a dimension. An appropriate tool to measure poverty in such a situation is fuzzy set theory. Essential to the notion of fuzzy set theory is a membership function. A membership function is used to map the position of a person with respect to achievements of the person in different dimensions. The values of a membership function are regarded as membership grades or values and these values are limited between 0 and 1. If a person is fully deprived in a dimension, that is, his achievement is at the minimum level, then the function takes on the value 1. In contrast, if the person's achievement is not below the dimensional threshold limit, the membership grade is 0. When a person/surveyor is unclear about the status of achievement in a dimension then the membership function assigns a grade lying between 0 and 1. It decreases as the achievement level increases from the minimum level to the threshold cutoff. A membership function can be linear or non-linear, but it must possess the property that its values are bounded between 0 and 1.

Chapter 8 of the volume presents a rigorous discussion on the axioms, including the one involving the Atkinson–Bouruignon type inter-dimensional association, for a multidimensional poverty index in a fuzzy set up. It is clearly indicated how standard multidimensional poverty indices can be reformulated in a fuzzy framework. A characterization of a fuzzy membership function is also presented. Often the choice of a threshold limit for a dimension in a multidimensional poverty measurement analysis may involve ambiguity. It may vary in a certain range. This in turn raises the possibility that the poverty ranking of two alternative social matrices for alternative choices of threshold limits may not be the same. The ninth chapter of the volume, a joint contribution of Bourguignon and Chakravarty, published in a volume edited by Basu and Kanbur (Oxford University Press, 2008), looks for necessary and sufficient conditions under which poverty ordering of two social matrices will be the same when poverty threshold limits are allowed to vary within a broad range. The ranking conditions depend explicitly on the nature of inter-dimensional association. This notion of poverty ordering is known as poverty-threshold ordering, which contrasts with poverty-measure ordering that establishes conditions for ranking of social distributions when threshold limits are assumed to be fixed but variability of functional forms of poverty indicators is allowed. (For parallel single dimensional rankings, see Atkinson 1987; Foster and Shorrocks 1988.)

Often it becomes necessary to dichotomize individual achievements in a dimension using a binary variable that takes on the values 0 and 1, where a value of 1 indicates that the person under consideration is deprived in the dimension, and a value 0 means that the person has no feeling of deprivation with respect to the dimension. For instance, sometimes it becomes necessary to know whether a person has a desired level of literacy, his income exceeds a certain limit, he likes the environment in his workplace; and so on. If the person is found to possess the desired level of literacy, his income exceeds the given limit and likes the environment in the workplace; then he is non-deprived in each of the three dimensions and the value 0 can be assigned to indicate his non-deprivation in each case. On the other hand, if he is deprived in a dimension, for instance, if he does not possess the desired level of literacy, then the value 1 can be assigned to indicate this deprivation. Note that such dichotomizations of dimensional achievements apply to both ordinal and non-ordinal dimensions. Examples of dimensions of the latter category can be income, wealth, etc. and the former category include dimensions like self-reported health status, environment in workplace, etc. We refer to the total number of dimensions $c$ in which a person is deprived as his deprivation count. If $d$ stands for the number of dimensions of well-being, then the person's functioning score, the number of dimensions in which he is non-deprived, is given by $(d-c)$.

The next three chapters of the volume, based on the counting approach (Atkinson 2003), rely on binary representation of dimensions of well-being. Of these the tenth chapter, written jointly with Conchita D'Ambrosio, published in Review of Income and Wealth, 2006, presents a formal treatment of the notion of social exclusion, an area to which Atkinson contributed significantly. Social exclusion means relegation of one or more population subgroups and individuals to socially disadvantageous positions, where disadvantage may arise with respect to one or more dimensions of well-being. Examples of such dimensions can be health, literacy, income, and social rights (e.g. communing with friends, access to banking facilities, labor market participation), etc. In other words, social exclusion is a denial of human rights and it segregates people from social relations, thus, blocking them from full participation in normal activities of the society. It is a combined result of personal deprivations in terms of individuals' exclusion from regular participation in society functionings. It is a failure of the society to provide basic rights of human living conditions. Thus, social exclusion arises from the absence of consumption of the individuals due to inability to afford, not due to their preferences. The affected individuals become socially isolated and unimportant. Gender, caste, ethnic discrimination may translate into social exclusion. From general perspective, it may be defined as the process that excludes people from complete participation in the society in which they live. Hence socially excluded individuals are unable to enjoy the minimal standard of well-being. (For a recent treatment, see Atkinson et al. 2017.)

The chapter presents a formal treatment of social exclusion in an axiomatic framework. It also investigates the implications of a social exclusion dominance relation in terms of aggregate exclusion measures and a T-transformation, a transformation reflecting egalitarianism. The essay clearly argues that social exclusion should not be equated with multidimensional inequality or poverty.

Material deprivation is concerned with economic tightness arising from inability of an individual to reach minimal consumption in dimensions representing material living conditions. Qualitative dimensions such as whether a person is sick or not do not come under the purview of analysis of material deprivation. While multidimensional poverty, in addition to, material dimensions takes into non-material dimensions like communing with friends also, material deprivations looks into living conditions in former dimensions only. In their report prepared for the Commission of Economic Performance and Social Progress, formed at the initiative of the French Government, Stiglitz et al. (2009) suggested the inclusion of dimensions indicating material comfort for evaluation of well-being of a population from a multidimensional perspective.

In the eleventh essay of the volume, prepared jointly with Walter Bossert and Conchita D'Ambrosio, published in Review of Income and Wealth, 2013, an analytical discussion on material deprivation is presented. A person is assumed to be materially deprived if he is found to be deprived in at least one dimension. This contrasts with the intersection method of identification of material deprivation which requires deprivation in all the dimensions. The material deprivation score of a person is defined as the number of dimensions in which he happens to be deprived. The essay characterizes a social material deprivation index as a weighted sum of individual material deprivation scores and investigates its properties. The index characterized is quite general in the sense that it includes an arbitrary number of dimensions and no specific definition of materialistic dimensions is used. It is also employed to evaluate material deprivation in the European Union. Various combinations of materialistic dimensions can be used to illustrate our general index. However, in the essay, for illustrative purpose, the set of materialistic dimensions proposed by the European Union are considered.

Stochastic dominance is a standard tool for ordering of social situations, for instance, welfare ranking of income distributions (Atkinson 1970), ranking risky prospects on the basis of rate of returns (Levy 2006; Chakravarty 2013) etc. The variables considered are generally assumed to be of continuous type. But as we have argued earlier, often dichotomization becomes necessary to indicate a person's achievements in dimensions like health, literacy, etc. There can be a clear division of the total number of dimensions into functioning score, the number of dimensions in which the person's achievements are at the respective desired levels, and the deprivation count, the number of dimensions in which he is deprived. Consequently, the functioning score of a person is a non-negative integer varying between 0 and the total number of dimensions of well-being. The twelfth chapter of the volume, written jointly with Claudio Zoli, published in Journal of Economic Theory, 2012, identifies analytically the necessary and sufficient conditions under which one vector of functioning scores integer generalized Lorenz dominates that of another. The integer generalized Lorenz curve of a vector of functioning scores is the plot of cumulative functioning scores, divided by the population size, against cumulative population shares, when the scores are ranked from the lowest to the highest. If the generalized integer Lorenz curve of a vector of functioning scores lies nowhere below that of another, we say that the former integer generalized Lorenz dominates the latter. This is also same as the stipulation that the former second-order integer dominates the latter. It is rigorously shown that if the vector of functioning scores of one population dominates that of another by the above criterion, then the former can be obtained from the latter by a sequence of transformations satisfying monotonicity and non-increasingness of marginal social evaluation, where a social evaluation function is a real valued function defined on the set of vectors of functioning scores. The converse is also true. According to monotonicity, if the functioning score of a person increases by 1, then social evaluation of the profile of functioning scores cannot reduce. Non-increasingness of marginal social evaluation demands that an increase in the functioning score of a person by 1 has higher impact on social evaluation the lower is the score of the person. These two conditions are also equivalent to the requirement that the generalized Gini social evaluation function cannot assume a lower value for the former profile than for the latter one. If the total number of functioning scores of the two profiles are the same, then our result can be regarded as integer counterpart to a well-known result on welfare ranking in income distribution literature (see Atkinson 1970; Rothschild and Stiglitz 1970).

The final chapter of the volume, prepared jointly with Maria Ana Lugo, for Oxford Handbook of Well-Being and Policy (edited by Adler and Fleurbaey 2016), presents a survey of multidimensional indicators of welfare, inequality, and poverty. Given that well-being of a population is a multidimensional phenomenon, multidimensional economic inequality summarizes the level of dispersion arising from the distribution of achievements in different dimensions of well-being among individuals in a society. For both inequality and poverty, two different approaches are analyzed. The first is a direct approach which begins by specifying a set of desirable postulates for a general indicator and the indices under consideration are scrutinized on the basis of these postulates. The second approach defines a measure of well-being at the outset and an underlying index is defined at the next step.

Aggregation of dimension-by-dimension indicators of inequality or poverty does not give us a true picture of the desired objective since this dashboard-based approach ignores a noteworthy feature of analysis of multidimensional well-being, possible correlation, a measure of inter-dimensional association.

Atkinson's multidimensional inequality index, which can be regarded as a multidimensional translation of the single dimensional Atkinson index, determines the proportion of total achievements in each dimension that could be saved if the society distributed the totals for different dimensions equally among persons without any loss of welfare. It also gives the fraction of welfare lost through unequal distribution of totals of different dimensional achievements. The chapter presents a conscientious discussion on this quantifier of multidimensional inequality.

I wish to express sincere gratitude to my coauthors Walter Bossert, François Bourguignon, Nachiketa Chattopadhyay, Conchita D'Ambrosio, Joseph Deutsch, Maria Ana Lugo, Zoya Nissanov, Jacques Silber and Claudio Zoli for generously permitting me to include our joint contributions in this volume. I sincerely thank Anjan Mukherji who went through an earlier draft of this introductory chapter and offered several suggestions. Nandish Chattopadhyay generated the figure files and MS Word versions of some of the chapters were prepared by Chunu Ram Saren that were available as journal articles in published form. It is a pleasure for me to acknowledge the help I received from them.

## References

Adler, M. D., & Fleurbaey, M. (Eds.). (2016). *Oxford handbook of well-being and public policy*. New York: Oxford University Press.

Atkinson, A. B. (1970). On the measurement of inequality. *Journal of Economic Theory, 2*, 244–263.

Atkinson, A. B. (1987). On the measurement of poverty. *Econometrica, 55*, 749–764.

Atkinson, A. B. (2003). Multidimensional deprivation: Contrasting social welfare and counting approaches. *Journal of Economic Inequality, 1*, 51–65.

Atkinson, A. B. (2007). Measuring top incomes: Methodological issues. In A. B. Atkinson & T. Piketty (Eds.), *Top incomes over the twentieth century* (pp. 18–42). Oxford: Oxford University Press.

Atkinson, A. B., & Bourguignon, F. (1982). The comparison of multidimensioned distributions of economic status. *Review of Economic Studies, 49,* 183–201.

Atkinson, A. B., & Bourguignon, F. (2001). Poverty and inclusion from a world perspective. In J. E. Stiglitz & P. A. Muet (Eds.), *Governance, Equity and Global Markets*. New York: Oxford University Press.

Atkinson, A. B., Guio, A. -C., & Marlier, E. (Eds.). (2017). *Monitoring social inclusion in Europe*. Luxembourg: European Union.

Berenger, V., & Bresson, F. (Eds.). (2013). *Monetary poverty and social exclusion around the Mediterranean Sea*. New York: Springer.

Blackorby, C., & Donaldson, D. (1980a). A theoretical treatment of indices of absolute inequality. *International Economic Review, 21,* 107–136.
Blackorby, C., & Donaldson, D. (1980b). Ethical indices for the measurement of poverty. *Econometrica, 58,* 1053–1060.
Calvo, S., & Dercon, S. (2009). Chronic poverty and all that: The measurement of poverty over time. In T. Addison, D. Hulme, & R. Kanbur (Eds.), *Poverty dynamics: Interdisciplinary perspectives*. Oxford: Oxford University Press.
Calvo, C., & Dercon, S. (2013). Vulnerability of individual and aggregate poverty. *Social Choice and Welfare, 41,* 721–740.
Chakravarty, S. R. (1983). A new index of poverty. *Mathematical Social Sciences, 6,* 307–313.
Chakravarty, S.R. (2013). *An outline of financial economics*. New York: Anthem Press.
Chakravarty, S. R. (2018). *Analyzing multidimensional well-being*. New Jersey: Wiley.
Dasgupta, P., Sen, A. K., & Starrett, D. (1973). Notes on the measurement of inequality. *Journal of Economic Theory, 6,* 180–187.
Dutta, I., Foster, J. E., & Mishra, A. (2011). On measuring vulnerability to poverty. *Social Choice and Welfare, 37,* 743–761.
Foster, J. E., Greer, J., & Thorbecke, E. (1984). A class of decomposable poverty measures. *Econometrica, 42,* 761–766.
Foster, J. E., & Shorrocks, A. F. (1988). Poverty orderings. *Econometrica, 56,* 173–177.
Foster J. E., & Jin Y. (1998). Poverty orderings for the Dalton utility-gap measures. In S.P, Jenkins, A. Kapteyn & B. Van Praag (eds.). *The distributions of welfare and household production: International Perspective* (pp.268–285). Cambridge: Cambridge University Press.
Jenkins, S. P. (2000). Modeling household income dynamics. *Journal of Population Economics, 13,* 529–567.
Klasen, S.(Eds.). (2018). *Measuring poverty*. Cheltenham: Edward Elgar.
Kolm, S. C. (1969). The optimal production of social justice. In J. Margolis & H. Guitton (Eds.), *Public economics* (pp. 145–200). London: Macmillan.
Lasso de la Vega, M. C., Urrutia, A. M., & Sarachu, A. (2009). '*The Bourguignon and Chakravarty multidimensional poverty family: A characterization*'. ECINEQ WP 2009–109.
Lasso de la Vega, M. C., & Urrutia, A. M. (2011). Characterizing how to aggregate the individuals' deprivations in a multidimensional framework. *Journal of Economic Inequality, 9,* 183–194.
Levy, H. (2006). *Stochastic dominance, investment decisions making under uncertainty, second edition*. New York: Springer.
Peichl, A., Schaefer, T., & Scheicher, C. (2010). Measuring richness and poverty: A micro data application to Europe and Germany. *Review of Income and Wealth, 56,* 597–619.
Piketty, T., & Saez, E. (2006). The evolution of top incomes: A historical and international perspective. *American Economic Review, 96,* 200–205.
Pyatt, G. (1987). Measuring welfare, poverty and inequality. *Economic Journal, 97,* 459–467.
Rodgers, J. R., & Rodgers, J. L. (1993). Chronic poverty in the United States. *Journal of Human Resources, 28*, 25–54.
Rothschild, M., & Stiglitz, J. E. (1970). Increasing risk: I, A definition. *Journal of Economic Theory, 3,* 225–243.
Rothschild, M., & Stiglitz, J. E. (1973). Some further results on the measurement of inequality. *Journal of Economic Theory, 6,* 188–204.
Sen, A. K. (1973). *On economic inequality*. New York: Norton.
Sen, A. K. (1976). Poverty: An ordinal approach to measurement. *Econometrica, 44,* 219–231.
Sen, A. K. (1992). *Inequality re-examined*. Cambridge, MA: Harvard University Press.
Shorrocks, A. F. (1995). Revisiting the Sen poverty index. *Econometrica, 63,* 1225–1230.
Stiglitz, J. E., Sen, A., & Fitoussi, J.-P. (2009). *Report by the Commission on the Measurement of Economic Performance and Social Progress*, CMEPSP.

Vélez, C. E., & Robles, M. (2008). Determining the parameters of axiomatically derived multi-dimensional poverty indices: An application based on reported well-being in Colombia. In N. Kakwani & J. Silber (Eds.), *Quantitative approaches to multidimensional poverty measurement* (pp. 210–225). New York: Palgrave Macmillan.

Zheng, B. (1997). Aggregate poverty measures. *Journal of Economic Surveys, 11*, 123–162.

# Ethically Flexible Measures of Poverty

**Satya R. Chakravarty**

**Abstract** This paper introduces new measures of both relative and absolute poverty using the notion of representative income of a community corresponding to the censored income distribution. These new measures satisfy the monotonicity and transfer axioms proposed by Sen (1976) in all cases.
**Abstract** *Des mesures de pauvrete' e'thiquement flexibles. Ce me'moire pre'sente des measures nouvelles de lapauvrete' relative et absolute\`a partir de la notion de revenu representatif d'une communaute' correspondant \`a la re'partition du revenu censure' au sens de Takayama. Ces mesures nouvelles satisfont aux axiomes de monotonicite' et de transfert propose'par* Sen (1976) *dans tous les cas.*

## 1 Introduction

This study proposes new indices for the measurement of poverty through a social welfare approach, building on the papers by Takayama (1979), Blackorby and Donaldson (1980a), and Clark et al. (1981). Blackorby and Donaldson constructed their poverty index employing a social evaluation function defined on the incomes of the poor. With their poverty index it is possible that a transfer of income from a poor person to the richest poor person may actually reduce the value of the index if the transfer enables its recipient to cross the poverty line, thus violating what is known as the transfer axiom (see the following section). Takayama defined the censored income distribution as one where all incomes above the poverty line are set equal to the poverty line, and he then used the Gini index of the censored income distribu-

The author is grateful to Professor N. Bhattacharya for his valuable guidance in preparing the paper. The author also thanks Professors A. B. Atkinson, David Donaldson, Bhaskar Dutta and Amartya Sen for their comments. Special thanks are due to two anonymous referees, whose comments on an earlier draft considerably improved the paper. I sincerely thank John Wiley & Sons for kindly permitting me to reprint this article published in Canadian Journal of Economics, Volume 16, 1983.

S. R. Chakravarty (✉)
Indian Statistical Institute, Kolkata 700108, India
e-mail: satyarchakravarty@gmail.com

 
S. R. Chakravarty (ed.), *Poverty, Social Exclusion and Stochastic Dominance*, Themes in Economics, https://doi.org/10.1007/978-981-13-3432-0_2

tion as an index of poverty. But this index violates the monotonicity axiom (see the next section). The same difficulty arises with the other indices based on the same approach proposed by Hamada and Takayama (1977). Clark, Hemming, and Ulph defined the social evaluation function over the censored income distribution and used a Blackorby–Donaldson type approach to construct their poverty index. However, they did so only for the symmetric mean of order $\alpha(< 1)$ social evaluation function.

In this paper, we recognize that the Clark, Hemming, and Ulph approach does not depend upon the use of such a restricted social evaluation function and we present the general approach implicit in the Clark, Hemming, and Ulph example. All the indices introduced here will satisfy both the monotonicity and transfer axioms. We propose measures of the relative as well as the absolute variety. The relative measures are related to the Atkinson–Kolm–Sen (AKS) relative inequality indices (see Atkinson 1970; Kolm 1969; Sen 1973) and the absolute measures to the Blackorby–Donaldson (BD) absolute inequality indices (see Blackorby and Donaldson 1980b), if applied to the censored income distribution. The social evaluation functions that we employ here are *strictly S-concave*.[1] That is, if two censored income distributions have the same mean and if one is more unequal than the other (by the Lorenz criterion), then the former is ranked as worse than the latter by the social evaluation function. For a given poverty line, this property is preserved in the indices we suggest for poverty measurement.

## 2 Properties for a Measure of Poverty

With a population of size $n$, the distribution of incomes is represented by a vector $y = (y_1, y_2, \ldots, y_n)$, where $y_i \geq 0 \forall\, i = 1, 2, \ldots, n$. Let us assume that the incomes are arranged in nonincreasing order, that is, $y_1 \geq y_2 \geq \cdots \geq y_n$. Let $q(\leq n)$ be the number of the poor who have incomes not above the poverty line $z$ (given exogenously).

A poverty index which is assumed to be a nonnegative scalar function of $y$, and $z$ is said to be a relative poverty index or an absolute poverty index according as it satisfies (a) or (b).

(a) The value of the poverty index remains unchanged when all the incomes and the poverty line itself are multiplied by the same positive scalar.
(b) The value of the poverty index remains unchanged when the same amount of income is added to or subtracted from all the incomes and the poverty line itself.

A poverty index $P(y, z)$—whether a relative index or an absolute index—is required to satisfy the following properties:

---

[1] A numerical function $f$ defined on $R^n$ (the $n$-dimensional Euclidean space) is said to be $S$-concave if $f(yB) \geq f(y)$ for all $y \in R^n$ and for all bistochastic matrices $B$ of order $n$. $f$ is strictly $S$-concave if the inequality is strict whenever $yB$ is not a permutation of $y$. It can be shown that (Berge 1963) S-concavity implies symmetry; and that symmetry and quasiconcavity imply S-concavity, but the reverse is not true.

1. $P(y, z)$ is independent of the incomes of the rich. (This is a strong justification for basing the poverty index on the censored income distribution.)
2. $P(y, z)$ is increasing in $z$.
3. Given other things, a reduction in income of a person below the poverty line must increase the poverty index (Monotonicity Axiom).
4. Given other things, a pure transfer of income from a person below the poverty line to anyone who is richer must increase the poverty index, unless the number of persons below the poverty line is strictly reduced by the transfer (*Weak Transfer Axiom*).
5. Given other things, a pure transfer of income from a person below the poverty line to anyone who is richer must increase the poverty index (*Strong Transfer Axiom*).
6. $P(y, z)$ is left unchanged by a permutation of the incomes (*Impartiality*).
7. $P(y, z)$ is jointly continuous in $(y, z)$.

Property 1 states that income variations of any individual above the poverty line do not change the poverty index unless the individual falls below the poverty line. Property 2 demands that the index of poverty should increase as the poverty line representing the subsistence income level is raised. Properties 3, 4, and 5 have been discussed in the literature (see, e.g., Sen 1976, 1977, 1979; Chakravarty 1980, 1981; Kakwani 1980) and need no fresh discussion. Property 6 is unavoidable as long as income recipients are not distinguished by anything other than income. In addition to the above properties, the poverty index may be required to satisfy the population symmetry axiom, which is stated as follows: "If the same population is replicated several times, then the poverty index should be the same for the original income distribution and for the distribution obtained through replication." This axiom is parallel to Dalton's (1920) principle of population for inequality indices.

## 3 Relative Measures of Poverty

Before we propose the new index, we shall briefly discuss the AKS relative inequality indices, the Takayama and Hamada–Takayama indices, and the Blackorby–Donaldson index.

### *3.1 The AKS Relative Inequality Indices*

Throughout the third section, we shall assume that $W$, the social evaluation function, is *continuous, increasing, strictly S-concave and homothetic*. Homotheticity means $W$ should be of the form

$$W = \phi(\bar{W}(y)), \tag{1}$$

where $\phi$ is increasing in its argument and $\bar{W}$ is positively linearly homogeneous.

The AKS representative income ($\xi$) of the population is that income that, if distributed equally, is ethically indifferent (indifferent as measured by the social evaluation function) to $y$ and is implicitly defined by

$$W(\xi\, 1_n) = W(y), \tag{2}$$

where $1_n$ is the $n$-co-ordinated vector of ones. Solving (2) (uniquely) for $\xi$, we get

$$\xi = E(y), \tag{3}$$

where $E$ is a particular numerical representation of $W$. $E$ is homogeneous of degree one.

Letting $\lambda > 0$ be the mean of the distribution $y$, the AKS inequality index is defined as

$$I(y) = 1 - E(y)/\lambda. \tag{4}$$

Clearly, $I$ is homogeneous of degree zero; that is, it is a relative index. Further, $I$ is strictly S-convex (it agrees with Lorenz quasi-ordering) if $W$ is strictly $S$-concave and, in this case, it is symmetric and ranges between zero and one, attaining the value of zero at equality. Given a functional form for $I$, we can find $E$ and $W$ from (4), (3), and (1).

## *3.2* The Takayama and Hamada–Takayama Indices

Takayama (1979) defined the censored income distribution $y^*$ corresponding to $y$ as

$$\begin{aligned} y^* &= \left(y_1^*, y_2^*, \ldots, y_n^*\right) \\ &= \left(z, z, \ldots, z, y_{n-q+1}, \ldots, y_n\right). \end{aligned} \tag{5}$$

He defined the Gini coefficient $I_G^*$ of the censored income distribution $y^*$ as the Gini coefficient of poverty of distribution $y$.

$$\begin{aligned} I_G^*(y) &= \frac{1}{2\,n^2\,\lambda^*} \sum_{i=1}^{n} \sum_{j=1}^{n} \left|y_i^* - y_j^*\right| \\ &= 1 - \frac{1}{n^2\,\lambda^*} \sum_{i=1}^{n} \sum_{j=1}^{n} (2i - 1) y_i^*, \end{aligned} \tag{6}$$

where $\lambda^* = \frac{1}{n} \sum\limits_{i=1}^{n} y_i^*$.

Other measures of relative inequality have been applied to the censored income profile to derive corresponding measures of poverty in Hamada and Takayama (1977).

To show that all such indices violate the monotonicity axiom[2] we assume, for simplicity, that all the incomes are below the poverty line.[3] Now suppose all the incomes are multiplied by some positive scalar c such that all of them remain below the poverty line. Then a poverty measure should increase or decrease according as $c$ is less than or greater than unity. But the Takayama and Hamada–Takayama measures remain invariant under such circumstances. Hence we have the following theorem.

**Theorem 1** If a relative inequality index defined on the censored income distribution is used as a relative poverty index (the Takayama and Hamada–Takayama approach), the poverty index will violate the monotonicity axiom.

## 3.3 The Blackorby–Donaldson Index

In the case of the Blackorby–Donaldson poverty index we shall additionally assume that the social evaluation function $W$ is completely strictly recursive (any group of poorer people is strictly separable from the richer ones).[4] This particular requirement allows the "representative income of the poor" to be defined for each possible $q$ and to be independent of the incomes of the rich. The representative income of the poor $\xi_p$ is given by

$$W\left(y_1, y_2, \ldots, y_{n-q}, \xi_p, \xi_p, \ldots, \xi_p\right) = W(y). \quad (7)$$

Since $W$ is completely strictly recursive, $\xi_p$ is independent of $\left(y_1, y_2, \ldots, y_{n-q}\right)$, and we may write

$$\xi_p = E^q\left(y_{n-q+1}, \ldots, y_n\right), \quad (8)$$

where $E^q$ is homogeneous of degree one.

Blackorby and Donaldson (1980a) considered

$$B(y, z) = q/n\left[1 - \xi_p/z\right], \quad (9)$$

as a general relative poverty index. $B$ $(y, z)$ is Sen's (1976) index if the evaluation is done with the Gini social evaluation function of the poor (see Blackorby and

[2]Kakwani (1981) demonstrates that Takayama's index violates the monotonicity axiom only when the poverty line strictly exceeds the median of the income distribution.

[3]In such a case, if all the incomes assume a common value, then the Takayama and Hamada Takayama indices take the value zero, irrespective of the common income value. This result is clearly undesirable.

[4]For a detailed discussion of the notion of recursivity, see Blackorby et al. (1978, ch. 6).

Donaldson 1980a, b). The Gini function[5] is not completely strictly recursive, but complete strict recursivity is only a minimal requirement for $B(y, z)$.

The index $B(y, z)$ suffers from a number of defects; apart from the requirement that the social evaluation function is completely strictly recursive. First, $B(y, z)$ is not continuous. To prove this, let $y_{n-q+1} = z$ and $y_{n-q+2} < z$. The income profile is $y^0 = \left(y_1, \ldots, y_{n-q}, z, y_{n-q+2}, \ldots y_n\right)$. We now raise $y_{n-q+1}$ by $\tau > 0$ lowering the number of poor to $(q - 1)$. The new income profile is $y^\tau = \left(y_1, \ldots, y_{n-q}, z + \tau\, y_{n-q+2}, \ldots y_n\right)$. Let $\xi_p^0$ and $\varsigma_p^\tau$ denote the representative incomes of the poor corresponding to the income profiles $y^0$ and $y^\tau$, respectively. Since $W$ is strictly recursive, we have

$$W(y^\tau) = W\left(y_1, \ldots, y_{n-q}, z + \tau,\ \xi_p^\tau, \ldots, \xi_p^\tau\right) \tag{10}$$

and

$$\begin{aligned} W\left(y^0\right) &= W\left(y_1, \ldots, y_{n-q}, z, \xi_p^\tau, \ldots, \xi_p^\tau\right) \\ &= W\left(y_1, \ldots, y_{n-q}, \xi_p^0, \ldots, \xi_p^0\right). \end{aligned} \tag{11}$$

By strict $S$-concavity, $\xi_p^\tau < z\left(\text{since } y_{n-q+2} < z\right)$ and

$$\xi_p^0 < ((q-1)\,\xi_p^\tau + z)/q. \tag{12}$$

Now

$$\begin{aligned} B\left(y^0, z\right) &= (q/n)\left[\left(\left(z - \xi_p^0\right)/z\right)\right] \\ &> (q/n)\left[1 - ((q-1)\xi_p^\tau + z)/qz\right] \\ &= (q/n)\left[\left(qz - (q-1)\xi_p^\tau - z\right)/qz\right] \\ &= ((q-1)/n)\left[\left(z - \xi_p^\tau\right)/z\right] \\ &= B(y^\tau, z). \end{aligned} \tag{13}$$

Equation (13) must hold for all $\tau > 0$. But $B\left(y^0, z\right)$ is independent of $\tau$, and, because of independence of the incomes of the rich (guaranteed by strict recursivity), so is $B(y^\tau, z)$. Therefore, continuity of $B$ requires $B\left(y^0, z\right) > B\left(y^0, z\right)$, a contradiction.[6]

We now show that $B(y, z)$ violates the strong transfer axiom. Consider the income profile $\bar{y} = \left(y_1, \ldots, y_{n-q}, z - \upsilon/q, z - 2\upsilon/q, \ldots, z - ((q-1)\upsilon)/q, z - \upsilon\right)$ where $\upsilon > 0$ is small. Transfer $\upsilon$ amount of income from the poorest person to the richest poor person. The new income profile is $y^\upsilon = \left(y_1, \ldots, y_{n-q}, z + ((q-1)\upsilon)/q, z - 2\upsilon/q, \ldots, z - ((q-1)\upsilon)/q, z - 2\upsilon\right)$.

[5] For a discussion, see Blackorby and Donaldson (1978).

[6] The author thanks one of the referees for pointing to the discontinuity aspect of $B(y, z)$

Denote the representative incomes of the poor corresponding to the distributions $\bar{y}$ and $y^{\upsilon}$ by $\bar{\xi}_p$, and $\xi_p^{\upsilon}$, respectively. Since the social evaluation function is continuous and $\upsilon > 0$ is arbitrary, we can make $(z - \bar{\xi}_p)$ very close to $(z - \xi_p^{\upsilon})$ so that the inequality

$$(q/n)\left[(z - \bar{\xi}_p)/z\right] < ((q-1)/n)\left[(z - \xi_p^{\upsilon})/z\right] \tag{14}$$

does not hold. This shows that $B(y, z)$ violates the strong transfer axiom.

We summarize the above results in the following theorem.

**Theorem 2** The Blackorby–Donaldson relative poverty index violates (i) continuity and (ii) the strong transfer axiom.

## 3.4 *The New Index*

Let $\xi^*$ denote the representative income corresponding to the censored income distribution $y^* = (y_1^*, \ldots, y_n^*)$. So

$$\begin{aligned} \xi^* &= E(y_1^*, y_2^*, \ldots, y_n^*) \\ &= E(z, z, \ldots, z, y_{n-q+1}, \ldots, y_n). \end{aligned} \tag{15}$$

Our new relative poverty index $Q$ is the proportionate gap between the poverty line $z$ and the representative income $\xi^*$ corresponding to $y^*$; that is,

$$Q = (z, y) = (z - \xi^*)/z. \tag{16}$$

The index $Q$ lies in the interval [0, 1], the lower and upper limits being attained, respectively, when $y_i \geq z\,\forall = 1, 2, \ldots, n$ and when $y_i = 0\,\forall i = 1, 2, \ldots, n$. Since $E$ is homogeneous of degree one, we can rewrite $Q(y, z)$ as

$$Q(y, z) = 1 - E(1, 1, \ldots, 1, y_{n-q+1}/z, \ldots, y_n/z). \tag{17}$$

Since $E$ is increasing, $Q$ is increasing in $z$. It is obvious that $Q$ satisfies continuity.

The claim that $Q$ satisfies the monotonicity axiom follows from increasingness of $E$. Since $E(y^*)$ is strictly $S$-concave, it ranks any Lorenz superior censored income distribution with the same mean as $y^*$ as better than $y^*$. This is equivalent to the condition that $y^*$ is obtained from the Lorenz superior distribution by a finite sequence of transformations transferring income from the worse off persons to the better off persons (see Dasgupta et al. 1973, Theorem 1, 181–3). This shows that $Q$ satisfies the weak and strong versions of the transfer axiom. Impartiality of $Q$ follows from symmetry of $W$, which is a consequence of S-concavity. We therefore have proved the following.

**Theorem 3** The new relative poverty index $Q\ (y, z)$ satisfies all the properties listed (1–7) in the second section.

The specific functional form of $W$ will determine whether the index satisfies the population symmetry axiom or not.

Our next result is as follows.

**Theorem 4** If the social evaluation function is completely strictly recursive, then $Q\ (y, z)$ and $B\ (y, z)$ are related by

$$B(y, z) < Q(y, z) < \left(z - \xi_p\right)/z \tag{18}$$

as long as $\xi_p < z$ and $q < n$.

*Proof* Using complete strict recursivity, we have

$$\begin{aligned} \xi^* &= E\left(z, \ldots, z, y_{n-q+1}, \ldots, y_n\right) \\ &= E\left(z, \ldots, z, \xi_p, \ldots, \ldots \xi_p\right). \end{aligned} \tag{19}$$

By strict $S$-concavity, we have

$$\xi^* < \left(q\, \xi_p + (n - q)z\right)/n. \tag{20}$$

$$\begin{aligned} \therefore\ Q(y, z) &= \left(z - \xi^*\right)/z \\ &> \left(nz - q\xi_p - (n - q)z\right)/nz \\ &= \left(nz - q\, \xi_p - nz + qz\right)/nz \\ &= q/n\left[\left(z - \xi_p\right)/z\right]. \end{aligned} \tag{21}$$

In (19), since $\xi_p < z$ and $E$ is strictly $S$-concave, $\xi^* > \xi_p$. Hence

$$Q(y, z) = \left(z - \xi^*\right)/z < \left(z - \xi_p\right)/z \tag{22}$$

and (18) is established.[7]

Note that the bounds is (18) are actually attained with $W(y) = \min\{y_i\}$ (the maximum criterion) and $W(y) = \sum_{i=1}^{n} y_i$ (which is $S$-concave but not strictly so).

We can rewrite $Q$ in (16) as

$$Q(y, z) = 1 - \left(\lambda^*(1 - I^*(y))\right)/z, \tag{23}$$

[7] The author is grateful to one of the referees for this result.

where $I^*(y)$ is the AKS inequality index based on $y^*$. Therefore, for two censored income distributions $x^*$ and $y^*$ with the same mean $\lambda^*$, we have

$$Q(y,z) \geq Q(x,y) \Leftrightarrow I^*(y) \geq I^*(x). \tag{24}$$

It is now clear that given (16), to every homothetic social evaluation function there corresponds a different relative poverty index. These indices will differ only in the manner in which the amount of relative inequality in the censored income distribution is taken into account. Therefore, the index $Q$ is a fairly natural translation of a relative inequality index of a censored income distribution into a relative poverty index.

*Examples* 1. Consider the social evaluation function that corresponds to the single-parameter Ginis (Donaldson and Weymark 1980). Then

$$\bar{W}_\beta(y^*) = \frac{1}{n^\beta}\sum_{i=1}^{n}\left[i^\beta - (i-1)^\beta\right]y_i^*, \tag{25}$$

where $\beta > 1$. The requirement $\beta > 1$ is necessary and sufficient for $\bar{W}_\beta(y^*)$ to be strictly $S$-concave in $y^*$. The associated poverty index is

$$Q_\beta(y,z) = 1 - \frac{1}{n^\beta z}\sum_{i=1}^{n}\left[i^\beta - (i-1)^\beta\right]y_i^*. \tag{26}$$

The distributional sensitivity of $Q_\beta$ increases as $\beta$ increases. When $\beta = 2$, $\bar{W}_2(y^*)$ is the Gini social evaluation function for the censored income distribution and when $\beta \to \infty$, $W_\infty(y^*) = \min\{y_i^*\}$ (the maximin social evaluation function producing $Q_\infty(y,z) = 1 - \min_i\{y_i^*\}/z$, the relative maximin index.

2. Assume that the social evaluation function is the symmetric mean of order $\alpha$, then

$$\begin{aligned} E_\alpha(y^*) &= \left[\frac{1}{n}\sum_{i=1}^{n}(y_i^*)^\alpha\right]^{1/\alpha}, \quad \alpha < 1, \alpha \neq 0, \\ &= \prod_{i=1}^{n}\left(y_i^*\right)^{1/n}, \quad \alpha = 0. \end{aligned} \tag{27}$$

The corresponding poverty index is

$$Q_\alpha(y,z) = 1 - \left(\left[\frac{1}{n}\sum_{i=1}^{n}(y_i^*)^\alpha\right]^{1/\alpha}\right)/z, \quad \alpha < 1, \alpha \neq 0,$$

$$= 1 - \left( \prod_{i=1}^{n} \left(y_i^*\right)^{1/n} \right) / z, \quad \alpha = 0. \tag{28}$$

which is the measure of Clark, Hemming, and Ulph. A transfer from person $i$ to person $j$ will increase $Q_\alpha$, by a larger amount, the richer is person $j$. The smaller the value of $\alpha$ the more is the sensitivity of $Q_\alpha$ to transfers. As $\alpha \rightarrow -\infty$,

$$E_{-\infty}\left(y^*\right) = \min_i \left\{y_i^*\right\}$$

and the associated poverty index is the relative maximin index.

# 4 Absolute Measures of Poverty

In this section, we shall assume that $W$ is continuous, increasing, strictly $S$-concave, and translatable. In the case of the Blackorby–Donaldson poverty index, we shall further assume that $W$ is completely strictly recursive. $W$ is translatable if it can be written as

$$W(y) = \phi\left(\hat{W}(y)\right), \tag{29}$$

where $\phi$ is increasing in its argument and $\hat{W}$ is unit translatable. $\hat{W}$ is said to be unit-translatable if

$$\hat{W}(y + a 1_n) = \hat{W}(y) + a, \tag{30}$$

where $\alpha$ is any scalar such that $y + \alpha\ 1_n$ is in the domain of definition of $W$. The overall representative income $\xi$ can be written as

$$\xi = F(y), \tag{31}$$

where $F$ is unit translatable. If $W$ is completely strictly recursive, we can write $\xi_p$ as

$$\xi_p = F^q\left(y_{n-q+1,}, \ldots, y_n\right), \tag{32}$$

where $F^q$ is unit translatable.

We now present results analogous to those presented in the third section. We start with a discussion of the BD absolute inequality index. The BD inequality index corresponding to $W$ is defined as

$$A(y) = \lambda - F(y). \tag{33}$$

$A$ is an absolute index (i.e., it is invariant with respect to equal absolute changes in all incomes), because $F$ is unit-translatable. Further, $A$ is strictly $S$-convex (it agrees with Lorenz quasi-ordering) if $W$ is strictly $S$-concave, and in this case it is symmetric, nonnegative, and equal to zero at equality. Given a functional form for $A$, we can find $W$ from (33), (31), and (29).

At this stage, one might consider the absolute measures of inequality, when applied to the censored income profile, as absolute measures of poverty. However, the approach is not a fruitful one in view of theorem 5, which is easy to demonstrate.

**Theorem 5** If an absolute inequality index defined on the censored income distribution is used as an absolute poverty index, the poverty index will violate the monotonicity axiom.

Blackorby and Donaldson (1980a) suggested the use of

$$D(y,z) = q\left[z - \xi_p\right], \tag{34}$$

as a general absolute poverty index. The following theorem, whose proof is completely analogous to that of Theorem 2, shows that as an absolute poverty index $D(y, z)$ is not a suitable candidate.

**Theorem 6** The Blackorby–Donaldson absolute poverty index violates (i) continuity and (ii) the strong transfer axiom.

In contrast, as a general absolute poverty index we introduce the measure

$$\begin{aligned} T(y,z) &= z - \xi^* \\ &= z - F(z, \ldots, z, y_{n-q+1}, \ldots, y_n). \end{aligned} \tag{35}$$

$T$ lies between zero and $z$. The index $T$ measures the per capita poverty. In a censored income profile if each person were given $(z - \xi^*)$ amount of money, then the index would be zero (since $F$ is unit-translatable) at an aggregate cost of $nT(y, z)$. Hence $nT(y, z)$ gives the money unit cost of poverty. Therefore, we can also use the index

$$\bar{T}(y,z) = n\left(z - \xi^*\right) \tag{36}$$

as an absolute poverty index. This index measures total absolute poverty rather than per capita poverty. The specific functional form of $W$ determines whether the per capita index will satisfy the population symmetry axiom or not. If the per capita index meets this axiom, then replicating the population would raise $\bar{T}(y, z)$ in proportion to $n$. The following theorems can be proved easily

**Theorem 7** The new absolute poverty index $T(y, z)$ satisfies all the properties listed (1–7) in the second section.

**Theorem 8** If $W$ is completely strictly recursive, then $D(y, z)$ and $T(y, z)$ are related by

$$D(y,z) < nT(y,z) < n\big(z - \xi_p\big), \tag{37}$$

as long as $\xi_p < z$ and $q < n$.
We can rewrite $T$ in (35) as

$$T(y,z) = z - \lambda^* + A^*(y), \tag{38}$$

where $A^*(y)$ is the BD absolute inequality index defined on $y^*$. Therefore, for two censored income distributions $y^*$ and $x^*$ with the same mean $\lambda^*$, we have

$$T(y,z) \geq T(x,y) \Leftrightarrow A^*(y) \geq A^*(x). \tag{39}$$

An absolute poverty index that depends on absolute differentials only exists for every translatable social evaluation function defined on the censored income distribution.

*Examples* 1. Let the social evaluation function correspond to the single-parameter Ginis:

$$\hat{W}_\beta\big(y^*\big) = \frac{1}{n}\sum_{i=1}^{n}\big[i^\beta - (i-1)^\beta\big]y_i^*, \tag{40}$$

where $\beta > 1$. This social evaluation function is homothetic as well as translatable. The associated poverty index is

$$T_\beta(y,z) = z - \frac{1}{n^\beta}\sum_{i=1}^{n}\big[i^\beta - (i-1)^\beta\big]y_i^*. \tag{41}$$

For $\beta = 2$, the index becomes the absolute Gini index of poverty, and $\beta \rightarrow \infty$, $T_\infty(y,z) = z - \min_i\{y_i^*\}$, the absolute maximin index.

2. Another alternative of interest arises from the Kolm-Pollak social evaluation function. Its implicit poverty index is

$$\begin{aligned} T_{KP}(y,z) &= z - \left[\frac{-1}{\theta}\log\left((1/n)\sum_{i=1}^{n} e^{-\theta y_i^*}\right)\right] \\ &= \frac{1}{\theta}\log\left[\frac{1}{n}\sum_{i=1}^{n} e^{\theta(z-y_i^*)}\right], \end{aligned} \tag{42}$$

where $\theta > 0$. Here $\theta$ is a free parameter which determines the curvature of the social indifference surfaces. As $\theta$ increases, the measure attaches more weight to transfers lower down the income scale. As $\theta \to \infty$, $T_{KP}$ approaches the absolute maximin index.

The general measure introduced in this section incorporates an absolute measure of inequality of a censored income profile for purposes of measurement of poverty. To every translatable social evaluation function there corresponds a particular index. These indices will differ in the way they take account of the absolute inequality in the censored income distribution.

## 5 Conclusions

While the Takayama and Hamada–Takayama indices do not satisfy the monotonicity axiom and Blackorby–Donaldson's ethical indices do not satisfy the transfer axiom, the general ethical indices introduced in this paper satisfy both the axioms. These indices make use of the notion of representative income of the population corresponding to the censored income distribution. To every homothetic social evaluation function there corresponds a relative poverty index of the type and for every translatable social evaluation function there exists a corresponding absolute poverty index.

## References

Atkinson, A. B (1970). On the measurement of inequality. *Journal of Economic Theory, 2,* 244–263.
Berge, C. (1963). *Topological spaces*. Edinburgh: Oliver and Boyd.
Blackorby, C., & Donaldson, D. (1978). Measures of relative equality and their meaning in terms of social welfare. *Journal of Economic Theory, 18,* 59–80.
Blackorby, C., & Donaldson, D. (1980a). Ethical indices for the measurement of poverty. *Econometrica, 48,* 1053–1060.
Blackorby, C., & Donaldson, D. (1980b). A theoretical treatment of indices of absolute inequality. *International Economic Review, 20,* 107–136.
Blackorby, C., Primont, D., & Russell, R. (1978). *Duality, separability and functional structure: Theory and economic applications*. North Holland: Amsterdam.
Chakravarty, S. R. (1980). New indices for the measurement of poverty. Paper presented at the Fourth World Congress of the Econometric Society. Aix-en-Provence, France.
Chakravarty, S. R. (1981). On measurement of income inequality and poverty (Unpublished Ph.D. thesis). Indian Statistical Institute, Calcutta.
Clark, S., Hemming, R., & Ulph, D. (1981). On indices for the measurement of poverty. *Economic Journal, 91,* 515–525.
Dalton, H. (1920). The measurement of inequality of incomes. *Economic Journal, 30,* 348–361.
Dasgupta, P., Sen, A., & Starrett, D. (1973). Notes on the measurement of inequality. *Journal of Economic Theory, 6,* 180–187.
Donaldson, D., & Weymark, J. A. (1980). A single-parameter generalisation of the Gini indices of inequality. *Journal of Economic Theory, 22,* 67–86.
Hamada, K., & Takayama, N. (1977). Censored income distribution and the measurement of poverty. *Bulletin of the International Statistical Institute, 47,* Book 1.

Kakwani, N. (1980). *Income inequality and poverty: Methods of estimation and policy applications*. Oxford University Press.

Kakwani, N. (1981). Note on a new measure of poverty. *Econometrica, 49,* 525–526.

Kolm, S. C. (1969). The optimal production of social justice. In J. Margolis & H. Guitton (Eds.), *Public economics*. London: Macmillan.

Sen, A. K. (1973). *On economic inequality*. Oxford University Press.

Sen, A. K. (1976). Poverty: An ordinal approach to measurement. *Econometrica, 44,* 219–231.

Sen, A. K. (1977). Social choice theory: A re-examination. *Econometrica, 45,* 53–89.

Sen, A. K. (1979). Issues in the measurement of poverty. *Scandinavian Journal of Economics*.

Takayama, N. (1979). Poverty, income inequality and their measures: Professor Sen's axio matic approach reconsidered. *Econometrica, 47,* 747–759.

# On Shorrocks' Reinvestigation of the Sen Poverty Index

**Satya R. Chakravarty**

**Abstract** This paper demonstrates that the Shorrocks (Econometrica 63:225–1230, 1995) modification of the Sen (Econometrica 44:219–231, 1976) poverty index drops out as a particular case of the Chakravarty (Canadian Journal of Economics 16:74–85, 1983) general ethical index of poverty.

**Keywords** Sen index · Shorrocks modification · Chakravarty general ethical index

In a pioneering article, Sen (1976) argued that a poverty index should meet two desirable properties: the monotonicity axiom, which requires poverty to increase if the income of a poor person decreases; and the transfer axiom, which demands that poverty should increase under a transfer of income from a poor person to anyone who is richer. He also axiomatically derived a poverty index that, for a large number of poor persons, is given by

$$S(y, z) = HI + H(1 - I)G, \tag{1}$$

where $y = (y_1, y_2, \dots, y_n)$, $y_1 \le y_2 \le \dots \le y_n$, is the income distribution in an $n$-person economy; $z > 0$ is the poverty line; $I = \sum_{i=1}^{q} (z - y_i)/qz$, the income gap ratio, with $q$ being the number of poor persons, that is, $y_i \le z$ for $i = 1, \dots, q$, $y_i > z$ for $i = q + 1, \dots, n$; $H = q/n$, the head-count ratio; and $G = 1 - \sum_{i=1}^{q} (2(q - i) + 1)y_i/mq^2$, the Gini index for the poor, with $m$ being their mean income. In the literature, $S(y, z)$ is popularly referred to as the *Sen index*.

Blackorby and Donaldson (1980) offered an alternative interpretation and a generalization of $S(y, z)$ as an ethical index. Unfortunately, the Sen–Blackorby–Donaldson poverty indices violate continuity and the transfer axiom [Chakravarty (1983,

For comments and suggestions, I am grateful to two anonymous referees, Diganta Mukherjee, and Tony Shorrocks.
I offer my sincere gratitude to the Wiley-Blackwell for allowing me to reprint this article published in Econometrica, Volume 65, 1997.

S. R. Chakravarty (✉)
Economic Research Unit, Indian Statistical Institute, 203 B. T. Road, 700108 Kolkata, India
e-mail: satyarchakravarty@gmail.com



S. R. Chakravarty (ed.), *Poverty, Social Exclusion and Stochastic Dominance*, Themes in Economics, https://doi.org/10.1007/978-981-13-3432-0_3

1990)], Chakravarty (1983) proposed a general ethical index that avoids these shortcomings.

In a recent article, Shorrocks (1995) suggested a modification of the Sen index which meets continuity, the monotonicity, and the transfer axioms. It can also be interpreted in terms of the area under the inverse generalized Lorenz curve for poverty gaps. We show that this modification is in fact a particular case of the general index introduced by Chakravarty (1983). To see this, define the censored income $y_i^*$ associated with $y_i$ as min $(y_i, z)$. Thus, the censored income distribution $y^*$ corresponding to $y$ is obtained by replacing all non-poor incomes by the poverty line. Let $W$ be the continuous, increasing, strictly $S$-concave, homothetic social evaluation function (SEF) defined on the income distributions. The representative income $y_i^*$ corresponding to $y^*$ is that level of income which, if given to each person, will make the distribution $y^*$ ethically indifferent.

Finally,

$$W(y_f^*, \ldots, y_f^*) = W(y^*). \tag{2}$$

The general ethical index proposed by Chakravarty (1983) is given by

$$C(y, z) = 1 - \frac{y_f^*}{z}. \tag{3}$$

Now, suppose that the evaluation in (2) is done with respect to the Gini SEF. Then $y_f^* = \sum_{i=1}^{n} (2(n-i)+1)y_i^*/n^2$, which, when substituted in (3), gives

$$\begin{aligned} C(y, z) &= \sum_{i=1}^{n} (2(n-i)+1)(z - y_i^*)/n^2 z \\ &= \sum_{i=1}^{q} (2(n-i)+1)(z - y_i)/n^2 z, \end{aligned} \tag{4}$$

the Shorrocks modification of the Sen index.

Though the index (4) has been proposed earlier in the literature, Shorrocks' analytical derivation along with its graphical interpretation enriches our understanding of the issue substantially.

## References

Biackorby, C., & Donaldson, D. (1980). Ethical indices for the measurement of poverty. *Econometrica, 48,* 1053–1060.

Chakravarty, S. R. (1983). Ethically flexible measures of poverty. *Canadian Journal of Economics, 16,* 74–85.

Chakravarty, S. R. (1990). *Ethical social index numbers*. London: Springer.

Sen, A. K. (1976). Poverty: An ordinal approach to measurement. *Econometrica, 44,* 219–231.

Shorrocks, A. F. (1995). revisiting the sen poverty index. *Econometrica, 63,* 1225–1230.

# A New Index of Poverty

**Satya R. Chakravarty**

**Abstract** This paper introduces a new index of poverty. The index satisfies all the axioms for 'a good index of poverty'.

**Keywords** Measurement of poverty · A new index based on the "utility gaps" of the poor

## 1 Introduction

In measuring the incidence of poverty, the most widely used statistic is the proportion of population that falls below the poverty line. But this index does not reflect the intensity of poverty suffered by the poor. As an alternative, the aggregate value of the difference between the incomes of the poor and the poverty line has been considered. This index is insensitive to transfers of income among the poor so long as nobody crosses the poverty line as a result of such transfers. In his pioneering paper, Sen (1976) introduced a superior (ordinal) index of poverty. Alternatives and variations of Sen's index have been proposed in the literature (see Sect. 4 for a discussion). But almost all of the existing indices have one or more shortcomings.

This paper introduces a new poverty index that avoids many of the shortcomings of other indices. Moreover, the index possesses some attractive properties, e.g., attaching greater weight to transfers lower down the income scale and decomposability.

I am grateful to Elsevier for generously permitting me to reprint this article published in Mathematical Social Sciences, Volume 6, 1983.

S. R. Chakravarty (✉)
Economic Research Unit, Indian Statistical Institute, 203, B. T. Road, 700108 Kolkata, India
e-mail: satyarchakravarty@gmail.com

 
S. R. Chakravarty (ed.), *Poverty, Social Exclusion and Stochastic Dominance*,
Themes in Economics, https://doi.org/10.1007/978-981-13-3432-0_4

## 2 Axioms for a Good Index of Poverty

With a population of size $n$, the distribution of incomes is represented by a vector $y = (y_1, y_2, \ldots, y_n)$, where $y_i \geq 0 \forall_i = 1, 2, \ldots, n$. We assume that the incomes are arranged in nondecreasing order, i.e., $y_1 \leq y_2 \leq \ldots \leq y_n$, $q(\leq n)$ is the number of the poor who have incomes below the poverty line $z$ (given exogenously).

A poverty index $P$ which is assumed to be a nonnegative scalar function of $y$ and $z$ should satisfy the following properties:

(i) Continuity ($C$): $P(y, z)$ is jointly continuous in $(y, z)$.

(ii) Independence of the incomes of the rich (IIR): Given the number of people, the number of poor and the poverty line, $P(y, z)$ is independent of the incomes of the rich.

(iii) Scale invariance (SI): $P(y, z)$ remains unchanged if all the incomes and the poverty line itself are multiplied by the same positive scalar.[1]

(iv) *Normalization* ($N$): If all n persons have zero income, then $P(y, z)$ takes the value unity[2]

(v) *Increasingness in subsistence income* (ISI): $P(y, z)$ is increasing in $z$.

(vi) *Monotonicity* ($M$): Given other things, a reduction in income of a person below the poverty line must increase $P(y, z)$.

(vii) Transfer ($T$): Given other things, a transfer of income from a poor person to anyone who is richer increases $P(y, z)$.[3]

(viii) Diminishing transfer (DT): If a transfer of a fixed amount of income takes place from the $i$th poor with income $y_i$ to a poor with income $(y_i + h)$, then for a given $h > 0$, the magnitude of increase in $P(y, z)$ decreases as $i$ increases. This axiom gives more weight to transfers of income at the lower end of the distribution than at the upper ends. There is a considerable discussion of a similar axiom in the literature on income inequality (see Atkinson 1970; Sen 1973; Kolm 1976).

(ix) *Impartiality* ($I$): $P(y, z)$ is left unchanged by a permutation of the incomes. This axiom is unavoidable as long as income recipients are not distinguished by anything other than income.

(x) *Decomposability* ($D$): If the population is divided into two or more mutually exclusive groups or regions, then the overall poverty index equals the weighted

[1]Strictly speaking, a poverty index satisfying axiom Sl is called a relative poverty index. On the other hand, a poverty index is called an absolute poverty index if it remains unchanged when the same amount of income is added to or subtracted from all the incomes and the poverty line itself. For a detailed discussion, see Blackorby and Donaldson (1980a) and Chakravarty (1983).

[2]This axiom rules out any utility function which is undefined for zero incomes, e.g. a logarithmic utility function.

[3]Axioms $M$ and $T$ were introduced by Sen (1976) (but not used in the derivation of his index). Sen (1977, 1979, 1981) questioned the merit of using a transfer axiom that allows the possibility of a change in the number of persons below the poverty line occurring as a result of transfers considered in the axiom, and opted for a weak transfer (WT) axiom. Sen stated his weak transfer axiom as: Given other things, a transfer of income from a poor person to a richer poor person that does not change the number of poor increases $P(y, z)$.

average of the poverty indices for different groups, the weights being the population shares of different groups.

If the population is partitioned into groups according to some characteristic (e.g., age, sex, race, occupation, and educational standard), then a poverty index satisfying axiom $D$ is useful in analyzing the influence of poverty within each group on the aggregate poverty. This helps us to inquire into factors contributing to poverty using income data and in choosing and implementing policies for the reduction of poverty.

In deriving the new index, we shall use only axioms $N$ and SI. The other axioms will be shown to be satisfied by the new index.

## 3 The New Index

Let $U_i$ denote the utility function of individual $i$. We assume that $U_i$ depends only on $y_i$ . We further assume that $U_i's$ are the same for all, i.e., $U_i(\cdot) = U(\cdot)$ and that $U$ is increasing and strictly concave. Let $h_i = (U(z) - U(y_i))$ denote the utility gap of individual $i$. Obviously, $h_i$s are positive for the poor and nonpositive for others.

For a given income configuration y, the index of poverty $Q$ is defined as the normalized aggregate utility gap of the poor. That is,

$$Q(y, z) = A\left[\sum_{i=1}^{q} U(z) - U(y_i)\right], \tag{1}$$

where $A > 0$ is the coefficient of normalization. Therefore, given $z$, $Q$ can be regarded as a (cardinal) measure of distance separating the income profile of the poor from the social state $z1_q$, where $1_q$ is the $q$-coordinated vector of ones.

**Theorem** *The only poverty index of the form* (1) *satisfying axioms N and* SI *is given by*

$$Q(y, z) = \frac{1}{n}\sum_{i=1}^{q}\left[1 - \left(\frac{y_i}{z}\right)^e\right], \tag{2}$$

*where* $0 < e < 1$.

*Proof* $Q$ in (1) satisfying axiom $N$ gives

$$A = \frac{1}{n[U(z) - U(0)]}, \tag{3}$$

which on substitution in (1) yields

$$Q(y, z) = \frac{\sum_{i=1}^{q} [(U(z) - U(y)]}{n[U(z) - U(0)]} \tag{4}$$

$$= \frac{1}{n} \sum_{i=1}^{q} \left[ 1 - \frac{f(y_i)}{f(z)} \right], \quad (5)$$

where $f(x) = U(z) - U(x)$.

For $n = 1$ and $0 < y_1 < z$ by axiom *SI* the index depends only on $y_1/z$. But for this special case the index in (5) is $1 - [f(y_1)/f(z)]$. That is, $f(y_1)/f(z)$ depends on $y_1/z$. Therefore, $f(x)/f(s)$ is of the form $g(x/s)$ for some continuous function $g$. This shows

$$f(x) = \beta x^e, \quad (6)$$

where $\beta$ and $e$ are constants (see Aczel 1966, p. 144). Increasingness and strict concavity of $f(\cdot)$ require that $\beta > 0$ and $0 < e < 1$. Substituting $U(x) = \alpha + \beta x^e$, where $a = U(0)$, in (4) we get the desired form of $Q$. This establishes the necessity part of the theorem. The sufficiency can be verified by checking that $Q$ in (2) satisfies axioms SI and *N*. □

The poverty index $Q$ has the following properties:

(i) It lies in the interval [0, 1], the lower limit is attained in the case when there is no person below the poverty line and the upper limit in the extreme case described in axiom *N*.
(ii) It remains invariant under affine transformations of $U(\cdot)$.[4]
(iii) It satisfies axioms *C*, IIR, ISI, *M*, *I*, and *D*.
(iv) When $0 < e < 1$, $Q$ embodies a social evaluation function which is strictly concave in the incomes of the poor and axioms *T* and WT are satisfied. The change in $Q$ due to a transfer of income between two individuals depends on the difference in the marginal utilities of the individuals concerned. Therefore, $Q$ satisfies axiom DT. As $e$ decreases, $Q$ becomes more sensitive to transfers lower down the income scale.
(v) For a given $y$ and a poverty line $z$, $Q$ increases as $e$ increases, ($e$–1) it may be noted, is the constant elasticity of marginal utility with respect to income.

## 4 A Comparison with the Existing Indices

Sen's index is the normalized weighted sum of the income gaps $g_i = (z - y_i)$ of the poor, the weight of $g_i$ being the rank of $i$ in the interpersonal income ordering of the poor. Kakwani (1980) proposed a generalization of Sen's index where the weight of $g_i$ is the $r$th power of the income rank used in Sen's index. The motivation for introducing the new index is to enable it to satisfy the axiom DT. Sen's index corresponds to $r = 1$ making it, as Kakwani puts it, "equally sensitive to a transfer

[4]This goes well beyond the ordinal information restriction imposed by Sen.

of income at all income positions". But as Clark et al. (1981) have pointed out, the use of this index involves the search for an appropriate value of $r$ because different values of $r$ would be needed for different distributions to meet axiom DT.

Blackorby and Donaldson (1980a) offered an alternative interpretation and a generalization of Sen's index. As a general poverty index, they introduced the index

$$B(y, z) = \frac{q}{n}\left[\frac{z - y_f^p}{z}\right], \tag{7}$$

where $y_f^p$ is the *representative income of the poor.*[5] $y_f^p$ is implicitly defined by

$$F(y_f^p.1_q) = F(y^p), \tag{8}$$

where $y^P$ is the income vector of the poor and $F$ is their ordinal social evaluation function. It is assumed that $F$ is *continuous, increasing, strictly S-concave*[6] and homothetic.[7]

It is clear that to every homothetic social evaluation function[8] there corresponds a different poverty index of the form (7). For example, suppose that $y_j^p$ is determined from the social evaluation function $\phi\left(\sum_{i=1}^{q} y_i(q+1-i)^r\right)$, where $\phi' > 0$ and $r \geq 1$. Then $B$ is Kakwani's index. The index $B$ may decrease if a disequalizing transfer enables its recipient to cross the poverty line, thus violating the transfer axiom (see Chakravarty 1981, 1983). For Sen's index this behavior was pointed out in Sen (1977).[9]

With a view to accommodating deprivation relative to individuals above the poverty line, Takayama (1979) defined the censored income distribution as one where all incomes above the poverty line are set equal to the poverty line, and then used the Gini index of the censored income distribution as an index of poverty. Other indices of inequality have been applied to the censored income distribution to derive corresponding measures of poverty in Hamada and Takayama (1977). But all such indices violate axiom $M$ (see Sen 1979, 1981; Chakravarty 1981, 1983). In contrast

[5]For the population as a whole this representative income is the same as the Atkinson-Kolm-Sen equally distributed equivalent income. See Atkinson (1970), Kolm (1969) and Sen (1973). Also, see Blackorby and Donaldson (1978, 1980b) and Weymark (1981).

[6]$F$ is $S$-concave if $F(y^p R)$ for all bistochastic matrics $R$ of order $q$. Strict $S$-concavity requires a strict inequality whenever $y^p R$ is not a permutation of $y_p$. It can be shown that (Berge 1963) $S$-concavity implies symmetry; and that symmetry and quasi-concavity imply $S$-concavity but the reverse is not true. An $S$-concave function ranks any Lorenz superior distribution of income with the same mean as no worse, a strictly $S$-concave function ranks it as better.

[7]Homotheticity of $F$ is necessary and sufficient for $B$ to satisfy axiom SI. Hornotheticity means $F$ should be of the form $\phi(F^*(y^p))$, where ¢ is increasing in its argument and $F^*$ is positively linearly homogeneous.

[8]Blackorby and Donaldson pointed out the need for complete strict recursivity (strict separability of a special kind that permits us to rank distributions of income among the poor independently of the incomes of the rich) of the social evaluation function.

[9]Sen (1979, p. 302) argued that such behavior of an index may be treated as reasonable.

to Kakwani's and Takayama's indices, Clark et al. defined a new poverty index as the proportionate gap between $z$ and the equally distributed equivalent income according to the social evaluation function:

$$V(y^*) = \frac{1}{\beta} \sum_{i=1}^{n} (y_1^*)^\beta, \tag{9}$$

where $y^* = (y_1^*, y_2^*, \ldots y_n^*)$ is the censored income distribution corresponding to $y$ and $\beta < 1$. The resulting index is

$$H(y, z) = 1 - \left[ \frac{\frac{1}{n} \sum_{i=1}^{n} (y_i^*)^\beta}{z} \right]^{1/\beta}. \tag{10}$$

The index $H$ satisfies axioms *M*, *T*, *WT*, and *DT*. But it becomes independent of $\beta$ when all the $n$ persons are poor and have the same positive income. Independently of how low the incomes of the poor are, the index remains unaffected by changes in the value of the parameter $\beta$. Of course, this is no more than what Clark et al. said about their second index

$$K(y, z) = \frac{q}{nz} \left[ \frac{1}{q} \sum_{i=1}^{q} g_i^\varepsilon \right]^{\frac{1}{\varepsilon}}, \tag{11}$$

where $\varepsilon > 1$.[10] It is not clear how serious this criticism is. Denoting the equally distributed equivalent income of the population according to some continuous, increasing, strictly *S*-concave, homothetic social evaluation function defined on the censored income distribution by $y_t^*$ the index $H$ becomes a special case of the general ethical index

$$L(y, z) = 1 - (y_f^*/z) \tag{12}$$

if the evaluation is done with the symmetric mean of order $\beta (< 1)$ social evaluation function (see Chakravarty 1983).

## 5 Conclusions

In this paper, we have suggested a new index of poverty. The index has been defined as the normalized "aggregate utility gap" of the poor. The index satisfies Sen's monotonicity and transfer axioms, and also attaches greater weight to transfers of income

[10] The index $K$ behaves in the same way as $B$ with respect to axiom $T$ (see Chakravarty 1981).

at the lower end of the income distribution. Moreover, if the population is partitioned into groups, then the index can be decomposed into components that reflect the partition.

**Acknowledgements** The author thanks A. B. Atkinson, N. Bhattacharya, C. Blackorby, B. Dutta, and A. K. Sen for comments. The author also thanks an anonymous referee whose comments on an earlier draft improved the paper.

## References

Aczel, J. (1966). *Lectures on functional equations and their applications*. New York: Academic Press.
Atkinson, A. B. (1970). On the measurement of inequality. *Journal of Economic Theory, 2,* 244–263.
Berge, C. (1963). *Topological spaces*. Edinburgh: Oliver and Boyd.
Blackorby, C., & Donaldson, D. (1978). Measures of relative equality and their meaning in terms of social welfare. *Journal of Economic Theory, 18,* 59–80.
Blackorby, C., & Donaldson, D. (1980a). Ethical indices for the measurement of poverty. *Econometrica, 48,* 1053–1060.
Blackorby, C., & Donaldson, D. (1980b). A theoretical treatment of indices of absolute inequality. *International Economic Review, 20,* 107–136.
Chakravarty, S. R. (1981). *On measurement of income inequality and poverty*, Unpublished Ph.D. Thesis. Indian Statistical Institute.
Chakravarty, S. R. (1983). Ethically flexible measures of poverty. *Canadian Journal of Economics, 16,* 74–85.
Clark, S., Hemming, R., & Ulph, D. (1981). On indices for the measurement of poverty. *Economic Journal, 91,* 515–526.
Hamada, K., & Takayama, K. (1977). Censored income distribution and the measurement of poverty. *Bulletin of the International Statistical Institute, 47.*
Kakwani, N. (1980). On a class of poverty measures. *Econometrica, 48,* 437–446.
Kolm, S. C. (1969). The optimal production of social justice, In: J. Margolis & H. Guitton (Eds.), *Public economics.* London: Macmillan.
Kolm, S. C. (1976). Unequal inequalities II. *Journal of Economic Theory, 13,* 82–111.
Sen, A. K. (1973). *On economic inequality*. Oxford: Clarendon Press.
Sen, A. K. (1976) Poverty: An ordinal approach to measurement. *Econometrica, 44*, 219–231.
Sen, A. K. (1977). Social choice theory: A re-examination. *Econometrica, 45,* 55–89.
Sen, A. K. (1979). Issues in the measurement of poverty. *Scandinavian Journal of Economics, 91,* 285–307.
Sen, A. K. (1981). *Poverty and famines: An essay on entitlement and deprivation*. London: Oxford University Press.
Takayama, N. (1979). Poverty income inequality and their measures: Professor Sen's axiomatic approach reconsidered. *Econometrica, 47,* 747–759.
Weymark, J. A. (1981). Generalised Gini inequality indices. *Mathematical Social Sciences, I,* 409–430.

# Reference Groups and the Poverty Line: An Axiomatic Approach with an Empirical Illustration

**Satya R. Chakravarty, Nachiketa Chattopadhyay, Joseph Deutsh, Zoya Nissanov and Jacques Silber**

**Abstract** A recent trend in the study of poverty is to consider a relative poverty line, one that is responsive to the nature of the income distribution. We develop an axiomatic approach to the determination of an amalgam poverty line. Given a reference income (e.g., the mean or the median), the amalgam poverty line becomes a weighted average of the absolute poverty line and the reference income, where the weights depend on the policy maker's preferences for aggregating the two components. The paper ends with an empirical illustration comparing urban and rural areas in the People's Republic of China and India.

**Keywords** Absolute poverty · Amalgam threshold · India · People's Republic of China · Poverty line · Relative poverty

**JEL Classifications** D31 · D63 · I32

---

Kind permission received from Emerald Publishing for reprinting this article from Research On Economic Inequality, Volume 24, 2017, is acknowledged thankfully.

---

S. R. Chakravarty (✉) · N. Chattopadhyay
Indian Statistical Institute, Kolkata 700108, India
e-mail: satyarchakravarty@gmail.com

N. Chattopadhyay
e-mail: ncstat@yahoo.com

J. Deutsh · J. Silber
Department of Economics, Bar-Ilan University, 52900 Ramat-Gan, Israel
e-mail: yosef.deutsch@gmail.com

J. Silber
e-mail: jsilber_2000@yahoo.com

Z. Nissanov
Department of Economics and Business Management, Ariel University, Ariel, Israel
e-mail: zoya_n@hotmail.com



S. R. Chakravarty (ed.), *Poverty, Social Exclusion and Stochastic Dominance*, Themes in Economics, https://doi.org/10.1007/978-981-13-3432-0_5

## 1 Introduction

Even in the early years of the twenty-first century, removal of poverty remains one of the major goals of economic policy in many countries of the world. A wide variety of poverty indices have been proposed in the literature and the determination of an income or consumption threshold on which the definition of poverty relies has been a debatable issue for quite some time (see among others, Ruggles 1990; Ravallion 1994; Citro and Michael 1995). A distinction is made between an "absolute poverty line", which has a fixed real value over time and is given exogenously, and a "relative poverty line" which is responsive to the income distribution.[1] The major distinction between the relative and absolute thresholds arises not from specification of their values but from how the values change under changes in the distribution.

In fact virtually all developing countries use absolute poverty lines, whereby any standard measure of poverty decreases if all incomes grow at the same rate (leaving relative inequality unchanged). Following Ravallion et al. (1991), the World Bank thus used a \$1 per day poverty line for the developing world and this threshold was updated by Ravallion et al. (2009) to \$1.25 a day at 2005 purchasing power parity (PPP). Deaton (2010) argued that many problems are involved in the calculation of a global poverty line and correction for international price differences using PPP exchange rates. More recently the World Bank adopted a new international poverty line equal to \$1.90 (see, Ferreira et al. 2015).

Developed countries, especially the OECD countries, on the other hand use a constant proportion of mean or median income as the poverty line so that an equi-proportionate increase in all incomes leaves the poverty level unchanged. This is called a strongly relative poverty measure (SR). Such an approach requires, however, quite implausible assumptions, namely that people are concerned solely with relative deprivation and/or that the costs of social inclusion can fall to nearly zero in the poorest places.

Various attempts have been made to incorporate relativity in poverty measurement. Some studies suggested adjusting poverty lines across demographic subgroups. The idea of equivalence scale has as well been used for determining a relative poverty line.[2] More recently, Kakwani (2011) employed consumer theory to construct food and nonfood poverty thresholds.

An original approach was taken by Ravallion and Chen (2011) who introduced the concept of weakly relative poverty. They argued that selecting a strongly relative

[1]Examples of relative poverty lines include 50% of the median (Fuchs 1969) and 50% of the mean (O'Higgins and Jenkins 1990). Atkinson and Bourguignon (2001) considered a relative poverty line equal to the mean income (or expenditure) multiplied by 0.37. Chen and Ravallion (2001) preferred to use 0.33 instead of 0.37 as the multiplicative factor. The EU standard set poverty line as 60% of the median. In contrast, the US official poverty, which is largely due to Orshansky (1965), is based on family pre-tax income and an absolute poverty threshold. Currently, a new supplemental poverty measure (SPM) which uses more general definitions and adjustments for family size and composition, has been introduced in 2011. India uses separate absolute poverty lines for rural and urban sectors. (See Subramanian 2011, for a recent discussion.)

[2]See, for example, Blackorby and Donaldson (1994) and Foster (1998) for further discussion.

poverty measure (SR) in terms of the costs of social exclusion, where an implicit assumption is made according to which this cost is proportional to mean income, may not be tenable in the case of the developing world. They therefore proposed a weakly relative poverty line (WR) whose elasticity with respect to the mean income is positive with unity as its upper bound. In their model, they made a distinction between an income and a welfare space and assumed that $\overline{V} = V\left(Z, \left(\frac{Z}{M}\right)\right)$, where $\overline{V}$ is the fixed welfare poverty line, $Z$ is the income poverty line and $M$ is the mean or median income. For a non-welfarist interpretation of relative poverty line, they proposed a generalization of the Atkinson and Bourguignon (AB) approach. The AB approach links the physical survival needs to absolute poverty line and the social inclusion needs to the relative line. Ravallion and Chen (2011) specified that $Z = Z^* + \Psi(M)$, where $Z^*$ and $\Psi(M)$ are, respectively, the minimum expenditure required to assure the basic consumption needs and the cost of the incremental social needs beyond basic consumption. This ensures domination of absolute lines at low consumption levels (developing world) while the poverty line becomes relative beyond some higher level (developed world) and sets up a framework to make global poverty comparisons.

In another paper, Chen and Ravallion (2013) argued that there may in fact be two quite different reasons why poverty lines might vary systematically with the average consumption or income of a society. One reason is that there may be a common underlying poverty level of welfare, but that the level of consumption needed to attain it varies, stemming from social effects. The other reason does not require such effects, but rather postulates that social norms vary, implying different reference levels of welfare. Furthermore, the choice between these two interpretations has implications concerning the choice of relative versus absolute poverty lines. If one thinks that it is really only social norms that differ, with welfare depending solely on one's own consumption, then one would probably prefer an absolute measure, imposing a common norm (though one may want to consider more than one possible line). If however one is convinced that there are social effects on welfare, then one would be more inclined to use a relative line in the consumption or income space, anchored to a common welfare standard. The weakly relative poverty measures entail that the poverty line only rises with the mean above some critical value and it then does so with elasticity less than one. A process of distribution-neutral growth will then reduce the incidence of weakly relative poverty. The absolute measure is only obtained as a special case for sufficiently poor countries. Ideas quite similar to those expressed in Ravallion and Chen (2011) and Chen and Ravallion (2013) may be found in Ravallion (2008) and Ravallion (2012).

An obvious place to look for identifying the parameters of a schedule of weakly relative poverty lines is the set of national poverty lines found across developing countries. It then appears that national poverty lines among developing countries show a systematic nonnegative relationship with the average consumption of a country. Given that the determination of the poverty line is still a disputable matter, we wish to propose an axiomatic approach to the calculation of a relative poverty line. It is assumed that the poverty line is relative in the income/consumption space. Our approach follows a long tradition of identifying welfare with utility. Utility depends on the absolute income and the relative income, that is, income relative to some reference standard. There is in fact a vast literature that stresses the importance of incorporating relative position in decision-making analysis (see, Duesenberry 1949; Kahneman and Tversky 1991; Frank 1985, 1999; Clark and Oswald 1996; Easterlin 2001; Falk and Knell 2004; Ferrer-i-Carbonell 2005). The focus on relative economic position in utility analysis has also been recognized in the theory of relative deprivation (Runciman 1966).[3]

In this paper, we assume that individual utility is increasing, concave in absolute income but decreasing, convex in the reference standard (see, Clark and Oswald 1998). Our analysis relies on a general reference income level, of which some proportions of mean or median income can be special cases. An additive form and a multiplicative form of the utility function are characterized using two different sets of intuitively reasonable axioms. Now, suppose a reference income is given. We then employ a utility-consistency condition to determine the poverty line uniquely in terms of a reference income and a given poverty line. More precisely, given a reference income and a person with income equal to an arbitrarily set poverty line, who is just poor, we determine the level of the corresponding utility. We then consider an alternative setting where the person is again just poor, that is, with income at some alternative poverty line. However, in this situation, his utility is not affected by the reference income. Since the effect of the reference income on utility is captured through the absolute or relative divergence of a person's income with the reference income, the annulment of the effect is obtained by setting his own income to be his reference income. Utility-consistency requires that the person is equally satisfied in both positions. In other words, we equate the utility in this later state of affairs with the level of utility derived for the arbitrarily set poverty line and reference income situation to determine the arbitrary poverty line uniquely. This assumption of equal satisfaction is quite plausible because in each case the individual is at the existing poverty line income.

It may be worthwhile to note that the idea of utility-consistency goes back a long way in classical welfare measurement. The interpretation of the poverty line as a money metric of utility can be found in Blackorby and Donaldson (1987). A more recent treatment of the issue in the context of poverty analysis can be found in Kakwani (2011).

An innovative feature of our paper is that, for either form of the utility function, the new poverty line becomes an amalgam, a weighted average, of the given poverty line and the reference income. Therefore, our derivation allows the possibility of a change in the question "absolute or relative?" to "how much relative?" A second novelty of our contribution is that Foster's (1998) suggestion for a "hybrid" poverty threshold, a weighted geometric mean of a relative threshold and an absolute threshold, can be supported by our utility-consistency condition. Thus, our suggestion bears a close similarity with that of Foster (1998) and hence can as well be treated as a hybrid approach.

[3]See also, Yitzhaki (1979), Berrebi and Silber (1985), Chakravarty and Moyes (2003), Bossert and D'Ambrosio (2007) and Zheng (2007).

Another attractive feature of our framework is that some of the suggestions that exist in the literature (e.g., Atkinson-Bourguignon (2001) and EU standard) for basing the poverty line directly on some location parameter, such as the mean or median, become particular cases of our formulation.

The paper is organized as follows. Section 2 develops the theoretical framework. The main contribution of this section is that we characterize the utility functions using both the ratio and difference form comparisons. For the sake of completeness, Sect. 2 also provides a systematic comparison of our framework with the approach of Blackorby–Donaldson (1987). Next, Sect. 3 gives a short empirical illustration based on separate data on rural and urban areas in the People's Republic of China and India. Section 4 then briefly concludes.

## 2 Formal Framework

The model relies on two assumptions about an individual's utility function. The first assumption specifies that utility depends in part on the individual's absolute income. According to the second assumption, utility also depends on the relative income, income relative to some reference standard. This latter condition is one way of ensuring that utility partly depends on his relative position (or "status") in the society in terms of some attribute of wellbeing. Such assumptions about utility functions are quite common in the literature (see, for example, Clark and Oswald 1998). As Clark and Oswald (1998) suggested, relativity can be incorporated into the framework by having difference comparisons or ratio comparisons.

Let $x$ and $m$, respectively, be the absolute income and reference income of an individual in the society. Both $x$ and $m$ are assumed to be drawn from the finite nonnegative nondegenerate interval $[0, \infty)$, that is, $x, m \in [0, \infty)$. The reference income $m$ can be treated as a positional good and it is assumed that $x$ does not exceed the reference income.[4] Examples of $m$ can be the mean and the median incomes in the population or some positive scalar transformations of them.

Let $U$ denote the nonconstant real valued utility function of the individual. Following Clark and Oswald (1998), the function $U(x, m)$ is assumed to be increasing, concave in $x$ and decreasing, convex in $m$. Increasingness and concavity assumptions in absolute income are quite standard.[5] Suppose a person with a low income regards the income level $m$ as his targeted income. He may be optimistic about receiving this income by working hard and/or receiving some subsidy. An increase in $m$ might increase his difficulty to fulfil the objective of receiving the higher targeted income. This means that his additional utility from an increase in $m$ will be negative, that is,

---

[4]For a somewhat different position, see Hopkins (2008).

[5]The concavity assumption, which we have made following Clark and Oswald (1998), can definitely be replaced by strict concavity and a similar analysis can be developed. See Remark 1 at the end of this section.

$U$ is decreasing in $m$. Convexity means that his dissatisfaction from an increase in $m$ increases at a nondecreasing rate. Assume also that $U(.)$ is differentiable.

The difference form comparison demands that the utility function should be of the form $U(x, x - m)$. The argument $x - m$ can be thought of as capturing dis-utility from comparison. That is, in this case the determinant of relative status depends on difference $x - m$. Since $x, m \in [0, \infty)$ and $x \leq m$, it is clear that $x - m \in (-\infty, 0]$.

We now propose the following axioms for a utility function $U : [0, \infty) \times (-\infty, 0] \rightarrow R$ involving difference form comparison, where $R$ is the set of real numbers.

**Linear Translatability (LIT)**: For any real $c$ such that $x + c \in [0, \infty)$, $U(x + c, (x + c) - (m + c)) = U(x, x - m) + kc$, where $k > 0$ is some scalar.

**Linear Homogeneity (LIH)**: For any $c \in (0, \infty)$, $U(cx, cx - cm) = cU(x, x - m)$.

Since under equal increase of the absolute and reference incomes the relative status $(x - m)$ remains unchanged but the absolute income increases, individual utility should increase. LIT is a simple way of specifying this increment. It demands that when the absolute and reference incomes are changed by a given amount, then utility changes by a constant time of the given amount. In other words, it shows how utility changes when the absolute and reference incomes are diminished or augmented by the same amount. This axiom can be treated as an absolute counterpart to LIH, which says that an equi-proportionate change in the absolute and the reference incomes changes utility equi-proportionately. This postulate is weaker than the requirement that $U$ is increasing in $x$.

In the literature, on income inequality measurement, a social welfare function that satisfies linear homogeneity and linear translatability simultaneously is called a compromise welfare function. The Gini welfare function is an example of a welfare function of this type (see Blackorby and Donaldson 1980). Such welfare functions are helpful for measuring economic distance between income distributions, which quantifies well-being of one population relative to that of another (see Chakravarty and Dutta 1987).

**Proposition 1** The only utility function that satisfies LIT and LIH is of the form

$$U(x, x - m) = (k - a)x + am, \tag{1}$$

where $k > 0$ is same as in LIT and $a < 0$ is a constant.

*Proof* By LIT $U(x - x, x - x - m + x) = U(x, x - m) - kx$. We rewrite this equation as $U(x, x - m) = U(0, -m + x) + kx$. By LIH it follows that $U(0, -m + x) = (m - x)U(0, -1) = a(m - x)$, where $a = U(0, -1)$. Hence $U(x, x - m) = (k - a)x + am$. Decreasingness of $U$ in $m$ requires that $a < 0$. This establishes the necessity part of the proposition. The sufficiency part can be checked easily. □

The weights $(k - a)$ and $a$ in (1) provide a simple way of capturing the mixture of two effects. For $a = 0$ the preferences are private and self-interested. This becomes ensured under the mild condition that $k > 0$. The individual does not look at his position in terms of the reference income. He does not care about what other individuals are doing. It also follows that $U$ is concave in $x$ and convex in $m$ under the restrictions $(k - a) > 0$ and $a < 0$. The utility function in (1) is a particular form of the "*additive comparisons model*" suggested by Clark and Oswald (1998). However, no characterization has been developed by them.

Let us now consider a situation in which an individual does not compare his/her absolute income with the reference income because the reference income itself is identical to the absolute income. If we denote this absolute income by $z_0$, then from (1) we have, $U(z_0, 0) = kz_0$. This absolute income can be taken as the current poverty line. The utility corresponding to some arbitrary poverty line $z_1$ and the reference income $m$ will then be given by $U(z_1, z_1 - m) = (k - a)z_1 + am$. Let us now find the income $z_1$ which would guarantee the individual a level of utility identical to the utility level $U(z_0, 0)$. That is, the level of happiness that the person had in the earlier scenario when he was enjoying the poverty line income remains the same in the present case characterized by a new poverty line and a reference income. Equality of the two utility levels can be justified on the ground that in both circumstances the individual's income coincides with the poverty line income. We refer to this as a utility-consistency condition. (See Blackorby and Donaldson 1987, and Kakwani 2011). To understand this further, suppose for a given time point the absolute poverty line is well-defined at $z_0$. Suppose now the distribution changes. Given a reference income $m$, if we want to determine a poverty line $z_1$ that will keep the utility of the person at the old poverty line unchanged, we should readjust the poverty line. The readjustment is done by equating the utility levels.

Equating the two expressions $U(z_0, 0)$ and $U(z_1, z_1 - m)$, we get

$$z_1 = qz_0 + (1 - q)m, \tag{2}$$

where $q = \frac{k}{(k-a)}$. Given that $a < 0$, we can say that the revised poverty line is a convex mixture, a weighted average, of the existing poverty line and the specified reference income. For a 1 unit increase in the living standard ($m$), $(1 - q)$ represents the increase in the threshold $z_1$. Therefore, $q$ may be interpreted as a policy parameter in the sense that it reflects the relative importance of the current poverty line in getting its revised estimate. As the weight $q$ increases from 0 to 1, more and more importance is assigned to the current poverty line in the averaging in (2). For $q = 1, z_1$ coincides with the existing poverty line $z_0$, whereas for $q = 0, z_1$ becomes the reference income $m$. A compromise choice for $q$ is $q = 0.5$.

As Clark and Oswald (1998) argued, an alternative specification can be a '*ratio comparisons model*'. In this case the individual's utility depends directly on the absolute income $x$ and also on the relative factor $\frac{x}{m}$. Thus, in this case the determinant of the status is the ratio $\frac{x}{m}$. We consider a general form of the utility function $U\left(x, f\left(\frac{x}{m}\right)\right)$, where $f$ is a positive valued and increasing transformation of the ratio $\frac{x}{m}$. This is a fairly general version of a ratio comparisons model. As before, we maintain the assumptions that $U$ is increasing, concave in $x$ and decreasing, convex in $m$. By our formulation, $U$ is increasing in $f\left(\frac{x}{m}\right)$.

In order to characterize a particular form of the utility function which we wish to use for determining a poverty line in the ratio comparisons framework, we consider the following axioms for $U : (0, \infty) \times (0, \infty) \rightarrow R_{++}$, where $R_{++}$ is the strictly positive part of $R$.

Linear Homogeneity (LIH): For any $\left(x, f\left(\frac{x}{m}\right)\right) \in (0, \infty) \times (0, \infty)$, $U\left(cx, f\left(\frac{cx}{cm}\right)\right) = cU\left(x, f\left(\frac{x}{m}\right)\right)$, where $c > 0$ is arbitrary.

Since $f\left(\frac{x}{m}\right)$ remains unaltered under positive scale transformation of the absolute income $x$ and the reference income $m$, LIH shows how utility should be adjusted under such transformation of the variables.

Normalization (NOM): If $x = 1$, then $U\left(x, f\left(\frac{x}{m}\right)\right) = f\left(\frac{1}{m}\right)$.

Constancy of Marginal Utility of Reference Income (CMR): $\frac{\partial U\left(x, f\left(\frac{x}{m}\right)\right)}{\partial m} = -\theta < 0$.

Continuity (CON): $U$ is continuous in its arguments.

NOM is a cardinality principle which says that if the individual's income is 1, then corresponding utility value is given simply by the transformed value $f\left(\frac{1}{m}\right)$ of the ratio $\frac{1}{m}$. Variants of this are certainly possible. But given that the income is fixed at 1, the utility should be dependent on the ratio $\frac{1}{m}$ in a negative monotonic way and NOM ensures this. Continuity assures that minor observational errors in incomes will not change utility abruptly. CMR reflects the view that with an increase in reference income utility decreases at a nonincreasing rate, an assumption we have made at the outset of this section. While alternative possibilities definitely exist, CMR is quite simple and easy to understand.

Axioms LIH, NOM, CMR, and CON uniquely identify a specific functional form of the utility function.

**Proposition 2** The only utility function $U : (0, \infty) \times (0, \infty) \rightarrow R_{++}$ that satisfies LIH, NOM, CMR and CON is of the form

$$U\left(x, f\left(\frac{x}{m}\right)\right) = x\left(\beta - \frac{\theta m}{x}\right), \tag{3}$$

where $\beta > \theta > 0$ are constants such that $U\left(x, f\left(\frac{x}{m}\right)\right) > 0$.

*Proof* Let us denote the ratio $\frac{x}{m}$ by $A$. LIH implies that

$$U(cx, f(A)) = cU(x, f(A)), \tag{4}$$

where $c > 0$. This equality holds for all $x > 0$ and $c > 0$. Consequently, for any $c > 0$ it holds for $x = 1$ also.

Now, given $x = 1$, using NOM in (4), we get

$$U(c.1, f(A)) = cU(1, f(A)) = cf(A). \tag{5}$$

From (5) it follows that

$$c = \frac{U(c, f(A))}{f(A)}. \tag{6}$$

Plugging the value of $c$ from (6) into (4) we get

$$U(cx, f(A)) = cU(x, f(A)) = \frac{U(c, f(A))}{f(A)} U(x, f(A)). \tag{7}$$

Let

$$V(x, f(A)) = \frac{U(x, f(A))}{f(A)}. \tag{8}$$

From (7) and (8) it now follows that

$$\begin{aligned} V(cx, f(A)) &= \frac{U(cx, f(A))}{f(A)} \\ &= \frac{1}{f(A)}\left[\frac{U(c, f(A))}{f(A)} U(x, f(A))\right] \\ &= \left[\frac{U(c, f(A))}{f(A)}\right]\left[\frac{U(x, f(A))}{f(A)}\right] \\ &= V(c, f(A))V(x, f(A)). \end{aligned} \tag{9}$$

Now, define $g_{f(A)}(x) = V(x, f(A))$ so that we can rewrite (9) as

$$g_{f(A)}(cx) = g_{f(A)}(c)g_{f(A)}(x). \tag{10}$$

Given $A$, by non-constancy of $U$ we rule out the trivial solutions $g_{f(A)}(t) = 0$ and $g_{f(A)}(t) = 1$ of the functional Eq. (10). Since $U$ (hence $g$) is positive valued, we can take logarithmic transformation on both sides of (10) to get

$$\log\left(g_{f(A)}(cx)\right) = \log\left(g_{f(A)}(c)\right) + \log\left(g_{f(A)}(x)\right). \tag{11}$$

Substitution of $c = \mathrm{e}^u$ and $x = \mathrm{e}^v$ into (11) yields the functional equation

$$\log\left(g_{f(A)}\left(\mathrm{e}^{u+v}\right)\right) = \log\left(g_{f(A)}\left(\mathrm{e}^u\right)\right) + \log\left(g_{f(A)}\left(\mathrm{e}^v\right)\right). \tag{12}$$

Define $h_{f(A)}(t) = log\left(g_{f(A)}\left(\mathrm{e}^t\right)\right)$, where $t \in R$. CON implies continuity of $h_{f(A)}$. Then the functional Eq. (12) reduces to

$$h_{f(A)}(u+v) = h_{f(A)}(u) + h_{f(A)}(v), \tag{13}$$

of which the only continuous solution is $h_{f(A)}(u) = \delta u$, where $\delta$ is a nonzero constant that depends on $f(A)$ (Aczel 1966, p. 34). Using $h_{f(A)}(u) = \delta u$, in the definition of $h_{f(A)}(t)$, we get $log\left(g_{f(A)}(\mathrm{e}^u)\right) = \delta u$ and with $u = \log t$, it follows that $g_{f(A)}(t) = t^{\delta}$. From the definition of $g_{f(A)}$ it then follows that

$$V(x, f(A)) = x^{\delta(f(A))}. \tag{14}$$

Using the definition of $V(x, f(A))$ in (14) we get

$$U(x, f(A)) = x^{\delta(f(A))} f(A). \tag{15}$$

LIH ensures that $\delta(f(A)) = 1$, which in turn shows that

$$U(x, f(A)) = xf(A) = xf\left(\frac{x}{m}\right). \tag{16}$$

From (16), by CMR, it now follows that $f'\left(\frac{x}{m}\right)\frac{x^2}{m^2} = -\theta$, which gives $f\left(\frac{x}{m}\right) = \beta - \theta\frac{m}{x}$, where $\beta$ is the constant of integration and $f'$ is the derivative of $f$. Substituting this form of $f$ in (16) we get $U\left(x, f\left(\frac{x}{m}\right)\right) = x\left(\beta - \frac{\theta m}{x}\right)$.

Now, when $x = m$, we have $U(m, f(1)) = m(\beta - \theta)$ which becomes positive only when $\beta > \theta$ (since $m > 0$). Since the functional form $U\left(x, f\left(\frac{x}{m}\right)\right) = x\left(\beta - \frac{\theta m}{x}\right)$ holds for all $x \leq m$, we must choose $\beta > \theta > 0$ such that $U$ becomes positive unambiguously. This establishes the necessity part of the proposition. The sufficiency can be checked easily. □

Clark and Oswald (1998) specified, without characterization, a utility function which is additively separable in the absolute income $x$ and the relative income $\frac{x}{m}$. However, the functional form we have characterized is of product type in its arguments. The essential idea of dependence of the utility function on the relative as well as absolute statuses is well-maintained in our characterized form also. Further, our form becomes additively separable under the logarithmic transformation.

As in the additive case, we now wish to determine the value of $z_1$ such that $U\left(z_0, f\left(\frac{z_0}{z_0}\right)\right) = U\left(z_1, \frac{z_1}{m}\right)$. For the characterised form of $f\left(\frac{x}{m}\right)$, in view of (3), this equality becomes, $z_0(\beta - \theta) = z_1\left(\beta - \theta\frac{m}{z_1}\right)$, from which we get

$$z_1 = wz_0 + (1-w)m, \tag{17}$$

where $w = \frac{\beta - \theta}{\beta}$. Since $\beta > \theta > 0$, it follows that $0 < w < 1$. Thus, as in (2), here also the revised poverty line becomes a compound of the existing poverty line and the reference income. The parameter $w$ has the same policy interpretation as in (2). Thus, irrespective of the form of the utility function, we have the same procedure of generating a relative poverty line from an existing poverty line and a reference income. For an observed income distribution, $\beta$ and $\theta$ can be taken as $\beta = \frac{u}{l} + 1$ and $\theta = 1$, where $l > 0$ and $u$ are, respectively, the lower and upper bounds on income. The corresponding utility function turns out to be $x\left(\beta - \frac{m}{x}\right)$.

Since in general $m > z_0$, and $z_1$ is a weighted average of $z_0$ and $m$, it follows that $z_1 > z_0$. Therefore, in order to provide illustrations of our characterized poverty line, we have to choose hybrid poverty lines greater than the absolute poverty line. (See also the discussion below on the suggestions put forward by Atkinson and Bourguignon 2001; EU and Foster 1998).[6]

The choice of the weight $w$ is evidently related to that of the parameters. Assuming that the function $f$ may be written as $f(x/m) = \beta - (m/x)$, we can express $U$ as $U = x\beta - m$, from which we derive that $\mathrm{d}U = \frac{\partial U}{\partial x}\mathrm{d}x + \frac{\partial U}{\partial m}\mathrm{d}m = \beta\mathrm{d}x - \mathrm{d}m$ so that for a given utility level, $\frac{\mathrm{d}m}{\mathrm{d}x} = \beta$.

There are very few papers in the literature on subjective welfare that have estimated the simultaneous impact on happiness, ceteris paribus, of an increase in one's own income and in that of the reference group's income. One of these papers is a very recent study by Clark et al. (2013). In Table 4 of their paper the authors report the results of a regression where the dependent variable refers to satisfaction with income. It then appears that the coefficient of own income is about three times as high as that of self-reported reference income, and of opposite sign. This would imply that the value of $\beta$ is around 3 and, as a consequence, the value of the weight $w$ would be equal to (2/3). We now show that some of the existing suggestions for treating the poverty line as some fraction of the mean or median income can be accommodated in our framework. The EU standard set poverty line as 60% of the median is equivalent to choosing a particular weight for the reference income in our formulation. If we take $(1 - w) = \frac{0.6m - z_0}{m - z_0}$ in (17), where in $m$ is the median, then we get the poverty line set by the EU. Likewise, for $(1 - w) = \frac{0.37m - z_0}{m - z_0}$, where $m$ now stands for the mean, we get the Atkinson-Bourguignon (2001) relative poverty line.

It will now be worthwhile to compare our proposal with Foster's (1998) recommendation for a hybrid threshold. If $m$ represents the median, then the threshold $\alpha\, m$, where $0 < \alpha < 1$, is a general relative cutoff (Citro and Michael 1995). If we denote $\alpha\, m$ by $z_m$, then Foster (1998) suggested the use of a weighted geometric mean of the absolute threshold $z_0$ and the relative threshold $z_m$, namely, $z_0^{\rho} z_m^{1-\rho}$ as a threshold limit, where $0 < \rho < 1$ is a constant. A 1% increase in the living standard $m$ increases the poverty line by $\rho$% (see also Fisher 1995). Now, assume that the individual utility function is of the form $U\left(x, \frac{x}{m}\right) = x^{\rho}\left(\frac{x}{m}\right)^{1-\rho}$, $0 < \rho < 1$ is a constant. This utility function is increasing, concave in absolute income but decreasing convex in the reference level. Then our utility-consistency condition reveals that $z_1 = z_0^{\rho} z_m^{1-\rho}$, the hybrid cutoff advocated by Foster (1998). Thus, the Foster proposition can be justified by our utility-consistency condition.

[6]However, in order to increase the flexibility of the choice of the poverty line, it may be worthwhile to choose hybrid lines that are less than the absolute line. This would be fulfilled if $m < z_0$ and hence requires a different structure.

**Remark 1** The two forms of $U$ given by $U(x, m) = (k - a)x^\delta + am^\delta$ and $U(x, m) = x^\delta\left(\beta - \left(\frac{m}{x}\right)^\delta\right)$, where $a < 0$, $k > 0$, $0 < \delta < 1$ and $\beta - \left(\frac{m}{x}\right)^\delta > 0$, are increasing and strictly concave in absolute income but decreasing and strictly convex in reference income. For each of these two specifications of $U$, by the utility-consistency condition, we have $z_1 = \left(sz_0^\delta + (1-s)m^\delta\right)^{\frac{1}{\delta}}$, where $0 < s < 1$. Thus, we have examples of two different utility functions each of which leads to the same hybrid poverty lines. For $\delta = 1$, $z_1$ coincides with (2), whereas as $\delta \to 0$, it becomes Foster's hybrid poverty line. This form of $z_1$ is known as a quasilinear mean. Such a form has been characterized by Chakravarty (2011) as a generalized human development index using several dimensions of human well-being. A similar characterization can be developed in the current context.

We now make a systematic comparison between utility-consistency (equating $U(z_0, 0)$ with $U(z_1, z_1 - m)$, and $U\left(z_0, f\left(\frac{z_0}{z_0}\right)\right)$ with $U\left(z_1, \frac{z_1}{m}\right)$) and the Blackorby–Donaldson (1987) formulation. In their framework, preferences are assumed to be represented by a real valued utility function whose image is $u = U(y, \lambda)$, where $U$ is the utility that each member of the family derives with the characteristic $\lambda \in B$ when the household consumption is $y$, where $B$ is the set of household characteristics. The parameter $\lambda \in B$ enables to take into account economies of consumption due to household consumption. Household preferences remain unaltered if we consider an increasing function $\overline{U}$ of $U$, that is, $\overline{U} = L(U(y, \lambda), \lambda)$, where $L$ is increasing in its first argument for all $\lambda \in B$. However, interpersonal comparison of utility cannot be achieved only by household preferences. Some external value judgement has to be imposed on a particular $U$ that makes interpersonal comparisons possible. As Blackorby and Donaldson (1987) pointed out, one such judgement is provided by a set poverty consumption bundles $\{y(\lambda)|\lambda \in B\}$. This judgement requires that $u^r = U(y(\lambda), \lambda)$, for all $\lambda \in B$, where $u^r$ is the poverty utility level corresponding to $U$. This equation becomes meaningful if and only if $L(u^r, \lambda^1) = L(u^r, \lambda^2)$ for all $\lambda^1, \lambda^2 \in B$. Given that two utility functions satisfy $u^r = U(y(\lambda), \lambda)$, if they also satisfy $L(u^r, \lambda^1) = L(u^r, \lambda^2)$, then they are said to fulfil informational invariance for interpersonal comparisons with respect to reference utility indexed by $u^r$. As Blackorby and Donaldson (1987) argued, $L$ must be independent of $\lambda$ for interpersonal comparisons to be meaningful.[7]

Thus, the essential idea of equating two utility levels is the same in both the cases. While in our case two utility values are equated to determine a hybrid poverty line, in the Blackorby–Donaldson structure this is done for a given poverty consumption bundle in order to determine the necessary and sufficient condition for interpersonal utility comparison.

---

[7] A taxonomy of information invariance and interpersonal comparisons can be found in Sen (1977) and Blackorby et al. (1984).

## 3 An Empirical Illustration

In this section, we present several measures of the extent of poverty in rural and urban areas of the People's Republic of China and India, when an "amalgam poverty line", a weighted average of an absolute poverty line and of the mean or median income, is introduced. As absolute poverty line, we have used a monthly income of \$38 (at 2005 PPP) which corresponds to \$1.25 per day, as originally suggested by Ravallion et al. (2009). We assumed various possible weights. More precisely, we supposed that the weight $w$ given to the absolute poverty line [the weight of the median or of the mean being then $(1 - w)$], could be 1, 0.9, 0.66, and 0.5.

The database consisted of information on the income shares of ten deciles in the rural and urban areas of the two countries mentioned previously. Two computation methods were used. The first one is based on an algorithm originally proposed by Kakwani and Podder (1973) allowing one to estimate the Lorenz curve for each country and year on the basis of these 10 observations (income shares). On the basis of this Lorenz curve, it was then easy to find out which percentage of the population had an income (or expenditure level) smaller than that corresponding to some poverty line. The second approach used an algorithm proposed by Shorrocks and Wan (2009), which allows to "ungroup" income distributions, that is, to derive, for example, the share of each centile when the only data available originally are the income shares of deciles.

In Table 1, we present the values of the headcount ratio (in percentage) in the rural and urban areas in the People's Republic of China and India, under several possible scenarios. We give two sets of results: those based on the Shorrocks and Wan (2009) algorithm (part A) and those derived from the Kakwani and Podder approach (part B). In parentheses, we give also bootstrap confidence intervals. As expected, for a given weight, the headcount ratio is higher when the weight $(1 - w)$ refers to the mean rather than the median. Needless to say, the headcount ratio increases with the weight $w$. Looking at the bootstrap confidence intervals it appears that these differences are always significant, except in the case of a weight of 90% given to the \$38 poverty line when the Kakwani and Podder approach is implemented. In this specific case, the adjusted headcount ratio is the same whether a weight of 10% is given to the mean or the median income. Table 1a, b show also that, whatever weights are selected, the headcount ratio is higher in rural than in urban India. The percentage of poor is also higher in rural than in urban China. These differences are clearly significant, as can be checked by looking at the corresponding confidence intervals. Note also that whereas with the regular \$38 poverty line, there is almost no urban poverty in China, when some weight is given to the mean or median income when defining the poverty line, the headcount ratio becomes significant, being even higher than 30% when the weight of the mean is equal to 50%. The differences between the urban and rural sectors are much less striking in India, poverty being quite high in both areas.

We then combined the data on the headcounts given in Table 1 with the data on the total population around 2010, to derive an estimate of the total number of poor in the urban and rural areas of each of the two countries examined. These results are

**Table 1** Headcount ratios (in percentages) under various scenarios

A- The Shorrocks and Wan (2009) approach

| Weighting scheme (weight given to the absolute poverty line) | People's Republic of China, rural areas (2009) Shorrocks and Wan approach | People's Republic of China, urban areas (2009) Shorrocks and Wan approach | India, rural areas (2010) Shorrocks and Wan approach | India, urban areas (2010) Shorrocks and Wan approach |
|---|---|---|---|---|
| Absolute poverty line: $38<br>It is weighted with the median | | | | |
| 100% | 20.48<br>(19.38;21.62) | 0.26<br>(0.12;0.42) | 34.34<br>(33.04;35.68) | 29.18<br>(27.94;30.46) |
| 90% | 23.92<br>(22.84;24.98) | 1.42<br>(1.10;1.74) | 36.04<br>(34.84;37.24) | 31.22<br>(30.08;32.38) |
| 66% | 31.18<br>(30.18;32.12) | 10.70<br>(9.86;11.54) | 39.88<br>(38.82;40.82) | 36.48<br>(35.52;37.42) |
| 50% | 36.30<br>(35.36;37.14) | 20.58<br>(19.62;21.56) | 42.46<br>(41.64;43.22) | 40.04<br>(39.22;40.88) |
| Absolute poverty line: $38<br>It is weighted with the mean | | | | |
| 90% | 27.04<br>(25.82;28.30) | 2.14<br>(1.76;2.56) | 38.20<br>(36.86;39.56) | 34.04<br>(32.76;35.38) |
| 66% | 40.60<br>(39.28;41.96) | 17.74<br>(16.68;18.80) | 46.70<br>(45.34;48.14) | 45.24<br>(43.88;46.66) |
| 50% | 49.40<br>(48.02;50.82) | 30.58<br>(29.32;31.86) | 52.16<br>(50.78;53.56) | 52.04<br>(50.64;53.46) |

(continued)

**Table 1** (continued)

B- The Kakwani and Podder (1973) approach

| Weighting scheme (weight given to the absolute poverty line) | People's Republic of China, rural areas (2009) Kakwani and Podder approach | People's Republic of China, urban areas (2009) Kakwani and Podder approach | India, rural areas (2010) Kakwani and Podder approach | India, urban areas (2010) Kakwani and Podder approach |
|---|---|---|---|---|
| Absolute poverty line: $38<br>It is weighted with the median | | | | |
| 100% | 21.35<br>(20.45;22.25) | 0.15<br>(0.15;0.15) | 33.05<br>(32.45;33.55) | 27.85<br>(27.05;28.45) |
| 90% | 25.15<br>(24.35;25.85) | 0.15<br>(0.15;0.15) | 34.95<br>(34.45;35.45) | 30.55<br>(29.85;31.05) |
| 66% | 33.15<br>(32.55;33.55) | 15.85<br>(14.95;16.55) | 39.35<br>(38.95;39.65) | 36.45<br>(36.05;36.85) |
| 50% | 37.75<br>(37.35;38.15) | 26.25<br>(25.65;26.75) | 42.05<br>(41.75;42.25) | 40.05<br>(39.75;40.35) |
| Absolute poverty line: $38.<br>It is weighted with the mean. | | | | |
| 90% | 26.55<br>(25.75;27.25) | 0.15<br>(0.15;0.15) | 35.65<br>(35.05;36.15) | 31.65<br>(30.95;32.25) |
| 66% | 37.05<br>(36.45;37.65) | 20.35<br>(19.45;21.15) | 41.55<br>(41.05;41.85) | 39.85<br>(39.35;40.25) |
| 50% | 42.95<br>(42.45;43.45) | 31.75<br>(31.05;32.35) | 45.15<br>(44.75;45.45) | 44.65<br>(44.25;45.05) |

*Note* (The Shorrocks-Wan approach) The complete income distributions were derived on the basis of data on the shares of the deciles in total income. The first column gives the weight (in percentage) given to the absolute poverty line ($38), the complement (in percentage) giving the weight given to the median or the mean of the income distributions. Bootstrap confidence intervals (2.5–97.5%) are given in parentheses. These bootstrap results are based on 4000 random samples of the ungrouped distribution with 5000 individuals

*Note* (The Kakwani-Podder approach) The complete income distributions were derived on the basis of data on the shares of the deciles in total income. The first column gives the weight (in percentage) given to the absolute poverty line ($38), the complement (in percentage) giving the weight given to the median or the mean of the income distributions. Bootstrap confidence intervals (5–95%) are given in parentheses. These bootstrap results are based on 1000 samples of 1000 individuals given in Table 2, together with the corresponding confidence intervals. To simplify the presentation, we give only results based on the Shorrocks and Wan algorithm. It is then easy to compare the number of poor under various scenarios with those obtained on the basis of a weight $w$ equal to 1 (so that the "amalgam poverty line" is also equal to \$38). Here also we observe a very important increase in the number of poor in urban areas in China, when the poverty line depends on the median or mean income.

Finally, Table 3 gives the income gap ratios in the rural and urban areas of the People's Republic of China and India under the various scenarios, the results being again based on the Shorrocks and Wan algorithm. This index is an indicator of poverty depths of different individuals. Here, also the income gap ratio increases with the weight given to the median or mean income, whether in India or in the People's Republic of China. The income gap ratio is much smaller in urban than in rural areas of the People's Republic of China but this is not true for India since when the weight given to the mean or median income becomes higher, the income gap ratio, becomes higher in urban than in rural areas.

Note finally that when multiplied by the poverty line and the total number of poor, this summary measure has a direct policy interpretation in the sense that the multiplied formula determines the total amount of money required to put all the poor persons at the poverty line. Now, for a given country and area, with a given poverty line and the reference income, we determine the amalgam poverty line using a specific weighting scheme. Given an amalgam poverty line, we can then directly estimate the amount of money necessary to place the poor persons of a given area in a given country at its poverty line, using the country's area income gap ratio from Table 3 and the number of poor from Table 2.

## 4 Conclusions

We have followed Clark and Oswald's (1998) suggestion that an individual cares about his absolute position (his own income) and his relative position (his own income in comparison with a reference income, such as the mean or the median). Two different forms of the utility function that depend on a person's absolute and relative statuses have been characterized. These two utility functions have been employed to determine a relative poverty line endogenous to the income distribution. It turns out that in either case, the relative poverty line becomes a combination, a weighted mean, of a given poverty line and a reference income, where the weights add up to one. This is similar in spirit to Foster's (1998) hybrid poverty threshold, a weighted geometric mean of a relative and an absolute cutoff point. This weight enables a policy maker to express his preference for absolute or relative poverty. Interestingly enough, some of the existing suggestions for the choice of the relative poverty line drop out as special cases of our general approach. The empirical illustration has shown that no matter how we define the "amalgam poverty line" the extent of poverty is generally smaller in the People's Republic of China than in India.

**Table 2** Number of poor (in million) in rural and urban areas of the People's Republic of China and India, depending on the weighting scheme

| Country and area | $38;median;100% | $38;median;90% | $38;median;66% | $38;median;50% | $38;mean;90% | $38;mean;66% | $38;mean;50% |
|---|---|---|---|---|---|---|---|
| People's Republic of China, rural areas (2009) | 143.77 (136.05;151.77) | 167.92 (160.34;175.36) | 218.88 (211.86;225.48) | 254.83 (248.23;260.72) | 189.82 (181.26;198.67) | 285.01 (275.75;294.56) | 346.79 (337.10;356.76) |
| People's Republic of China, urban areas (2009) | 1.70 (0.78;2.74) | 9.27 (7.18;11.36) | 69.87 (64.39;75.36) | 134.39 (128.12;140.79) | 13.97 (11.49;16.72) | 115.84 (108.92;122.76) | 199.69 (191.46;208.05) |
| India, rural areas (2009) | 285.71 (274.89;296.86) | 299.85 (289.87;309.84) | 331.80 (322.98;339.62) | 353.27 (346.44;359.59) | 317.82 (306.68;329.14) | 388.54 (377.23;400.52) | 433.97 (422.49;445.62) |
| India, urban areas (2009) | 107.67 (103.10;112.40) | 115.20 (111.00;119.48) | 134.61 (131.07;138.08) | 147.75 (144.72;150.85) | 125.61 (120.88;130.55) | 166.94 (161.92;172.18) | 192.03 (186.86;197.27) |

*Note* The heading of each column shows that the poverty line is assumed to be equal to $38 and it also indicates which other indicator is weighted (median or mean) and which weight is given to the absolute poverty line. The computations were based on the Shorrocks and Wan (2009) approach

**Table 3** Poverty Gap Ratios in the rural and urban areas of the People's Republic of China and of India, depending on the weighting scheme

| Country and area | \$38;median;100% | \$38;median;90% | \$38;median;66% | \$38;median;50% | \$38;mean;90% | \$38;mean;66% | \$38;mean;50% |
|---|---|---|---|---|---|---|---|
| People's Republic of China, rural areas (2009) | 0.2319 (0.2228;0.2409) | 0.2473 (0.2387;0.2560) | 0.2840 (0.2758;0.2928) | 0.3043 (0.2959;0.3130) | 0.2621 (0.2540;0.2707) | 0.3217 (0.3136;0.3296) | 0.3533 (0.3458;0.3610) |
| People's Republic of China, urban areas (2009) | 0.1251 (0.0708;0.1894) | 0.1495 (0.1229;0.1796) | 0.1981 (0.1857;0.2107) | 0.2465 (0.2357;0.2567) | 0.1567 (0.1338;0.1814) | 0.2240 (0.2136;0.2345) | 0.2832 (0.2746;0.2920) |
| India, rural areas (2009) | 0.2192 (0.2123;0.2264) | 0.2234 (0.2167;0.2305) | 0.2336 (0.2269;0.2409) | 0.2414 (0.2346;0.2482) | 0.2292 (0.2225;0.2361) | 0.2530 (0.2468;0.2594) | 0.2704 (0.2641;0.2767) |
| India, urban areas (2009) | 0.2527 (0.2248;0.2605) | 0.2651 (0.2576;0.2728) | 0.2862 (0.2785;0.2942) | 0.3004 (0.2921;0.3083) | 0.2765 (0.2691;0.2842) | 0.3182 (0.3109;0.3255) | 0.3460 (0.3387;0.3531) |

*Note* If $z$ is the poverty line and $\overline{x_P}$ is the mean income of the poor, then the poverty gap ratio $PGR$ is defined as $PGR = \frac{z-\overline{x_P}}{z}$
The bootstrap confidence intervals (2.5–97.5%) are based on 4000 random samples of the ungrouped distribution with 5000 individuals

**Acknowledgements** For comments and suggestions, the authors first thank participants to the ADB (Asian Development Bank) International Workshop on "Untold side of the Asian Poverty Reduction Story", Southwest University, People's Republic of China, November 19–20 2013, in particular B. Zheng for helpful discussions and comments. The authors wish also to thank Bhaskar Dutta and participants to the UNU-WIDER Development Conference on "Inequality—measurement, trends, impacts, and policies", Helsinki, September 5–6 2014. Finally the authors are grateful to Iva Sebastian-Samaniego of the Asian Development Bank for helping them with the computations based on the Shorrocks-Wan algorithm.

## Appendix 1: On Shorrocks and Wan's (2009) "Ungrouping Income Distributions"

Assume a Lorenz curve with $(m+1)$ coordinates $(p_k^*, L_k^*)$ where $p_k^*$ and $L_k^*(k = 1, \ldots, m)$ (refer respectively to the cumulative shares in the total population and in total income of income classes 1 to $k$, while $p_0^* = L_0^* = 0$. These Lorenz coordinates can, for example, refer to decile shares published on a given country. Since often the corresponding average income is not available, it will be assumed to be equal to 1 so that the mean income $\mu_k^*$ of class $k$ will be expressed as

$$\mu_k^* = \frac{L_k^* - L_{k-1}^*}{p_k^* - p_{k-1}^*} \quad k = 1, 2, \ldots\ldots, m. \tag{18}$$

The goal is to obtain a synthetic sample of $n$ equally weighted observations whose mean value is 1 and which are conform to the original data. These $n$ observations are therefore partitioned into $m$ non-overlapping and ordered groups having each $m_k = n\left(p_k^* - p_{k-1}^*\right)$ observations. Call $x_{ki}$ the $i^{th}$ observation in class $k$, the sample mean of this class being $\mu_k$.

The algorithm proposed by Shorrocks and Wan (2009) includes two stages.

The first step consists of building an initial sample with unit mean which is generated from a parametric form fitted to the grouped data [see, for example, Ryu and Slottje (1999), for a survey of various parameterizations of the Lorenz curve].[8]

In the second stage the algorithm adjusts the observations generated in the initial sample to the true values available from the grouped data. More precisely the initial sample value $x_j$, assumed to belong to class $k$, is transformed into an intermediate value $\widehat{x_j}$ via the following rule:

$$\frac{\widehat{x_j} - \mu_k^*}{\mu_{k+1}^* - \mu_k^*} = \frac{x_j - \mu_k}{\mu_{k+1} - \mu_k}. \tag{19}$$

For the first class we will write that

---

[8] Shorrocks and Wan chose to generate the initial sample on the basis of a lognormal distribution. For more details, see, Shorrocks and Wan (2009).

$$\frac{\widehat{x_j}}{\mu_1^*} = \frac{x_j}{\mu_1} \quad \text{for} \quad x_j \leq \mu_1, \tag{20}$$

while for the last class we have

$$\frac{\widehat{x_j}}{\mu_m^*} = \frac{x_j}{\mu_m} \quad \text{for} \quad x_j \geq \mu_m. \tag{21}$$

Obviously in the next iteration the intermediate values $\widehat{x_j}$ are themselves transformed into new values until the algorithm produces an ordered sample which exactly replicates the properties of the original grouped data. Convergence is in fact very quickly obtained.

## Appendix 2: The Kakwani and Podder (1973) Approach

Let $L$ refer to the height of the Lorenz curve (cumulative income share) and $z$ to the corresponding abscissa (cumulative population share). Kakwani and Podder (1973) proposed then the following equation for the Lorenz curve (and showed that such a formulation satisfies all the desired properties of a Lorenz curve):

$$lnL = -h + lnz + hz. \tag{22}$$

It is hence possible to derive the value of the parameter $h$ by regressing $lnL$ on $lnz$ and $z$.

From (22) we also derive that

$$L = \mathrm{e}^{lnz+h(z-1)} = \mathrm{e}^{lnz}\mathrm{e}^{h(z-1)} = z\mathrm{e}^{h(z-1)}. \tag{23}$$

Remembering that the slope along the Lorenz curve is equal to the ratio of the income corresponding to this point of the Lorenz curve to the mean income, we can apply (23) to the poverty line and write that

$$\begin{aligned} \frac{\partial L}{\partial z} = \left(\frac{\text{poverty line}}{\text{mean}}\right) &= \mathrm{e}^{h(z-1)} + zh\mathrm{e}^{h(z-1)} \\ &= \mathrm{e}^{h(z-1)}(1 + zh). \end{aligned} \tag{24}$$

We are therefore looking for the population share $z$ for which the equation below holds

$$\ln\left(\frac{\text{poverty line}}{\text{mean}}\right) = h(z-1) + \ln(1 + zh), \tag{25}$$

that is,

$$\ln(\text{poverty line}) = \ln(\text{mean}) + h(z - 1) + \ln(1 + zh). \tag{26}$$

Given the poverty line selected, the mean income and the parameter $h$ determined previously, it is easy to derive the value of $z$ for which (26) holds, that is, the headcount ratio corresponding to the chosen poverty line.

## References


Aczel, J. (1966). *Lectures on functional equations and their applications*. New York: Academic Press.

Atkinson, A. B., & Bourguignon, F. (2001). Poverty and inclusion from a world perspective. In J. E. Stiglitz & P. A. Muet (Eds.), *Governance, equity and global markets*. Oxford: Oxford University Press.

Berrebi, Z. M., & Silber, J. (1985). Income inequality indices and deprivation: A generalisation. *Quarterly Journal of Economics, 100,* 807–810.

Blackorby, C., & Donaldson, D. (1980). A theoretical treatment of indices of absolute inequality. *International Economic Review, 21,* 107–136.

Blackorby, C., & Donaldson, D. (1987). Welfare ratios and distributional sensitive cost-benefit analysis. *Journal of Public Economics, 34*(3), 265–290.

Blackorby, C., & Donaldson, D. (1994). Measuring the cost of children: A theoretical framework. In R. Blundell, I. Preston, & I. Walker (Eds.), *The measurement of household welfare* (pp. 51–69). Cambridge: Cambridge University Press.

Blackorby, C., Donaldson, D., & Weymark J. A. (1984). Social choice theory with interpersonal utility comparisons: A diagrammatic introduction. *International Economic Review, 25,* 327–356.

Bossert, W., & D'Ambrosio, C. (2007). Dynamic measures of individual deprivation. *Social Choice and Welfare, 28,* 77–88.

Chakravarty, S. R. (2011). A reconsideration of the trade-offs in the new human development index. *Journal of Economic Inequality, 9,* 471–474.

Chakravarty, S. R., & Dutta, B. (1987). A note on measures of distance between income distributions. *Journal of Economic Theory, 41,* 185–188.

Chakravarty, S. R., & Moyes, P. (2003). Individual welfare, social deprivation and income taxation. *Economic Theory, 21,* 843–869.

Chen, S., & Ravallion, M. (2001). How did the world's poorest fare in the 1990s? *Review of Income and Wealth, 47,* 283–300.

Chen, S., & Ravallion, M. (2013). More relatively-poor people in a less absolutely-poor world. *Review of Income and Wealth, 59*(1), 1–28.

Citro, C. F., & Michael, R. T. (1995). *Measuring poverty: A new approach*. Washington, DC: National Academy Press.

Clark, A. E., & Oswald, A. J. (1996). Satisfaction and comparison income. *Journal of Public Economics, 51,* 359–381.

Clark, A. E., & Oswald, A. J. (1998). Comparison-concave utility and following behaviour in social and economic settings. *Journal of Public Economics, 70,* 133–155.

Clark, A., Senik, C., & Yamada K. (2013). *The Joneses in Japan: Income comparisons and financial satisfaction*. Discussion Paper No. 866, Institute of Social and Economic Research, Osaka University, Japan.

Deaton, A. (2010). Price indexes, inequality, and the measurement of world poverty. *American Economic Review, 100,* 5–34.

Duesenberry, J. S. (1949). *Income, saving and the theory of consumer behaviour*. Cambridge, MA: Harvard University Press.

Easterlin, Richard A. (2001). Income and happiness: Towards a unified theory. *Economic Journal, 111,* 465–484.

Falk, A., & Knell, M. (2004). Choosing the Joneses: Endogenous goals and reference standards. *Scandinavian Journal of Economics, 106,* 417–435.

Ferreira, F. H. G., Chen, S., Dabalen, A., Dikhanov, Y., Hamadeh, N., & Jolliffe, A. et al. (2015). *A Global Count of the Extreme Poor in 2012: Data Issues, Methodology and Initial Results*. IZA DP No. 9442.

Ferrer-i-Carbonell, A. (2005). Income and well-being: An empirical analysis of the comparison income effect. *Journal of Public Economics, 89,* 997–1019.

Fisher, G. M. (1995). "*Is there such a thing as an absolute poverty line over time?*", Mimeo, U.S. Department of Health and Human Services, Washington, DC.

Foster, J. E. (1998). Absolute versus relative poverty. *American Economic Review, 88,* 335–341.

Frank, R. H. (1985). *Choosing the right pond*. Oxford: Oxford University Press.

Frank, R. H. (1999). *Luxury Fever*. New York: The Free Press.

Fuchs, V. (1969). Comment on measuring the size of the low-income population. In L. Soltow (Ed.), *Six papers on the size distribution of wealth and income* (pp. 198–202). New York: National Bureau of Economic Research.

Hopkins, E. (2008). Inequality, happiness and relative concerns: What actually is their relationship? *Journal of Economic Inequality, 6,* 351–372.

Kahneman, D., & Tversky, A. (1991). Loss aversion in riskless choice: A reference-dependent model. *The Quarterly Journal of Economics, 106,* 1039–1061.

Kakwani, N. C. (2011). A new model for constructing poverty thresholds. In J. Deutsch & J. Silber (Eds.), *The Measurement of Individual Well-Being and Group Inequalities: Essays in Memory of Z.M. Berrebi*. London: Routledge.

Kakwani, N. C., & Podder, N. (1973). On the estimation of lorenz curve from grouped observations. *International Economic Review, 14,* 278–292.

O'Higgins, M., & Jenkins, S. (1990). Poverty in the EC: Estimates for 1975, 1980 and 1985. In R. Teekens & B. M. S. van Praag (Eds.), *Analysing poverty in the European Community: Policy issues, research options, and data sources* (pp. 187–212). Luxembourg: Office of Official Publications of the European Communities.

Orshansky, M. (1965). Counting the poor: Another look at the poverty profile. *Social Security Bulletin, 28,* 3–29.

Ravallion, M. (1994). *Poverty comparisons*. Chur, Switzerland: Harwood.

Ravallion, M. (2008). Poverty lines. In S. N. Durlauf & L. E. Blume (Eds.), *The New Palgrave Dictionary of Economics* (2nd ed).

Ravallion, M. (2012). Poverty lines across the world. In P. Jefferson (Ed.), *Oxford Handbook of the Economics of Poverty*.

Ravallion, M., Datt, G., & van de Walle, D. (1991). Quantifying absolute poverty in the developing world. *Review of Income and Wealth, 37,* 345–361.

Ravallion, M., Chen, S., & Sangraula, P. (2009). Dollar a day revisited. *The World Bank Economic Review, 23,* 163–184.

Ravallion, M., & Chen, S. (2011). Weakly relative poverty. *Review of Economics and Statistics, 93*(4), 1251–1261.

Ruggles, P. (1990). *Drawing the line*. Washington, DC: Urban Institute Press.

Runciman, W. G. (1966). *Relative deprivation and social justice*. London: Routledge.

Ryu, H. K., & Slottje, D. S. (1999). Parametric approximations to the Lorenz curve. In J. Silber (Ed.), *Handbook on income inequality measurement*. Dordrecht, The Netherlands: Kluwer Academic Publishers.

Sen, A. K. (1977). Social choice theory: A re-examination. *Econometrica, 45*.

Shorrocks, A., & Wan, G. (2009). Ungrouping income distributions. Synthesizing samples for inequality and poverty analysis. In K. Basu & R. Kanbur (Eds.), *Arguments for a better world. Essays in Honor of Amartya Sen, Volume 1, Ethics, welfare and measurement* (pp. 414–434). Oxford: Oxford University Press. (Chapter 22).

Subramanian, S. (2011). The poverty line: Getting it wrong again. *Economic and Political Weekly, 46*, 37–42.

Yitzhaki, S. (1979). Relative deprivation and the Gini coefficient. *The Quarterly Journal of Economics, 93*, 321–324.

Zheng, B. (2007). Utility-gap dominances and inequality orderings. *Social Choice and Welfare, 28*, 255–280.

# Poverty and Time

**Walter Bossert, Satya R. Chakravarty and Conchita D'Ambrosio**

**Abstract** We examine the measurement of individual poverty in an intertemporal context. Our aim is to capture the importance of persistence in a state of poverty and we characterize a corresponding individual intertemporal poverty measure. Our first axiom requires that intertemporal poverty is identical to static poverty in the degenerate single-period case. The remaining two properties express decomposability requirements within poverty spells and across spells in order to reflect the persistence issue. In addition, we axiomatize an aggregation procedure to obtain an intertemporal poverty measure for societies and we illustrate our new index with an application to EU countries.

**Keywords** Intertemporal poverty measurement · Equity

**JEL Classification** D63

---

Permission granted by Springer Nature to reprint this article from Journal of Economic Inequality, Volume 10, 2012, is acknowledged with thanks.

---

W. Bossert (✉)
Department of Economics and CIREQ, University of Montreal, Montreal, Canada
e-mail: walter.bossert@umontreal.ca

S. R. Chakravarty
Indian Statistical Institute, Kolkata 700108, India
e-mail: satyarchakravarty@gmail.com

C. D'Ambrosio
Université du Luxembourg, Maison des Sciences Humaines, 11, Porte des Sciences, L-4366 Esch-sur-Alzette, Luxembourg
e-mail: conchita.dambrosio@uni.lu



S. R. Chakravarty (ed.), *Poverty, Social Exclusion and Stochastic Dominance*, Themes in Economics, https://doi.org/10.1007/978-981-13-3432-0_6

## 1 Introduction

In a seminal contribution, Sen (1976) distinguished two fundamental issues in poverty measurement, namely, (i) identifying the poor among the total population; and (ii) constructing an index of poverty using the available information on the poor. The first problem has been solved in the literature by setting a poverty line (which may or may not depend on the income distribution under consideration) and identifying as poor the individuals whose incomes fall below this threshold. To address the second issue, the aggregation problem, many indices have been proposed capturing not only the fraction of the population that is poor (*the head-count ratio*), that is, the incidence of poverty, but also the extent of individual poverty and the inequality among those who are poor.

The literature on poverty measurement has advanced to a high degree of sophistication since Sen (1976). However, there remain substantial issues to be addressed. One of these issues is concerned with the measurement of intertemporal poverty as opposed to limiting attention to single-period considerations. For instance, consider an observer comparing two individuals both of whom are poor today to the same degree. Suppose that, while the first was not poor in any of the previous two periods, the second individual experienced poverty in both previous periods in addition to the present. Is the degree of intertemporal poverty of those two individuals the same? This does not seem to be the case—the second individual is poorer as soon as the entire intertemporal income distribution is taken into consideration. Now consider again two individuals both of whom are poor today to the same degree but the first was poor also last year, while the second was out of poverty last year but in poverty the year before that. Is the intertemporal poverty of those two individuals the same? Again, we believe not. Both individuals were poor twice (and we are assuming that they were poor to the same degree) but the first individual experienced poverty in two consecutive periods while the second did not.

The relative degree of overall poverty when comparing the two individuals over time depends on the role and evaluation of *persistence* in a state of poverty. To us, the negative effects of being in poverty are cumulative, hence a two-period poverty spell is much harder to handle than two one-period spells that are interrupted by one (or more) period(s) out of poverty. We believe that intertemporal information should not be neglected in assessing individual poverty. Nowadays, the availability of panel data for most of the countries in the world makes it possible for researchers to expand the information set when evaluating poverty. In addition to poverty lines, per-period poverty values and inequality among the poor, the lengths of individual poverty spells can be incorporated. We propose a way to add this time dimension to the information used in poverty measurement.

Temporal incidence and its consequences have also been analyzed in other contexts such as demography, marketing, and unemployment; see Arranz and Cantó (2010) for some references on the first two areas. The *Journal of Economic Inequality* has published a mini-symposium on unemployment in 2009. We refer the reader to its introduction (Lambert 2009) for an exhaustive summary of the literature and to the articles on the topic by Sengupta (2009) and Shorrocks (2009a, b) contained in it.

There are several approaches to the measurement of chronic poverty (some of which are discussed below). Without going into specifics at this stage, it may nevertheless be useful to distinguish our notion of persistence of poverty from what we think of as being in chronic poverty. Generally speaking, we think of chronic poverty as a term to apply to situations in which an individual is in a state of poverty for a "large" *total* proportion of the number of time periods under consideration. This, we think, does not necessarily mean that attention is paid to the duration of poverty spells given a total number of periods spent in poverty. Our notion of persistence explicitly takes the duration of these spells into consideration by assigning, in a sense to be made precise once our formal framework is introduced, higher weights to longer spells. In other words, chronic poverty occurs when there is a frequent recurrence of poverty states while persistent poverty requires in addition to frequency that poverty manifests itself in periods that are consecutive.

This paper is similar in spirit to Hoy and Zheng (2006) but the individual intertemporal poverty measure we characterize differs from theirs due to the properties that are deemed relevant to capture the role of time and persistence. Hoy and Zheng (2006) demand that aggregating first across individuals and then across time periods should be equivalent to aggregating in the reverse order—first across time periods for each single individual and then across members of the society. This leads to a notion of *path independence*. In contrast to Hoy and Zheng (2006), we consider the phenomenon of persistence to be crucial in assessing individual intertemporal poverty. Aggregating across individuals first means that this information is lost when we reach the second stage of aggregation. Hence we characterize an index of intertemporal poverty for each member of the society under analysis and then aggregate across members of society.

Foster (2009) expresses a similar view in proposing chronic poverty indices by aggregating first across time. In contrast to our contribution, persistence in the state of poverty is not assigned any relevance. The measures Foster (2009) proposes—generalizations of the Foster–Greer–Thorbecke (1984) class that allows for time to matter—do satisfy a property of *time anonymity* under which the sequencing of incomes in individual intertemporal profiles does not affect poverty. Foster (2009) defines an individual as chronically poor if his income is below the poverty line for at least a given number of periods. Thus, in addition to a poverty line, there is a second cut off point in defining the chronically poor—a point defined in terms of the incidence of poverty over time. As is the case for our contribution, the order of aggregation matters in Foster's approach—to identify the chronically poor, the first aggregation step has to be performed across periods for each individual. The individual Foster indices are means over time of per-period Foster–Greer–Thorbecke indices. The aggregate indices are obtained by calculating average poverty among the chronically poor. Recall that, in Foster (2009), only individuals who are poor for at least a given number of periods are considered. Thus, if an individual is poor, but rarely so, it is treated in the analysis as one of the individuals who are never poor. This is not the case in the present contribution. We do not restrict our sample to chronically poor individuals, hence we take into account spells of poverty of any length.

The path-independence property mentioned above can be called into question in other models of social evaluation as well. For example, in a framework where well-being is to be aggregated across time and across individuals, aggregating across individuals first means that, in the second step of the procedure, we do not have information on the period of life of an *individual—only aggregate* per-period information is available. Hence, a given per-period level of individual wellbeing has to be treated in the same way, no matter in which period of life this level is achieved. This seems to be rather counter-intuitive and restrictive, and the same reasoning applies to the issue of intertemporal poverty measurement considered here. See, for instance, Blackorby et al. (1996, 2005) for discussions.

Porter and Quinn (2008) and Calvo and Dercon (2009) consider intertemporal measures of individual poverty as well. Porter and Quinn (2008, p. 27) propose one class of measures with the property that "fluctuations in wellbeing have a greater negative impact, the poorer the individual." Calvo and Dercon (2009) suggest measures some of which allow for different treatment of different time periods by means of discounting. They also address the persistence issue but the proposed measure is very different from ours and deals only with poverty in the immediately preceding period without allowing the entire history of individuals to matter.

It seems to us that the negative effects of being in poverty are cumulative. Empirical evidence is in favor of this view. Individuals who have been persistently poor are often discriminated against and "have little access to productive assets and low capabilities in terms of health, education and social capital" (Chronic Poverty Research Center 2004, p. 3). In addition, there is true state dependence in poverty status since the chances of being poor in the future are higher for individuals who are already poor, even after controlling for individual heterogeneity, observed and unobserved. "For example, the experience of poverty itself might induce a loss of motivation, lowering the chances that individuals with given attributes escape poverty in the future" (Cappellari and Jenkins 2004, p. 598). Arranz and Cantó (2010), using longitudinal data for Spain, show that poverty spell accumulation and the duration of past spells have negative effects on poverty exit rates. Bradbury et al. (2001) report that children who have been poor for a long time are worse off than those who are poor in a single period only. Walker (1995, p. 103) writes that "When poverty predominantly occurs in long spells(…)the poor have virtually no chance of escaping from poverty and, therefore, little allegiance to the wider community." Past poverty spells are also found to affect the current evaluation of poverty, over and above the individual current income status; see, among others, Castilla (2010).

The empirical and econometric literature on poverty measurement has long recognized the importance of being able to distinguish between chronic and transitory poverty and proposes alternative methods for capturing the relevant phenomenon; for surveys of this literature, see, among others, Rodgers and Rodgers (1993) and Jenkins (2000). Numerous applied contributions provide a detailed description of poverty persistence in various countries and help in shaping social policies but the measures used are established in an ad hoc fashion without much of a theoretical foundation. Our paper contributes to this literature by filling this gap. Specifically, some of the empirical literature involving persistence in poverty proceed by counting the proportion of people being poor in each period. Alternatively, the percentage of "long" poverty spells or the sequence of multiple spells is used as a crude measure of intertemporal poverty. In order to try to include information on the intensity of poverty, some authors capture the temporal aspect of individual poverty by using a measure of permanent income and then applying standard (static) indices of poverty such as members of the Foster–Greer–Thorbecke class to the resulting distribution of permanent incomes. See, for instance, Rodgers and Rodgers (1993, p. 31) who use as permanent income "the maximum sustainable annual consumption level that the agent could achieve with his or her actual income stream over the same $T$ years, if the agent could save and borrow at prevailing interest rates."

The main purpose of this paper is to provide an axiomatic foundation for the measurement of intertemporal poverty that differs from earlier approaches such as those of Hoy and Zheng (2006), Porter and Quinn (2008), Calvo and Dercon (2009) and Foster (2009) in the way persistence is taken into consideration. Our measure pays attention to the length of individual poverty spells by assigning a higher level of poverty to situations where, ceteris paribus, poverty is experienced in consecutive rather than separated periods. The length of breaks between spells is also accounted for by associating longer breaks between spells with lower intertemporal poverty. In the theoretical part of the paper, we provide a characterization of our new measure. Furthermore, we characterize aggregate intertemporal poverty as the arithmetic mean of the individual intertemporal poverty indices. We do not restrict attention to environments with a fixed poverty line—we allow for any method to obtain individual per-period poverty indicators; in particular, the commonly-used procedure of using a percentage of average or median income as the poverty line is compatible with our setup, and this is the procedure that is used in the applied part of this paper.

We use our new aggregate index as well as measures suggested in the earlier literature to illustrate the commonalities and the differences with alternative approaches. The application pertains to poverty patterns among EU countries in the years from 1994 to 2001.

## 2 Individual Intertemporal Poverty Measures

This paper is concerned with the intertemporal aggregation of per-period individual poverty indicators (such as relative poverty gaps or their square values) over time and the across society aggregation of these individual measures into a social measure of intertemporal poverty. We begin with a discussion of individual intertemporal poverty and its link to what we refer to as persistence.

Suppose that individual poverty indicators are observed in each of a non-empty and finite set of consecutive periods. A standard way of generating these per period indicators consists of defining them, in each period, as the difference between a (constant or income-distribution-dependent) poverty line and the individual's income divided by the poverty line if the income is below this poverty line and as equal to zero otherwise. We do not need to commit to a specific way of obtaining these indicators and treat them, for simplicity, as the primary inputs for our analysis.

Our individual poverty index depends on the length of the spells in which a person remains poor. Clearly, the definition of a poverty spell is context specific. The choice of the reference period is important for defining a poverty spell and there is a minimum length of time for which poverty should persist. In fact, it is quite similar to the issue of unemployment duration of a person. As Shorrocks (2009a, b) points out, there can be different approaches to the measurement of unemployment duration. In our case, a person may be asked whether its income is currently below the poverty line and whether it has been so for a specified length of time. If, for instance, the answer is that the person's income is indeed below the poverty line and has been for a year, the poverty spell is one year. We may also consider a person as unemployed as well as poor if during a time spell its income has been below a threshold level. In this case, the duration of unemployment and poverty coincide. The analysis considered in our paper applies to any well-defined poverty spell.

The novel feature we suggest in intertemporal poverty measurement is to take into consideration the length of the poverty spells an individual is subjected to. For example, suppose two per-period individual poverty profiles are compared, where the first profile is given by (1/3,1/2,1/4,1/2,0) and the second by (1/3,0,1/2,1/4,1/2). We claim that individual intertemporal poverty should be higher in the first than in the second: in the second profile, the individual experiences a break from being in poverty rather than being poor in four *consecutive* periods.

Moreover, the length of spells out of poverty matters in the sense that a longer break between poverty spells is better than a shorter break if the lengthening of the break by adding a period out of poverty is the only change when moving from one profile to another. For instance, suppose we have two per-period individual poverty profiles (1/2,0,1/3,1/4,0,1/2) and (1/2,0,0,1/3,1/4,0,1/2). According to our hypothesis, the first of these profiles is associated with a higher value of individual intertemporal poverty. The two profiles involve an identical triple of spells—namely, a one-period spell with a per-period poverty of 1/2, a two-period spell with poverty values of 1/3 and 1/4, and another one-period spell with poverty 1/2. However, there is one zero-poverty period separating the spells in the first profile but a break of two periods in the second and, thus, intertemporal poverty is lower in the second option.

The above two properties are not sufficient to narrow down the class of possible measures to any significant degree; they are merely monotonicity conditions that are satisfied by a large class of measures. For that reason, although we note that these are properties of importance, they need to be supplemented by further restrictions with some intuitive appeal. We employ notions of decomposability in our axioms, and these properties represent a (we think, very plausible) way of formalizing a notion of individual intertemporal poverty that conforms to the features illustrated in the above examples. Of course, these are not the only possibilities of doing so but, given that decomposability properties have a long and well-established standing in the theory of social index numbers, they appear to constitute a well-motivated choice.

As is apparent from the formal definition of our axioms, they accommodate the features alluded to above by requiring different types of decompositions depending on whether we decompose a profile across spells or within a single spell.

Comparisons of poverty profiles of different length (and profiles coming from societies of possibly different populations and population sizes) are possible according to our measure; this is essential in order to perform international comparisons involving data sets with different sampling periods. These comparisons can be performed because our index is invariant to replications of an individual poverty profile with respect to time. For instance, if a two-period poverty profile of a person is replicated twice, then our individual poverty index remains unchanged; see also the time replication invariance principle suggested by Shorrocks (2009).

Let $\Omega = \cup_{T \in N} R_+^T$. For $T \in N$, an individual per-period individual poverty profile of dimension $T$ is a vector $p_i \in R_+^T$, where $p_i^t$ is individual $i$'s poverty experienced in period $t \in \{1, \ldots, T\}$. An individual intertemporal poverty measure is a function $P_i : \Omega \to R_+$ where, for all $p_i \in \Omega$, $P_i(p_i)$ is the intertemporal poverty experienced by person $i$. We choose the domain consisting of the union of the entire spaces $R_+^T$ merely for expositional convenience. All of our arguments go through if this rich space is replaced with a subset of $R_+^T$ containing the origin—for example, we can deal with environments where per-period poverty can assume the values zero and one only (one when the individual is below the per-period poverty line, zero otherwise).

The result of this section consists of a characterization of an individual intertemporal poverty measure that reflects the length-of-spell hypothesis mentioned above. This basic idea also motivates a characterization in the context of deriving measures of social exclusion from measures of individual deprivation (Bossert et al. 2007), where similar considerations apply. However, the axioms we employ are different and we obtain a different measure as a consequence.

According to the measure, we propose in this paper, individual intertemporal poverty is calculated as the weighted average of the individual per-period poverty values where, for each period, the weight is given by the length of the spell to which this period belongs. An alternative weighting scheme is proposed by Roope (2010), where the weight assigned to a period is equal to the number of periods of relative affluence directly preceding it.

Consider any $T \in N$ and $p_i \in R_+^T$. For $t \in \{1, \ldots, T\}$ such that $p_i^t > 0$, let $D^t(p_i)$ be the maximal number of consecutive periods including $t$ with positive per-period poverty values. Fort $t \in \{1, \ldots, T\}$ such that $p_i^t = 0$, let $D^t(p_i)$ be the maximal number of consecutive periods including $t$ with zero per-period poverty. To illustrate this definition, consider the profile $p_i = (1/2, 0, 0, 1/3, 1/4, 0, 1/2) \in R_+^7$. The length of the first poverty spell is one and, thus, $D^1(p_i) = 1$. This is followed by a non-poverty spell of length two, which implies $D^2(p_i) = D^3(p_i) = 2$. The next two periods are periods in poverty and we obtain $D^4(p_i) = D^5(p_i) = 2$. Period 6 is a single period out of poverty and, thus, $D^6(p_i) = 1$. Finally, there is a one-period poverty spell and we have $D^7(p_i) = 1$.

Our individual intertemporal poverty measure is now defined as

$$P_i^*(p_i) = \frac{1}{T}\sum_{\tau=1}^{T} D^\tau(p_i)p_i^\tau \tag{1}$$

for all $T \in N$ and for all $p_i \in R_+^T$. Returning to our earlier examples, the individual intertemporal poverty associated with the relevant profiles is

$$P_i^*\left(\frac{1}{3}, \frac{1}{2}, \frac{1}{4}, \frac{1}{2}, 0\right) = \frac{1}{5}.\left(4.\left(\frac{1}{3} + \frac{1}{2} + \frac{1}{4} + \frac{1}{2}\right) + 1.0\right) = \frac{19}{15},$$
$$P_i^*\left(\frac{1}{3}, 0, \frac{1}{2}, \frac{1}{4}, \frac{1}{2}\right) = \frac{1}{5}.\left(1.\frac{1}{3} + 1.0 + 3.\left(\frac{1}{2} + \frac{1}{4} + \frac{1}{2}\right)\right) = \frac{49}{60},$$
$$P_i^*\left(\frac{1}{2}, 0, \frac{1}{3}, \frac{1}{4}, 0, \frac{1}{2}\right) = \frac{1}{6}.\left(1.\frac{1}{2} + 1.0 + 2.\left(\frac{1}{3} + \frac{1}{4}\right) + 1.0 + 1.\frac{1}{2}\right) = \frac{13}{36},$$
$$P_i^*\left(\frac{1}{2}, 0, 0, \frac{1}{3}, \frac{1}{4}, 0, \frac{1}{2}\right) = \frac{1}{7}.\left(1.\frac{1}{2} + 2.0 + 2.\left(\frac{1}{3} + \frac{1}{4}\right) + 1.0 + 1.\frac{1}{2}\right) = \frac{13}{42}.$$

$P_i^*$ treats persistence in the way we suggest in the introduction and at the beginning of this section: *ceteris paribus*, longer breaks between spells reduce individual intertemporal poverty and longer poverty spells increase individual intertemporal poverty. As mentioned earlier, this measure represents one possible way of doing so, and the reason we focus on it is that, in addition to these monotonicity properties, $P_i^*$ satisfies notions of decomposability that we consider to be very natural in this setting.

The weight function $D^\tau$ has an interesting implication in terms of the severity of poverty. As the number of consecutive periods in which a person remains in poverty increases, $D^\tau$ increases which, in turn, implies an increase in the value of the individual poverty index. This becomes evident from the first two examples following Eq. 1.

The first property we impose on an individual intertemporal poverty measure requires that, in degenerate cases where there is only one period, individual intertemporal poverty and individual per-period poverty coincide.

*One-period equivalence* For all $p_i \in R_+$,

$$P_i(p_i) = p_i.$$

In agreement with many issues involving social index numbers (see, for instance, Ebert and Moyes (2000), in the context of individual deprivation measurement), we impose decomposability properties. As opposed to the standard single-period approach, we are dealing with a richer domain and wish to distinguish features across spells and within spells. Across spells, that is, in situations where two groups of periods in poverty are separated by at least one period with zero poverty, we require individual intertemporal poverty to be equal to a weighted average of poverty experienced in each spell, where the weights are given by the proportional lengths of the two spells. The scope of the axiom is restricted to separate spells due to one of the features we want to highlight—the importance of the lengths of poverty spells and the lengths of spells out of poverty. This requirement captures the main novel feature of our approach: the length of a spell emerges as an important criterion when assessing intertemporal poverty.

*Across-spells average decomposability*. For all $T \in N\backslash\{1\}$, for all $p_i \in R_+^T$ and for all $t \in \{1, 2, \ldots, T-1\}$, if $p_i^t = 0$ or $p_i^{t+1} = 0$, then

$$P_i(p_i) = \frac{t}{T} P_i(p_i^1, \ldots, p_i^t) + \frac{T-1}{T} P_i(p_i^{t+1}, \ldots, p_i^T).$$

This axiom can be illustrated using poverty profile in the fourth example following Eq. 1. For $t = 2$, the axiom demands that

$$P_i(p_i) = P_i\left(\frac{1}{2}, 0, 0, \frac{1}{3}, \frac{1}{4}, 0, \frac{1}{2}\right) = \frac{2}{7} P_i\left(\frac{1}{2}, 0\right) + \frac{5}{7} P_i\left(0, \frac{1}{3}, \frac{1}{4}, 0, \frac{1}{4}\right).$$

The second decomposability property applies to situations where there is but a single poverty spell—that is, the individual is in poverty in all $T$ periods. In particular, we impose an additive-decomposability axiom that focuses on total rather than average poverty when the single spell is separated into two sets of periods.

*Single-spell additive decomposability*. For all $T \in N\backslash\{1\}$ for all $p_i \in R_{++}^T$ and for all $t \in \{1, 2, \ldots, T-1\}$

$$P_i(p_i) = P_i(p_i^1, \ldots, p_i^t) + P_i(p_i^{t+1}, \ldots, p_i^T).$$

To illustrate this axiom suppose that the poverty profile is (1/2,1/3,1/4,1/2). Then the axiom demands that

$$P_i(p_i) = P_i\left(\frac{1}{2}, \frac{1}{3}, \frac{1}{4}, \frac{1}{2}\right) = P_i\left(\frac{1}{2}, \frac{1}{3}\right) + P_i\left(\frac{1}{4}, \frac{1}{2}\right).$$

The novelty in our approach is that we distinguish between decomposability across and within spells: (i) averages matter across spells to take into consideration the hypothesis that, *ceteris paribus*, longer breaks between spells are associated with lower degrees of intertemporal poverty, and (ii) totals matter within spells so that, ceteris paribus, longer poverty spells lead to higher intertemporal poverty. As usual, these decomposability properties impose an additive structure on the measure.

The axioms introduced above characterize $P_i^*$. We obtain

**Theorem 1** *An individual intertemporal poverty measure $P : \Omega \to R_+$ satisfies one period equivalence, across-spells average decomposability and single-spell additive decomposability if and only if $P_i = P_i^*$.*

Proof 'If.' That $P_i^*$ satisfies one-period equivalence is straightforward to verify.

To prove across-spells average decomposability, let $T \in N\backslash\{1\}$, $p_i \in R_+^T$ and for all $t \in \{1, 2, \ldots, T-1\}$ be such that $p_i^t = 0$ or $p_i^{t+1} = 0$. By definition of $P_i^*$ we have

$$\frac{t}{T} P_i^*(p_i^1, \ldots, p_i^t) + \frac{T-t}{T} P_i^*(p_i^{t+1}, \ldots, p_i^T) \\ = \frac{1}{T} \sum_{\tau=1}^{t} D^\tau(p_i^1, \ldots, p_i^t) p_i^\tau + \frac{1}{T} \sum_{\tau=t+1}^{T} D^\tau(p_i^{t+1}, \ldots, p_i^T) p_i^\tau. \quad (2)$$

Because $p_i^t = 0$ or $p_i^{t+1} = 0$, it follows that $D^\tau(p_i^1, \ldots, p_i^t) = D^\tau(p_i)$ for all $\tau \in \{1, \ldots, t\}$ such that $p_i^t > 0$ and $D^\tau(p_i^{t+1}, \ldots, p_i^T) = D^\tau(p_i)$ for all $\tau \in \{t+1, \ldots, T\}$ such that $p_i^t > 0$. Therefore, Eq. 2 implies.

$$\frac{t}{T} P_i^*(p_i^1, \ldots, p_i^t) + \frac{T-t}{T} P_i^*(p_i^{t+1}, \ldots, p_i^T) = \frac{1}{T} \sum_{t=1}^{T} D^\tau(p_i) p_i^\tau = P_i^*(p_i),$$

as was to be established.

Let $T \in N\backslash\{1\}$, $p_i \in R_{++}^T$ and $t \in \{1, \ldots, T-1\}$. By definition of $P_i^*$ and because $D^\tau(p_i) = T$ for all $\tau \in \{1, \ldots, T\}$, $D^\tau(p_i^1, \ldots, p_i^t) = t$ for all $\tau \in \{1, \ldots, t\}$ and $D^\tau(p_i^{t+1}, \ldots, p_i^T) = T - t$ for all $\tau \in \{t+1, \ldots, T\}$, it follows that

$$P_i^*(p_i) = \frac{1}{T} \sum_{\tau=1}^{T} D^\tau(p^i) = \sum_{\tau=1}^{T} p_i^\tau = \sum_{\tau=1}^{t} p_i^\tau + \sum_{\tau=t+1}^{T} p_i^\tau \\ = \frac{1}{t} \sum_{\tau=1}^{t} D^\tau(p_i^1, \ldots, p_i^t) p_i^\tau + \frac{1}{T-t} \sum_{\tau=1+1}^{T} D^\tau(p_i^{t+1}, \ldots, p_i^T) p_i^\tau \\ = P_i^*(p_i^1, \ldots, p_i^t) + P_i^*(p_i^{t+1}, \ldots, p_i^T)$$

and single-spell additive decomposability is proven.

'Only if.' Now suppose $P^i$ satisfies the axioms of the theorem statement. Let $T \in N$ and $p_i \in R_+^T$.

If $T = 1$, $P_i(p_i) = p_i = P_i^*(p_i)$ follows immediately from one-period equivalence.

Now consider the case $T \geq 2$.

If $p_i^\tau = 0$ for all $\tau \in \{1, 2, \ldots, T\}$, repeated application of one-period equivalence and across-spells average decomposability implies $P_i(p_i) = 0 = P_i^*(p_i)$.

If $p_i^\tau > 0$ for all $\tau \in \{1, 2, \ldots, T\}$, we have $D^\tau(p_i) = T$ for all $\tau \in \{1, 2, \ldots, T\}$. By repeated application of one-period equivalence and single-spell additive decomposability,

$$P_i(p_i) = P_i(p_i^1, \ldots, p_i^{T-1}) + P_i(p_i^T) = P_i(p_i^1, \ldots, p_i^{T-1}) + p_i^T$$

$$\vdots$$

$$= \sum_{\tau=1}^{T} p_i^{\tau} = \frac{1}{T} \sum_{t=1}^{T} D^{\tau}(p_i) p_i^{\tau} = P_i^*(p_i)$$

because $D^{\tau}(p_i) = T$ for all $\tau \in \{1, \ldots, T\}$.

Finally, suppose there exist $\tau, \tau' \in \{1, \ldots, T\}$ such that $p_i^{\tau} > 0$ and $p_i^{\tau'} = 0$. In this case, we can decompose $p_i$ into spells in and out of poverty. Without loss of generality, suppose the first spell is associated with a positive level of per-period poverty. Thus, there exist $K \in N \backslash \{1\}$, and $t^1, \ldots, t^K \in \{1, 2, \ldots, T\}$ such that $\sum_{k=1}^{K} t^k = T, p_i^1, \ldots, p_i^{t^1} > 0, p_i^{t^1+1} = \cdots = p_i^{t^1+t^2} = 0$, etc. The $t^k$ are the lengths of the spells in poverty for all odd $k$ and the length of the spells out of poverty for all even $k$. By applying across-spells average decomposability as many times as necessary, we obtain

$$P_i(p_i) = \frac{t^1}{T} P_i\left(p_i^1, \ldots, p_i^{t^1}\right) + \cdots + \frac{t^K}{T} P_i\left(p_i^{t^1+\cdots+t^{K-1}+1}, \ldots p_i^T\right). \quad (3)$$

Applying one-period equivalence and single-spell additive decomposability, we obtain

$$\frac{t^k}{T} P_i\left(p_i^{t^1+\cdots+t^{k-1}+1}, \ldots p_i^{t^1+\cdots+t^k}\right) = \frac{t^k}{T} P_i\left(p_i^{t^1+\cdots+t^{k-1}+1} + \cdots p_i^{t^1+\ldots+t^k}\right) \text{ for all odd } k. \quad (4)$$

Analogously, using one-period equivalence and across-spells average decomposability as many times as needed, it follows that

$$\frac{t^k}{T} P_i\left(p_i^{t^1+\cdots+t^{k-1}+1}, \ldots p_i^{t^1+\cdots+t^k}\right) = 0 \text{ for all even } k. \quad (5)$$

Recall that the $t^k$ are the lengths of the spells in and out of poverty and, thus, substituting Eqs. 4 and 5 back into Eq. 3 yields Eq. 1. □

## 3 Aggregate Intertemporal Poverty Measures

Given the individual intertemporal poverty measures $P_i^*$ for each individual in a society, we use an aggregate intertemporal poverty index to obtain an overall measure of poverty that allows us to compare intertemporal poverty across societies, possibly involving different sampling periods and different populations and population sizes. Although it is possible to define an aggregate intertemporal measure from first principles (that is, using individual per-period poverty indicators as the basic objects to be aggregated into overall poverty), we proceed by implicitly assuming that the intertemporal aggregation is performed first (see the discussion in the introduction) and the second step consists of aggregating these indicators across individuals in a society to arrive at an overall measure of intertemporal poverty. This choice is motivated primarily by our desire to keep the exposition simple.

To describe the second part of the aggregation process, let $\Pi = \cup_{n \in N} R^n_+$ and consider a function $P : \Pi \to R_+$, to be interpreted as a measure that assigns an aggregate value of intertemporal poverty to each vector of individual intertemporal poverty values.

The aggregate intertemporal poverty measure we propose is defined as average individual intertemporal poverty, that is, we employ the index $P^*$ defined by

$$P^*(p) = \frac{1}{n} \sum_{i=1}^{n} p_i \tag{6}$$

for all $n \in N$ and for all $p \in R^n_+$. We view aggregate poverty as an *ordinal* variable and, thus, any increasing transformation of $P^*$ can equivalently be employed. Of course, *individual* intertemporal poverty measures must contain more than ordinal and interpersonally non-comparable information—clearly, the definition of $P^*$ is incompatible with the assumption that the $\boldsymbol{p}$ carry ordinally measurable and interpersonally non-comparable information only. We provide a characterization of $P^*$ that is based on results in population ethics due to Blackorby et al. (2002, 2005). However, we provide a self-contained proof because the domain we consider here is different from the one in these contributions. We note that, although we use the indices $P_i^*$ in the application discussed in the following section, our characterization is valid for any way of defining the individual intertemporal poverty values $p_i$.

The first axiom is a weak monotonicity property. It requires that, in situations where the level of individual intertemporal poverty is equal across individuals, aggregate intertemporal poverty is increasing in individual intertemporal poverty. The scope of the axiom is restricted to comparisons involving a given population size. For any $n \in N$, let $1_n$ denote the vector consisting of $n$ ones.

*Minimal increasingness*. For all $n \in N$ and for all $a, b \in R_+$, if $a > b$, then

$$P(a\,1_n) > P(b\,1_n).$$

Minimal increasingness is a very mild monotonicity requirement because it applies to equal distributions of individual intertemporal poverty and to fixed-population size comparisons only.

The second axiom we impose on $\boldsymbol{P}$ is an impartiality property with respect to increases or decreases in individual poverty. If a single individual's intertemporal poverty level changes by a given amount, it does not matter whose poverty changes. Let $n \geq 2$. We use the notation $1^j_n$ for the vector $w \in R^n_+$ such that $w_j = 1$ and $w_i = 0$ for all $i \in \{1, \ldots, n\} \setminus \{j\}$.

*Incremental equity*. For all $n \in N \backslash \{1\}$ for all $p \in R^n_+$, for all $d \in R^n_+$ and for all $j, k \in \{1, \ldots, n\}$ with $j \neq k$, if $\left(p + d1^j_n\right) \in R^n_+$ and $\left(p + d1^k_n\right) \in R^n_+$, then

$$P\left(p + d1^j_n\right) = P\left(p + d1^k_n\right).$$

Incremental equity incorporates a notion of anonymity in terms of gains and losses in individual poverty. If there is an increase or decrease of a given value in individual intertemporal poverty, the measure is insensitive to the identity of the person experiencing this gain or loss. Clearly, gains and losses of poverty values have to be comparable across individuals in order for this axiom to be well-defined. In particular, poverty has to employ *translation-scale comparable* values; see, for instance, Blackorby et al. (1984) and Bossert and Weymark (1099) for a discussion.

Minimal increasingness and incremental equity together characterize ordinal aggregate poverty measures based on average (or total) individual poverty for any fixed population size; see Blackorby et al. (2002, 2005). However, further axioms are needed to extend this characterization to the entire domain $\Pi$, that is, to aggregate poverty comparisons that may involve different population sizes. One possibility is to require that average individual poverty is a *critical level* for any poverty vector $p \in \Pi$; see, again, Blackorby et al. (2005) for a detailed discussion. That is, aggregate poverty is unaffected if an individual with average poverty is added to a given distribution $p \in \Pi$. This reflects the position that aggregate poverty is a per-capita notion, a view that is shared in most of the literature on poverty measurement.

*Average critical levels*. For all $n \in N$ and for all $p \in R^n_+$

$$P\left(p, \frac{1}{n}\sum_{i=1}^{n} p_i\right) = P(p).$$

Recall that the arguments $p_i$ of $\boldsymbol{P}$ are themselves intertemporal aggregates of individual per-period poverty values and, thus, all information concerning per-period poverty lines has already been fully taken into consideration when arriving at the individual intertemporal poverty indices. Thus, treating average poverty as a critical level does not conflict in any way with whatever method is chosen to identify these per-period poverty lines.

The three axioms defined above characterize the class of all aggregate poverty measures that are ordinally equivalent to $P^*$. The axioms can be motivated further by noting that they are implied by other properties with intuitive interpretations. For instance, minimal increasingness is a consequence of standard increasingness, incremental equity is implied by a fixed-population information-invariance property and average critical levels are implied by increasingness, the existence of critical levels and a variable-population information-invariance condition; see Blackorby et al. (2005, Chaps. 4, 5 and 6) for a detailed discussion.

**Theorem 2** *An aggregate intertemporal poverty measure* $\boldsymbol{P}$ *satisfies minimal increasingness, incremental equity and average critical levels if and only if* $\boldsymbol{P}$ *is an increasing transformation of* $P^*$.

*Proof* That any increasing transformation of $P^*$ satisfies minimal increasingness, incremental equity and average critical levels is straightforward to verify.

Conversely, suppose that $P$ satisfies the three axioms.

If $n = 1$, minimal increasingness alone implies the result.

Now let $n \geq 2$. Consider $p \in R^n_+$ and $j, k \in \{1, \ldots, n\}$ with $j \neq k$, and suppose $d \in R_+$ is such that $p_j \geq d$. By incremental equity.

$$P\big(p - d1^j_n + d1^k_n\big) = P\big(p - d1^j_n + d1^j_n\big) = P(p). \tag{7}$$

Let $p \in R^n_+$ and suppose, without loss of generality, that $p_1 \geq p_2 \geq \cdots \geq p_n$. By (repeated if necessary) application of Eq. 7, it follows that

$$\begin{aligned} P(p) &= P\left(p_1 - \left(p_1 - \frac{1}{n}\sum_{i=1}^n p_i\right), p_2, \ldots, p_n + \left(p_1 - \frac{1}{n}\sum_{i=1}^n p_i\right)\right) \\ &= P\left(\frac{1}{n}\sum_{i=1}^n p_i, p_2, \ldots, p_n + p_1 - \frac{1}{n}\sum_{i=1}^n p_i\right) \\ &\;\vdots \\ &= P\left(\frac{1}{n}\sum_{i=1}^n p_i, \frac{1}{n}\sum_{i=1}^n p_i, \ldots, \sum_{i=1}^n p_i - \frac{n-1}{n}\sum_{i=1}^n p_i\right) \\ &= P\left(\left(\frac{1}{n}\sum_{i=1}^n p_i\right)1_n\right). \end{aligned}$$

Together with minimal increasingness, this implies

$$\begin{aligned} P(p) \geq P(q) &\Leftrightarrow P\left(\left(\frac{1}{n}\sum_{i=1}^n p_i\right)1_n\right) \geq P\left(\left(\frac{1}{n}\sum_{i=1}^n q_i\right)1_n\right) \\ &\Leftrightarrow \frac{1}{n}\sum_{i=1}^n p_i \geq \frac{1}{n}\sum_{i=1}^n q_i \\ &\Leftrightarrow P^*(p) \geq P^*(q) \end{aligned} \tag{8}$$

for all $n \in N$ and for all $p, p \in R^n_+$. Thus, all fixed-population-size comparisons must be performed according to $P^*$.

Now consider $n, m \in N$ such that $n \neq m$, $p \in R^n_+$ and $q \in R^n_+$. Without loss of generality, suppose $n > m$. By (repeated if necessary) application of average critical levels, we obtain

$$P(q) = P\left(q, \frac{1}{m}\sum_{i=1}^{m} q_i\right) = \cdots = P\left(q, \left(\frac{1}{m}\sum_{i=1}^{m} q_i\right)1_{n-m}\right)$$

and, therefore,

$$P(p) \geq P(q) \Leftrightarrow P(p) \geq P\left(q, \left(\frac{1}{m}\sum_{i=1}^{m} q_i\right)1_{n-m}\right). \tag{9}$$

Because $p$ and $\left(q, \left((1/m)\sum_{i=1}^{m} q_i\right)1_{n-m}\right)$ have the same population size $n$, Eq. 8 implies

$$P(p) \geq P\left(q, \left(\frac{1}{m}\sum_{i=1}^{m} q_i\right)1_{n-m}\right) \Leftrightarrow \frac{1}{n}\sum_{i=1}^{n} p_i \geq \frac{1}{n}\left(\sum_{i=1}^{m} q_i + \frac{n-m}{m}\sum_{i=1}^{m} q_i\right)$$
$$\Leftrightarrow \sum_{i=1}^{n} p_i \geq \sum_{i=1}^{m} q_i + \frac{n-m}{m}\sum_{i=1}^{m} q_i$$

which implies

$$P(p) \geq P\left(q, \left(\frac{1}{m}\sum_{i=1}^{m} q_i\right)1_{n-m}\right) \Leftrightarrow \frac{1}{n}\sum_{i=1}^{n} p_i \geq \frac{1}{m}\sum_{i=1}^{m} q_i.$$

By Eq. 9, we obtain

$$P(p) \geq P(q) \Leftrightarrow \frac{1}{n}\sum_{i=1}^{n} p_i \geq \frac{1}{m}\sum_{i=1}^{m} q_i \Leftrightarrow P^*(p) \geq P^*(q)$$

which completes the proof. □

## 4 An Application to European Countries

The purpose of this section is to illustrate the aggregate measure of poverty, $P^*$ as defined in Eq. 6 with individual intertemporal poverty measures $p_i$ given by $P_i^*(p_i)$, using the European Community Household Panel (ECHP). We base our analysis on all the waves available in ECHP, which cover the period from 1994 to 2001. The surveys are conducted at a European national level. We do not aim at providing an accurate analysis of poverty persistence in EU countries, hence we take the available years as such without considering the presence of any measurement errors and the possibility that poverty spells are censored at the beginning or at the end of the sample we observe. For a discussion of these estimation techniques see, among others, Bane and Ellwood (1986) and Jenkins (2000). The ECHP is an ambitious effort at collecting information on the living standards of the households of the EU member states using common definitions, information collection methods, and editing procedures. It contains detailed information on incomes, socio-economic characteristics, housing amenities, consumer durables, social relations, employment conditions, health status, subjective evaluation of well-being, etc. Of the 15 EU member states, we could not consider Sweden since the data for this country is cross-sectional only. For Finland and Austria, data were not available for all the waves. While the former joined from wave three onwards, the Austrian data are available beginning with the second wave. The full ECHP data format for the UK, Germany, and Luxembourg is available only for the years 1994–1996. We therefore use the ECHP data format derived from national surveys instead. These data are available for the UK and Germany for 1994–2001; for Luxembourg, on the other hand, they are available from 1995 onwards only. For this reason, Luxembourg, like Austria, was included from the second wave onwards. The unit of our analysis is the individual. The calculation uses required sample weights. Since we are interested in analyzing poverty spells and the effect of persistence in the state of poverty, we consider only individuals that were interviewed in all the waves for each country. The variable studied is net yearly household income equivalized using the OECD modified equivalence scale in order to account for different household size and composition. For each country and for each period in the sample, the poverty line is set to 60% of the national median. Thus, for any given per-period income distribution $y^t$, the poverty line in this period, $z^t(y^t)$, is given by 0.6 times the median of $y^t$. An individual is classified as poor if its income is strictly below the poverty line.

For the per-period individual poverty indicators, we choose three among those most commonly used in empirical studies, namely, the normalized relative gaps raised to the power $\alpha \in \{0, 1, 2\}$ so that, for any period $t \in N$,

$$p_i^t = \begin{cases} \frac{(z^t(y^t)-y_i^t)^\alpha}{z^t(y^t)} & \text{if } y_i^t < z^t(y^t), \\ 0 & \text{if } y_i^t \geq z^t(y^t). \end{cases}$$

When $\alpha = 0$, the individual poverty indicator captures only the number of periods spent in poverty. In this case, $p_i^t$ assumes the value one for those in poverty and zero for everybody else. This individual index is similar in spirit to the head-count ratio. When $\alpha = 1$ we consider not only the incidence of poverty but also its intensity since we take into account how poor each poor individual is, expressed as a proportion of the poverty line. In this case, the index resembles the normalized poverty gap. When $\alpha = 2$, the normalized gaps are squared. As a result, we give more importance to poorer individuals as opposed to those poor whose income is less distant from the poverty line.

We compare the values of the index we propose with those obtained with a weight equal to one independently of the duration of the spell. In this case persistence does not play a role. This is the only case where aggregating first across time and then across individuals produces exactly the same results as the reverse order of aggregation does, that is, aggregating first across individuals and then across time. The aggregate index coincides with the average of per-period standard poverty indices. If, in addition, $\alpha = 0$, the aggregate index is the average of the per-period head-count ratios; if $\alpha = 1$, it is the average of the aggregate normalized poverty gap indices; and, lastly, if $\alpha = 2$, it is the average of the aggregate squared normalized poverty gaps.

The results are contained in Table 1, while in Table 2 we report the rankings of the countries under alternative indices. In the first column, the names of the countries are reported while the following pairs of columns present poverty indicators for the three different values of $\alpha$. The first column of each pair contains the values of the index where persistence does not play any role. The values of the index we propose in this paper are reported in the second column of each pair. The results show that persistence in a state of poverty does play a role in poverty measurement. It constitutes relevant information and its omission would not give a correct picture of the phenomenon. The rankings of the countries change, particularly in the center of the rankings. Portugal, followed by Greece, is indeed always the poorest country among those under analysis. At the opposite end the Netherlands is always the least poor when $\alpha = 0$ while Denmark followed by Finland is the least poor for the other values of the parameter $\alpha$. The majority of rank changes are observed for $\alpha = 0$. In this case Denmark, Austria and particularly Spain improve their position by one, two and three slots respectively, while Finland, Germany, Luxembourg and Ireland move one position down. The UK sees its position worsen by two. For $\alpha = 1$, no country experiences a movement of more than one position. In particular, Luxembourg and the Netherlands, Germany and Austria, Italy and Spain switch places in the rankings.

**Table 1** Aggregate intertemporal poverty in EU member states, with (yes) and without (no) weights for persistence (index values)

| Country | $\alpha = 0$ | | $\alpha = 1$ | | $\alpha = 2$ | |
|---|---|---|---|---|---|---|
| | No | Yes | No | Yes | No | Yes |
| Denmark | 0.096 | 0.327 | 0.017 | 0.060 | 0.006 | 0.018 |
| Finland | 0.094 | 0.356 | 0.018 | 0.069 | 0.006 | 0.022 |
| Luxembourg | 0.114 | 0.468 | 0.021 | 0.092 | 0.006 | 0.026 |
| Netherlands | 0.087 | 0.298 | 0.023 | 0.079 | 0.012 | 0.038 |
| Ireland | 0.187 | 0.768 | 0.035 | 0.148 | 0.011 | 0.046 |
| Austria | 0.116 | 0.422 | 0.028 | 0.111 | 0.012 | 0.049 |
| Belgium | 0.134 | 0.534 | 0.031 | 0.127 | 0.013 | 0.052 |
| France | 0.144 | 0.583 | 0.033 | 0.141 | 0.013 | 0.054 |
| Germany | 0.107 | 0.434 | 0.028 | 0.121 | 0.013 | 0.056 |
| UK | 0.176 | 0.750 | 0.048 | 0.217 | 0.022 | 0.100 |
| Spain | 0.190 | 0.702 | 0.058 | 0.233 | 0.029 | 0.0119 |
| Italy | 0.181 | 0.721 | 0.058 | 0.257 | 0.031 | 0.140 |
| Greece | 0.201 | 0.827 | 0.067 | 0.306 | 0.033 | 0.153 |
| Portugal | 0.220 | 1.005 | 0.071 | 0.357 | 0.037 | 0.188 |

**Table 2** Aggregate intertemporal poverty in EU member states, with (yes) and without (no) weights for persistence (ranking)

| Country | $\alpha = 0$ | | $\alpha = 1$ | | $\alpha = 2$ | |
|---|---|---|---|---|---|---|
| | No | Yes | No | Yes | No | Yes |
| Denmark | 3 | 2 | 1 | 1 | 1 | 1 |
| Finland | 2 | 3 | 2 | 2 | 2 | 2 |
| Luxembourg | 5 | 6 | 3 | 4 | 3 | 3 |
| Netherlands | 1 | 1 | 4 | 3 | 5 | 4 |
| Ireland | 11 | 12 | 9 | 9 | 4 | 5 |
| Austria | 6 | 4 | 6 | 5 | 6 | 6 |
| Belgium | 7 | 7 | 7 | 7 | 8 | 7 |
| France | 8 | 8 | 8 | 8 | 9 | 8 |
| Germany | 4 | 5 | 5 | 6 | 7 | 9 |
| UK | 9 | 11 | 10 | 10 | 10 | 10 |
| Spain | 12 | 9 | 12 | 11 | 11 | 11 |
| Italy | 10 | 10 | 11 | 12 | 12 | 12 |
| Greece | 13 | 13 | 13 | 13 | 13 | 13 |
| Portugal | 14 | 14 | 14 | 14 | 14 | 14 |

For $\alpha = 2$, Ireland and the Netherlands switch positions while Germany moves below both Belgium and France. From a social policy point of view, the discovery of this temporal characteristic of poverty should lead to different recommendations: in a country like Germany, for example, where poverty is more persistent, policies should aim at helping individuals and households to escape from poverty; in the Netherlands, on the other hand, poverty is more transitory and a more effective policy would be one preventing individuals from becoming poor.

## 5 Concluding Remarks

Time is an important aspect of individual lives. Experiences are accumulated over lifetimes and the assessment of the impact a poverty spell has on a person's situation may very well differ according to what happened to the individual in previous periods. The index of intertemporal poverty that we propose aims at including experiences in addition to the incidence of poverty and inequality among those who are poor when measuring poverty. The results of our simple application to EU countries show that a different picture can emerge when we value individual experiences.

Clearly, we do not claim that our index is the only plausible measure of intertemporal poverty, just as no one would, we believe, declare the Gini coefficient to be the only possible choice as a tool to measure income inequality, to the exclusion of all other measures. However, we view our proposal as an attractive option and we think the properties used in its characterization have some strong intuitive appeal.

We restrict attention to the intertemporal aggregation of per-period overall poverty in this paper. Clearly, our approach can be modified easily in order to obtain measures of chronic poverty based on the idea underlying our new index. For instance, any particular definition of chronic poverty can be accommodated by adding a *duration* criterion and declaring an individual to be chronically poor if there is at least one poverty spell of at least that duration and then perform the aggregation over individuals by calculating the arithmetic mean of the poverty values only of all those satisfying this criterion.

Another possible extension that may be of interest is the inclusion of a component capturing the psychological effects of gains and losses in income, in addition to the features that are already accounted for in the individual per-period poverty values.

Further work could be done by performing statistical inference with the index we propose and by considering the possibility that poverty spells are censored when estimating intertemporal poverty.

**Acknowledgements** We thank two anonymous referees, Luc Christiaensen, James Foster, Itzhak Gilboa, Stephan Klasen, Rajiv Sethi, Tony Shorrocks, Philippe van Kerm, Paolo Verme, and participants at several conferences and seminars for useful comments and discussions. Financial support from the Social Sciences and Humanities Research Council of Canada and MIUR (Prin 2007) is gratefully acknowledged.

## References

Arranz, J. M., & Cantó, O. (2010). *Measuring the effects of spell recurrence on poverty dynamics*. UNU-WIDER Working Paper No. 2010/72.

Bane, M. J., & Ellwood, D. T. (1986). Slipping into and out of poverty: The dynamics of spells. *Journal of Human Resources, 21,* 1–23.

Blackorby, C., Bossert, W., & Donaldson, D. (1996). Intertemporally consistent population ethics: Classical utilitarian principles. In K. J. Arrow, A. K. Sen, & K. Suzumura (Eds.), *Social choice re-examined* (Vol. 2, pp. 137–162). London: Macmillan.

Blackorby, C., Bossert, W., & Donaldson, D. (2002). Utilitarianism and the theory of justice. In K. J. Arrow, A. K. Sen, & K. Suzumura (Eds.), *Handbook of social choice and welfare* (Vol. 1, pp. 543–596). Amsterdam: Elsevier.

Blackorby, C., Bossert, W., & Donaldson, D. (2005). *Population issues in social choice theory, welfare economics, and ethics*. Cambridge: Cambridge University Press.

Blackorby, C., Donaldson, D., & Weymark, J. A. (1984). Social choice with interpersonal utility comparisons: A diagrammatic introduction. *International Economic Review, 25,* 327–356.

Bossert, W., D'Ambrosio, C., & Peragine, V. (2007). Deprivation and social exclusion. *Economica, 74,* 777–803.

Bossert, W., Weymark, J. A. (2004). Utility in social choice. In S. Barberà, P. Hammond, & C. Seidl (Eds.), *Handbook of utility theory* (vol. 2: Extensions, pp. 1099–1177). Kluwer, Dordrecht.

Bradbury, B., Jenkins, S. P., & Micklewright, J. (Eds.). (2001). *The dynamics of child poverty in industrialised countries*. Cambridge: Cambridge University Press.

Calvo, C., & Dercon, S. (2009). Chronic poverty and all that: The measurement of poverty over time. In T. Addison, D. Hulme, & R. Kanbur (Eds.), *Poverty dynamics* (pp. 29–59). Oxford: Oxford University Press.

Cappellari, L., & Jenkins, S. P. (2004). Modelling low income transitions. *Journal of Applied Economics, 19,* 593–610.

Castilla, C. (2010). *Subjective poverty and reference-dependence*. UNU-WIDER Working Paper No. 2010/76.

Chronic Poverty Research Center. (2004). *The Chronic Poverty Report No. 2004–05*. Downloaded from www.chronicpoverty.org.

Ebert, U., & Moyes, P. (2000). An axiomatic characterization of Yitzhaki's index of individual deprivation. *Economic Letters, 68,* 263–270.

Foster, J. E. (2009). A class of chronic poverty measures. In T. Addison, D. Hulme, & R. Kanbur (Eds.), *Poverty dynamics* (pp. 59–77). Oxford: Oxford University Press.

Foster, J. E., Greer, J., & Thorbecke, E. (1984). A class of decomposable poverty indices. *Econometrica, 52,* 761–766.

Hoy, M., Zheng, B. (2006). *Measuring lifetime poverty*. Paper Presented at the 8th International Meeting of the Society for Social Choice and Welfare, Istanbul.

Jenkins, S. P. (2000). Modelling household income dynamics. *Journal of Population Economics, 13,* 529–567.

Lambert, P. J. (2009). Mini-symposium: The 1990, 1992 and 1993 papers on distributionally sensitive measures of unemployment by Manimay Sengupta and Anthony Shorrocks. *Journal of Economic Inequality, 7,* 269–271.

Porter, C., & Quinn, N. N. (2008). *Intertemporal poverty measurement: Trade offs and policy options*. Paper Presented at the IARIW 2008 Conference in Portorož.

Rodgers, J. R., & Rodgers, J. L. (1993). Chronic poverty in the United States. *Journal of Human Resources, 28,* 25–54.

Roope, L. (2010). Intertemporal poverty measures: The impact of affluence and principles of aggregation. Paper Presented at the 10th International Meeting of the Society for Social Choice and Welfare, Moscow.

Sen, A. K. (1976). Poverty: An ordinal approach to measurement. *Econometrica, 44,* 219–231.

Sengupta, M. (2009). Unemployment duration and the measurement of unemployment. *Journal of Economic Inequality, 7,* 273–294.

Shorrocks, A. (2009a). Spell incidence, spell duration and the measurement of unemployment. *Journal of Economic Inequality, 7,* 295–310.

Shorrocks, A. (2009b). On the measurement of unemployment. *Journal of Economic Inequality, 7,* 311–327.

Walker, R. (1995). The dynamics of poverty and social exclusion. In G. Room (Ed.), *Beyond the threshold* (pp. 102–128). Bristol: The Policy Press.

# The Measurement of Multidimensional Poverty

**François Bourguignon and Satya R. Chakravarty**

**Abstract** Many authors have insisted on the necessity of defining poverty as a multidimensional concept rather than relying on income or consumption expenditures per capita. Yet, not much has actually been done to include the various dimensions of deprivation into the practical definition and measurement of poverty. Existing attempts along that direction consist of aggregating various attributes into a single index through some arbitrary function and defining a poverty line and associated poverty measures on the basis of that index. This is merely redefining more generally the concept of poverty, which then essentially remains a one-dimensional concept. The present paper suggests that an alternative way to take into account the multidimensionality of poverty is to specify a poverty line for each dimension of poverty and to consider that a person is poor if he/she falls below at least one of these various lines. The paper then explores how to combine these various poverty lines and associated one-dimensional gaps into multidimensional poverty measures. An application of these measures to the rural population in Brazil is also given with poverty defined on income and education.

**Keywords** Multidimensional · Poverty measure

## 1 Introduction

Poverty has been in existence for many years and continues to exist in a large number of countries. Therefore, targeting of poverty alleviation remains an important issue in many countries. In order to understand the threat that the problem of poverty poses,

---

It is a pleasure to acknowledge the permission granted by Springer Nature to reprint this article from Journal of Economic Inequality, Volume 1, 2003.

---

F. Bourguignon (✉)
Paris School of Economics, 48 Bd Jourdan, 75014 Paris, France
e-mail: efrancois.bourguignon@psemail.eu

S. R. Chakravarty
Indian Statistical Institute, 203, Barrackpore Trunk Road, Kolkata 700108, India
e-mail: satyarchakravarty@gmail.com

 
S. R. Chakravarty (ed.), *Poverty, Social Exclusion and Stochastic Dominance*, Themes in Economics, https://doi.org/10.1007/978-981-13-3432-0_7

it is necessary to know its dimension and the process through which it seems to be deepened. A natural question that arises here is how to quantify the extent of poverty. In an important contribution, Sen (1976) viewed the poverty measurement problem as involving two exercises: (i) the identification of the poor, and (ii) aggregation of the characteristics of the poor into an overall indicator. In the literature, the first problem has been solved mostly by the income (or consumption) method, which requires the specification of a subsistence income level, referred to as the poverty line. A person is said to be poor if his/her income falls below the poverty line. On the aggregation issue, Sen (1976) criticised two crude poverty measures, the head count ratio (proportion of persons with incomes less than the poverty line) and the income gap ratio (the gap between the poverty line and average income of the poor, expressed as a proportion of the poverty line), because they are insensitive to the redistribution of income among the poor and the former also remains unaltered if the position of a poor worsens. He also suggested a more sophisticated index of poverty using an axiomatic approach.[1]

However, the well-being of a population and, hence its poverty, which is a manifestation of insufficient well-being, depend on both monetary and non-monetary variables. It is certainly true that with a higher income or consumption budget a person may be able to improve the position of some of his/her monetary and non-monetary attributes. But at the same time, it may be the case that markets for some non-monetary attributes do not exist, for example, with some public good. It may also happen that markets are highly imperfect, for instance, in the case of rationing. Therefore, income as the sole indicator of well-being is inappropriate and should be supplemented by other attributes or variables, e.g., housing, literacy, life expectancy, provision of public goods and so on. The need for such a multidimensional approach to the measurement of inequality in well-being was already emphasised, among others, by Kolm (1977), Atkinson and Bourguignon (1982), Maasoumi (1986) and Tsui (1995). Concerning poverty, Ravallion (1996) argued in a recent paper that four sets of indicators can be defended as ingredients for a sensible approach to poverty measurement. These are: (i) real expenditure per single adult on market goods, (ii) non-income indicators as access to non-market goods, (iii) indicators of intra-household distribution such as child nutritional status and (iv) indicators of personal characteristics which impose constraints on the ability of an individual, such as physical handicap. In other words, a genuine measure of poverty should depend on income indicators as well as non-income indicators that may help in identifying aspects of welfare not captured by incomes.

We can cite further rationales for viewing the problem of measurement of well-being of a population from a multidimensional structure. For instance, the basic needs approach advocated by development economists regards development as an improvement in an array of human needs and not just as growth of income-see Streeten (1981). There exists a debate about the importance of low incomes as a

[1]Alternatives and variations of the Sen index have been suggested, among others, by Takayama (1979), Blackorby and Donaldson (1980), Kakwani (1980), Clark et al. (1981), Foster et al. (1984), Chakravarty (1990), and Bourguignon and Fields (1997).

determinant of under-nutrition-see Lipton and Ravallion (1995). Finally, well-being is intrinsically multidimensional from the view point of 'capabilities' and 'functionings', where functionings deal with what a person can ultimately do and capabilities indicate the freedom that a person enjoys in terms of functionings—Sen (1985, 1992). In the capability approach functionings are closely approximated by attributes such as literacy, life expectancy, etc. and not by income per se. An example of multidimensional measure of well-being in terms of functioning achievements is the Human Development Index suggested by UNDP (Streeten 1981). It aggregates at the country level functioning achievements in terms of the attributes life expectancy, per capita real GDP and educational attainment rate.

For reasons stated above, we deviate in the present paper from the single dimensional income approach to the measurement of poverty and adopt an alternative approach which is of multidimensional nature. In our multidimensional framework instead of visualising poverty or deprivation using income or consumption as the sole indicator of well-being, we formalise it in terms of functioning failures, or, more precisely, in terms of shortfalls from threshold levels of attributes themselves. We then examine various aggregation rules which permit to quantify the overall magnitude of poverty using these shortfalls. It may be important to note that the threshold levels are determined independently of the attribute distributions. In this sense the concept of poverty measurement we explore here is of 'absolute' type.

We begin the paper by discussing the problem of identifying the poor in Sect. 2. Section 3 then suggests reasonable properties for a multidimensional poverty index. Since we view poverty measurement from a multidimensional perspective, a very important issue that needs to be discussed is the trade off among attributes. It is shown that the possibility/impossibility of such trade offs drops out as an implication of different postulates for a multidimensional measure of poverty. This is presented in Sect. 4 of the paper. Section 5 introduces some functional forms for a multidimensional poverty measure whereas Sect. 6 shows how they may be practically implemented by considering the evolution of 'income/education poverty' in rural Brazil. Section 7 concludes.

## 2 Identification of the Poor

The purpose of this section is to determine the set of poor persons. We begin with notational definitions. With a population of size $n$, person $i$ possesses an $m$-row vector of attributes, $x_i \in R^m_+$, where $R^m_+$ is the non-negative orthant of the Euclidean $m$-space $R^m$. The vector $x_i$ is the $i$th row of a $n \times m$ matrix $X \in M^n$, where $M^n$ is the set of all $n \times m$ attribute matrices whose entries are non-negative reals. The $(i, j)$th entry of $X$ gives the quantity of attribute $j$ possessed by person $i$. Therefore, the $j$th column of $X$ gives a distribution of attribute $j$ among $n$ persons. Let $M = \cup_{n \in N} M^n$, where $N$ is the set of positive integers. For any $X \in M$, we write $n(X)$—or, $n$—for the corresponding population size. It should be noted that quantitative specifications of different attributes preclude the possibility that a variable can be of qualitative type—for instance, of the type whether a person is ill or not.

A simple way of dealing with the multidimensionality of poverty is to assume that the various attributes of an individual may be aggregated into a single cardinal index of 'well-being' and that poverty may be defined in terms of that index. In other words, an individual can be said poor if his/her index of aggregate well-being falls below some poverty line. However, such an approach would be severely restrictive and would mostly amount to considering multidimensional poverty as single dimensional income poverty, with some appropriate generalisation of the concept of 'income'. Although there sometimes may be a good justification for such an approach,[2] this is the case that we do not want to consider here because it is conceptually strictly equivalent to the case of income poverty. The fundamental point in all what follows is that a multidimensional approach to poverty defines poverty as a shortfall from a threshold on each dimension of an individual's well-being. In other words, the *issue of the multidimensionality of poverty arises because individuals, social observers or policy-makers want to define a poverty limit on each individual attribute: income, health, education,* etc. All the arguments presented in this paper are based on this idea.[3]

In agreement with this basic principle, a direct method to check whether a person is poor in the multidimensional framework where he/she is characterised by m attributes is to see whether he/she has the subsistence or threshold level of each attribute. Let z $\in$ Z be a vector of thresholds, or 'minimally acceptable levels'—Sen (1992), p. 139—for different attributes,[4] where $Z$ is a subset of $R^m_+$.The problem is now to determine whether a person, $i$, is poor or not on the basis of his/her, $x_i$ and the vector $z$.

One unambiguous way of counting the number of poor in this context is to identify those for whom the levels of all attributes fall below the corresponding thresholds. But this definition does not exhaust the entire set of poor persons. For example, an old beggar certainly cannot be regarded as rich because of his longevity, though the above notion excludes him from the set of poor. Therefore, this definition seems to be inappropriate.

More generally, person $i$ may be called poor with respect to attribute $j$ if $x_{ij} < z_j$. Person $i$ is regarded as rich if $x_{ij} \geq z_j$ for all $j$. Analogously, attribute $j$ for person $i$ is said to be meagre or non-meagre according as $x_{ij} < z_j$ or $x_{ij} \geq z_j$.For any X $\in$ M, let $S_j(X)$ (or $S_j$) be the set of persons who are poor with respect to attribute $j$. One may argue that the total number of poor persons can be obtained by adding the number of people in $S_j$ over $j$. But this procedure may lead to double counting. To see this, suppose that there are two attributes, 1 and 2. The subsistence levels

---

[2]Tsui (2002) provides an axiomatic justification of such an approach. Note also that this approach may go quite beyond aggregating a few goods or functionings through using appropriate prices or weights. For instance Pradhan and Ravallion (2000) tried to integrate into the analysis unobserved welfare determinants summarised by reported subjective perception of poverty.

[3]Note that poverty limits in all dimensions are defined independently of the quantity of other attributes an individual may enjoy. For a more general statement see Duclos et al. (2001).

[4]Using the same attributes as UNDP (1990), empirical examples of these threshold quantities could be an income of 1$ (ppp corrected) a day, primary education, and 50 year life expectancy.

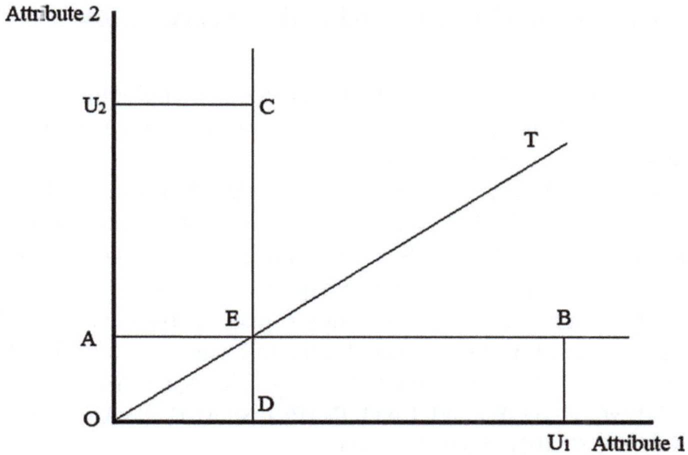


**Fig. 1** Poverty regions

$z_1$ and $z_2$ are represented by the lines CD and AB respectively in Fig. 1. $U_1$ and $U_2$ are upper bounds on the quantities of the attributes. Clearly the total number of poor in this two-attribute case becomes the number of persons for whom the attribute quantities lie inside the space (OABU1 + ODCU2). This shows that the number of persons in OAED is counted twice in this calculation. The double counting may be avoided if we subtract OAED from (OABU1 + ODCU2). But with an increase in the number of attributes the number of sets on which double counting occurs will increase. Consequently, given that we should avoid double counting, determination of the total number of poor using $S_j^{'}s$ will be very intricate.

A simpler way of defining poverty and counting the number of poor is to explicitly account for the possibility of being poor in any poverty dimension. A straightforward way of doing so is to define the poverty indicator variable:

$$\begin{aligned} &\rho(x_i; z) = 1 \ \text{ if} \exists j \in (1, 2, \ldots, m) : x_{ij} < z_j \text{ and} \\ &\rho(x_i; z) = 0, \text{ otherwise.} \end{aligned} \tag{1}$$

Then the number of poor is simply given by:

$$\sum_{i=1}^{n} \rho(x_i; z). \tag{2}$$

For further reference and in line with the preceding arguments, it will be convenient to adopt the following definitions. The region OAED in Fig. 1, where person $i$ is poor with respect to both attributes, will be called the '*two-dimensional poverty*' region (PR2). In contrast, the spaces AECU2 and DEBU1 can be called the 'one-dimensional poverty regions' (PR1) because the quantity of only one of the attributes is above the subsistence level in these spaces.

## 3 Properties for a Multidimensional Poverty Index

In this section, we lay down the postulates for a measure of multidimensional poverty. A formal statement of all these postulates is given in the Appendix to this paper. The following discussion is essentially verbal.

A multidimensional poverty index is a non-constant function $P : M \times Z \rightarrow R^t$. For any $X \in M$, $z \in Z$, $P(X : z)$ gives the extent of poverty associated with the attribute matrix $X$ and thresholds $z$. Thus, though we view the poverty measurement problem from a multidimensional perspective, we indicate the magnitude of overall poverty by a real number. The index $P$ may be assumed to satisfy certain postulates. A first set of postulates includes the following: STRONG FOCUS (SF), WEAK FOCUS (WF), SYMMETRY (SM), MONOTONICITY (MN), CONTINUITY (CN), PRINCIPLE OF POPULATION (PP), SCALE INVARIANCE (SI), and SUBGROUP DECOMPOSABILITY (SD).

These postulates are straight generalisations of the desiderata suggested for a single dimensional poverty index.[5] As such, most of them are little debatable. SF demands that for any two-attribute matrices $X$ and $Y$, if $Y$ is obtained from $X$ by changing some non-poor attainment quantities so that the set of poor persons as well as their attribute levels below the relevant thresholds remain the same, then the poverty levels associated with $X$ and $Y$ must be equal. In other words, we say that the poverty index is independent of the non-poor attribute quantities. Therefore, *SF* does not allow the possibility that a person can give up some amount of a non-meagre attribute to improve the position of a meagre attribute. If one views poverty in terms of deprivation from thresholds, then SF is quite reasonable. In contrast to *SF*, *WF*, the weak version of the focus axiom, says that the poverty index is independent of the attribute levels of the non-poor persons only. *SM* states that any characteristic of persons other than the quantities of attributes used to define poverty is unimportant for measuring poverty. According to *MN* if the position of person $i$ who is poor with respect to attribute $j$ improves then overall poverty should not increase. It may be noted that the improvement may make the beneficiary non-poor with respect to the attribute under consideration. Continuity (CN) requires $P$ to vary continuously with $x_{ij}$s and is essentially a technical requirement. Continuity ensures in particular that the poverty index will not be oversensitive to minor observational errors on quantities of attributes. *PP* is necessary for cross population comparisons of poverty. SI says that the poverty index should be invariant under scale transformation of attributes and thresholds. In other words, what matters for poverty measurement is only the relative distance at which the quantities of all attributes are from their poverty thresholds. SD shows that if the population is partitioned into several subgroups with respect to some homogeneous characteristic, say age, sex, race, region, etc., then the overall poverty is the population share weighted average of subgroup poverty levels. Therefore,

[5]For discussion of properties for a single dimensional poverty index, see among others, Foster (1984), Donaldson and Weymark (1986), Cowell (1988), Chakravarty (1990), Foster and Shorrocks (1991) and Zheng (1997).

SD enables us to calculate percentage contributions of different subgroups to total poverty and hence to identify the subgroups that are most afflicted by poverty.[6]

We now consider postulates which may less easily be generalised to a multidimensional framework or are specific to it. We first focus on redistribution criteria that involve a transfer of a fixed amount of some attribute from one person to another. We say that matrix $X$ is obtained from $Y$ by a Pigou–Dalton progressive transfer of attribute $j$ from one poor person to another if the two matrices $X$ and $Y$ are exactly the same except that the richer poor $i$—with respect to attribute $j$—has $\theta$ units less of attribute $j$ in $Y$ than in $X$ whereas poorer poor $t$ has $\theta$ units more. Equivalently, we say that $Y$ results from $X$ through a regressive Pigou–Dalton transfer in attribute $j$. It is quite reasonable to argue that under such a progressive (regressive) transfer poverty should not increase (decrease). This is what is demanded by the one-dimensional transfer principle (OTP).

A straightforward extension of that principle that generalises in a simple manner the Pigou–Dalton transfer principle used in income poverty measurement, is a variant of the following multidimensional transfers principle introduced by Kolm (1977). The Kolm property says that the distribution of a set of attributes summarised by some matrix $X$ is more equal than another matrix $Y$ (whose rows are not identical) if and only if $X = BY$, where $B$ is some bistochastic matrix[7] and $X$ cannot be derived from $Y$ by permutation of the rows of $Y$. Intuitively, multiplication of $Y$ by $\mathbf{B}$ makes the resulting distribution less concentrated. In effect, this transformation is equivalent to replacing the original bundles of attributes of any pair of individuals by some convex combination of them. Following Tsui (2002), the analogous property applied to the set of poor is the multidimensional transfer principle (MTP). There is no more poverty with $X$ than with $Y$ if $X$ is obtained from $Y$ simply by redistributing the attributes of the poor according to the bistochastic transformation.[8]

Instead of the single dimensional and multidimensional transfer principles OTP and MTP, we now consider a redistributive criterion involving two attributes, but without tying down the proportions in which they are exchanged as in MTP. For this, suppose two persons, $i$ and $t$, are in the two-dimensional poverty space associated with attributes $j$ and $k$, and $i$ has more of $k$ but less of $j$. Let us interchange the amounts of attribute $j$ between the two persons. As person $i$ who had more of $k$ has now more of $j$ too, there is an increase in the correlation of the attributes within the population. It is reasonable to expect that such a switch will not decrease or increase poverty according to the two attributes correspond to similar or different aspects of poverty. The non-decreasing poverty under correlation increasing switch (NDCIS) postulate says that poverty cannot decrease with such correlation increasing switches. The

---

[6]For further discussion, see Tsui (2002) and Chakravarty et al. (1998). Also it may be noted that that SD is not the same as subgroup consistency discussed in Foster and Shorrocks (1991).

[7]A square matrix is called a bistochastic matrix if each of its entries is non-negative and each of its rows and columns sums to one. Evidently, a permutation matrix is a bistochastic matrix but the converse is not necessarily true.

[8]It is well-known that the one-dimensional Pigou–Dalton transfer principle is connected to Lorenz dominance through the Hardy–Little wood–Polya theorem. No such theorem is available in the multiattribute case.

converse property will be denoted by NICIS. The exact meaning of both postulates will be discussed more explicitly in the next section.

## 4 Implications of Properties

This section discusses some implications of the properties suggested in the previous section.

In the rest of this paper, we will consider mostly subgroup decomposable measures. A trivial implication of SD is that a poverty index defined on $M^n$ can be written as:

$$P(X; z) = \frac{1}{n} \sum_{i=1}^{n} p(x_i; z),$$

In this expression $p(x_i; z)$ may clearly be interpreted as the level of poverty associated with a single person $i$ possessing attribute vector $x_i$. Most of our arguments in this section are presented in terms of this 'individual poverty function'.

Our first proposition, whose proof is easy, makes a simple but extremely important observation about the shape of an isopoverty contour in a single dimensional poverty region.

**Proposition 1** *Under SF, the isopoverty contours of an individual in a one-dimensional poverty space are parallel to the axis that shows the quantities of the attribute with respect to which he/she is poor.*

This proposition is extremely important because it conveys the essence of multidimensional poverty measurement. If one insists on defining a poverty threshold *independently for each attribute*, then at the same time one cannot suppose that the poverty shortfall in a given attribute may be compensated and possibly eliminated by increasing the quantity of another attribute indefinitely above its threshold level. If I am poor because my income is below the poverty limit, a very long life expectancy cannot make my poverty disappear. More precisely, Proposition 1 does not allow trade off between meagre and non-meagre attribute quantities of a person.

Things are slightly different when using WF rather than SF. Since WF assumes that the poverty index is independent of attribute levels of non-poor persons only, it does not rule out the possibilities of trade offs. WF ignores information on attributes of non-poor persons but, unlike SF, takes into account the non-poor attributes of a poor person, that is, of a person who has at least one poor attribute. Therefore, we can no longer have straight line isopoverty contours in one-dimensional poverty spaces if we assume WF.

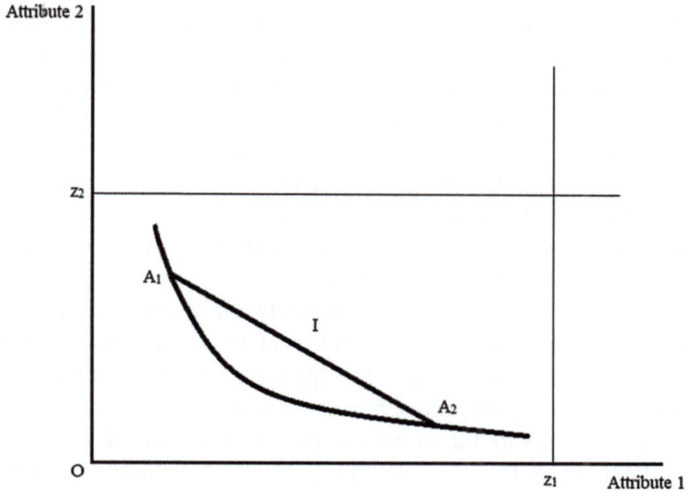


**Fig. 2** Convexity of isopoverty contour

In fact, if we assume convexity of isopoverty contours in single dimensional poverty regions,[9] then the following variant of Proposition 1 emerges.

**Proposition 1*** *Under WF, the convex isopoverty contours in single dimensional poverty regions have vertical and horizontal asymptotes.*

The reasoning behind this proposition is as follows. Although trade off is allowed under WF in one-dimensional poverty spaces, poverty is never eliminated. That is, there is a positive lower bound of the poverty index along any vertical or horizontal axis in the poverty space. This means that the contour becomes a horizontal or a vertical line asymptotically. However, this property leads to analytically difficult problems and we shall be working mostly with SF in what follows.

**Proposition 2** *(Convexity of isopoverty contours). Suppose that $m = 2$ and that the poverty index satisfies MN, CN, SD, and OTP or MTP. Then the is poverty contours in the two-dimensional poverty region are decreasing convex to the origin.*

*Proof* That the is poverty contour is decreasing is guaranteed by MN. The convexity makes use of OTP or MTP. Denote the two attributes for which contours are to be examined by 1 and 2. Since we will restrict our attention to the two-dimensional space only, let us suppose that $x_{ij} < z_j$ for $j = 1, 2$ and for two persons 1 and 2. Let their attributes $(x_{11}, x_{12})$ and $(x_{21}, x_{22})$ be represented by points $A_1$ and $A_2$ in Fig. 2. Consider a transfer of attributes between these two persons which makes their bundles identical. Under SD, the change in the overall poverty index is given by:

$$\Delta P = \frac{1}{n}[2.p((x_{11} + x_{21})/2), (x_{12} + x_{22})/2; z) - p(x_{11}, x_{12}; z) - p(x_{21}, x_{22}; z)]. \quad (3)$$

[9]Convexity of the contours implicitly assumes that MTP holds throughout the entire poverty space.

Both OTP and MTP imply that this expression is non-positive. If I is the midpoint of the segment $A_1A_2$ in Fig. 2, CN and MN then imply that I lies above the isopoverty contour going through the bundle $A_1$ or $A_2$, where individual poverty is maximum. If $A_1$ and $A_2$ are on the same isopoverty contour it follows that all bundles on the segment $A_1A_2$ lie on isopoverty contours with lower poverty. □

This proposition shows that non-increasingness of the marginal rate of substitution between two attributes for a person in the two-dimensional poverty region is an implication of OTP or MTP. The notion of substitutability between attributes in something different and will be taken up below.

It should be clear that under SF, the poverty indifference curves in the one-dimensional poverty regions will be either horizontal or vertical straight lines depending on which axis of the graph represents quantities of which attribute. Given the shapes of the curves in the respective poverty spaces, we can combine them to generate isopoverty contours for the entire domain. Continuity enables us to connect the curves over the intervals $[z_1 - \varepsilon, z_1]$ and $[z_2 - \varepsilon, z_2]$, by continuous curves, where $\varepsilon > 0$ is infinitesimally small. We show the combined graphs in Fig. 3. $Q_1$, $Q_2$, and $Q_3$ are three overall isopoverty curves. The poverty levels associated with $Q_1$, is higher than that corresponds to $Q_2$, and $Q_2$ represents more poverty than $Q_3$.

In the preceding proposition, OTP and MTP have an identical role. It is clear, however, that requiring validity of the transfers principle for all attributes is more demanding than that for one attribute only. Therefore, the set of poverty indices satisfying OTP must be more restrictive than those satisfying MTP. Our next proposition shows that indeed the former includes only those individual poverty functions that are additive across components.

**Proposition 3** (*Additivity*). *Suppose that a subgroup decomposable poverty index satisfying OTP possesses first-order partial derivatives. Then it is additive across attributes, that is,*

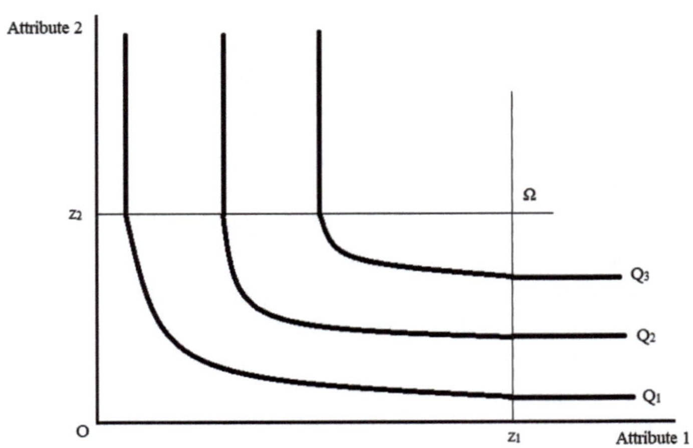


**Fig. 3** Poverty indifference curves in different poverty regions

$$P(X; z) = \frac{1}{n}\sum_{i=1}^{n}\sum_{j=1}^{m} p^j(x_{ij}; z_j), \tag{4}$$

where $p^j()$ is the individual poverty function associated with attribute $j$.

*Proof* For simplicity let us consider the two-person, two-attribute case. But one may check that the result remains valid in the general case too.

Consider two individuals 1 and 2 with attribute levels $(x_{11}, x_{12})$ and $(x_{21}, x_{22})$ respectively. Then for $(x_{11} < x_{21})$ OTP implies the following:

$$p(x_{11} - \varepsilon, x_{12}) + p(x_{21} + \varepsilon, x_{22}) - p(x_{11}, x_{12}) - p(x_{21}, x_{22}) \geq 0$$

for all $(x_{12}, x_{22}, \varepsilon > 0)$.

Letting ε tend towards 0 and taking limits leads to:

$$p_1(x_{21}, x_{22}) - p_1(x_{11}, x_{12}) \geq 0 \text{ for all } (x_{12}, x_{22}, \text{ and } x_{11} < x_{21}), \tag{5}$$

where $p_1()$ is the partial derivative of $p$ ()with respect to its first argument. Define now:

$$\begin{aligned} g(t) &= \text{Max } p_1(t, s) \text{ for } s \in [0, \infty] \text{ and} \\ h(t) &= \text{Min } p_1(t, s) \text{ for } s \in [0, \infty). \end{aligned} \tag{6}$$

Then (5) implies,

$$h(x_{21}) - g(x_{11}) \geq 0 \text{ for all } x_{11} < x_{21}. \tag{7}$$

But, by definition of $g$ () and $h$ () in (6), we have

$$\begin{aligned} h(x_{11}) - g(x_{11}) &\leq 0 \text{ for all } x_{11} \text{ and} \\ h(x_{21}) - g(x_{21}) &\leq 0 \text{ for all } x_{21}. \end{aligned} \tag{8}$$

Allowing $x_{11}$ to tend towards $x_{21}$ from below shows a contradiction between (7) and (8), unless $h(t) = g(t)$ for all $t.h(t) = g(t)$ implies that $p_1(t, s)$ is independent of $s$, which in turn shows that $p(t, s)$ can be written as $p_1(t) + p_2(s)$. □

Using (4) we can determine the shares of different attributes to total poverty. If a poverty index exhibits additivity in conjunction with SD, then we have a two-way poverty breakdown and can calculate the contributions of alternative subgroups to aggregate poverty with respect to different attributes. Consequently, identification of the subgroup-attribute combinations that are more susceptible to poverty can be made. Isolation of such subgroup-attribute combinations becomes important in designing antipoverty policies when a society's limited resource does not enable it to eliminate poverty for an entire subgroup or for a specific attribute.[10] We shall study later the practical implications of this additivity property and see that they may not always be convenient.

We finally consider the last transfer properties introduced in the preceding section, non-decreasing (non-increasing) poverty under correlation increasing switch. To understand this issue, define substitutability as proximity in the nature of attributes. A correlation increasing switch means that a person who has higher amount of one attribute gets higher amount of the other through a rank reversing transfer. If attributes are close to each other—i.e. they are substitutes—such a transfer should not decrease poverty. The poorer person cannot compensate the lower quantity of one attribute by a higher quantity of the other. A similar argument can be provided for the complementarity case. Atkinson and Bourguignon (1982) argued rigorously that welfare should not increase under a correlation increasing switch if the attributes involved in the switch are substitutes, where substitute attributes are such that the marginal utility of one attribute decreases when the quantity of the other increases. The equivalent definition in terms of the individual poverty function $p(x; z)$—assuming that this function is twice differentiable—is that two attributes $j$ and $k$ are substitutes whenever $p_{jk}(x; z) > 0$ for all $x$. In other words, poverty decreases less with an increase in attribute $j$ for persons with larger quantities of $k$. For instance, the drop in poverty due to a unit increase in income is less important for people who have an educational level close to the education poverty threshold than for persons with very low education, if income and education are considered as substitutes. On the contrary, the drop in poverty is larger for persons with higher education if these two attributes are supposed to be complements. Thus, the equivalent of the Atkinson and Bourguignon property in the case of poverty is:

**Proposition 4** *Under SD, non-decreasing (non-increasing) poverty under increasing correlation switch holds for attributes which are substitutes (complements) in the individual poverty function.*

Of course, we observe that with P() in (4), attributes are neither substitutes nor complements. As expected OTP makes the properties NDCIS or NICIS irrelevant. However, this is not the case with MTP. There will be indices satisfying MTP and NICIS and others satisfying MTP and NDCIS. Tsui (2002) argued that a poverty index should be unambiguously non-decreasing under a correlation increasing switch. But there is no a priori reason for a person to regard attributes as substitutes only. Some of the attributes can as well be complements.

[10]For a numerical illustration of this two-way decomposability formula, see Chakravarty et al. (1998).

## 5 Some Functional Forms for Multidimensional Poverty Indices

Assuming that we may require multidimensional poverty indices to satisfy MN, FC, CN, and SD, the preceding section led us to distinguish poverty indices satisfying OTP from those satisfying MTP. Further, among the latter, there are indices that meet NDCIS (NICIS) but not NICIS (NDCIS). In this section, we consider simple functional forms for poverty indices from these three sets, imposing in addition scale invariance. We will start from the two-dimensional case and try to generalise whenever this is possible.

*The Set of Additive Multidimensional Poverty Indices*

As seen above, poverty indices satisfying OTP are additive so that the general form of the individual poverty function in the two-dimensional case is simply:

$$p(x_{i1}, x_{i2}; z_1, z_2) = \begin{cases} f_1\left(\frac{x_{i1}}{z_1}\right) & \text{if } x_{i1} < z_1 \text{ and } x_{i2} \geq z_2, \\ f_1\left(\frac{x_{i1}}{z_1}\right) + f_2\left(\frac{x_{i2}}{z_2}\right) & \text{if } x_{i1} < z_1 \text{ and } x_{i2} < z_2, \\ f_2\left(\frac{x_{i2}}{z_2}\right) & \text{if } x_{i1} < z_1 \text{ and } x_{i2} \geq z_2, \end{cases} \tag{9}$$

where $f_j()$ are continuous, decreasing and convex function such that $f_j(u) = 0$ for $u \geq 1$. Note that homogeneity with respect to $x$ and $z$ results from the *SI* property. Equation (9) may also written under a more compact form as:

$$p(x_{i1}, x_{i2}; z_1, z_2) = f_1\left(\frac{x_{i1}}{z_1}\right).S_1^i + f_2 f_2\left(\frac{x_{i2}}{z_2}\right).S_2^i, \tag{10}$$

where $S_j^i$ is the indicator function such that $S_j^i = 1$ if $i \in S_j$ and $S_j^i = 0$, otherwise.

In the general case of m attributes and n individuals, the expression for the poverty index $P$ corresponding to Eq. (10) becomes:

$$P(X; z) = \frac{1}{n} \sum_{j=1}^{m} \sum_{i \in S_j} f_j\left(\frac{x_{ij}}{z_j}\right), \tag{11}$$

where $X \in M^n, n \in N, z \in Z$ are arbitrary, $f_j : [0, \infty[ \to R^1$ is continuous, non-increasing, convex and $f_j(t) = 0$ for all $t \geq 1$.

To illustrate the preceding formula let us choose:

$$f_j(t) = a_j(1-t)^{\theta_j}, \quad 0 \leq t < 1, \tag{12}$$

where $\theta_j > 1$ and $a_j(> 0)$ may be interpreted as the 'weight' given to attribute $j$ in the overall poverty index. Then the resulting measure is:

$$P_\theta(X;z) = \frac{1}{n}\sum_{j=1}^{m}\sum_{i\in S_j} a_j\left(1-\frac{x_{ij}}{z_j}\right)^{\theta_j}, \tag{13}$$

This is a simple multidimensional extension of the Foster–Greer–Thorbecke (Foster et al. 1984) index. If $\theta_j = 1$ for all $j$, then $P_\theta$ becomes a weighted sum of poverty gaps in all dimensions. On the other hand, if $\theta_j = 2$ for all $j$, then

$$P_2(X;z) = \frac{1}{n}\sum_{j=1}^{m} a_j, F_j.[A_j^2 + (1-A_j^2).V_j^2), \tag{14}$$

where $F_j$ is the population size in $S_j$ as a fraction of $n$, $A_j$ is the average relative poverty shortfall of persons in $S_j$ and $V_j$ is the coefficient of variation of the distribution of attribute $j$ among those in $S_j$.

It may be important to note that though the use of $S_j$ sets for determining the number of poor leads to double counting, their use in the construction of a poverty index of the form (11) (excluding the headcount ratio) does not involve this problem. The reason behind this is that we are not counting the number of poor but aggregating their poverty shortfalls in the various dimensions. However, as mentioned earlier, these measures are not sensitive to a correlation increasing switch.

*Non-additive Poverty Indices Satisfying MTP*

As seen above, a more general family of poverty indices is that satisfying MTP rather than OTP. It may be obtained in the two-dimensional case from isopoverty contours which are convex to the origin. These poverty contours may be generated by taking non-decreasing and quasi-concave transformations of the relative shortfalls of the two attributes. The following functional form for the individual poverty function $p\,(x;z)$ is a compact way of representing the isopoverty contours shown in Fig. 3:

$$p(x;z) = I\left[\text{Max}\left(1-\frac{x_1}{z_1},0\right), \text{Max}\left(1-\frac{x_2}{z_2},0\right)\right], \tag{15}$$

where $I\,(u_1,u_2)$ is an increasing, continuous, quasi-concave function with $I\,(0,0) = 0$. The corresponding poverty index becomes:

$$P(X;z) = \frac{1}{n}\sum_{i=1}^{n} I\left[\text{Max}\left(1-\frac{x_{i1}}{z_1},0\right), \text{Max}\left(1-\frac{x_{i2}}{z_2},0\right)\right], \tag{16}$$

Clearly, the additive case analysed above is a particular case of (16) where $I(u_1,u_2) = f_1(u_1) + f_2(u_2)$. Different forms of the poverty index may now be generated from alternative specifications of $I$ (). An appealing specification may be derived from the CES form:

$$I(u_1,u_2) = f[(a_1, u_1^\theta + a_2.u_2^\theta)^{1/\theta}], \tag{17}$$

where $f$ () is an increasing and convex function such that $f(0) = 0$, $a_1$ and $a_2$ are positive weights attached to the two attributes and $\theta$ permits to parameterise the elasticity of substitution between the shortfalls of the various attributes. Note, however, that in order to generate isopoverty contours convex to the origin in the two-dimensional region of the space of attributes, (17) must lead to isopoverty contours that are concave to the origin in the space of shortfalls. This is what is shown in Fig. 3 when is poverty contours are looked at from the origin, $O$, or from the no-poverty point, $\Omega$. This concavity requirement imposes that $\theta > 1$ in (17).

The full specification of poverty indices based on the individual poverty function (17) is obtained by combining (16) and (17).

$$P(X; z) = \frac{1}{n}\sum_{i=1}^{n} f\left[\left\{a_1\left[\text{Max.}\left(1 - \frac{x_{i1}}{z_1}, 0\right)\right]^{\theta} + a_2\left[\text{Max.}\left(1 - \frac{x_{i2}}{z_2}, 0\right)\right]^{\theta}\right\}^{1/\theta}\right]. \quad (18)$$

This index seems a rather flexible functional form consistent with MTP. Note, however, that it is not clear a priori whether it satisfies NDCIS or NICIS. It is easy to see that MTP implies that $\theta > 1$, which in turn implies that the cross second derivative of $I$ () is negative. However, the two shortfalls may still be complement in determining poverty depending on the shape of the function $f$ ().[11]

Three particular cases of (18) are worth stressing. The first case is when θ tends towards infinity so that the substitutability between the two shortfalls or equivalently the two attributes in the definition of poverty tends towards zero. In that case, the isopoverty contours become rectangular curves even within the two-dimensional poverty space. This is the shape shown in Fig. 4. It is interesting to note that in this case the two attributes must necessarily combine within the two-dimensional poverty space in the same proportions as the threshold levels $z_1$ and $z_2$.[12] The expression for the poverty index then becomes:

$$P(X; z) = \frac{1}{n}\sum_{i=1}^{n} f\left[\text{Max.}\left\{\text{Max}\left(1 - \frac{x_{i1}}{z_1}, 0\right), \text{Max}\left(1 - \frac{x_{i1}}{z_1}, 0\right)\right\}\right]$$
$$= \frac{1}{n}\sum_{j=1}^{2}\sum_{i \in I_j} f\left(1 - \frac{x_{ij}}{z_j}, 0\right), \quad (19)$$

[11]To see this, note that the cross second derivative of the individual poverty function $p(x_1, x_2; z_1, z_2)$ writes with obvious notation: $p_{12} = f'.I_{12} + f''.I_1.I_2$. The condition $\theta > 1$ implies that $I_{12}$ is negative, but $p_{12}$ may still be positive because of the second term on the RHS.

[12]If this were note the case, a point like B in Fig. 4 could be the summit of a rectangular isopoverty contour, which is obviously contradictory since poverty is zero for high values of an attribute on the vertical branch and non-zero on the horizontal branch.

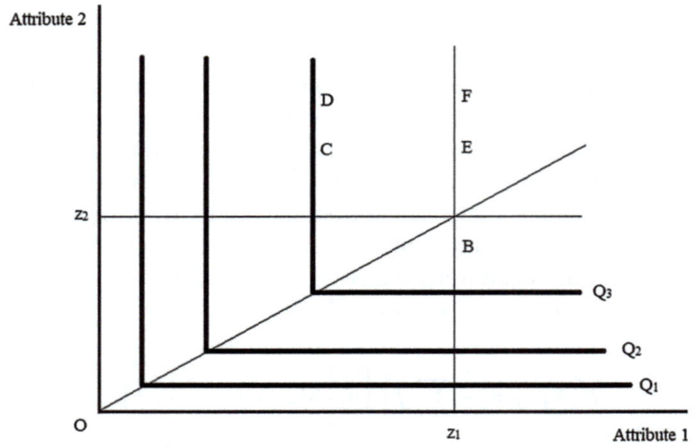


**Fig. 4** Rectangular isopoverty contours

where

$$I_1 = \left\{ i : \frac{x_{i1}}{z_1} \leq \text{Min}\left[\frac{x_{i2}}{z_2}, 1\right] \right\}, \quad I_2 = \left\{ i : \frac{x_{i2}}{z_2} \leq \text{Min}\left[\frac{x_{i1}}{z_2}, 1\right] \right\}.$$

These two sets may be called 'exclusive poverty sets' where two-dimensional poverty is transformed into one-dimensional poverty with respect to the attribute that is the farthest away from its poverty line. Expression (19) is analogous to that for additive poverty indices except that the poverty sets $S_j$ are replaced by the sets $I_j$, and the poverty functions are the same for the various attributes. The extreme parsimony of this family of poverty indices is to be noted. It actually requires no more than the knowledge of the threshold levels and a conventional one-dimensional poverty index $f$ (), for instance, the well-known Foster–Greer–Thorbecke $P_a$ index. Of course, these poverty indices satisfy MTP and NICIS.

The second particular case is at the other extreme when the two-attributes are perfect substitutes in the two-dimensional poverty space. The isopoverty contour is then a straight line in that space which connects the horizontal and vertical straight lines in one-dimensional poverty spaces, as in Fig. 5. The general expression of the corresponding poverty indices is:

$$P(X; z) = \frac{1}{n} \sum_{i=1}^{n} f\left[ a_1 \text{Max}\left(1 - \frac{x_{i1}}{z_1}, 0\right) + a_2 \text{Max}\left(1 - \frac{x_{i2}}{z_2}, 0\right)\right], \qquad (20)$$

where, again, $f()$ may be any one-dimensional poverty index, like the Foster—Greer–Thorbecke $P_a$ index, and, as before, the positive coefficients $a_j$ represent the weight given to the attributes and determine the slope of the isopoverty contour in the two-dimensional poverty space. Poverty indices of type (20) satisfy MTP and

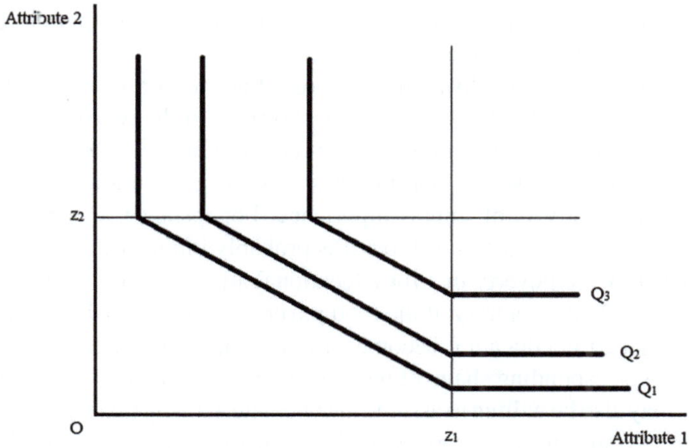


**Fig. 5** Isopoverty contours for perfect substitutes

NDCIS or NICIS depending on whether the one-dimensional poverty function $f()$ is concave or convex.

A third particular case of (18) is obtained by using the Foster–Greer–Thorbecke $P_a$ index for the function $f$ (). One then obtains:

$$P_a^\theta(X;z) = \frac{1}{n}\sum_{i=1}^{n}\left[a_1\left[\mathrm{Max}\left(1-\frac{x_{i1}}{z_1},0\right)\right]^\theta + a_2\left[\mathrm{Max}\left(1-\frac{x_{i2}}{z_2},0\right)\right]^\theta\right]^{a/\theta}, \tag{21}$$

where α is a positive parameter. The interpretation of that measure is straightforward. The poverty shortfalls in the two dimensions are first aggregated into some 'average' shortfall through function $I$ () with a particular value of θ and the coefficients $a_j$. Multidimensional poverty is then defined as the average of that aggregate shortfall, raised to the power α, over the whole population. This seems to be the measure the closest to one-dimensional poverty measurement concepts and the simplest generalisation of these concepts. With $\alpha = 0$, (21) yields the multidimensional headcount. With $\alpha = 1$, $P_a^\theta$ becomes a multidimensional poverty gap obtained by some particular averaging of the poverty gaps in the two dimensions. Higher values for α may be interpreted, as in the one-dimensional case, as higher aversion towards extreme poverty. An interesting property of that $P_a^\theta$ measure is that it satisfies NDCIS or NICIS depending on whether α is greater or less than θ.

These three families of poverty indices may easily be generalised to any number of attributes. However, doing so implies assuming the same elasticity of substitution between attributes, and therefore the resulting poverty indices are NDCIS or NICIS for all pairs of attributes. This may not be very satisfactory and other more complex specifications have to be designed to avoid this.

Another interesting generalisation of the preceding measures consists of assuming that the substitutability between the poverty shortfalls in the two attributes changes with the extent of poverty. When some one is very poor in one of the two dimensions, one may be willing to assume that the elasticity of substitution between the two dimensions of poverty is of minor importance. For instance, if a person is 50% below the poverty line in terms of food, it is probably immaterial whether he/she is 10 or 20% below the poverty line for educational attainment for evaluating his/her overall poverty. On the contrary, if the food poverty gap is only 10%, then the extent of the poverty gap in education becomes a more important determinant of overall poverty. The corresponding shape of the isopoverty contours is shown in Fig. 6.

But one may also be willing to assume the opposite, namely that the substitutability between the two attributes decreases with the extent of poverty. Analytically, a simple way of allowing for this dependency between the substitutability of attributes and the extent of poverty consists of making the $\theta$ parameter in (18) a function of the level of poverty. Within a $P_a$ framework, individual poverty is then defined implicitly by the following equation:

$$\left[\left[\text{Max}\left(1-\frac{x_{i1}}{z_1},0\right)\right]^{a(p)}+\left[\text{Max}\left(1-\frac{x_{i2}}{z_2},0\right)\right]^{a(p)}\right]^{a/a(p)}$$
$$= P(x_{i1}, x_{i2}, z_1, z_2). \tag{22}$$

where $a\,(p)$ is a function that describes how attribute substitutability changes with the extent of poverty. Obvious candidates for this function are $a\,(p) = 1/p$ and $a\,(p) = 1/(1-p)$, assuming $p$ is normalised so as to lie between 0 and 1. With

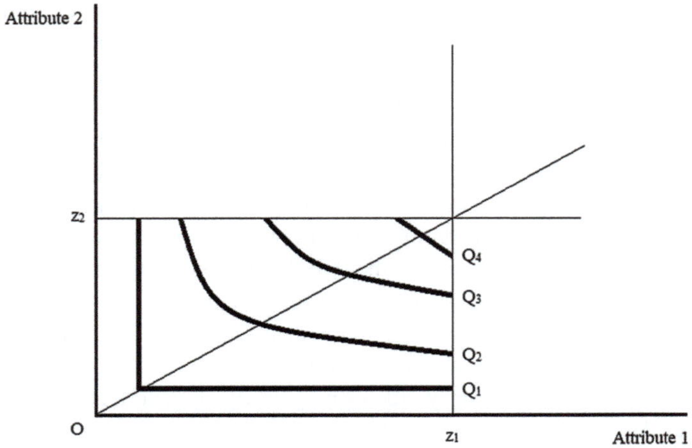


**Fig. 6** Variability of substitutability and isopoverty contours

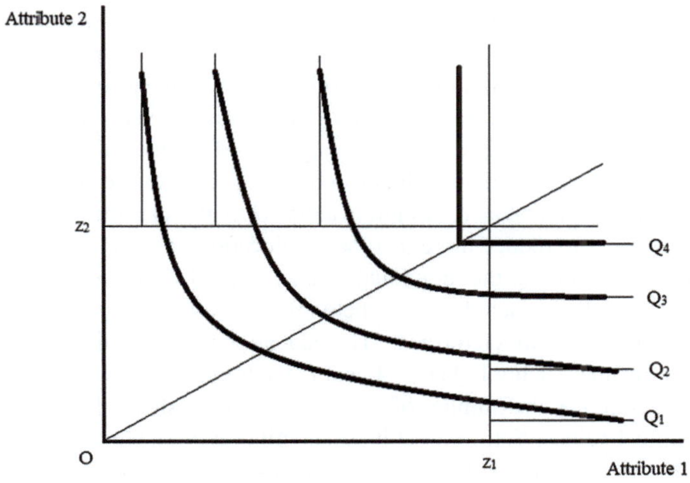


**Fig. 7** Isopoverty contours under the weak focus axiom

these functions, solving numerically Eq. (22) is not difficult. It leads to poverty functions with the same properties as (21), except for the fact that correlation increasing switches may now increase or decrease overall poverty depending on whether they are performed among very poor or moderately poor persons. We shall refer to these indices respectively as $P_a^{1/p}$ and $P_a^{1/(1-p)}$.

It is worth stressing that all preceding multidimensional poverty indices actually rely on the $SF$ postulate. In effect, it may be shown that the weak focus postulate ($WF$) rules out functional forms of poverty indices that are additive as well as the CES-like $P_a^{\theta}$ measures, or even their varying substitutability generalisations, $P_a^{1/p}$ and $P_a^{1/(1-p)}$. As a matter of fact we have not been able to find relatively simple functions leading to isopoverty contours consistent with $WF$ as shown in Fig. 7, and the other properties of the individual poverty function $p$ ().

## 6 An Example of Application

To illustrate the use of the preceding measures as well as the concepts behind them, we analye here the evolution of multidimensional poverty in rural Brazil during the 1980s. Poverty includes two dimensions: income on the one hand and educational attainment on the other. The analysis is performed on the rural population only, because this is where Brazilian poverty tends to concentrate. It is also restricted to the adult population, so as to avoid the problem of imputing some final educational level to children who are still going to school. Samples from the PNAD household surveys for the years 1981 and 1987 are being used.[13] The reason for choosing these years is that they happen to correspond to an increase in income poverty in the rural population. So, we felt it could be interesting to use the measures presented in the previous section to see whether this increase in income poverty had possibly been compensated by a drop in educational poverty. But, of course, this issue of the trade off between these two particular dimensions of poverty would also arise in very different contexts. For instance, designing antipoverty policies may require deciding whether it is better to reduce more income or education poverty.

Poverty is measured at the individual level. Each individual is given the income per capita within the household he/she belongs to. The income poverty threshold is 2$ a day, at1985 ppp corrected prices. The educational poverty threshold is defined as the end of primary school, that is, 4 years of schooling. The educational poverty shortfall is defined as the number of years of schooling short of that level. It may thus take only 4 values. Yet, we treat it as a continuous variable.

The first two columns of Table 1 show the level of poverty as measured by the conventional $P_a$ measures separately for income and education. It may be seen that income poverty increased from 1981 to 1987, whereas education poverty fell. The "alpha = 0" rows show that there were 40.5% of rural adults below the poverty line in 1981 whereas 74.4% had not completed primary school. Six years later these proportions were 42.1 and 68% respectively, indicating an increase in income poverty and a fall in education poverty. The poverty gap ("alpha = 1") and higher levels of the $P_a$ measures show the same evolution.

We now consider multidimensional poverty measures of the $P_a^\theta$ type, with $\alpha$ taking the same values as for the one-dimensional poverty measures that we just reviewed and $\theta$ taking the values 1, which corresponds to perfect substitutability as in (20) above, 2 and 5. We also use the varying substitutability measures, $P_a^{1/p}$ and $P_a^{1/(1-p)}$. The evaluation of multidimensional poverty for 1981 and 1987 according to these various measures are reported in Table 1 for two sets of weights for the income and education attributes. The first set gives equal weights to the two dimensions whereas the second gives more weight to income.

Consider first the first two rows which correspond to headcount poverty measures. In the multidimensional case, the headcount corresponds to individuals who are poor either in terms of income or in terms of education. Accordingly, there were 79.7% poor in 1981 versus 75.6% in 1987. From these figures and the headcounts in one dimension, it is easy to derive the proportion of people who were poor in both dimensions. They were 35.2% in 1981 and 34.4% in 1987.

Reading down the other rows, one may check that the multidimensional $P_a^\theta$ measures—as well as the measures with variable substitutability—are commensurate with the one-dimensional $P_a$ measures for income and education. There is nothing surprising here. As noted above, the multidimensional $P_a^\theta$ measures are designed in such a way that they may be interpreted as some particular mean of one-dimensional measures. This mean depends on the weighing coefficients, $a_1$ and $a_2$, but also on the

[13]Irrespectively of the fact that rural incomes are known to be imperfectly observed in PNAD–see for instance Elbers et al. (2001). The calculations below must therefore be taken as mostly illustrative.

**Table 1** Multidimensional measurement of poverty with $P_\alpha^\theta$, $P_\alpha^{1/p}$ and $P_\alpha^{1/(1-p)}$ measures. Income/education poverty in rural Brazil, 1981–1987 (percent)

| Multidimensional income/education poverty | | | | | | | | | | | | |
|---|---|---|---|---|---|---|---|---|---|---|---|---|
| One-dimensional poverty | | | Income weight = 50%, education weight = 50% | | | | | Income weight = 80%, education weight = 20% | | | | |
| Aversion for poverty | Income | Education | Theta = 1 | Theta=2 | Theta=5 | $1/p$ | $1/(1-p)$ | Theta = 1 | Theta=2 | Theta=5 | $1/p$ | $1/(1-p)$ |
| Alpha = 0 (headcount) | | | | | | | | | | | | |
| 1981 | **40.52** | 74.41 | 79.7 | 79.7 | 79.7 | 79.7 | 79.7 | 79.7 | 79.7 | 79.7 | 79.7 | 79.7 |
| 1987 | **42.07** | 67.99 | 75.65 | 75.65 | 75.65 | 75.65 | 75.65 | 75.65 | 75.65 | 75.65 | 75.65 | 75.65 |
| Alpha = 1 (poverty gap) | | | | | | | | | | | | |
| 1981 | **15.93** | 57.82 | 36.87 | 45.63 | 53.28 | 43.8 | 55.18 | **24.31** | 33.7 | 46 | 35.67 | 30.02 |
| 1987 | **17.64** | 52.93 | 35.82 | 42.83 | 49.97 | 41.57 | 51.4 | **24.7** | 32.82 | 43.56 | 34.52 | 29.8 |
| Alpha = 2 | | | | | | | | | | | | |
| 1981 | **8.48** | 51.23 | *20.67* | 29.86 | 40.92 | 31.07 | 28.97 | ***11.15*** | **17.03** | 30.24 | 24.25 | **11.84** |
| 1987 | **9.66** | 46.87 | *20.24* | 28.27 | 38.12 | 29.45 | 27.53 | ***11.97*** | **17.11** | 28.65 | 22.46 | **12.69** |
| Alpha = 3 | | | | | | | | | | | | |
| 1981 | **5.21** | 47.97 | ***12.87*** | *20.94* | 33.29 | 24.39 | 15.38 | ***6.43*** | ***9.59*** | 21.02 | 17.22 | **6.66** |
| 1987 | **6.02** | 43.86 | ***12.96*** | *19.98* | 30.9 | 23.07 | 15.26 | ***7.12*** | ***9.94*** | 19.96 | 16.56 | **7.38** |
| Alpha = 5 | | | | | | | | | | | | |
| 1981 | **2.47** | 44.68 | ***6.12*** | *11.27* | 23.57 | 17.4 | 6.58 | ***2.94*** | ***3.86*** | 10.91 | 11.4 | **3** |
| 1987 | **2.89** | 40.84 | ***6.49*** | *11* | 21.86 | 16.37 | 6.96 | ***3.34*** | ***4.22*** | 10.48 | 10.86 | **3.41** |

Cells in bold refer to cases where there is more poverty in 1987 than in 1981. Cells in italics refer to cases where the NICIS property hold ($\alpha > \theta$)

substitutability parameter, $\theta$. So, multidimensional measures is higher when more weight is given to education because one-dimensional poverty is higher for education, as shown in the first two columns of Table 1. But multidimensional poverty also tends to increase when the substitutability of the two attributes fall, or equivalently the $\theta$ parameter increases. As suggested by the argument leading to (19) above, this is because low substitutability between the two attributes give more weight for each observation to the attribute with the largest shortfall.

Bold figures in Table 1 correspond to situations where poverty measures indicate more poverty in 1987 than in 1981. We see that this occurrence is more frequent when the weight given to the income dimension is higher. There is nothing really surprising here since we have seen that there was more poverty, in a one dimension sense, with income than with education. It is more interesting to notice that poverty appears to be higher in 1987 than in 1981 when the poverty aversion parameter, $\alpha$, is high enough, although the value of that parameter for which this happens is not systematically shown in the table. This is true for each value of the substitutability parameter, $\theta$, as well as for both systems of weights. This is true also with the variable substitutability measure, $P_a^{1/(1-p)}$. A possible explanation for this pattern would be that the worsening of the bi-dimensional income/education distribution in rural Brazil may have its roots at the very bottom of the distribution, where poverty is more severe. In other words, income losses may have been more serious predominantly for people with low income and low education.

Regarding the correlation between the two dimensions of poverty, still a more interesting feature in Table 1 is the fact that poverty tends to be higher in 1987 in cases where the NICIS property holds. It was seen in the previous section that the $P_a^{\theta}$ measure was such that poverty would increase with increasing correlation switches when $a < \theta$. It happens in Table 1 that cases where poverty is higher in 1987 than in 1981 occur only when the opposite is true. This suggests that the increase in one-dimensional income poverty was accompanied by a drop in the correlation with educational levels.

The varying substitutability measures give still another information. First, it may be seen that 1987 never exhibits more poverty than 1981 with the $P_a^{1/p}$ measure. It does however with the $P_a^{1/(1-p)}$ measure for high values of $\alpha$ when both dimensions have equal weight and much sooner when more weight is put on the income dimension. This evolution is consistent with the idea that income losses were more pronounced for poorer people with a larger income than education shortfall. With the $P_a^{1/(1-p)}$ there is limited substitutability for them and the drop in income could not be compensated by a possible increase in the educational level.

This interpretation of the figures reported in Table 1 would need to be confirmed by a more careful analysis of the bi-dimensional distribution of education and income in rural Brazil. Within the present framework, what matters is that measures directly inspired from the familiar one-dimensional $P_a$ poverty indices and enlarged through a reduced set of parameters—2 parameters in the case of $P_a^{\theta}$ and a single one in the case of $P_a^{1/p}$ or $P_a^{1/(1-p)}$—permit to describe adequately the extent of poverty in a multidimensional perspective.

# 7 Conclusion

We have explicitly argued in this paper why poverty should be regarded as the failure to reach 'minimally acceptable' levels of different monetary and non-monetary attributes necessary for a subsistence standard of living. That is, poverty is essentially a multidimensional phenomenon. The problems of counting the number of poor in this framework and then combining the information available on them into a statistic that summarises the extent of overall poverty have been discussed rigorously. Using different postulates for a measure of poverty, shapes of isopoverty contours of a person have been derived in alternative dimensions. This in turn establishes a person's nature of trade off between attributes in different poverty spaces.

We make a distinction between additive and non-additive poverty measures satisfying the strong version of the 'Focus Axiom', which demands independence from non-poor attribute quantities in poverty measurement. One problem with additive measures is that they are insensitive to a correlation increasing switch. A correlation increasing switch requires giving more of one attribute to a person who has already more of another. A finer subdivision among non-additive measures is possible depending on whether a measure decreases or increases under such a switch. Specific functional forms have been proposed that fit these various properties depending on the value of a small number of key parameters and generalizing in an easy way the familiar $P_a$ family. As an illustration, the resulting measures have been used to evaluate the evolution of income/education poverty in rural Brazil in the 1980s.

# Appendix: Formal Statement of the Axioms Used in the Paper

Strong Focus (SF). For any $n \in N$, $(X, Y) \in M^n, z \in Z, j \in \{1, 2, \cdots, m\}$, if (i) for any $i$ such that $x_{ij} \geq z_j, y_{ij} = x_{ij} + \delta$, where $\delta > 0$, (ii) $y_{tj} = x_{tj}$ for all $t \neq i$, and (iii) $y_{is} = x_{is}$, for all $s \neq j$ and for all $i$, then $P\,(Y; z) = P\,(X; z)$.

Weak Focus (WF). For any $n \in N$, $(X, Y) \in M^n, z \in Z$, if for some $i$, $x_{ik} \geq z_k$, for all $k$ and (*i*) for any $j \in \{1, 2, \ldots, m\}$, $y_{ij} = x_{ij} + \delta$, where $\delta > 0$, (ii) $y_{it} = x_{it}$ for all $t \neq j$ and (iii) $y_{rs} = x_{rs}$ for all $r \neq i$ and $s$ then $P(Y; z) = P(X; z)$.

Symmetry (SM): For any $(X; z) \in M \times Z$, $P(X; z) = P(\Pi X; z)$, where $\Pi$ is any permutation matrix of appropriate order.

Monotonicity (MN). For any $n \in N$, $(X, Y) \in M^n, z \in Z, j \in \{1, 2, \cdots, m\}$, if (i) for any $i$ $y_{ij} = x_{ij} + \delta$, where $x_{ij} < z_j, \delta > 0$, (ii) $y_{tj} = x_{tj}$ for all $t \neq i$, and (iii) $y_{is} = x_{is}$, for all $s \neq j$ and for all *i*, then $P(Y; z) \leq P(X; z)$.

Continuity (CN): For any $z \in Z$, $P()$ is continuous on $M$.

Principle of Population (PP). For any $(X; z) \in M \times Z, k \in N$, $P(X^k; z) = P(X; z)$, where $X^k$ is the *k*-fold replication of *X*.

Scale Invariance (SI). For any $(X; z) \in M \times Z, k \in N, P(X; z) = P(X'; z')$ where $X' = X\Lambda, z' = z\Lambda$, $\Lambda$ being the diagonal matrix diag $(\lambda_1, \cdots, \lambda_m), \lambda_i > 0$ for all $i$.

Subgroup Decomposability (SD). For any $X^1, X^2, \ldots, X^K \in M$ and $z \in Z$:

$$P^n(X; z) = \sum_{i=1}^{K} \frac{n_i}{n} P^{n_i}(X^i; z),$$

where $X \in M$ is the attribute matrix $\begin{bmatrix} X^1 \\ X^2 \\ \\ \\ X^k \end{bmatrix}$ witn $n$ rows and $m$ columns, $n_i$ is the population size corresponding to $X^i$ and $n = \sum_{i=1}^{K} n_i$.

Definition of a Pigou–Dalton Progressive Transfer. Matrix $X$ is said to be obtained from $Y \in M^n$ by a *Pigou–Dalton progressive transfer of attribute j* from one poor person to another if for some persons $i, t$: (i) $y_{tj} < y_{ij} < z_j$, (ii) $x_{ij} - y_{ij} = y_{ij} - x_{ij} > 0$, $x_{ij} \geq x_{tj}$, (iii) $x_{rj} = y_{rj}$ for all $r \neq i$, $t$ and (iv) $x_{rk} = y_{rk}$ for all $k \neq j$ and all r.

One-dimensional Transfer Principle (OTP). For all n ∈ N and $Y \in M^n$, if $X$ is obtained from $Y$ by a Pigou–Dalton progressive transfer of some attribute between two poor, then $P(X; z) \leq P(Y; z)$, where z ∈ Z is arbitrary.

Multidimensional Transfer Principle (MTP). For any $(Y; z) \in M \times Z$,if $X$ is obtained form $Y$ by multiplying $Y_p$ by a bistochastic matrix $B$ and $BY_p$ is not a permutation of the rows of $Y_p$, then $P(X; z) \leq P(Y; z)$, given that the attributes of the non-poor remain unchanged, where $Y_p$ is the bundle of attributes possessed by the poor as defined with the attribute matrix $Y$.

Definition of a Correlation Increasing Switch. For any $X \in M^n, n \geq 2$, $(j, k) \in \{1,2,\ldots,m\}$, suppose that for some $i, t, x_{ij} < x_{tj} < z_j$ and $x_{tk} < x_{ik} < z_k$. $Y$ is then said to be obtained from $X$ by a 'correlation increasing switch' between two poor if: (i) $y_{ij} = x_{tj}$, (ii) $y_{tj} = x_{ij}$; (iii) $y_{rj} = x_{rj}$ for all $r \neq i, t$, and (iv) $y_{rs} = x_{rs}$ for all $s \neq j$ and for all $r$.

Non-decreasing Poverty Under Correlation Increasing Switch (NDCIS). For any $n \in N$ and $n \geq 2$, $X \in M^n$, z ∈ Z, if $Y$ is obtained from $X$ by a correlation increasing switch, then $P(Y; z) \geq P(X; z)$.

The converse property is denoted by NICIS.

## References


Atkinson, A., & Bourguignon, F. (1982). The comparison of multidimensioned distributions of economic status. *The Review of Economic Studies, 49,* 183–201.

Blackorby, C., & Donaldson, D. (1980). Ethical indices for the measurement of poverty. *Econometrica, 48,* 1053–1060.

Bourguignon, F., & Fields, G. S. (1997). Discontinuous losses from poverty, generalized $P_\alpha$ measures, and optimal transfers to the poor. *Journal of Public Economics, 63,* 155–175.
Chakravarty, S. R. (1990). *Ethical Social Index Numbers*. London: Springer-Verlag.
Chakravarty, S. R., Mukherjee, D., & Ranade, R. (1998). On the family of subgroup and factor decomposable measures of multidimensional poverty. *Research on Economic Inequality, 8,* 175–194.
Clark, S., Hemming, R., & Ulph, D. (1981). On indices for the measurement of poverty. *The Economic Journal, 91,* 515–526.
Cowell, F. A. (1988). Poverty measures, inequality and decomposability. In D. Bös, M. Rose, & C. Seidl (Eds.), *Welfare and efficiency in public economics*. London: Springer-Verlag.
Donaldson, D., & Weymark, J. A. (1986). Properties of fixed population poverty indices. *International Economic Review, 27,* 667–688.
Duclos, J.-Y., Sahn, D., & Younger, S. (2001). *Robust multi-dimensional poverty comparisons*. Mimeo: Cornell University.
Elbers, C., Lanjouw, J., Lanjouw, P., & Leite, P. G. (2001). *Poverty and inequality in Brazil: new estimates from combined PPV-PNAD data*. World Bank, DECRG, Mimeo.
Foster, J. E. (1984). On economic poverty: A survey of aggregate measures. In R. L. Basman & G. F. Rhodes (Eds.), *Advances in econometrics* (Vol. 3). Connecticut: JAI Press.
Foster, J., Greer, J., & Thorbecke, E. (1984). A class of decomposable poverty measures. *Econometrica, 52,* 761–765.
Foster, J., & Shorrocks, A. F. (1991). Subgroup consistent poverty indices. *Econometrica, 59,* 687–709.
Kakwani, N. C. (1980). On a class of poverty measures. *Econometrica, 48,* 437–446.
Kolm, S. C. (1977). Multidimensional egalitarianisms. *Quart. J. Econom., 91,* 1–13.
Lipton, M., & Ravallion, M. (1995). Poverty and policy. In J. Behrman & T. N. Srinivasan (Eds.), *Handbook of development economics* (Vol. 3). Amsterdam: North-Holland.
Maasoumi, E. (1986). The measurement and decomposition of multidimensional inequality. *Econometrica, 54,* 771–779.
Pradhan, M., & Ravallion, M. (2000). Measuring poverty using qualitative perceptions of consumption adequacy. *Review of Economics and Statistics, 82*(3), 462–471.
Ravallion, M. (1996). Issues in measuring and modelling poverty. *Economic Journal, 106,* 1328–1343.
Sen, A. K. (1976). Poverty: An ordinal approach to measurement. *Econometrica, 44,* 219–231.
Sen, A. K. (1985). *Commodities and capabilities*. Amsterdam: North-Holland.
Sen, A. K. (1992). *Inequality reexamined*. Cambridge, MA: Harvard University Press.
Streeten, P. (1981). *First things first: Meeting basic human needs in developing countries*. New York: Oxford University Press.
Takayama, N. (1979). Poverty, income inequality and their measures: Professor Sen's axiomatic approach reconsidered. *Econometrica, 47,* 747–759.
Tsui, K. Y. (1995). Multidimensional generalizations of the relative and absolute indices: The Atkinson–Kolm-Sen approach. *Journal of Economic Theory, 67,* 251–265.
Tsui, K. Y. (2002). Multidimensional poverty indices. *Social Choice and Welfare, 19,* 69–93.
UNDP. (1990). *Human development report*. Oxford University Press, New York.
Zheng, B. (1997). Aggregate poverty measures. *Journal of Economic Surveys, 11,* 123–162.

# A Family of Unit Consistent Multidimensional Poverty Indices

**Satya R. Chakravarty and Conchita D'Ambrosio**

**Abstract** This paper characterizes a family of subgroup decomposable unit consistent multidimensional poverty indices. Unit consistency requires that poverty rankings should remain unaltered when dimensions are expressed in different measurement units. The characterized family is a simple generalization of a family of unit consistent income poverty index suggested by Zheng (Economic Theory 31:113–142, 2007b). The paper also illustrates the index numerically using Turkish data. Journal of Economic Literature Classification No.: D63.

**Keywords** Multidimensional poverty measurement · Unit consistency

## 1 Introduction

Removal of poverty is still one of the primary aims of economic policy in many countries of the world. In order to judge the efficacy of a targeted poverty alleviation policy, it becomes necessary to know the dimension of poverty, that is, how much poverty is there and changes in level of poverty over time. The policy formulator also needs to identify the causal factors of poverty. All these require the quantification of

This paper was prepared for the workshop on Multidimensional Poverty and Pro-poor Growth in the MENA Countries, Nice, June 11–12, 2009. We thank participants for suggestions and the organizers, Valérie Bérenger and Florent Bresson for comments and for providing the dataset. We also thank two anonymous referees for comments and suggestions.
This article published in a volume entitled 'Monetary Poverty and Social Exclusion around the Mediterranean Sea', Springer Nature, 2013, is being reprinted with a generous consent of Springer Nature. Heartfelt acknowledgement goes to the publisher for the consent.

S. R. Chakravarty
Indian Statistical Institute, Kolkata, India
e-mail: satyarchakravarty@gmail.com

C. D'Ambrosio (✉)
Université du Luxembourg, Maison des Sciences Humaines, 11, Porte des Sciences, L-4366 Esch-sur-Alzette, Luxembourg
e-mail: conchita.dambrosio@uni.lu

 
S. R. Chakravarty (ed.), *Poverty, Social Exclusion and Stochastic Dominance*, Themes in Economics, https://doi.org/10.1007/978-981-13-3432-0_8

the extent of poverty. More precisely, we need an indicator of poverty that becomes helpful in analyzing these issues.

In his pioneering contribution, Sen (1976) regarded the poverty measurement problem as involving two distinct but unrelated exercises: (i) the identification of the poor and (ii) the aggregation of the characteristics of the poor into an overall indicator that will specify the extent of poverty. In the literature, the first problem is generally solved by the income method, which requires the specification of an income poverty line, the level of income required for subsistence standard of living. A person is regarded as poor if his income falls below the poverty line. Sen (1976) criticized two crude indicators of poverty, the head-count ratio (proportion of persons in poverty) and the income gap ratio (the shortfall of the ratio between the average income of the poor and the poverty line from unity), because of their insensitivity to a transfer of income between two poor persons and the former also does not change under a reduction in the income of a poor. Sen (1976) also developed an axiomatic characterization of a more sophisticated index of poverty.[1]

However, Sen (1992) argued that the proper space for social evaluation is that of functionings, the various things, such as literacy, housing, health, provision of public goods, adequate nourishment, essential services, communing with friends, a person cares about. Capability set of a person provides information on the set of functionings that a person could achieve. This shows that well-being is intrinsically multidimensional from the capability-functioning perspective. Consequently, poverty being a manifestation of insufficient well-being, is a multidimensional phenomenon as well. In this context, poverty is regarded as a problem of capability failure.

In the basic needs approach, which regards development as an improvement in the array of human needs (Streeten 1981), poverty is a consequence of lack of human needs. The social exclusion approach also regards poverty as a multidimensional issue. It refers to exclusion of individuals "from ordinary living patterns, customs and activities" (Townsend 1979, p. 31). The implicit process is generally regarded as a dynamic process whose end product is the exclusion of the concerned individuals from full participation. It is a relative concept in the sense that it is defined relative to the standard of the given society (Atkinson 1998). Social exclusion incorporates the process aspect of capability failure (Sen 2002).[2]

In view of the above discussion, we assume that each person is characterized by a vector of attributes that correspond to different dimensions of human life and a direct identification method of the poor checks whether the person has "minimally acceptable levels" (Sen 1992, p. 139) or threshold levels of this set of attributes. Thus, the direct method looks at poverty from a multidimensional perspective, more precisely, in terms of shortfalls of attribute quantities from respective threshold levels. These threshold levels are determined independently of the attribute distributions.

---

[1]Alternatives and variations of the Sen index have been suggested, among others, by Takayama (1979), Blackorby and Donaldson (1980), Kakwani (1980), Clark et al. (1981), Chakravarty (1983a, b, 1997), Thon (1983), Foster et al. (1984), Hagenaars (1987) and Shorrocks (1995).

[2]See Sen (1981, 1985), Ravallion (1996), Tsui (2002) and Bourguignon and Chakravarty (2003) for further discussion on multidimensionality of poverty.

The objective of this paper is to characterize axiomatically a family of unit consistent multidimensional poverty indices. According to unit consistency, poverty rankings remain unaffected when all the attribute quantities and threshold levels are expressed in differing measuring units. For instance, suppose that income and life expectancy are two dimensions of human life. Then unit consistency demands that the ranking of two attribute distributions when income is measured in dollars and life expectancy in years should be the same when income is measured in euros and life expectancy in months. Unit consistency is a reasonable property and demands invariance of poverty rankings when units of measurement of dimensions change. To understand this, assume, for simplicity, that there are two dimensions of well-being, income, and life expectancy. Now, consider the problem of poverty rankings between two countries. Suppose income is measured in the currency of country I and life expectancy is measured in years. It turns out that country I is regarded as more poverty stricken than country II. Next, suppose we decide to measure income in the currency of country II and life expectancy in months. Unit consistency then demands that the poverty ranking of the two countries remains unaltered because of these changes in the units of measurement. Clearly, ratio scale invariance, which demands invariance of poverty under ratio scale transformations of attribute quantities and threshold levels, implies unit consistency. But the converse is not true. That is, there are poverty indices that satisfy unit consistency but not ratio scale invariance. Thus, without unit consistency the problem of inconsistency in ranking may arise if we consider indices that are not ratio scale invariant. It is also important to note the difference between ratio scale invariance and unit consistency: while the former is a cardinal property, the latter is an ordinal requirement (see Zheng 2007a, b).

Zheng (2007a) characterized a family of income distribution-based unit consistent poverty indices. This family is a two-parameter generalization of the Clark et al. (1981) and Chakravarty (1983a) indices. Our unit consistent multidimensional index is a generalization of the Zheng index to the multivariate set up.

Section 2 of the paper lays down the postulates for an index of multidimensional poverty. In Sect. 3 we characterize the family of unit consistent indices. Section 4 contains an application of the index to Turkish data. Finally Sect. 5 concludes.

## 2 Postulates for an Index of Multidimensional Poverty

In this section we set out the properties for a multidimensional poverty index. Let $\Re^m_{++}$ be the positive orthant of the $m$-dimensional Euclidean space $\Re^m$. For a set of $n$-persons, person $i$ possesses a vector $(x_{i1}, x_{i2}, \ldots, x_{im}) = x_i \in \Re^m_{++}$ of $m$ attributes. The vector $x_i$ is the $i$th row of an $n \times m$ distribution matrix $X \in M^n$, where $M^n$ is the set of all $n \times m$ matrices whose entries are positive real numbers. The $j$th column $x_{.j}$ of $X \in M^n$ represents the distribution of attribute $j$ $(j = 1, 2, \ldots, m)$ among the $n$ persons. Let $M = \cup_{n \in N} M^n$, where $N$ is the set of all positive integers. For any $n \in N$, $X \in M^n$, we write $n(X)$ (or $n$) for the corresponding population size. We restrict our attention to $\Re^m_{++}$ in order to avoid the problem that the welfare function $\prod_{j=1}^{m} x_{ij}^{c_j}$ of person $i$ based on different consumption levels becomes zero if consumption of one attribute is zero. This happens irrespective of how large or small the consumption levels of the other attributes are.

In this multivariate set up, a threshold or cut off is defined for each attribute. These thresholds represent the minimal quantities of the $m$ attributes required for maintaining a subsistence standard of living. Let $z = (z_1, \ldots, z_m) \in Z$ be the vector of given thresholds, where $Z$ is a nonempty subset of $\Re^m_{++}$. The quantitative specification of different attributes exclude the possibility that a dimension can be of qualitative type, for instance, whether a person is ill or not.

In this structure, the $i$th person is regarded as poor or non-poor with respect to attribute $j$, or equivalently, attribute $j$ is meager or non-meager for him, according as $x_{ij} < z_j$ or $x_{ij} \geq z_j$ and he is called non-poor if $x_{ij} \geq z_j$ for all $j$. For any $X \in M^n$, let $S_j(X)$ (or $S_j$) be the set of persons who are poor or deprived with respect to attribute $j$, where $n \in N$ is arbitrary. As Bourguignon and Chakravarty (2003) argued, in order to count the number of poor in a simple way, it is convenient to define a poverty indicator variable as follows:

$$\begin{aligned} \rho(x_i; z) &= 1 \text{ if} \exists\, j \in \{1, 2, \ldots, m\} : x_{ij} < z_j, \\ &= 0, \quad \text{otherwise.} \end{aligned} \tag{1}$$

Then the number of poor in the multidimensional framework is given by:

$$n_p(X) = \sum_{i=1}^{n} \rho(x_i; z). \tag{2}$$

The identification method defined in (1) is known as the union method of identification. This contrasts with the intersection method which identifies a person as poor if he is deprived in all dimensions (see Bourguignon and Chakravarty 2003, 2008). Alkire and Foster (2007) considered an intermediate identification method which regards a person as poor if he is deprived in at least $k$ dimensions, where $1 \leq k \leq m$. This method includes the union and intersection methods as special cases when $k = 1$ and $k = m$.

A multidimensional poverty index $P$ is a non-constant real valued function defined on $M \times Z$. For any $X \in M, z \in Z$, the functional value $P(X; z)$ determines the extent of poverty associated with the distribution matrix $X$ and the cut off vector $z$.

Most of the properties we consider below, following Chakravarty et al. (1998), Tsui (2002), Bourguignon and Chakravarty (2003, 2008), Chakravarty (2009) and Chakravarty and Silber (2008), are immediate generalizations of different postulates proposed for an income poverty index.[3] All properties apply for any arbitrary $P$ and any positive integer $n$.

---

[3]For discussion on properties of an income poverty index, see Sen (1976), Foster et al. (1984), Donaldson and Weymark (1986), Cowell (1988), Seidl (1988), Chakravarty (1990, 2009), Foster and Shorrocks (1991), Bourguignon and Fields (1997) and Zheng (1997).

**Focus (FOC)**: *For any* $(X; z) \in M \times Z$ *and for any person i and attribute j such that* $x_{ij} \geq z_j$, *an increase in* $x_{ij}$, *given that all other attribute levels in X remain fixed, does not change the poverty value* $P(X; z)$.[4]

**Normalization (NOM)**: *For any* $(X; z) \in M \times Z$ *if* $x_{ij} \geq z_j$ *for all i and j, then* $P(X; z) = 0$.

**Monotonicity (MON)**: *For any* $(X; z) \in M \times Z$, *any person i and attribute j such that* $x_{ij} < z_j$, *an increase in* $x_{ij}$, *given that other attribute levels in X remain fixed, does not increase the poverty value* $P(X; z)$.

**Principle of Population (POP)**: *For any* $(X; z) \in M \times Z$, $P(X; z) = P\left(X^{(l)}; z\right)$,

*where* $X^{(l)} = \begin{bmatrix} X^1 \\ X^2 \\ \\ \\ X^l \end{bmatrix}$ *with each* $X^i = X$ *and* $l \geq 2$ *is any integer.*

**Symmetry (SYM)**: *For any* $(X; z) \in M \times Z$, $P(X; z) = P(\pi X; z)$, *where* $\pi$ *is any* $n \times n$ *permutation matrix.*[5]

**Continuity (CON)**: $P(X; z)$ *is continuous in* $(X; z)$.

**Subgroup Decomposability (SUD)**: *For any* $X^1, X^2, \ldots, X^l \in M$ *and* $z \in Z$, $P(X; z) = \sum_{i=1}^{l} \frac{n_i}{n} P\left(X^i; z\right)$, *where* $X^{(l)} = \begin{bmatrix} X^1 \\ X^2 \\ \\ \\ X^l \end{bmatrix} \in M$, $n_i$ *is the population size associated with* $X^i$ $\sum_{i=1}^{l} n_i = n$.

**Non-decreasingness in Subsistence Levels of Attributes (NDS)**: *For any* $X \in M$, $P(X; z)$ *is non-decreasing in* $z_j$ *for all j.*

**Non-poverty Growth (NPG)**: *For any* $(X; z) \in M \times Z$, *if Y is obtained from X by adding a rich person to the society, then* $P(Y; z) \leq P(X; z)$.

**Ratio Scale Invariance (SCI)**: *For all* $(X^1; z^1) \in M \times Z$, $P\left(X^1; z^1\right) = P\left(X^2; z^2\right)$, *where* $X^2 = X^1\Omega$, $z^2 = z^1\Omega$ *and* $\Omega = \mathrm{diag}(\omega_1, \omega_2, \ldots \omega_m)$, $\omega_i > 0$ *for all i.*

According to **FOC** if a person is not deprived in an attribute, then giving him more of this attribute does not change the level of poverty, even if he is deprived in the other attributes. Thus, **FOC** rules out trade off between two attributes of a person who is deprived in one but non-deprived in the other. Thus, if life expectancy and a composite good are two attributes, more life expectancy above the threshold is of no use if the composite good is below its threshold. This, however, does not exclude the possibility of a trade off if a person is deprived in both the attributes.

[4]One may consider a weaker version of this axiom where the condition $x_{ij} \geq z_j$ applies simultaneously to all $j$. See Bourguignon and Chakravarty (2003).

[5]A $n \times n$ matrix with entries 0 and 1 is called a permutation matrix if each of its rows and columns sums to one.

**NOM** says that if all the persons in a society are non-poor, then the value of the index is zero. **MON** states that poverty does not increase if a person becomes less deprived in a dimension. This axiom implies Dimensional Monotonicity of Alkire and Foster (2007), which says that if deprivation in a dimension is completely eliminated, then poverty should not increase. Under **POP**, poverty remains unaltered if an attribute matrix is replicated several times. Since replication enables us to transform two different sized matrices into the same size, **POP** becomes helpful for inter-temporal and interregional poverty comparisons. **SYM** says that any characteristic other than the attribute quantities, for instance, the names of the individuals, is immaterial for poverty measurement. **CON** ensures that minor observational errors in attribute and threshold quantities will not generate an abrupt jump in the value of the poverty index. Therefore, a continuous poverty index will not be oversensitive to errors in observation on basic needs and threshold quantities. According to **SUD** for any partitioning of the population into several subgroups, say $l$, defined along ethnic, geographical or other lines, the overall poverty is the population share weighted average of subgroup poverty levels. The contribution of subgroup $i$ to overall poverty is $n_i P(X^i; z)/n$ and the overall poverty will precisely reduce by this amount if poverty in subgroup $i$ is eliminated. $(n_i P(X^i; Z)/nP(X; Z))100$ is the percentage contribution of subgroup $i$ to total poverty. Each of these statistics is regarded as useful to policymakers because they become helpful for identifying subgroups of the population that are more affected by poverty (see Anand 1997; Chakravarty 1983a, b, 2009; Foster et al. 1984; Foster and Shorrocks 1991). By repeated application of SUD we can write the poverty index as

$$P(X; z) = \frac{1}{n} \sum_{i=1}^{n} p\,(x_i; z). \tag{3}$$

Since $p\,(x_i; z)$ depends only on person $i$'s attributes, we call it, 'individual poverty function'. Evidently, $P$ in (3) is symmetric and population replication invariant.

Between two identical communities, the one with higher threshold levels of one or more attributes should not have a lower poverty because of higher deprivation of the poor resulting from increased subsistence quantities. This is what is demanded by **NDS**. According to **NPG**, poverty should not increase if a rich person migrates to the society. **SCI** means that the poverty index should remain invariant under scale transformations of attribute quantities and threshold levels. In other words, deprivation resulting from poverty is viewed in terms of proportionate shortfalls of attribute quantities from respective cut offs.

The next postulate is concerned with the redistribution of attributes. For $X, Y \in M$, with $X \neq Y$, $X$ is said to uniformly majorize $Y$ if $X = BY$ for some $n \times n$ bistochastic matrix which is not a permutation matrix.[6] This means that we transform the distribution matrix $Y$ into the matrix $X$ by some equalizing transfers. (See Kolm 1977; Tsui 2002; Savaglio 2006; Weymark 2006; Chakravarty 2009.)

[6]An $n \times n$ matrix with nonnegative entries is called a bistochastic matrix if each of its rows and columns sums to unity.

**Transfers Principle (TRP)**: *For any* $z \in Z$, $X, Y \in M$ *if X uniformly majorizes Y then* $P(X; z) \leq P(Y; z)$, *given that the transfers are among the poor.*

**TRP** shows that if we transform the distribution matrix *Y* into the matrix *X* by some equalizing operation among the poor, then poverty under *X* will not be higher than that under *Y*. It may be worthwhile to mention that this transfer axiom is not the only of generalizing the single dimensional transfers principle to the multidimensional set up (see Duclos et al. 2006).

We will now consider a property which deals with the essence of multidimensional poverty measurement through correlation between attributes. By taking into account the association of attributes, as captured by the degree of correlation between them, this postulate also underlines the difference between single and multidimensional poverty measurements. To illustrate the property, consider the two-person two-attribute case, where the two persons are deprived in both the dimensions. Suppose that $x_{11} > x_{21}$ and $x_{12} < x_{22}$. Now, let us consider a switch of attribute 2 between the two persons. This switch increases the correlation between the attributes because person 1 who had more of attribute 1 has now more of attribute 2 as well and that is why we refer to it as a correlation increasing switch between two poor persons. Next, suppose that attributes 1 and 2 are substitutes, that is, one attribute may compensate the lack of another in the definition of individual poverty. Then increasing the correlation between the attributes should increase poverty. Indeed, the switch just defined does not modify the mean of each attribute but reduces the extent to which the lack of one attribute may be compensated by the availability of the other. An analogous argument will establish that poverty should decrease under a correlation increasing switch if the two attributes are complements. If a poverty index does not change under a correlation increasing switch, then it treats the attributes as 'independents'. In the general case, the rearrangement of attributes are made in a way such that one of persons receives at least as much of every attribute as the other and more of at least one attribute(see Weymark 2006; Chakravarty 2009).

We state this principle formally as:

**Increasing Poverty Under Correlation Increasing Switch (IPC)**: *Under* **SUD**, *for any* $(X; z) \in M \times Z$, *if* $Y \in M$ *is obtained from X by a correlation increasing switch between two poor persons, then* $P(X; z) < P(Y; z)$ *if the two attributes are substitutes.*

The corresponding property which demands decreasingness of poverty under such switch, when the attributes are complements, is denoted by **DPC**.[7] We say that a poverty index is sensitive to a correlation increasing switch if it satisfies either **IPC** or **DPC**.

---

[7]For additional discussions on this issue, see Atkinson and Bourguignon (1982), Bourguignon and Chakravarty (1999, 2003) and Chakravarty (2009). Bourguignon and Chakravarty (1999) employed this property to examine the elasticity of substitution between proportional shortfalls of attributes from respective thresholds.

Finally, we consider the unit consitency axiom. It allows poverty values to vary when dimensional units change, provided that poverty orderings are not affected.

Formally,

**Unit Consistency (UCO)**: *For any* $X^1, X^2 \in M$ *and two given threshold vectors* $z^1, z^2 \in Z$, *if* $P(X^1; z^1) < P(X^2; z^2)$ *then* $P(X^1\Omega; z^1\Omega) < P(X^2\Omega; z^2\Omega)$ *for all* $\Omega = diag(\omega_1, \omega_2, \ldots \omega_m), \omega_i > 0$ *for all i.*

Clearly, all ratio scale invariant multidimensional poverty indices are unit consistent. However, as we will see in the next section, there exist unit consistent indices that are not ratio scale invariant.

## 3 The Characterization Theorem

For an income poverty index, Chakravarty (1983a) and Hagenaars (1987) interpreted poverty as the fraction of welfare losses due to the existence of poverty using the utilitarian and Gini type social welfare functions. In contrast, Chakravarty (1983b), Zheng (1993) and Chakravarty and Silber (2008) regarded it as the absolute amount of welfare loss. Here we take a similar approach.

**Definition 1**
*For any arbitrary* $n \in N$, $(X; z) \in M^n \times Z$, *a poverty index is defined as*

$$P(X; z) = W(\mathrm{Z_{n\times m}}) - W(\hat{X}), \tag{4}$$

*where* $\hat{X}$ *is the censored attribute matrix corresponding to X, that is,* $\hat{x}_{ij} = \min\{x_{ij}, z_j\}$, $Z_{n\times m}$ *is the* $n \times m$ *matrix each of whose rows is z and W is any non-decreasing real valued social welfare function defined on the set of all censored attribute matrices.*

Thus, *P* is the size of the welfare loss that results from shortfall of the attribute quantities of poor persons from the respective thresholds. At this stage, we do not impose any restriction on *W*. Note that by definition *P* satisfies **FOC** and **NOM**.

We can now present the following theorem.

**Theorem 1**
*Assume that the poverty index P is of the form* (4). *Then P satisfies* **CON**, **SUD**, **MON**, *and* **UCO** *and is sensitive to a correlation increasing switch if and only if it is of the form*

$$P(X; z) = \frac{\rho}{n\prod_{j=1}^{m} z_j^{c_j-\delta}} \sum_{i=1}^{n}\left[\prod_{j=1}^{m} z_j^{c_j} - \prod_{j=1}^{m} \hat{x}_{ij}^{c_j}\right], \tag{5}$$

*where $\delta$ is a real number and the parameters $\rho$ and $c_j$ have to be chosen such that $\rho c_j > 0$ for all $1 \leq j \leq m$. Furthermore,* **DPC** (**IPC**) *holds if and only if $\rho c_i c_j > 0 (\rho c_i c_j < 0)$, where $i \neq j = 1, 2, \ldots, m$.*

*Proof* For any $X \in M^n$, $\Omega = \text{diag}(\omega_1, \omega_2, \ldots \omega_m)$, let $Q(X; z) = P(X\Omega, z\Omega)$. **UCO** along with **CON** implies that if $P(X^1; z^1) = P(X^2; z^2)$ then $P(X^1\Omega; z^1\Omega) = P(X^2\Omega; z^2\Omega)$, that is, $Q(X^1; z^1) = Q(X^2; z^2)$. Furthermore, $P(X^1; z^1) < P(X^2; z^2)$ implies that $Q(X^1; z^1) < Q(X^2; z^2)$. This shows that $Q(X; z)$ is an increasing function of $P(X; z)$. Hence there exists an increasing function $g_{\omega_1,\ldots,\omega_m} : \Re^1 \to \Re^1$ such that $Q(X; z) = g_{\omega_1,\ldots,\omega_m}(P(X; z))$. Define $g : \Re^m_{++} \times \Re^1 \to \Re^1$ by $g(\omega_1, \ldots \omega_m; .) = g_{\omega_1,\ldots,\omega_m}(.)$. It then follows that

$$P(X\Omega; z\Omega) = Q(X; z) = g(\omega_1, \ldots \omega_m; P(X; z)). \tag{6}$$

Since by **CON**, minor changes in $\omega_i$'s generate minor changes in $P(X\Omega; z\Omega)$, it follows that $g$ is continuous in its first $m$ arguments. It is also increasing in the $(m + 1)$th argument. (See also Propositions 1 and 3 of Zheng 2007a and Proposition 1 of Diez et al. 2008.)

Following the structure of proof of Proposition 3 of Zheng (2007b) it can be shown that $P(X\Omega; z\Omega) = \left(\prod_{j=1}^m \omega_j\right)^\delta P(X; z)$. Define $G(X; z) = P(X; z) / \prod_{j=1}^m z_j^\delta$. Subgroup decomposability of $P$ implies that $G$ is subgroup decomposable.

As we have noted in (3), by repeated application of **SUD**, we can write any poverty index $P(X; z)$ as $\frac{1}{n}\sum_{i=1}^n p(x_i; z)$, where $X \in M^n$ and $p$ is the individual poverty function. This in turn shows that the poverty index given by (4) must be of the form

$$P(X; z) = \frac{1}{n}\sum_{i=1}^n \left[h(z) - h(\hat{x}_i)\right], \tag{7}$$

where $h : \Re^m_{++} \to \Re^1$. By **CON**, $h$ is continuous and **MON** demands that $h$ is non-decreasing.

Applying now Lemma 1, Theorems 3 and 4 of Tsui (1999) (see also Diez et al. 2008) to $G(X; z)$, when $P(X; z)$ is given by (7), we get the following form of the poverty index:

$$P(X; z) = G(X; z)\prod_{j=1}^m z_j^\delta = \frac{\rho}{n\prod_{j=1}^m z_j^{c_j-\delta}}\sum_{i=1}^n \left[\prod_{j=1}^m z_j^{c_j} - \prod_{j=1}^m \hat{x}_{ij}^{c_j}\right]. \tag{8}$$

It is easy to see that for **MON** to hold we require $\rho c_j > 0$ for all $j = 1, 2, \ldots, m$. Next, we can check easily that for **DPC** (**IPC**) to hold it is necessary that $\rho c_i c_j > 0 (\rho c_i c_j < 0)$, where $i \neq j = 1, 2, \ldots, m$. This establishes the necessity part of the theorem. The sufficiency is easy to check. ■

In the general case the restrictions on the parameters $\rho$ and $c_j$ for **TRP** to be fulfilled are quite complicated. However, it may be worthwhile to discuss the case for $m = 2$. The parametric restrictions that are required for fulfillment of all the postulates in this case are specified in the following corollary, which is easy to demonstrate.

**Corollary 1**
*Assume that the poverty index P is of the form* (4). *Then for $m = 2$, P satisfies* ***CON***, ***SUD***, ***MON*** *and* ***UCO*** *if and only if it is of the following form*

$$P(X;z) = \frac{\rho}{n \prod_{j=1}^{2} z_j^{c_j-\delta}} \sum_{i=1}^{n} \left[ \prod_{j=1}^{2} z_j^{c_j} - \prod_{j=1}^{2} \hat{x}_{ij}^{c_j} \right], \tag{9}$$

*where $\rho c_j > 0$ for $j = 1, 2$. Furthermore,* ***DPC (IPC)*** *holds if and only if $\rho c_i c_j > 0 \big(\rho c_i c_j < 0\big)$, where $i \neq j = 1, 2$. Finally, for* ***TRP*** *to hold it is necessary and sufficient that $\rho c_1(c_1 - 1) < 0$ and $c_1 c_2(1 - c_1 - c_2) < 0$.*

When the two attributes are complements, without loss of generality we may choose $\rho = 1$. Then for any choice of $c_1, c_2 \in (0.5,\ 1)$ all the conditions stipulated in Corollary 1 are satisfied. In contrast, if the two attributes are substitutes, we can set $\rho = -1$. Then for any choice of $c_1, c_2 \in (-1, -0.5)$, all of our required conditions are fulfilled. To understand this, observe that when $\rho = -1$, for IPC to hold we need $c_1 c_2 > 0$. The two TRP conditions are now $c_1(c_1 - 1) > 0$ (since $\rho = -1$) and $c_1 c_2(1 - c_1 - c_2) < 0$. These three inequalities are satisfied simultaneously for any choice of $c_1, c_2 \in (-1, -0.5)$. Note that for negative values of $c_1$ and $c_2$, the third bracketed term in (9) becomes non-positive.

Evidently, for any arbitrary number of dimensions the index satisfies **NDS** if and only if $\delta \geq 0$. **NPG** is obviously satisfied in the general case. Given $c_j$, $P$ in (8) satisfies **SCI** if $\delta = 0$. However, unit consistency is satisfied for all real values of $\delta$. Therefore, (8) gives us a large class of unit consistent multidimensional poverty indices. However, the family given by (5) does not satisfy translation invariance for any appropriate choice of $\delta$ and $c_j$, $1 \leq j \leq m$, that is, it does not remain invariant if the attribute quantity in any dimension and the threshold limit in the corresponding dimension change by an absolute amount. Given $\rho > 0$, even in the simple case when $\delta = c_j = 1$, where $1 \leq j \leq m$, its failure to satisfy translation invariance can be checked easily. (This particular case is not appealing because it does not meet **TRP**.) The reason behind this is that in the functional representation given by (5) the products of threshold limits and consumption levels of different attributes appear separately.

The index given by (8) has close similarity with an index suggested by Diez et al. (2008) (their Eq. (9)). However, they assumed only **IPC**, which in turn means that the scale parameter $\rho$ is negative. As we have noted in our framework $\rho$ is positive or negative depending on whether **DPC** or **IPC** holds. Another important difference is that while our index determines the size of welfare loss under a specific structure, they do not look at their index from such a perspective.

For $m = 1$, $P$ in (8) becomes the first member of the Dalton-Hagenaars class of unit consistent income poverty indices characterized by Zheng (2007b). Therefore, our index is a generalization of a single dimensional unit consistent poverty index suggested by Zheng (2007b) to the multi-attribute set up. The Zheng index itself is a two-parameter generalization of the Chakravarty (1983a) and the Clark et al. (1981) indices.

## 4 An Empirical Illustration

The purpose of this section is to illustrate the poverty index $P(X; z)$, as defined in (9), using the Household Income and Consumption Expenditure survey on Turkey.

We base our analysis on three years of available data: 2003, 2004 and 2005. The survey is collected by the State Institute of Statistics (SIS) of Turkey to provide information on household income, socio-economic status and consumption patterns of the population.

Only a few of the survey's variables on individual well-being are quantitative in nature. This situation is common to many other surveys, see for example the European Community Household Panel for EU countries or the more recent EU Statistics on Income and Living Conditions, where most of the variables that could be used to measure multidimensional poverty are of qualitative type.

We decided to focus on income and number of rooms in the house. The income variable we analyze is total disposable household income equivalized using the OECD equivalence scale. In the other dimension all individuals without at least one room in the dwellings were regarded as poor. As far as income in concerned, the poverty threshold level was set equal to \$4.3 in purchasing power parities per day, the threshold considered by the World Bank for medium-income countries. Purchasing power parities are from the OECD (http://www.oecd.org/std/ppp/). We subdivide the population by the geographic areas of residence, namely, rural and urban areas. Given complementarity between the attributes, we choose $\rho = 1$. Further, in order to assign equal weight to the two dimensions we assume that $c_1 = c_2 = .6$. Finally, values of $\delta$ chosen to provide the estimates are: $\delta = 0, 0.5, 1, 1.5, 2$. Sample weights were used in the computation of the indices.

Results for the entire country are contained in Table 1. Multidimensional poverty, as measured by the index we propose in this paper, decreased continuously over time. We note monotonicity of the index value with respect to the parameter $\delta$. Contributions of the rural and urban areas to total poverty, which are given as percentages of total poverty, are reported in Table 2. Complete elimination of poverty within an area will lower global poverty exactly by the percentage by which it contributes to total poverty. The picture is quite dismal for the rural area, for all values of $\delta$, more than 57% contribution comes from this area. In Tables 3 and 4 area-wise poverty values are presented and, as expected, the rural area turns out to be more poverty stricken

**Table 1** Multidimensional poverty, as measured by $P(X; z)$, for different values of $\delta$: results for Turkey

| Year | $P(X; z)$ with $\delta = 0$ | $P(X; z)$ with $\delta = 0.5$ | $P(X; z)$ with $\delta = 1$ | $P(X; z)$ with $\delta = 1.5$ | $P(X; z)$ with $\delta = 2$ |
|---|---|---|---|---|---|
| 2003 | 0.019 | 0.040 | 0.082 | 0.170 | 0.353 |
| 2004 | 0.016 | 0.034 | 0.070 | 0.146 | 0.303 |
| 2005 | 0.015 | 0.032 | 0.066 | 0.136 | 0.283 |

**Table 2** Percentage contributions to multidimensional poverty by geographic area groups

| Year | % Contribution of rural areas | % Contribution of urban areas | % Population of rural areas | % Population of urban areas |
|---|---|---|---|---|
| 2003 | 61.303 | 38.697 | 39.24 | 60.76 |
| 2004 | 66.972 | 33.028 | 38.62 | 61.38 |
| 2005 | 57.031 | 42.987 | 38.12 | 61.88 |

**Table 3** Multidimensional poverty, as measured by $P(X; z)$, for different values of $\delta$: results for the Rural Area

| Year | $P(X; z)$ with $\delta = 0$ | $P(X; z)$ with $\delta = 0.5$ | $P(X; z)$ with $\delta = 1$ | $P(X; z)$ with $\delta = 1.5$ | $P(X; z)$ with $\delta = 2$ |
|---|---|---|---|---|---|
| 2003 | 0.012 | 0.024 | 0.050 | 0.104 | 0.216 |
| 2004 | 0.011 | 0.023 | 0.047 | 0.098 | 0.203 |
| 2005 | 0.009 | 0.018 | 0.038 | 0.078 | 0.161 |

**Table 4** Multidimensional poverty, as measured by $P(X; z)$, for different values of $\delta$: results for the Urban Area

| Year | $P(X; z)$ with $\delta = 0$ | $P(X; z)$ with $\delta = 0.5$ | $P(X; z)$ with $\delta = 1$ | $P(X; z)$ with $\delta = 1.5$ | $P(X; z)$ with $\delta = 2$ |
|---|---|---|---|---|---|
| 2003 | 0.007 | 0.015 | 0.032 | 0.066 | 0.136 |
| 2004 | 0.005 | 0.011 | 0.023 | 0.048 | 0.100 |
| 2005 | 0.007 | 0.014 | 0.028 | 0.059 | 0.122 |

than the urban area. Thus, from the poverty reduction policy point of view the rural area deserves more attention than the urban area.

## 5 Conclusions

We have argued explicitly why poverty should be regarded as the failure to reach 'minimally acceptable' levels of functionings of well-being. That is, poverty should be measured in a multidimensional framework in terms of individual deprivations for different functionings from respective threshold levels. We then discussed certain desirable postulates for an indicator of poverty in such a framework.

Unit consistency is an important property of multidimensional inequality and poverty indices in the sense that use of different measurement units should not lead to inconsistent conclusions. We have made an attempt to characterize a class of unit consistent multidimensional poverty index under a specific structure. It is a generalization of one of the Zheng (2007b) single dimensional unit consistent poverty indices. An empirical illustration of the index using Turkish data was also provided.

## References


Anand, S. (1997). Aspects of poverty in Malaysia. *Review of Income and Wealth, 23,* 1–16.

Alkire, S., & Foster, J. E. (2007). *Counting and multidimensional poverty measurement.* OPHI Working Paper.

Atkinson, A. B. (1998). *Social exclusion, poverty and unemployment.* London School of Economics.

Atkinson, A. B., & Bourguignon, F. (1982). The comparison of multidimensioned distributions of economic status. *Review of Economic Studies, 49,* 183–201.

Blackorby, C., & Donaldson, D. (1980). Ethical indices for the measurement of poverty. *Econometrica, 58,* 1053–1060.

Bourguignon, F., & Chakravarty, S. R. (1999). A family of multidimensional poverty measures. In D. J. Slottjee (Ed.), *Advances in econometrics, income distribution and scientific methodology: Essays in honor of C.* Dagum, Berlin: Physica Verlag.

Bourguignon, F., & Chakravarty, S. R. (2003). The measurement of multidimensional poverty. *Journal of Economic Inequality, 1,* 25–49.

Bourguignon, F., & Chakravarty, S. R. (2008). Multidimensional poverty orderings theory and applications. In K. Basu & R. Kanbur (Eds.), *Welfare, development, philosophy and social science: Essays for Amartya Sen's 75th birthday (Volume 2: Development economics and policy).* Oxford: Clarendon Press.

Bourguignon, F., & Fields, G. (1997). Discontinuous losses from poverty, generalized $P_\alpha$ measures and optimal transfers to the poor. *Journal of Public Economics, 63,* 155–175.

Chakravarty, S. R. (1983a). A new index of poverty. *Mathematical Social Sciences, 6,* 307–313.

Chakravarty, S. R. (1983b). Ethically flexible measures of poverty. *Canadian Journal of Economics, 16,* 74–85.

Chakravarty, S. R. (1990). *Ethical social index numbers.* New York: Springer-Verlag.

Chakravarty, S. R. (1997). On Shorrocks' reinvestigation of the Sen poverty index. *Econometrica, 65,* 1241–1242.

Chakravarty, S. R. (2009). *Inequality, polarization and poverty: Advances in distributional analysis.* New York: Springer-Verlag.

Chakravarty, S. R., Mukherjee, D., & Ranade, R. (1998). On the family of subgroup and factor decomposable measures of multidimensional poverty. *Research on Economic Inequality, 8,* 175–194.

Chakravarty, S. R., & Silber, J. (2008). Measuring multidimensional poverty: The axiomatic approach. In N. Kakwani & J. Silber (Eds.), *Quantitative approaches to multidimensional poverty measurement.* London: Palgrave MacMillan.

Clark, S., Hamming, R., & Ulph, D. (1981). On indices for the measurement of poverty. *Economic Journal, 91,* 515–526.

Cowell, F. A. (1988). Poverty measures, inequality and decomposability. In D. Bos, M. Rose, & C. Seidl (Eds.), *Welfare and efficiency in public economics.* New York: Springer Verlag.

Diez, H., de la Vega, M. C. L., & Urrutia, A. M. (2007) Unit-consistent aggregative multidimensional inequality measures: A characterization. Working Paper No. 66. ECINEQ.
Diez, H., de la Vega, M. C. L., & Urrutia, A. M. (2008). Multidimensional unit- and subgroup consistent inequality and poverty measures: some characterization results. *Research on Economic Inequality, 16,* 189–211.
Donaldson, D., & Weymark, J. A. (1986). Properties of fixed-population poverty indices. *International Economic Review, 27,* 667–688.
Duclos, J.-Y., Sahn, D., & Younger, S. (2006). Robust multidimensional poverty comparisons. *Economic Journal, 116,* 943–968.
Foster, J. E., Greer, J., & Thorbecke, E. (1984). A class of decomposable poverty measures, *Econometrica, 42,* 761–766.
Foster, J. E., & Shorrocks, A. F. (1991). Subgroup consistent poverty indices. *Econometrica, 59,* 687–709.
Hagenaars, A. (1987). A class of poverty indices. *International Economic Review, 28,* 583–607.
Kakwani, N. C. (1980). On a class of poverty measures. *Econometrica, 48,* 437–446.
Kolm, S. C. (1977). Mulditimensional egalitarianisms. *Quarterly Journal of Economics, 91,* 1–13.
Ravallion, M. (1996). Issues in measuring and modeling poverty. *Economic Journal, 106,* 1328–1343.
Savaglio, E. (2006). Three approaches to the analysis of multidimensional inequality. In F. Farina & E. Savaglio (Eds.), *Inequality and economic integration*. London: Routledge.
Seidl, C. (1988). Poverty measurement: A survey. In D. Bos, M. Rose, & C. Seidl (Eds.), *Welfare and efficiency in public economics*. New York: Springer Verlag.
Sen, A. K. (1976). Poverty an ordinal approach to measurement. *Econometrica, 44,* 219–231.
Sen, A. K. (1981). *Poverty and famines*. Oxford: Clarendon Press.
Sen, A. K. (1985). *Commodities and capabilities*. Amsterdam: North Holland.
Sen, A. K. (1992). *Inequality re-examined*. Cambridge, MA: Harvard University Press.
Sen, A. K. (2002). *Rationality and freedom*. Cambridge: Harvard University Press.
Shorrocks, A. F. (1995). Revisiting the Sen poverty index. *Econometrica, 63,* 1225–1230.
Streeten, P. (1981). *First things first: Meeting basic human needs in developing countries*. New York: Oxford University Press.
Takayama, N. (1979). Poverty income inequality and their measures: Professor Sen's axiomatic approach reconsidered. *Econometrica, 47,* 749–759.
Thon, D. (1983). A poverty measure. *Indian Economic Journal, 30,* 55–70.
Townsend, P. (1979). *Poverty in the United Kingdom*. Harmondsworth: Penguin.
Tsui, K. Y. (1999). Multidimensional inequality and multidimensional generalized entropy measures: An axiomatic derivation. *Social Choice and Welfare, 16,* 145–157.
Tsui, K. Y. (2002). Multidimensional poverty indices. *Social Choice and Welfare, 19,* 69–93.
Weymark, J. A. (2006). The normative approaches to the measurement of multidimensional inequality. In F. Farina & E. Savaglio (Eds.), *Inequality and economic integration*. London: Routledge.
Zheng, B. (1993). An axiomatic characterization of the Watts poverty measure. *Economics Letters, 42,* 81–86.
Zheng, B. (1997). Aggregate poverty measures. *Journal of Economic Surveys, 11,* 123–162.
Zheng, B. (2007a). Unit-consistent decomposable inequality measures. *Economica, 74,* 97–111.
Zheng, B. (2007b). Unit-consistent poverty indices. *Economic Theory, 31,* 113–142.

# An Axiomatic Approach to Multidimensional Poverty Measurement via Fuzzy Sets

**Satya R. Chakravarty**

**Abstract** Often it may be difficult to judge the poverty/deprivation status of a person in a dimension of human wellbeing. An appropriate technique to evaluate poverty in such a situation is fuzzy set theory. This paper develops an axiomatic approach to the measurement of multidimensional poverty in a fuzzy set up. Rigorous discussion on a fuzzy membership function that determines the poverty position of a person in a dimension is presented. Fuzzy translations of multidimensional poverty axioms are formulated and analyzed with perfections. Fuzzy counterparts of several multidimensional poverty indices are suggested.

**Keywords** Multidimensional poverty · Fuzzy set approach · Membership function · Axioms · Indices · Characterization

## 1 Introduction

Poverty has been in existence for many years and continues to exist in a large number of countries of the World. Therefore, targeting of poverty alleviation remains an important policy issue in many countries. To understand the threat that the problem of poverty poses it is necessary to know the dimension of poverty and the process through which it seems to be deepened. In this context, an important question is: how to measure the poverty level of a society and its changes. In a pioneering contribution, Sen (1976) conceptualized the poverty measurement problem as involving two exercises: (i) the identification of the poor and (ii) aggregation of the characteristics of the poor into an overall indicator that quantifies the extent of poverty. In the literature, the income method has been used mostly to solve the first problem. It requires specification of a poverty line representing the income necessary for a subsistence

I am grateful to Sabina Alkire and Jacques Silber for bringing some important references to my attention and making them available to me.
Springer Nature's kind permission to reprint this article from its volume 'Fuzzy Set Approach to Multidimensional Poverty Measurement', 2006, is acknowledged with heartfelt gratitude.

S. R. Chakravarty (✉)
Economic Research Unit, Indian Statistical Institute, 203 B. T. Road, 700108 Kolkata, India
e-mail: satyarchakravarty@gmail.com



S. R. Chakravarty (ed.), *Poverty, Social Exclusion and Stochastic Dominance*, Themes in Economics, https://doi.org/10.1007/978-981-13-3432-0_9

standard of living. A person is said to be poor if his income falls below the poverty line. On the aggregation issue, Sen (1976) criticized two crude indicators of poverty, the head-count ratio (the proportion of persons with incomes below the poverty line) and the income gap ratio (the difference between the poverty line and the average income of the poor, expressed as a proportion of the poverty line), because they remain unaltered under a redistribution of income between two poor persons and the former also does not change if a poor person becomes poorer due to a reduction in his income. Sen (1976) also characterized axiomatically a more sophisticated index of poverty.[1]

However, the well-being of a population, and hence its poverty, which is a manifestation of insufficient well-being, is a multidimensional phenomenon and should therefore depend on both monetary and non-monetary attributes or components. It is certainly true that with a higher income or consumption budget a person may be able to improve the position of some of his non-monetary attributes of well-being. But it may happen that markets for certain non-monetary attributes do not exist. One such example is a public good like flood control or malaria prevention program in an underdeveloped country. Therefore, it has often been argued that income as the sole attribute of well-being is inappropriate and should be supplemented by other attributes, e.g., housing, literacy, life expectancy at birth, nutritional status, provision of public goods, etc.

We can provide further justifications for viewing the poverty measurement problem from a multidimensional perspective. In the basic needs approach, advocated by development economists, development is regarded as an improvement in the array of human needs, not just as growth of income alone (Streeten 1981). There is a debate about the importance of low income as a determinant of under-nutrition (Lipton and Ravallion 1995) and often it is argued to regard the population's failure to achieve a desirable nutritional status as an indicator of poverty (Osmani 1992). In the capability-functioning approach, where a functioning is what a person "succeeds in doing with the commodities and characteristics at his or her command" (Sen 1985, p. 10) and capabilities indicate a person's freedom with respect to functionings (Sen 1985, 1992), poverty is regarded as a problem of functioning failure. Functionings here are closely approximated by attributes like literacy, life expectancy, clothing, attending social activities, etc. The living standard is then viewed in terms of the set of available capabilities of the person to function. An example of a multidimensional index of poverty in terms of functioning failure is the human poverty index suggested by the UNDP (1997). It aggregates the country level deprivations in the living standard of a population for three basic dimensions of life, namely, decent living standard, educational attainment rate and life expectancy at birth. Chakravarty and Majumder (2005) axiomatized a generalized version of the human poverty index using failures in an arbitrary number of dimensions of life.

---

[1]Several contributions suggested alternatives and variations of the Sen index. See, for example, Takayama (1979), Blackorby and Donaldson (1980), Kakwani (1980a, 1980b), Clark et al. (1981), Chakravarty (1983a, b, c, 1997), Thon (1983), Foster et al. (1984), Haagenars (1987) and Shorrocks (1995).

In view of the above, in contrast to the income method, it has often been assumed in the literature that each person is characterized by a vector of basic need attributes (see, for example, Sen 1987, 1992; Ravallion 1996; Bourguignon and Chakravarty 1999, 2003; Atkinson 2003), and a direct method of identification of poor checks if the person has "minimally acceptable levels" (Sen 1992, p. 139) of different basic needs. Therefore, the direct method views poverty from a multidimensional perspective, more precisely, in terms of shortfalls of attribute quantities from respective threshold levels. These threshold levels are determined independently of the attribute distributions. A person is said to be poor with respect to an attribute if his consumption of the attribute falls below its minimally acceptable level. "In an obvious sense the direct method is superior to the income method, since the former is not based on particular assumptions of consumer behavior which may or may not be accurate" (Sen 1981, p. 26). If direct information on different attributes are not available, one can adopt the income method, "so that the income method is at most a second best" (Sen 1981, p. 26).

While the direct and income methods differ substantially in certain respects, they have one feature in common: each individual in the population must be counted as either poor or non-poor. The prospect of an intermediate situation is not considered by them. However, it is often impossible to acquire sufficiently detailed information on income and consumption of different basic needs and hence the poverty status of a person is not always clear cut. For instance, the respondents may be unwilling to provide exact information on income and consumption levels. There can be a wide range of threshold limits for basic needs which co-exist in reasonable harmony. The likelihood that relevant information is missing suggests that there is a degree of ambiguity in the concept of poverty. Now, if there is some ambiguity in a concept, "then a precise representation of that ambiguous concept must preserve that ambiguity" (Sen 1997, p. 121). Zadeh (1965) introduced the notion of fuzzy set with a view to tackling problems in which indefiniteness arising from a sort of ambiguity plays a fundamental role. Thus, given that the concept of poverty itself is vague, the poverty status of a person is intrinsically fuzzy. This shows that a fuzzy set approach to poverty measurement is sufficiently justifiable.

Fuzzy set theory-based approaches to the measurement of poverty has gained considerable popularity recently (see, for example, Cerioli and Zani 1990; Blaszczak-Przybycinska 1992; Dagum et al. 1992; Pannuzi and Quaranta 1995; Shorrocks and Subramanian 1994; Cheli and Lemmi 1995; Balestrino 1998; Betti and Verma 1998; Qizilbash 2002).[2]

However, a rigorous discussion on desirable axioms for a multidimensional poverty index in a fuzzy environment has not been made in the literature. The purpose of this paper is to fill in this gap. We also investigate how a variety of multidimensional poverty indices suggested recently (see, for example, Chakravarty et al. 1998;

[2]For applications of fuzzy set to inequality measurement, see Basu (1987) and Ok (1995). Fuzzy set theory is also helpful in analyzing the valuations of functioning vectors and capability sets (see, for example, Balestrino 1994; Balestrino and Chiappero Martinetti 1994; Chiappero Martinetti 1994, 1996, 2004; Casini and Bernetti 1996; Baliamoune 2003; Alkire 2005).

Bourguignon and Chakravarty 1999, 2003; Tsui 2002) can be reformulated in a fuzzy structure. These are referred to as fuzzy multidimensional poverty indices.

The paper is organized as follows. The next section begins by defining a fuzzy membership function that determines a person's poverty status in a dimension. A characterization of a particular membership function is also presented in this section Sect. 3 offers appropriate fuzzy reformulations of the axioms for a multidimensional poverty index. Section 4 shows how the conventional multidimensional poverty indices can be extended in a fuzzy framework. Finally, Sect. 5 concludes.

## 2 Fuzzy Membership Function

We begin by assuming that for a set of $n$-persons, the $i$th person possesses a $k$-vector $x_i = (x_{i1}, x_{i2}, \ldots, x_{ik}) \in R_+^k$ of attributes, where $R_+^k$ is the non-negative orthant of the $k$-dimensional Euclidean space $R^k$. The $j$th coordinate of the vector $x_i$ specifies the quantity of attribute $j$ possessed by person $i$. The vector $x_i$ is the $i$th row of a $n \times k$ matrix $X \in M^n$, where $M^n$ is the set of all $n \times k$ attribute matrices whose entries matrices whose entries are non-negative real numbers. The $j$th column of $X \in M^n$ gives the distribution of attribute $j(j = 1, 2, \ldots, k)$ among the $n$ persons. Let $M = \cup_{n \in N} M^n$, where $N$ is the set of positive integers. For any $X \in M$, we write $n(X)$ (or, $n$) for the associated population size.

In the conventional set up, the poverty status of person $i$ for attribute $j$ may be represented by a dichotomous function $\mu_j^*(x_{ij})$, which maps $x_{ij}$ into either zero or one, depending on whether he is non-poor or poor in the attribute, that is, whether $x_{ij} \geq z_j$ or, $x_{ij} < z_j$, where $z_j$ is the minimally acceptable or threshold level of attribute $j$. To allow for fuzziness in the poverty status, we consider a more general membership function $\mu_j : R_+^1 \rightarrow [0, 1]$ for attribute $j$ where $\mu_j(x_{ij})$ indicates the degree of confidence in the statement that person $i$ with consumption level $x_{ij}$ of attribute $j$ is possibly poor with respect to the attribute. Thus, $\mu_j$ is a generalized characteristic function, that is, one which varies uniformly between zero and one, rather than assuming just two values of zero and one (Zadeh 1965; Chakravarty and Roy 1985). We assume here that $\mu_j$ depends on $x_{ij}$ only. One can also consider a more general formulation where $\mu_j$ depends on the entire distribution (Cheli and Lemmi 1995). Since $\mu_j^*$ declares the poverty status of a person in dimension $j$ unambiguously, we refer to it as a crisp membership function.

Now, let $m_j > 0$ be the quantity of attribute $j$ at or above which a person is regarded as non-poor with certainty with respect to the attribute, that is, if, $x_{ij} \geq m_j$ then person $i$ is certainly non-poor in dimension $j$. (See Cerioli and Zani 1990 and Shorrocks and Subramanian 1994 for a similar assumption in the context of income based fuzzy poverty measurement). For instance, for life expectancy $m_j$ can be taken as the age level 60. Likewise, for the income dimension, it can be the level of mean per capita income. We assume here that $m_j$ coincides with one of the $x_{ij}$ values. For example, if a person with the mean level of attribute $j$, $\eta_j$, is considered as certainly non-poor in the attribute, then $m_j$ can be taken as the minimum value of

$x_{ij}$ which is at least as large as $\eta_j$. That is, $m_j = \min\{x_{ij}\}$, where $i \in \{1, 2, \ldots, n\}$ and $x_{ij} - \eta_j \geq 0$ Thus, we can say that the poverty extent of $x_{ij}$, as measured by $\mu_j$, is zero if $x_{ij} \geq m_j$, that is, $\mu_j(x_{ij}) = 0$ if $x_{ij} \geq m_j$. Similarly if $x_{ij} = 0$, then the poverty level associated with $x_{ij}$ is maximal, and hence $\mu_j(0) = 1$. Furthermore, a reasonable presumption is that a rise in $x_{ij}$ decreases the possibility of person $i$'s being poor in attribute $j$. Hence $\mu_j$ is assumed to be decreasing over $(0, m_j)$. It is also assumed to be continuous. The above properties of $\mu_j$ can now be summarized as follows:

$$\mu_j(x_{ij}) = \begin{cases} 1 \text{ if } x_{ij} = 0, \\ 0 \text{ if } x_{ij} \geq m_j. \end{cases} \tag{1}$$

It is decreasing over the interval $(0, m_j)$ and continuous everywhere. We write $\mu$ for the vector $(\mu_1, \mu_2, \ldots, \mu_k)$. Let $A$ be the set of vectors of membership functions of the form $\mu$.

An example of a suitable fuzzy membership function for attribute $j$ is:

$$\mu_j(x_{ij}) = \begin{cases} 1 & \text{if } x_{ij} = 0, \\ \left(\frac{m_j - x_{ij}}{m_j}\right)^{\theta_j} & \text{if } x_{ij} \in (0, m_j), \\ 0 & \text{if } x_{ij} \geq m_j. \end{cases} \tag{2}$$

where $\theta_j$ is a parameter.

It satisfies all the conditions laid down in (1). It is an individualistic function in the sense that it depends only on $x_{ij}$ and treats $m_j$ as a parameter.

Given $\mu_j$, let $S_{\mu_j}(X)$ (or, simply $S_{\mu_j}$) be the set of persons who are possibly poor in dimension $j$ in $X \in M^n$, where $n \in N$ is arbitrary, that is:

$$S_{\mu_j}(X) = \{i \in \{1, 2, \ldots, n\} | \mu_j(x_{ij}) > 0\}. \tag{3}$$

Attribute $j$ will be called possibly meager or certainly non-meager for person $i$ according as $i \in S_{\mu_j}(X)$ or $i \notin S_{\mu_j}(X)$. Person $i$ is referred to as certainly non-poor if $x_{ij} \geq m_j$ for all $j = 1, 2, \ldots, k$, that is, if $i \notin S_{\mu_j}(X)$ for all $j$.

It will now be worthwhile to characterize a fuzzy membership function. Such a characterization exercise will enable us to understand the membership function in a more elaborate way through the axioms used in the exercise. The following axioms are proposed for a general membership function $\mu_j : R^1_+ \to [0, 1]$ for attribute $j$.

(A1) Homogeneity of Degree Zero: $\mu_j$ is homogeneous of degree zero.
(A2) Linear Decreasingness: For any $x_{ij} \in [0, m_j)$ and $c_{ij} \in [0, m_j - x_{ij})$,

$$\mu_j(x_{ij}) - \mu_j(x_{ij} + c_{ij}) = \frac{c_{ij}}{m_j}.$$

(A3) Continuity: $\mu_j$ is continuous on its domain.
(A4) Maximality: $\mu_j(0) = 1$.

(A5) Independence of Non-meager Attribute Quantities: For all $x_{ij} \geq m_j$, $\mu_j(x_{ij}) = k$, where $k$ is a constant.

(A1) ensures that $\mu_j$ remains unaltered under equi-proportionate variations in quantities of attribute $j$. (A2) makes a specific assumption about decreasingness of the membership function. It says that the extent of reduction in the membership function resulting from an increase in $x_{ij}$ by $c_{ij}$ is the fraction $\frac{c_{ij}}{m_j}$. It is weaker than decreasingness assumption of the membership function over $\left(0, m_j\right]$. A membership function may as well decrease non-linearly. For instance, if $\theta_j > 1$, $\mu_j$ in (2) decreases at an increasing rate. (A3) means that $\mu_j$ should vary in a continuous manner with respect to variations in attribute quantities. (A4) specifies that $\mu_j$ should achieve its maximal value 1 when the level of the attribute is zero. Finally, (A5) shows insensitivity of $\mu_j$ to the attribute quantities of the persons who are certainly non-poor in the attribute through the assumption that the value of the membership function on $\left[m_j, \infty\right)$ is a constant. Thus, instead of assuming that the membership function takes on the value zero on $\left[m_j, \infty\right)$, we derive it as an implication of more primitive axioms.

**Proposition 1** *The only membership function that satisfies axioms (A1)–(A5) is*:

$$\mu_j(x_{ij}) = \begin{cases} 1 & \text{if } x_{ij} = 0, \\ \left(\frac{m_j - x_{ij}}{m_j}\right) & \text{if } x_{ij} \in \left(0, m_j\right), \\ 0 & \text{if } x_{ij} \geq m_j. \end{cases}$$

*Proof* In view of (A1), $\mu_j(x_{ij}) = \mu_j\left(\frac{x_{ij}}{m_j}\right)$. Hence (A2) becomes

$$\mu_j\left(\frac{x_{ij}}{m_j}\right) - \mu_j\left(\frac{x_{ij} + c_{ij}}{m_j}\right) = \frac{c_{ij}}{m_j}.$$

Since in the above equation $x_{ij} \in \left[0, m_j\right)$, is arbitrary, we can interchange the roles of $x_{ij}$ and $c_{ij}$ in it and derive that:

$$\mu_j\left(\frac{c_{ij}}{m_j}\right) - \mu_j\left(\frac{c_{ij} + x_{ij}}{m_j}\right) = \frac{x_{ij}}{m_j}.$$

These two equations imply that

$$\mu_j\left(\frac{x_{ij}}{m_j}\right) - \mu_j\left(\frac{c_{ij}}{m_j}\right) = \frac{c_{ij}}{m_j} - \frac{x_{ij}}{m_j}.$$

Letting $c_{ij} = 0$ in the above expression, we get:

$$\mu_j\left(\frac{x_{ij}}{m_j}\right) = \mu_j(0) - \frac{x_{ij}}{m_j},$$

from which in view of (A4) it follows that:

$$\mu_j\left(\frac{x_{ij}}{m_j}\right) = \frac{m_j - x_{ij}}{m_j}.$$

Applying (A1) to the above form of $\mu_j$ and using (A3), we note that $\mu_j(m_j) = 0$. This along with (A5) reveals that $k = 0$. Hence $\mu_j(x_{ij}) = 0$ for all $x_{ij} \geq m_j$. This establishes the necessity part of the proposition. The sufficiency is easy to check. Δ

Proposition 1 thus characterizes axiomatically the linear sub-case of the membership function in (2).

## 3 Properties for a Fuzzy Multidimensional Poverty Index

In this section, we lay down the postulates for a fuzzy multidimensional poverty index $P : M \times A \to R^1$. For all $n \in N$, the restriction of $P$ on $M^n \times A \to R^1$ is denoted by $P^n$. For any $X \in M^n$, $P^n(X; \mu)$ gives the extent of possible poverty (poverty, for short) level associated with $X$.

Sen (1976) suggested two basic postulates for an income poverty index. These are: (i) the monotonicity axiom, which requires poverty to increase under a reduction in the income of a poor, and (ii) the transfer axiom, which demands that poverty should increase if there is a transfer of income from a poor to anyone who is richer. Following Sen (1976) several other axioms have been suggested in the literature. (See, for example, Sen 1979; Foster 1984; Foster et al. 1984; Donaldson and Weymark 1986; Seidl 1988; Chakravarty 1990; Foster and Shorrocks 1991; Zheng 1997). Multidimensional generalizations of different postulates proposed for an income poverty index have been introduced, among others, by Chakravarty et al. (1998), Bourguignon and Chakravarty (1999, 2003) and Tsui (2002).

The axioms we suggest below for an arbitrary $P$ are fuzzy variants of the axioms presented in Chakravarty et al. (1998), Bourguignon and Chakravarty (1999, 2003) and Tsui (2002).

**Focus (FOC)**: For all $n \in N$; $X, \hat{X} \in M^n$; $\mu \in A$; if $S_{\mu_j}(X) = S_{\mu_j}\left(\hat{X}\right)$, $1 \leq j \leq k$ and $x_{ij} = \hat{x}_{ij}$ for all $i \in S_{\mu_j}(X)$, $1 \leq j \leq k$, then:

$$P^n(X; \mu) = P^n\left(\hat{X}; \mu\right).$$

**Normalization (NOM)**: For all $n \in N$; $X \in M^n$; $\mu \in A$; $j \in \{1, 2, \ldots, k\}$, if $S_{\mu_j}(X) = \varphi$, the empty set, then $P^n(X; \mu) = 0$.

**Monotonicity (MON)**: For all $n \in N$; $X, \hat{X} \in M^n$; $\mu \in A$; if $x_{rl} = \hat{x}_{rl}$ for all $r \in \{1, 2, \ldots, n\} \backslash \{i\}$, $l \in \{1, 2, \ldots, k\}$, $x_{il} = \hat{x}_{ll}$ for all $l \in \{1, 2, \ldots, k\} \backslash \{j\}$ and $x_{ij} > \hat{x}_{ij}$, where
$i \in S_{\mu_j}\left(\hat{X}\right)$, then $P^n(X; \mu) < P^n\left(\hat{X}; \mu\right)$.

**Transfers Principle (TRP)**: For all $n \in N$; $X, \hat{X} \in M^n$; $\mu \in A$; if $X$ is obtained from $\hat{X}$ by pre-multiplying $\hat{X}_p$ by a bistochastic matrix $B$ and $B\hat{X}_p$ is not a permutation of the rows of $\hat{X}_p$, then $P^n(X;\mu) < P^n\left(\hat{X};\mu\right)$, where $\hat{X}_p$ is the matrix of attribute quantities of possibly poor in $\hat{X}$, given that the bundles of attributes of the rich remain unaffected.[3]

**Principle of Population (POP)**: For all $n \in N$; $X \in M^n$; $\mu \in A$; $P^n(X;\mu) = P^n\left(\hat{X};\mu\right)$, where $\hat{X}$ is the $h-$ fold replication of $X$, $h \geq 2$ being an integer.

**Symmetry (SYM)**: For all $n \in N$, $X \in M^n$; $\mu \in A$ : $P^n(X;\mu) = P^n(\Pi X;\mu)$, where $\Pi$ is an $n \times n$ permutation matrix.

**Subgroup Decomposability (SUD)**: For $X^1, X^2, \ldots, X^h \in M$ and $\mu \in A$,

$$P^n(X;\mu) = \sum_{i=1}^{h} \frac{n_i}{n} P^{n_i}\left(X^i;\mu\right),$$

where $X$ is the attribute matrix $\begin{bmatrix} X^1 \\ X^2 \\ \\ \\ X^h \end{bmatrix}$ with $n$ rows and $k$ columns, $n_i$ is the population size corresponding to $X^i$ and $n = \sum_{i=1}^{h} n_i$.

**Continuity (CON)**: For all $n \in N$, $X \in M^n$; $\mu \in A$; $P^n(X;\mu)$ is continuous on $M^n$.

**Increasingness in Membership Functions (IMF)**: For all $n \in N$, $X \in M^n$; $\mu, \mu' \in A$ if $\mu_h = \mu'_h$ for all $h \in \{1, 2, \ldots, k\} \backslash \{j\}$, $S_{\mu_j}(X) = S_{\mu'_j}(X)$ and $\mu_j\left(x_{ij}\right) > \mu'_j\left(x_{ij}\right)$ for all $i \in S_{\mu_j}(X)$, then $P^n\left(X;\mu'\right) < P^n(X;\mu)$,

**Non-poverty Growth (NPG)**: For all $n \in N$; $X \in M^n$; $\mu \in A$ if $\hat{X}$ is obtained from $X$ by adding a certainly non-poor person to the society, then $P^{n+1}\left(\hat{X};\mu\right) < P^n(X;\mu)$ .

**Scale Invariance (SCI)**: For all $n \in N$, $X \in M^n$; $\mu \in A$ : $P^n(X;\mu) = P^n(X\Omega;\mu)$, where $\Omega$ is the diagonal matrix: diag $(\omega_1, \omega_2, \ldots, \omega_k)$, $\omega_i > 0$ for all $i = 1, 2, \ldots, k$.

**FOC**, which has similar spirit as (A5), states that, given the population size, the poverty index depends only on the attribute quantities of the persons who are possibly poor in different dimensions. Thus, if a person is certainly non-poor with respect to an attribute, then giving him more of this attribute does not change the intensity of poverty, even if he is possibly poor in the other attributes. Clearly, **FOC** rules out trade off between the two attributes of a person who is possibly poor with respect

[3]A square matrix of order $n$ is called a bistochastic matrix if its entries are non-negative and each of its rows and columns sums to one. A bistochastic matrix is called a permutation matrix if there is exactly one positive entry in each row and column.

to one but certainly non-poor with respect to the other. Thus, if life expectancy and composite good are the two attributes, more life expectancy in the domain in which it is certainly non-meager is of no use if the composite good is possibly meager. This, however, does not exclude the possibility of a trade off if both the attributes are possibly meager for a person. **NOM** is a cardinality property of the poverty index. It says that if all persons in a society are certainly non-poor, then the index value is zero. According to **MON**, poverty decreases if the condition of a poor improves. **MON** includes the possibility that the beneficiary may become certainly non-poor in the dimension concerned.

To understand **TRP**, let us recall a result from the literature on inequality measurement. Of two income distributions $u$ and $v$ of a given total over a given population size $n$, where $u$ is not a permutation of $v$, the former can be obtained from the latter through a sequence of rank preserving progressive transfers transferring incomes from the better off persons to those who are worse off if and only if $u = vB$ for some bistochastic matrix $B$ of order $n$ (Kolm 1969; Dasgupta et al. 1973). In the multidimensional context, Kolm (1977) showed that the distribution of a set of attributes summarized by some matrix $X$ is more equal than another matrix $\hat{X}$ (whose rows are not identical) if and only if $X = E\hat{X}$, where $E$ is some bistochastic matrix and $X$ cannot be derived from $\hat{X}$ by permutation of the rows of $\hat{X}$. Intuitively, multiplication of $\hat{X}$ by a bistochastic matrix makes the resulting distribution less concentrated. Following Kolm (1977), the analogous property applied to the set of possibly poor persons is **TRP**. It simply says that there is less possible poverty under $X$ than under $\hat{X}$, if the former is obtained from the latter by redistributing the attributes of the possibly poor using some bistochastic transformation.

Under **POP**, if an attribute matrix is replicated several times, then poverty remains unchanged. Since by replication we can transform two different sized matrices into the same size, **POP** is helpful for inter-temporal and interregional poverty comparisons. **SYM** demands anonymity. Any characteristic other than the quantities in different dimensions under consideration, for instance, the names of the individuals, is immaterial to the measurement of poverty. **CON**, which is similar to ($A3$), ensures that minor changes in attribute quantities will not give rise to an abrupt jump in the value of the poverty index. Therefore, a continuous poverty index will not be oversensitive to minor observational errors on basic need quantities.

**SUD** says that if a population is divided into several subgroups, say $h$, defined along ethnic, geographical or other lines, then the overall poverty is the population share weighted average of subgroup poverty levels. The contribution of subgroup $i$ to overall poverty is $\frac{n_i}{n} P^{n_i}(X^i;\mu)$ and overall poverty will precisely fall by this amount if poverty in subgroup $i$ is eliminated.

$\frac{n_i P^{n_i}(X^i;\mu)}{n P^n(X;\mu)} 100$ is the percentage contribution of subgroup $i$ to total poverty. Each of these statistics is useful to policy-makers because they become helpful for isolating subgroups of the population that are more susceptible to poverty (see Anand 1997; Chakravarty 1983a, b, c; Foster et al. 1984; Foster and Shorrocks 1991).

Between two identical communities, the one with higher membership function of an attribute should have a higher poverty because of higher possibility of individuals' being poor in that dimension. This is what **IMF** demands. A poverty index will be called $\mu$-monotonic if it satisfies **IMF**. According to **NPG** poverty should decrease if a person who is certainly rich joins the society. Thus, under **FOC**, **NPG** says that the poverty index is a decreasing function of the population size (see Kundu and Smith 1983; Subramanian 2002; Chakravarty et al. 2006). Finally, **SCI**, which parallels ($A1$), means that the poverty index is invariant under scale transformations of attribute quantities, that is, it is homogeneous of degree zero. Hence it should be independent of the units of measurement of attributes. Thus, if life expectancy is measured in months instead of in years, level of poverty remains unchanged.

We will now consider a property which takes care of the essence of multidimensional measurement through correlation between attributes. By taking into account the association of attributes, as captured by the degree of correlation between them, this property also underlines the difference between single and multidimensional poverty measurements. To illustrate the property, consider the two-person two-attribute case, where both the attributes are possibly meager for these persons. Suppose that $x_{11} > x_{21}$ and $x_{12} < x_{22}$. Now, consider a switch of attribute 2 between the two persons. This switch increases the correlation between the attributes because person 1 who had more of attribute 1 has now more of attribute 2 too and that is why we refer to it as a correlation increasing switch between two possibly poor persons. Formally, we have:

**Definition 1** For any $n \geq 2$; $X \in M^n$ ; $\mu \in A$ ; $j, h \in \{1, 2, \ldots, k\}$, suppose that for some $i, t \in S_{\mu_j}(X) \bigcap S_{\mu_h}(X)$, $x_{ij} < x_{tj}$ and $x_{th} < x_{ih}$. $\hat{X}$ is then said to be obtained from $X$ by a correlation increasing switch between two possibly poor persons if (i) $\hat{x}_{ij} = x_{tj}$, (ii) $\hat{x}_{tj} = x_{ij}$, (iii) $\hat{x}_{rj} = x_{rj}$ for all $r \neq i, t$ and (iv) $\hat{x}_{rs} = x_{rs}$ for all $s \neq j$ and for all $r$.

If the two attributes are substitutes, that is, if one attribute may compensate for the lack of another for a person who is possibly poor in both dimensions, then the switch should increase poverty. This is because the richer of the possibly poor is getting even better in the attributes which correspond to the similar aspect of poverty after the rearrangement. After the switch the poorer person is more unable to compensate the lower quantity of one attribute by the quantity of the other. Indeed, the switch just defined does not modify the marginal distribution of each attribute but reduces the extent to which the lack of one attribute may be compensated by the availability of the other. An analogous argument will establish that poverty should decrease under a correlation increasing switch if the two attributes are complements. (For more detailed arguments along this line, see Atkinson and Bourguignon 1982; Bourguignon and Chakravarty 2003). We state this principle formally for substitutes as:

**Increasing Poverty Under Correlation Increasing Switch (IPC)**: For all $n \in N$; $X \in M^n$; $\mu \in A$ if $\hat{X}$ is obtained from $X$ by a correlation increasing switch between two possibly poor persons, then $P^n(X; \mu) < P^n\left(\hat{X}; \mu\right)$ if the two attributes are substitutes.

The corresponding property which demands poverty to decrease under such a switch when the attributes are complements is denoted by **DPC**. If a poverty index does not change under a correlation increasing switch, then it treats the attributes as 'independents'.

## 4 The Subgroup Decomposable Fuzzy Multidimensional Poverty Indices

The objective of this section is to discuss the subgroup decomposable family of fuzzy multidimensional poverty indices. The necessity for a subgroup decomposable index arose from practical considerations. The use of such an index allows policy-makers to design effective, consistent national and regional antipoverty policies.

Repeated application of **SUD** shows that we can write a subgroup decomposable index as:

$$P^n(X;\mu) = \frac{1}{n}\sum_{i=1}^{n} p(x_i;\mu), \tag{4}$$

where $n \in N$; $X \in M^n$ and $\mu \in A$ are arbitrary. Since $p(x_i;\mu)$ depends only on person $i's$ consumption of the attributes, we call it 'individual poverty function'. If we define $p(x_i;\mu)$ as the weighted average of grades of membership of individual $i$ across dimensions, that is, if, $p(x_i;\mu) = \sum_{j=1}^{k}\delta_j\mu_j(x_{ij})$, where $0 < \delta_j < 1$ and $\sum_{j=1}^{k}\delta_j = 1$, then $P^n(X;\mu)$ in (4) becomes:

$$P^n(x_i;\mu) = \sum_{j=1}^{k}\delta_j\sum_{i\in S_{\mu_j}}\mu(x_{ij}). \tag{5}$$

The weight $\delta_j$ may be assumed to reflect the importance that we attach in our aggregation to dimension $j$. It may also be assumed to reflect the importance that the government assigns for alleviating poverty for that dimension. Since $\sum_{i\in S_{\mu_j}}\mu_j(x_{ij})$ gives the cardinality of the fuzzy set of the poor in the $j$th attribute (Dubois and Prade 1980, p. 30), $P^n$ in (5) is a weighted average of the proportions of possibly poor persons across dimensions. If $\mu_j$ coincides with the crisp membership function $\mu_j^*$, then the index in (5) becomes a weighted average of the proportions of persons who are poor in different dimensions.

We may interpret the formula alternatively as follows. $\mu_j(x_{ij})$ can be regarded as the extent of deprivation felt by person $i$ for being included in the set of persons who are possibly poor in attribute $j$. As his quantity of consumption of the attribute increases, deprivation decreases and $\mu_j(m_j) = 0$ shows the absence of this feeling at the level $m_j$. Therefore, $P^n$ is the population average of the weighted average of dimension—wise individual deprivations.

Defining $\frac{1}{n}\sum_{i\in S_{\mu_j}}\mu_j(x_{ij})$ as the possible poverty level associated with attribute $j$ and denoting it by $P^n(x_{.j};\mu_j)$, we can rewrite $P^n$ in (5) in a more compact way as:

$$P^n(X;\mu)=\sum_{j=1}^{k}\delta_j P^n(x_{.j};\mu_j). \tag{6}$$

This shows that $P^n(X;\mu)$ can also be viewed as a weighted average of attribute-wise (possible) poverty values. We refer to this property as 'Factor Decomposability'. The percentage contribution of dimension $j$ to total fuzzy poverty is $\frac{\delta_j P^n(x_{.j};\mu_j)}{P^n(X;\mu)}100.$. The elimination of poverty for the $j$th dimension will lower community poverty by the amount $\delta_j P^n(x_{.j};\mu_j)$.

We can use the two decomposability postulates to construct a two-way poverty profile and to calculate each attribute's poverty within each subgroup. This type of micro breakdown will help us to identify simultaneously the population subgroup(s) as well as attribute(s) for which poverty levels are severe and formulate appropriate antipoverty policies.

It will now be worthwhile to examine the behavior of $P^n$ given by (5) with respect to the axioms stated in Sect. 3. These axioms conveniently translate into constraints on the form of $\mu_j$ Evidently, $P^n$ in (5) is focused, normalized, monotonic, symmetric, population replication invariant, $\mu$-monotonic, continuous and correctly responsive to non-poverty growth. It satisfies **SCI** if and only if for each $j$, $\mu_j$ is homogeneous of degree zero, a condition fulfilled by the form given in (2). It is transfer preferring, that is, **TRP** holds if and only if $\mu_j$ is strictly convex over $(0;m_j)$ (see Marshall and Olkin 1979, p. 433). This means that the decline in the possibility of poverty with increase in quantities of attributes is the greatest at the lowest levels of the attribute. The membership function defined in (2) satisfies the convexity condition if $\theta_j\geq 2$. Finally, because of additivity across attributes it remains unchanged under a correlation increasing switch. We summarize these observations on the behavior of $P^n$ as follows:

**Proposition 2**
*The subgroup decomposable fuzzy multidimensional poverty index given by* (5) *satisfies the* **Focus, Normalization, Monotonicity, Principle of Population, Symmetry, Continuity, Increasingness in Membership Functions,** *and* **Non-Poverty Growth** *axioms. It fulfills the* **Scale Invariance** *axiom if and only if the membership functions for different attributes are homogeneous of degree zero. It meets the Transfers Principle axiom if and only if for each $j$, $\mu_j$ is strictly convex on the relevant part of the domain. Finally, it remains unchanged under a correlation increasing switch between two possibly poor persons.*

*To illustrate the general formula in* (5), *suppose that the membership function is of the form* (2). *In this case, the index is*:

$$P_{\theta}^{n}(X;\mu)=\frac{1}{n}\sum_{j=1}^{k}\delta_j\sum_{i\in S_{\mu_j}}\left(\frac{m_j-x_{ij}}{m_j}\right)^{\theta_j}. \tag{7}$$

where $\theta=(\theta_1,\theta_2,\ldots,\theta_k)$ which reflect different perceptions of poverty. This is a fuzzy counterpart to the multidimensional generalization of the Foster–Greer–Thorbecke (FGT) (1984) index considered by Chakravarty et al. (1998) and Bourguignon and Chakravarty (2003). For a given $X$, $P_\theta^n$ increases as $\theta_j$ increases, $1\le j\le k$. For $\theta_j=1$ for all $j$, $P_\theta^n$ becomes

$$P_{\theta}^{n}(X;\mu)=\sum_{j=1}^{k}\delta_j H_j I_j, \tag{8}$$

where $I_j$ is the average of the grades of membership of the persons in $S_{\mu_j}(X)$, that is, $I_j=\frac{1}{q_j}\sum_{i\in S_{\mu_j}}\left(\frac{m_j-x_{ij}}{m_j}\right)$ with $q_j$ being the cardinality of $S_{\mu_j}(X)$ and $H_j=\frac{q_j}{n}$ is the fuzzy head-count ratio in dimension $j$. Thus, for a given $H_j$, an increase in $I_j$, say, due to a reduction of $x_{ij}$, increases the index.

If $\theta_j=2$ for all $j$, $P_\theta^n$ can be written as:

$$P_{\theta}^{n}(X;\mu)=\sum_{j=1}^{k}\delta_j H_j\left[I_j^2+\left(1-I_j\right)^2C_j^2\right], \tag{9}$$

where $C_j^2=\frac{1}{q_j}\sum_{i\in S_{\mu_j}}\left(\frac{x_{ij}-\rho_j}{\rho_j}\right)^2$ is the squared coefficient of variation of the distribution of attribute $j$ among those for whom it is possibly meager, with $\rho_j=\frac{1}{q_j}\sum_{i\in S_{\mu_j}}x_{ij}$ being the mean of the distribution. Now, the squared coefficient of variation is an index of inequality of the concerned distribution. Clearly, given $I_j$ and $H_j$, $P_\theta^n$ in (9) reduces as $C_j$ reduces, say through a transfer from a less possibly poor to a more possibly poor. Thus, the decomposition in (9) shows that the poverty index is related in a positive monotonic way with the inequality levels of the possibly poor in different dimensions.

An alternative of interest arises from the following specification of the membership function:

$$\mu_j(x_{ij})=1-\left(\frac{x_{ij}}{m_j}\right)^{c_j}, \tag{10}$$

where for all $j$, $1\le j\le k$, $c_j\in(0,1)$. It satisfies all the conditions laid down in (1) along with homogeneity of degree zero and strict convexity. The associated poverty index is:

$$P_{c}^{n}(X;\mu)=\frac{1}{n}\sum_{j=1}^{k}\delta_j\sum_{i\in S_{\mu_j}}\left[1-\left(\frac{x_{ij}}{m_j}\right)^{c_j}\right] \tag{11}$$

where $c = (c_1, c_2, \ldots, c_k)$. This index is a fuzzy version of the multidimensional extension of the subgroup decomposable single dimensional Chakravarty (1983a) index suggested by Chakravarty et al. (1998). Given $X$, $P_c^n$ is increasing in $c_j$ for all $j$. For, $c_j = 1$, the index coincides with the particular case of the index in (9) when $\theta_j = 1, 1 \leq j \leq k$. On the other hand as $c_j \to 0$ for all $j$, $P_c^n \to 0$. As $c_j$ decreases over the interval (0, 1), $P_c^n$ becomes more sensitive to transfers lower down the scale of distribution along dimension $j$.

We may also consider a logarithmic formulation of the membership function that fulfils all conditions stated in (1):

$$\mu_j(x_{ij}) = \frac{\log\left(1 + \mathrm{e}^{\lambda_j\left(\frac{m_j - x_{ij}}{m_j}\right)}\right) - \log 2}{\log(1 + \mathrm{e}^{\lambda_j}) - \log 2}, \tag{12}$$

where $\lambda_j > 0$ is a parameter. The corresponding additive poverty index turns out to be:

$$P_\lambda^n(X; \mu) = \frac{1}{n}\sum_{j=1}^{k}\delta_j \sum_{i \in S_{\mu_j}} \frac{\log\left(1 + \mathrm{e}^{\lambda_j\left(\frac{m_j - x_{ij}}{m_j}\right)}\right) - \log 2}{\log(1 + \mathrm{e}^{\lambda_j}) - \log 2}, \tag{13}$$

where $\lambda$ is the parameter vector $(\lambda_1, \lambda_2, \ldots, \lambda_k)$. $P_\lambda^n$ can be regarded as a fuzzy sister of the multidimensional generalization of the Watts (1968) poverty index characterized by Tsui (2002). The parameter $\lambda_j$ determines the curvature of the poverty contour. An increase in $\lambda_j$ for any $j$ makes the fuzzy poverty contour more convex to the origin. If $\lambda_j \to 0$ for all $j$, then $P_\lambda^n \to 0$. In the particular case when $\theta_j = \lambda_j = 1$ for all $j$, the ranking of two attribute matrices $X, \hat{X} \in M^n$ by $P_\theta^n$ will be same as that generated by $P_\lambda^n$. Since $P_\lambda^n$ is transfer preferring for all $\lambda_j > 0$, it satisfies TRP even in this case. But $P_\theta^n$ does not fulfill TRP here.

There can be simple non-additive formulations of fuzzy multidimensional extensions of single dimensional subgroup decomposable indices. They satisfy SUD but not factor decomposability. Assuming that $\theta_j$ in (2) is constant across attributes, say equal to $\beta$, one such index can be:

$$P_{\alpha,\beta}^n(X; \mu) = \frac{1}{n}\sum_{i=1}^{n}\left[\sum_{j=1}^{k} a_j \mu_j(\bar{x}_{ij})\right]^{\frac{\alpha}{\beta}} = \frac{1}{n}\sum_{i=1}^{n}\left[\sum_{j=1}^{k} a_j \left(\frac{m_j - \bar{x}_{ij}}{m_j}\right)^{\beta}\right]^{\frac{\alpha}{\beta}} \tag{14}$$

where $\bar{x}_{ij} = \min(x_{ij}, m_j)$, $a_j > 0$ for all $j$ and $\alpha > 0$ is a positive parameter. $P_{\alpha,\beta}^n$ is the fuzzy counterpart to the multidimensional version of the FGT index suggested by Bourguignon and Chakravarty (2003). The interpretation of this index is quite straightforward. The membership functions in various dimensions are first aggregated into a composite membership using a particular value of $\beta$ and the coefficients $a_j$. Multidimensional fuzzy poverty is then defined as the average of that composite membership value, raised to the power $\alpha$, over the whole population. $P^n_{\alpha,\beta}$ satisfies IPC or DPC depending on whether $\alpha$ is greater or less than $\beta$. For $\alpha = 1$, it becomes the weighted sum of order $\beta$ of the membership grades and for a given $X$, it is increasing in $\beta$.

We may suggest an alternative to (14) using the membership function in (11). This form is defined by:

$$T^n_c(X;\mu) = \frac{1}{n}\sum_{i=1}^{n}\left(1 - \prod_{j=1}^{k}(1 - \mu_j(\bar{x}_{ij}))\right) = \frac{1}{n}\sum_{i=1}^{n}\left(1 - \prod_{j=1}^{k}\left(\frac{\bar{x}_{ij}}{m_j}\right)^{c_j}\right), \quad (15)$$

This is a fuzzy translation of the multidimensional generalization of the Chakravarty (1983a) index developed by Tsui (2002). In (15) for each person complements from unity of the grades of membership along various dimensions are subjected to a product transformation which is then averaged over persons after subtracting from its maximum value, that is, 1. Since $T^n_c$ is unambiguously decreasing under a correlation increasing switch between two possibly poor persons, it treats the concerned attributes unambiguously as complements, that is, it satisfies DPC.

Given a membership function $\mu_j$, there will be a corresponding multidimensional fuzzy poverty index that meets all the postulates considered in Sect. 2. These indices will differ only in the manner in which we use $\mu_j$ to aggregate membership grades of different persons along different dimensions into an overall indicator.

## 5 Conclusions

This paper has explored the problem of replacing the traditional crisp view of poverty status with a fuzzy structure which allows membership of poverty set or the possibility of poverty in different dimensions of life to take any value in the interval [0, 1]. Attempt was made to establish how standard multidimensional poverty indices might be translated into the fuzzy framework. Suggestions were made for suitable fuzzy analogues of axioms for a multidimensional poverty index, such as **Focus**, **Monotonicity**, **Transfers Principle**, and **Continuity**. We have also added a condition which requires poverty to increase if the possibility of poverty shifts upward along any dimension.

We will now make a comparison of our index with some existing indices. Assuming that the individual well-being depends only on income, Cerioli and Zani (1990) suggested the use of the arithmetic average of grades of membership of different individuals as a fuzzy poverty index. It 'represents the proportions of individuals "belonging" in a fuzzy sense to the poor subset' (Cerioli and Zani 1990, p. 282). Clearly, this index is similar in nature to $P^n$ given by (5). In a multidimensional framework, Cerioli and Zani (1990) introduced a transition zone for attribute $j$ over which the membership function declines from 1 to 0 linearly:

They then defined the membership function for person $i$ as

$$\mu_j(x_{ij}) = \begin{cases} 1 & \text{if } x_{ij} \le x_j^L, \\ \left(\frac{x_j^H - x_{ij}}{x_j^H - x_j^L}\right) & \text{if } x_{ij} \in \left(x_j^L, x_j^H\right), \\ 0 & \text{if } x_{ij} \ge x_j^H. \end{cases} \tag{16}$$

They then defined the membership function for person $i$ as $\frac{\sum_{j=1}^{k} \mu_j(x_{ij}) w_j}{\sum_{j=1}^{k} w_j}$ where $(w_1, w_2, \ldots, w_k)$ represents a system of weights.

In what has been called the "Totally Fuzzy and Relative" approach, Cheli and Lemmi (1995) defined the membership function for attribute $j$ as the distribution function, normalized (linearly transformed) so as to equal 1 for the poorest and 0 for the richest person in the population:

$$\mu_j(x_{ij}) = \begin{cases} 1 & \text{if } x_{ij} = x_j^{(s)}, \\ \mu_j\left(x_j^{(l-1)}\right) + \frac{F\left(x_j^{(l)}\right) - F\left(x_j^{(l-1)}\right)}{1 - F\left(x_j^{(l)}\right)} & \text{if } x_{ij} = x_j^{(l)} \\ 0 & \text{if } x_{ij} = x_j^{(1)}. \end{cases} \tag{17}$$

where $x_j^{(1)}, x_j^{(2)}, \ldots, x_j^{(s)}$ are modalities of dimension $j$ in increasing order with respect to the risk of poverty connected to them.

An alternative specification of the membership function for person $i$ arises if we replace $\mu_j$ in (16) by $\mu_j$ in (17). In either case, as Cerioli and Zani (1990) and Cheli and Lemmi (1995) suggested, under appropriate specification of weights, we can take:

$$C^n = \sum_{i=1}^{n} \frac{\sum_{j=1}^{k} \mu_j(x_{ij}) w_j}{n \sum_{j=1}^{k} w_j}, \tag{18}$$

as an indicator of poverty. Cerioli and Zani (1990) chose $w_j = \log\left(\frac{1}{p_j}\right)$, where $p_j$ is the proportion of persons with $j$th poverty symptoms, and Cheli and Lemmi (1995) preferred to use $w_j = \log\left(\frac{n}{\sum_{i=1}^{n} \mu_j(x_{ij})}\right)$. $C^n$ indicates the cardinality of the fuzzy subset of the poor as a proportion of the population size.

An important difference between $P^n$ in (5) and $C^n$ is that while $P^n$ is subgroup decomposable, $C^n$ is not. This is because $C^n$ depends on different kinds of rank orders. Precisely, because of this a poverty index based on a Gini type inequality index or welfare function is not subgroup decomposable. Examples are the Sen (1976), Kakwani (1980a) and Thon (1983) indices.

A rank preserving transfer of some quantity of an attribute from a possibly poor to a worse off person will not change the rank orders of the modalities in the concerned dimension. Therefore, satisfaction of the **Transfers Principle** by the general index $C^n$ will depend on the assumption about the weight system. Likewise, a rank preserving reduction in the quantity of an attribute will not change the rank orders of the modalities. Hence a similar argument holds concerning fulfillment of **Mono-**

**tonicity**. However, $C^n$ is normalized, symmetric, scale invariant (under appropriate choices of modalities) and responds correctly to non-poverty growth. It is continuous for the membership function in (16). Continuity for the membership function in (17) will hold if $F$ is continuous. To check whether it is population replication invariant, concrete specification of the weight sequence is necessary.

## References


Alkire, S. (2005). *Measuring the freedom aspects of capabilities*. Global Equity Initiative: Harvard University.

Anand, S. (1997). Aspects of poverty in Malaysia. *Review of Income and Wealth, 23,* 1–16.

Atkinson, A. B. (2003). Multidimensional deprivation: Contrasting social welfare and counting approaches. *Journal of Economic Inequality, 1,* 51–65.

Atkinson, A. B , & Bourguignon, F. (1982). The comparison of multidimensional distributions of economic status. *Review of Economic Studies, 49,* 183–201.

Balestrino, A. (1994). Poverty and functionings: Issues in measurement and public action. *Giornale degli economisti e Annali di economia, 53.*

Balestrino, A. (1998). Counting the poor in a fuzzy way: The head-count ratio and the monotonicity transfer axioms. *Notizie di Politeia, 14,* 77–86.

Balestrino, A., & Chiappero Martinetti, E. (1994). *Poverty, differentiated needs and information.* University of Pisa.

Baliamoune, M. (2003). *On the measurement of human well-being: Fuzzy set theory and Sen's capability approach.* Presented at the WIDER conference on Inequality. Poverty and Human Well-being, 30–31 May.

Basu, K. (1987). Axioms for fuzzy measures of inequality. *Mathematical Social Sciences, 14,* 69–76.

Betti, G., & Verma, V. K. (1998). *Measuring the degree of poverty in a dynamic and comparative context: A multidimensional approach using fuzzy set theory.* Working Paper n. 22, Department of Quantitative Methods, University of Siena.

Blackorby, C., & Donaldson, D. (1980). Ethical indices for the measurement of poverty. *Econometrica, 58,* 1053–1060.

Blaszczak-Przybycinska, I. (1992). Multidimensional statistical analysis of poverty in Poland. In: Polish Statistical Association and Central Statistical Office (Ed.), *Poverty measurement for economies in transition* (pp. 307–327). Warsaw.

Bourguignon, F., & Chakravarty, S. R. (1999). A family of multidimensional poverty measures. In D. J. Slottje (Ed.), *Advances in econometrics, income distribution and scientific methodology: essays in honor of C. Dagum* (pp. 331–344). Physica-Verlag, Heidelberg.

Bourguignon, F., & Chakravarty, S. R. (2003). The measurement of multidimensional poverty. *Journal of Economic Inequality, 1,* 25–49.

Casini, L., & Bernetti, I. (1996). Environment, sustainability and Sen's theory. University of Naples.

Cerioli, A., & Zani, S. (1990). A fuzzy approach to the measurement of poverty. In C. Dagum, & M. Zenga (Eds.), *Income and wealth distribution, inequality and poverty* (pp. 272–284). New York: Springer–Verlag.

Chakravarty, S. R. (1983a). Ethically flexible measures of poverty. *Canadian Journal of Economics, 16,* 74–85.

Chakravarty, S. R. (1983b). A new index of poverty. *Mathematical Social Sciences, 6,* 307–313.

Chakravarty, S. R. (1983c). Measures of poverty based on representative income gaps. *Sankhya, 45,* 69–74.

Chakravarty, S. R. (1990). *Ethical social index numbers*. New York: Springer–Verlag.

Chakravarty, S. R. (1997). On Shorrocks' reinvestigation of the Sen poverty index. *Econometrica, 65,* 1241–1242.

Chakravarty, S. R., & Majumder, A. (2005). Measuring human poverty: A generalized index and an application using basic dimensions of life and some anthropometric indicators. *Journal of Human Development, 6,* 275–299.
Chakravarty, S. R., & Roy, R. (1985). Measurement of fuzziness: A general approach. *Theory and Decision, 19,* 163–169.
Chakravarty, S. R., Mukherjee, D., & Ranade, R. (1998). On the family of subgroup and factor decomposable measures of multidimensional poverty. *Research on Economic Inequality, 8,* 175–194.
Chakravarty, S. R., Kanbur, R., & Mukherjee, D. (2006). Population growth and poverty measurement. *Social Choice and Welfare, 26,* 471–483.
Cheli, B., & Lemmi, A. (1995). A totally fuzzy and relative approach to the multidimensional analysis of poverty. *Economic Notes, 24,* 115–134.
Chiappero Martinetti, E. (1994). A new approach to evaluation of well-being and poverty by fuzzy set theory. *Giornale degli economisti e annali di economia, 53,* 367–388.
Chiappero Martinetti, E. (1996). Standard of living evaluation based on Sen's approach: Some methodological suggestions. *Politeia, 12,* 37–53.
Chiappero Martinetti, E. (2004). *Complexity and vagueness in the capability approach: Strength or weakness?* University of Pavia.
Clark, S., Hemming, R., & Ulph, D. (1981). On indices for the measurement of poverty. *Economic Journal, 91,* 515–526.
Dagum, C., Gambassi, R., & Lemmi, A. (1992). New approaches to the measurement of poverty. In Polish Statistical Association and Central Statistical Office (Ed.), *Poverty measurement for economies in transition* (pp. 201–226). Warsaw.
Dasgupta, P., Sen, A. K., & Starett, D. (1973). Notes on the measurement of inequality. *Journal of Economic Theory, 6,* 180–187.
Donaladson, D., & Weymark, J. A. (1986). Properties of fixed-population poverty indices. *International Economic Review, 27,* 667–688.
Dubois, D., & Prade, H. (1980). *Fuzzy sets and systems*. London: Academic Press.
Foster, J. E. (1984). On economic poverty measures: A survey of aggregate measures. In R. L. Basmann & G. F. Rhodes (Eds.), *Advances in econometrics* (Vol. 3). Connecticut: JAI Press.
Foster, J. E., & Shorrocks, A. F. (1991). Subgroup consistent poverty indices. *Econometrica, 59,* 687–709.
Foster, J. E., Greer, J., & Thorbecke, E. (1984). A class of decomposable poverty measures. *Econometrica, 42,* 761–766.
Haagenars, A. J. M. (1987). A class of poverty measures. *International Economic Review, 28,* 593–607.
Kakwani, N. C. (1980a). *Income inequality and poverty: methods of estimation and policy applications*. Oxford: Oxford University Press.
Kakwani, N. C. (1980b). On a class of poverty measures. *Econometrica, 48,* 437–446.
Kolm, S. C. (1969). The optimal production of social justice. In J. Margolis & H. Guitton (Eds.), *Public economics* (pp. 145–200). London: Macmillan.
Kolm, S. C. (1977). Multidimensional egalitarianism. *Quarterly Journal of Economics, 91,* 1–13.
Kundu, A., & Smith, T. E. (1983). An impossibility theorem on poverty indices. *International Economic Review, 24,* 423–434.
Lipton, M., & Ravallion, M. (1995). Poverty and policy. In: J. Behrman, & T. N. Srinivasan (Eds.), *Handbook of development economics* (Vol. 1.). North–Holland, Amsterdam.
Marshall, A. W., & Olkin, I. (1979). *Inequalities: Theory of majorization and its applications*. London: Academic Press.
Ok, E. (1995). Fuzzy measurement of income inequality: a class of fuzzy inequality measures. *Social Choice and Welfare, 12,* 111–136.
Osmani, S. (1992). Introduction In S. R. Osmani(Ed.), *Nutrition and poverty*. Oxford: Oxford University Press.

Pannuzi, N., & Quaranta, A. G. (1995). Measuring poverty: A study case in an Italian industrial city. *Research on Economic Inequality, 6*, 323–336.
Qizilbash, M. (2002). A note on the measurement of poverty and vulnerability in the South African context. *Journal of International Development, 14*, 757–772.
Ravallion, M. (1996). Issues in measuring and modeling poverty. *Economic Journal, 106*, 1328–1343.
Seidl, C. (1988). Poverty measurement: A survey. In D. Bos, M. Rose, & C. Seidl (Eds.), *Welfare efficiency in public economics*. New York: Springer-Verlag.
Sen, A. K. (1976). Poverty: On ordinal approach to measurement. *Econometrica, 44*, 219–231.
Sen, A. K. (1979). Issues in the measurement of poverty. *Scandinavian Journal of Economics, 81*, 285–307.
Sen, A. K. (1981). *Poverty and famines*. Oxford: Clarendon Press.
Sen, A. K. (1985). *Commodities and capabilities*. North–Holland, Amsterdam.
Sen, A. K. (1987). *Standard of living*. Cambridge: Cambridge University Press.
Sen, A. K. (1992). *Inequality re-examined*. Cambridge, MA: Harvard University Press.
Sen, A. K. (1997). *On economic inequality, with a substantial annexe by Foster J. E. and Sen A. K.* Oxford: Oxford University Press.
Shorrocks, A. F. (1995). Revisiting the Sen poverty index. *Econometrica, 63*, 1225–1230.
Shorrocks, A. F., & Subramanian, S. (1994). Fuzzy poverty indices. University of Essex.
Streeten, P. (1981). *First things first: Meeting basic human needs in developing countries*. Oxford: Oxford University Press.
Subramanian, S. (2002). Counting the poor: An elementary difficulty in the measurement of poverty. *Economics and Philosophy, 18*, 277–285.
Takayama, N. (1979). Poverty income inequality and their measures: Professor Sen's axiomatic approach reconsidered. *Econometrica, 47*, 749–759.
Thon, D. (1983). A poverty measure. *Indian Economic Journal, 30*, 55–70.
Tsui, K. Y. (2002). Multidimensional poverty indices. *Social Choice and Welfare, 19*, 69–93.
UNDP. (1997). *Human development report*. Oxford University Press.
Watts, H. (1968). An economic definition of poverty. In D. P. Moynihan (Ed.), *On understanding poverty* (pp. 16–329). New York: Basic Books.
Zadeh, L. A. (1965). Fuzzy sets. *Information and Control, 8*, 338–353.
Zheng, B. (1997). Aggregate poverty measures. *Journal of Economic Surveys, 11*, 123–162.

# Multidimensional Poverty Orderings: Theory and Applications

**François Bourguignon and Satya R. Chakravarty**

**Abstract** This paper generalizes the poverty ordering criteria available for single dimensional income poverty to the case of multidimensional welfare attributes. A set of properties to be satisfied by multidimensional poverty measures is first discussed. Then general classes of poverty measures based on these properties are defined. Finally, dominance criteria are derived such that a distribution of multidimensional attributes exhibits less poverty than another for all multidimensional poverty indices belonging to a given class. These criteria may be seen as a generalization of the single dimensional poverty-line criterion. However, it turns out that the way this generalization is made depends on whether attributes are complements or substitutes.

**Keywords** Poverty measurement · Multidimensional poverty ordering · Dominance

**JEL Codes** D3 · 132

---

An initial version of this paper has been presented in various seminars over the last couple of years. We thank participants to these seminars for helpful comments. They are too numerous to be mentioned and duly thanked by name. All remaining error in this paper is undoubtedly ours. The findings, interpretations, and conclusions expressed in this paper are entirely those of the authors, and do not necessarily represent the views of the World Bank and its affiliated organizations, or those of the Executive Directors of the World Bank or the governments they represent.

---

The kind consent of Oxford University Press to reprint this article from its volume 'Arguments for a Better World: Essays in Honor of Amartya Sen Volume II: Society, Institutions, and Development', 2009, is sincerely acknowledged.

---

F. Bourguignon (✉)
Paris School of Economics, Paris, France
e-mail: efrancois.bourguignon@psemail.eu

S. R. Chakravarty
Indian Statistical Institute, Kolkata 700108, India
e-mail: satyarchakravarty@gmail.com



S. R. Chakravarty (ed.), *Poverty, Social Exclusion and Stochastic Dominance*, Themes in Economics, https://doi.org/10.1007/978-981-13-3432-0_10

## 1 Introduction

Removal of poverty is one of the major aims of economic policy in many countries. In order to evaluate the efficacy of an antipoverty policy, it is necessary to observe the changes in the level of poverty over time. Therefore, the way level of poverty is measured is important both for an understanding of poverty and for policy applications. Since the publication of Sen's (1976) pioneering paper on poverty measurement, a great deal has been written on this subject. Over the last quarter century, research on poverty measurement has taken two close but distinct branches: construction of *measures of poverty* and *poverty orderings*. In both branches, income or consumption expenditures has been regarded as the only attribute of well-being. The first branch, following Sen (1976), is an attempt to develop alternative measures of poverty. A poverty measure aggregates the income shortfalls of the poor persons, persons, whose incomes fall below the poverty line representing the income necessary to maintain a subsistence standard of living. Several measures of poverty, including the one suggested by Sen (1976), are now available in the literature. They have been surveyed by various researchers (see, for example, Foster 1984; Seidl 1988; Chakravarty 1990; Foster and Sen 1997 and Zheng 1997).

The second branch of literature is concerned with rankings of income distributions based on multiple desiderata on poverty measurement. Since quite often the choice of a particular measure of poverty can be arbitrary, so can be the conclusions based on that measure. However, it may be possible to reduce the degree of arbitrariness by choosing all poverty measures that fulfill a set of reasonable postulates. That is, instead of choosing individual poverty measures we are choosing a set of criteria for poverty measures which in turn implicitly determines a class of measures. We can then check whether it is possible to rank two income distributions unambiguously by all members of this class. In a sense, this kind of research has grown out of presence of too many poverty measures. However, the use of a class of measures may not make all income distributions comparable, that is, there may be no unanimous agreement among these measures about the ranking of some income distributions. Thus, while a single measure of poverty completely orders all income distributions, the ordering generated by a family of measures is partial. For some distributions, it is not possible to say whether one has lower or higher poverty than another by all members of the family. Thus, we are forced to withhold our judgments on poverty comparison for some pairs of distributions. Following Zheng (1999) we refer to this notion of ordering as *poverty-measure ordering*. In an important contribution, Atkinson (1987) derived conditions on poverty-measure orderings for subgroup decomposable poverty measures with a common poverty line. Zheng (1999) extended Atkinson's results to a more restrictive class of poverty measures with the objective of increasing the completeness of poverty orderings. Atkinson (1992) and Jenkins and Lambert

(1993) considered poverty-measure orderings when the poverty line is adjusted for differences in family composition.[1]

Both for poverty measures and poverty orderings, the definition of a poverty line is crucial. The determination of such an income or consumption threshold that would define poverty has been an issue of debate for a long time. Quite often a significant degree of arbitrariness is involved in the construction of a poverty line. A poverty measure may rank two income distributions differently for two distinct poverty lines. Therefore, it becomes useful to see if two income distributions can be ranked unanimously by a given measure for all poverty lines in some reasonable interval. This establishes the second goal of research on partial poverty orderings which arises from uncertainty about the poverty line. This notion of ordering of distributions by a given poverty measure for a range of poverty lines is called *poverty-line* ordering (Zheng 1999). Foster and Shorrocks (1988a, b) and Foster and Jin (1996) characterized partial poverty-line orderings for several classes of poverty measures.

All these contributions regard income or consumption expenditures as the sole indicator of well-being. But poverty of a person also arises due to his/her insufficiency of different other attributes of well-being that are necessary to maintain a subsistence level of living. The basic needs approach considers development as an improvement in an array of human needs, not just growth of income. Wellbeing is intrinsically multidimensional from the capability–functionings perspective, where functionings refer to the various things a person may value doing (or being) and capability deals with the freedom to choose a particular set of functionings (Sen 1985, 1992). The valued functionings may vary from such elementary ones like health status or life expectancy, literacy, adequate nourishment, the availability of certain public goods and personal income to very complex activities or personal characteristics such as participation in the community life and having self-respect. This, in turn, means that poverty is essentially a multidimensional phenomenon and income is just one of its dimensions. It is certainly true that with a sufficiently high income, a person will be able to improve the position of some of his/her nonincome attributes. But income cannot buy everything. On the one hand, there may not be a market for some goods—for instance, flood control program in an underdeveloped economy. On the other hand, even if markets are available, prices may be too high for a person to afford consumption of different attributes above the corresponding thresholds representing subsistence level. Therefore, poverty should be viewed multidimensionally as the inability to achieve minimally acceptable or subsistence levels of income as well as nonincome indicators of welfare. Ravallion (1996) identified four sets of such indicators as ingredients for a sensible approach to poverty measurement (see also Bourguignon and Chakravarty 1999, 2003).[2]

[1] Spencer and Fisher (1992), Jenkins and Lambert (1997, 1998a, b) and Shorrocks (1998) characterized poverty dominance criteria involving poverty incidence, poverty intensity and inequality among the poor.

[2] An example of a multidimensional poverty indicator is the human poverty index suggested by the UNDP (1997). It aggregates country level deprivations in literacy, life expectancy and decent living standard.

While the literature on income poverty is already quite rich, research on multidimensional poverty measurement has just begun. Tsui (2002), Chakravarty et al. (1998), Bourguignon and Chakravarty (1999, 2003), Chakravarty (2006) and Chakravarty and Silber (2007) suggested several functional forms for multidimensional poverty indices. Bourguignon and Chakravarty (2003) also examined the shapes of isopoverty contours taking into account the idea of substitutability or complementarity between attributes, an important issue for multivariate poverty measures. However, partial poverty orderings in multidimensional context still remains an important area to be explored. This paper is a contribution to this area. More precisely, for given poverty threshold levels of attributes of well-being this paper provides *multidimensional poverty-measure orderings* corresponding to a class of multidimensional poverty measures satisfying a set of intuitively reasonable axioms.

The criteria obtained generalize, in a sensible way, single dimensional poverty-line orderings. A simple ordering criterion for two distributions defined in a single dimension is that the proportion of poor is not higher in the first than in the second distribution for all poverty lines below the actual threshold level. This property does extend to more than one dimension by considering all combinations of individual attributes' poverty lines below actual threshold levels.

Atkinson and Bourguignon (1982) argued explicitly how utility should change under a correlation increasing switch of attributes between two individuals. Using this as a postulate and applying the Atkinson–Bourguignon (1982) dominance results to the comparison of two-dimensional headcount ratios, we show that if the two attributes are substitutes, then the comparison should be made only in the region in which individuals lack both the attributes, that is, in the intersection of the sets in which the attribute quantities remain below the corresponding thresholds. On the other hand, if they are complements, the comparison should be in the union of the sets. That is, the definition of who is poor is then shown to depend on whether the various attributes that define multidimensional poverty may be considered as substitutes or complements. Interestingly enough, our study of multidimensional poverty ordering leads to a new view on the definition of multidimensional poverty itself.

It may be important to note that since the poverty limits of different attributes are given exogenously, the notion of poverty we are considering here is of absolute type and departs from the relative concept of poverty in which the limits are determined using consumption levels of those attributes in the whole population-typically the median or the mean. For instance, in the case of income poverty, a family with income less the half the median income may be regarded as relatively poor. However, the concept of absolute poverty is deemed to be more appropriate in a multidimensional context, even in the income dimension.[3]

In an interesting contribution, Atkinson (2003) brought out key differences between our approach and the 'counting approach', where the latter concentrates on the number of dimensions in which people suffer deprivation. He also explained how the counting approach can be put in an analytical framework like ours. Duclos

[3]Note than using median definition poverty thresholds become essentially ambiguous in a multidimensional setting. Things are less problematic with the means.

et al. (2002) considered bivariate poverty orderings under a different set of assumptions. They regarded the attributes only as substitutes. Their framework differs from ours because they assume dependence of the poverty line of one attribute on the other and viceversa, thus implicitly postulating some substitutability among the various dimensions of poverty and, in effect, getting closer to a single dimensional approach combining the two wellbeing attributes.

The present paper is organized as follows. The next section discusses the properties of a multidimensional poverty measure. Section 3 develops multidimensional poverty orderings for classes of poverty measures satisfying some subset of these properties. A graphical illustration of these orderings and their implications are provided in Sect. 4 for a simple stylized case. Finally, Sect. 5 concludes.

## 2 Properties for a Measure of Multidimensional Poverty

In this section, which relies on some of our previous work, we lay down the postulates for a multidimensional poverty index. As Sen (1976) suggested, two steps are involved in framing a poverty index. The first step is the identification of the poor, that is, the problem of counting the number of poor persons. Once the poor persons have been identified, the next step is to aggregate the income deviations of the poor from the poverty line into an overall device.

Since in this paper we are viewing poverty from a multivariate perspective, the identification problem will also be of multivariate type. For expositional ease we assume that there are only two attributes, 1 and 2. They are both supposed to be continuous. For example, attribute 1 can be the level of literacy or schooling and attribute 2 can be a composite good constituting all other basic needs of human life. Our analysis in this section easily generalizes to more than two attributes.

Let $R^2_+$ stand for the nonnegative orthant of the 2-dimensional Euclidean space $R^2$. For a set of $n$-persons, the $i$th person possesses a 2-vector $(x_{i1}, x_{i2}) = x_i \in R^2_+$ of attributes. The vector $x_i$ is the $i$th row of the $n \times 2$ matrix $X \in M^n$, where $M^n$ is the set of all $n \times 2$ matrices whose entries are nonnegative real numbers. The $j$th column $x_j$ of $X \in M^n$ gives the distribution of attribute $j$ ($j = 1, 2$) among the $n$ persons. Let $M = \cup_{n \in N} M^n$, where $N$ is the set of all positive integers. For any $X \in M$, we write $n(X)$ (or $n$) for the associated population size.

In this multivariate structure, a threshold is defined for each attribute. These thresholds represent the minimal quantities of the two attributes necessary for maintaining a subsistence level of living. Let $z = (z_1, z_2) \in Z$ be the vector of thresholds, where $Z$ is a nonempty subset of $R^2_{++}$, the strictly positive subset of $R^2_+$.

In this framework, person $i$ will be called poor with respect to attribute $j$ if $x_{ij} < z_j$ and he/she is called nonpoor if $x_{ij} \geq z_j$ for all $j$. The subset of $R^2_+$ corresponding to the set of persons who are poor with respect to attribute $j$ is denoted by $g_j$, which we call a single dimensional poverty space, $SDPS(z_j)$, where $j = 1, 2$. Adding together the numbers of poor in $g_1$ and $g_2$ will clearly overestimate the total number of poor. This is because people who are poor simultaneously in the two dimensions will be counted twice. This subset of $R^2_+$ in which each person's quantities of the two attributes remain below the corresponding threshold values, i.e. $x_{ij} < z_j$, for $j = 1, 2$, will be called the two dimensional poverty space, *TDPS* $(z_1, z_2)$. Figure 1 illustrates these concepts.

People in *TDPS* $(z_1, z_2)$ are certainly not rich. Hence, being poor along all dimensions might be a definition of multidimensional poverty. But it is also possible that a person has one attribute, say education, above its threshold; but the other attribute, the composite good, lies below the corresponding threshold. Such a person may not be called rich because of his/her high education. If we do not allow trade off between the two attributes, one of which has its quantities below the threshold and for the other the quantities are above the threshold, then another, possibly more satisfactory definition of poverty is that person $i$ is poor if $x_{ij} < z_j$ holds for at least one $j$. In fact, one of our axioms, Focus, rules out this type of trade off. As a practical example of this, we note that an old beggar cannot be regarded as rich because of his high longevity.

In terms of the *SDPS*$(z_j)$, the first definition is equivalent to considering all people in the *intersection* of the *SDPS*$(z_1)$ and *SDPS*$(z_2)$, which is *TDPS* $(z_1, z_2)$, as poor. With the second definition, poverty is defined by the *union* of the two *SDPS* regions. The next section will show that this distinction becomes crucial when considering multidimensional poverty orderings.

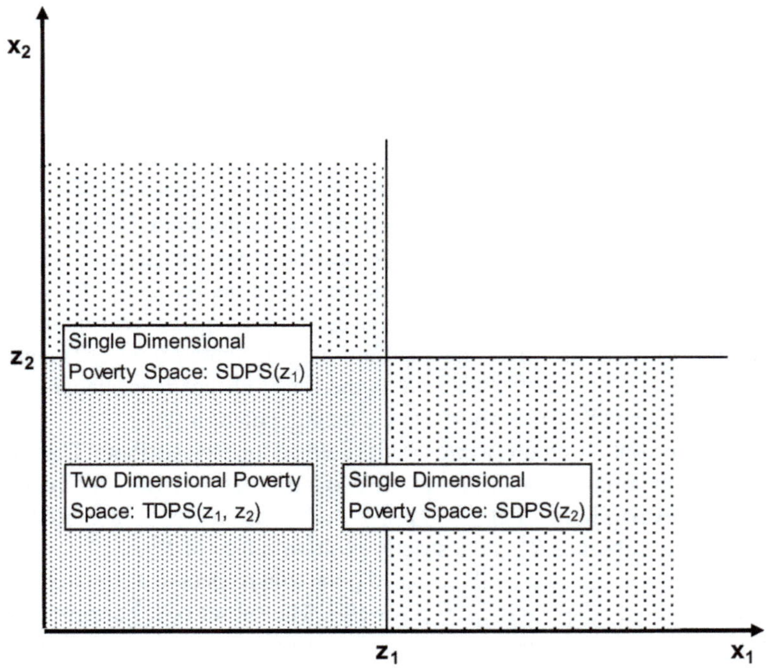


**Fig. 1** Alternative definitions of poverty in the two dimensional case

A multidimensional poverty measure $P^n$ is a nonconstant real-valued function defined on $M^n \otimes Z$. For any $X \in M^n$, $z \in Z$, the functional value $P^n(X; z)$ gives the extent of poverty associated with the attribute matrix $X$ and the threshold vector $z$.

Sen (1976) suggested two basic postulates for an income or a consumption poverty measure. They are: (i) the monotonicity axiom, which demands poverty not to decrease under a reduction in the income of a poor, and (ii) the transfer axiom, which requires that poverty should not decrease if there is a transfer of income from a poor person to anyone who has a higher income. Following Sen, variants of these two axioms and several other axioms have been suggested in the literature (see, for example, Foster et al. 1984; Donaldson and Weymark 1986; Chakravarty 1990; Foster and Shorrocks 1991 and Bourguignon and Fields 1997).

Following Tsui (2002) and Bourguignon and Chakravarty (1999, 2003), we now suggest some properties for an arbitrary measure $P^n$ which are immediate generalizations of an income/consumption poverty measure. All properties apply for any strictly positive $n$.

**Focus (FOC)**: For any $(X; z) \in M^n \otimes Z$ and for any person $i$ and attribute $j$ such that $x_{ij} \geq z_j$, an increases in $x_{ij}$, given that all other attribute levels in $X$ remain fixed, does not changes the poverty value $P^n(X; z)$.[4]
**Normalization (NOM)**: For any $(X; z) \in M^n \otimes Z$ if $x_{ij} \geq z_j$ for all $i$ and $j$, then $P^n(X; z) = 0$.
**Monotonicity (MON)**: For any $(X; z) \in M^n \otimes Z$, any person $i$ and attribute $j$ such that $x_{ij} < z_j$, an increase in $x_{ij}$, given that other attribute levels in $X$ remain fixed, does not increase the poverty value $P^n(X; z)$.
**Principle of Population (POP)**: For any $(X; z) \in M^n \otimes Z$, $P^n(X; z) = P^{nm}\left[X^{(m)}, z\right]$, where $X^{(m)}$ is the $m$-fold replication of $X$ and $m \geq 2$ is arbitrary.
**Symmetry (SYM)**: For any $(X; z) \in M^n \otimes Z$, $P^n(X; z) = P^n(\pi X; z)$, where $\pi$ is any permutation matrix of order $n$.[5]
**Subgroup Decomposability (SUD)**: For $X^i \in M^{n_i}, i = 1, 2, \ldots, k$; $z \in Z$, $P^n(X; z) = \sum_{i=1}^{k} \frac{n_i}{n} P^{n_i}(X^i; z)$, where $X \in M$ is the attribute matrix $\begin{bmatrix} X^1 \\ X^2 \\ \\ X^k \end{bmatrix}$ with $n$ rows and 2 columns and $\sum_{i=1}^{k} n_i = n$.
**Continuity (CON)**: For any $z \in Z$, $P^n$ is continuous on $M^n$.
**Transfers Principle (TRP)**: For any $z \in Z$, and $X, Y \in M^n$ if $X^P = BY^P$ and $BY^P$ is not a permutation of the rows of $Y^P$, where $X^P(Y^P)$ is the attribute matrix of the

[4]One may think of a stronger version of this axiom where the condition $x_{ij} \geq z_j$ would apply simultaneously to all $j$. See Bourguignon and Chakravarty (2003).

[5]A square matrix with entries 0 and 1 is called a permutation matrix if each of its rows and columns sums to one.

poor corresponding to $X$ ($Y$) and $B = (b_{ij})$ is some bistochastic matrix of appropriate order ($b_{ij} \geq 0$, $\sum_i b_{ij} = \sum_j b_{ij} = 1$), then $P^n(X; z) \leq P^n(Y; z)$.

**FOC** states that if a person is not poor with respect to an attribute, then giving him more of this attribute does not change the intensity of poverty, even if he/ she is poor in the other attribute. Thus, **FOC** rules out trade off between the two attributes in an *SDPS*. In other words, more education above the threshold is of no use if the composite good is below its threshold. This, however, does not exclude the possibility of a trade off in *TDPS*. **NOM** is a cardinality property of the poverty index. It says that if all persons in a society are nonpoor in both the dimensions, then the index value is zero. According to **MON**, poverty does not increase if the condition of a poor improves in any dimension. According to POP, if an attribute matrix is replicated several times, then poverty remains unchanged. Since by replication we can transform two different sized matrices into the same size, POP enables us to make for intertemporal and interregional poverty comparisons. **SYM** demands anonymity. Any characteristic other than the attributes under consideration, for instance, the names of the individuals, is immaterial for the measurement of poverty. **CON** ensures that minor changes in attribute quantities will not give rise to an abrupt jump in the value of the poverty index. Therefore, a continuous poverty index will not be oversensitive to minor observational errors on basic need quantities.

According to **SUD**, if a population is partitioned into several subgroups, say $k$, defined along ethnic, geographical or other lines, then the overall poverty is the population share weighted average of subgroup poverty levels. The contribution of subgroup $i$ to overall poverty is $n_i P(X^i; z)/n$ and overall poverty will exactly decrease by this amount if poverty in subgroup $i$ is eliminated. Thus, **SUD** is quite appealing from a policy point of view in the sense that it enables us to identify the subgroups that contribute most to overall poverty and hence to implement effective antipoverty policies. Using **SUD** we can write the poverty index as

$$P^n(X; z) = \frac{1}{n}\sum_{i=1}^{n} P^1(x_i; z) = \frac{1}{n}\sum_{i=1}^{n} p(x_i; z).$$

Since $p(x_i; z)$ depends only on person $i's$ attributes, we call it 'individual poverty function'. Finally, TRP shows that if we transform the attribute matrix $Y^P$ of the poor in $Y$ to the corresponding matrix $X^P$ in $X$ by some equalizing operation, then poverty in X will not be higher than that poverty in $Y$. Under **SUD**, **TRP** holds if and only if the individual poverty function is convex (Kolm 1977).

Let us now consider a property which takes care of the essence of multidimensional measurement through correlation between attributes. By taking into account the association of attributes, as captured by the degree of correlation between them, this property also brings out the distinguishing features between single and multidimensional poverty measurements. To illustrate the property, consider the two-person two-attribute case in Fig. 2. Suppose that $x_{11} > x_{21}$ and $x_{12} < x_{22}$. Now consider a switch of attribute 2 between the two persons. This switch increases the correlation between the attributes because person 1 who had more of attribute 1 has now more

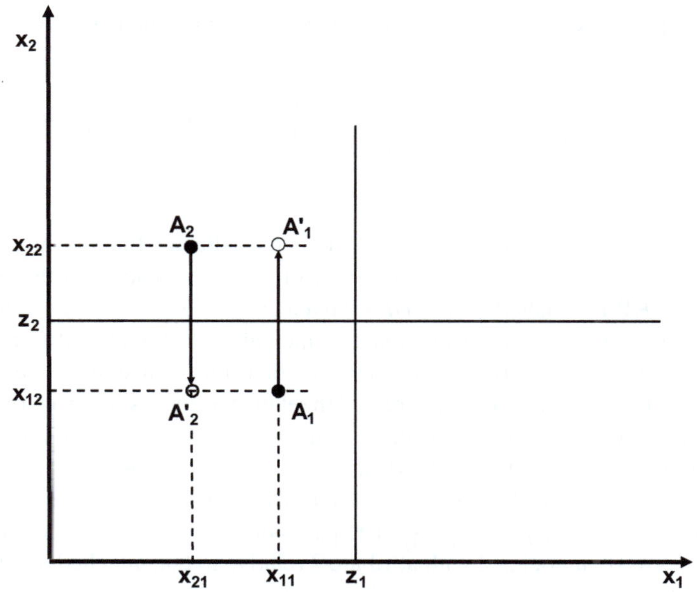


**Fig. 2** Correlation increasing switch: $(A_1, A_2) \rightarrow (A_1', A_2')$

of attribute 2 too. Now, suppose that attributes 1 and 2 are *substitutes*, or, in other words, that one attribute may compensate for the lack of another in the definition of individual poverty. Then, increasing the correlation between the two attributes must not decrease poverty. Indeed, the switch just defined does not modify the marginal distribution of each attribute but decreases the extent to which the lack of one attribute may be compensated by the availability of the other. A parallel argument will establish that poverty should not increase under a correlation increasing switch if the two attributes are complements.[6]

We state this principle formally for substitutes as:

**Nondecreasing Poverty Under Correlation Increasing Switch (NDP)**: For any $(X, z) \in M^n \otimes Z$, if $Y \in M^n$ is obtained from $X$ by a correlation increasing switch of an attribute between two persons who are poor in both attributes, then $P^n(X; z) \leq P^n(Y; z)$ if the two attributes are substitutes.

The analogous property which demands poverty not to increase under such a switch when the attributes are complements is denoted by **NIP**. Note that **NDP** and **NIP** hold in *TDPS* only and the implicit trade off never allows a person to cross the poverty limit of an attribute.

It may be worthwhile to give an example of a measure that satisfies all the above postulates. The following general form of a multidimensional poverty index which

[6]For further discussions on this issue, see Atkinson and Bourguignon (1982) and Bourguignon and Chakravarty (1999, 2003). Bourguignon and Chakravarty (1999) employed this property to examine the elasticity of substitution between proportional shortfalls of attributes from respective thresholds.

meets these properties has been suggested by Bourguignon and Chakravarty (1999):

$$P^n_{\alpha,\beta,b}(X;z) = \frac{1}{n}\sum_i \left[ I(x_{i1} < z_1)\left(1 - \frac{x_{i1}}{z_1}\right) + b^{\frac{\beta}{\alpha}} I(x_{i2} < z_2)\left(1 - \frac{x_{i2}}{z_2}\right)^{\beta}\right]^{\frac{\beta}{\alpha}}, \tag{1}$$

where $\alpha \geq 1$, $\beta \geq 1$ and $b > 0$, and $I()$ is an indicator function that takes on the value one or zero according as $x_{ij} < z_j$ or $x_{ij} \geq z_j$. The condition $\alpha \geq 1$ ensure that **TRP** is satisfied in an *SDPS*. Given $\alpha \geq 1$, $\beta \geq 1$ guarantees that **TRP** holds in TDPS $(z_1, z_2)$. An increase in the value of $\beta$ makes the contours of the individual poverty function more convex to the origin. Since in (1) the shortfalls $(z_1 - x_{i1})$ and $(z_2 - x_{i2})$ have been expressed in relative terms (as fractions of $z_1$ and $z_2$ respectively), the index satisfies a scale invariance condition—when all quantities of an attribute as well as its thresholds are multiplied by a positive scalar, poverty remains unchanged. The elasticity of substitution between the two relative shortfalls $(1 - x_{i1}/z_1)$ and $(1 - x_{i2}/z_2)$ is $\frac{1}{(\beta-1)}$. The parameter $b\,(> 0)$ shows the importance attached to poverty associated with attribute 2 relative to that attached to attribute 1.

The poverty index (1) is identical to the familiar Foster–Greer–Thorbecke (FGT), or "$P_\alpha$", index in the two *SDPSs*. In that sense, it is a straight generalization of that single dimensional poverty measure to the two dimensional case, with $\beta$ representing the substitutability between the two dimensions in TDPS$(z_1, z_2)$. For $1 \leq \beta \leq \alpha$, the two attributes are substitutes and the measure (1) satisfies **NDP**. For $\beta = 1$, there is a perfectly elastic trade off between the attributes in TDPS$(z_1, z_2)$. For $\beta > \alpha$, the measure satisfies **NIP** since the two attributes are then complements.[7] As $\beta \to \infty$, the resulting index becomes

$$P^n_{\alpha,\infty}(X;z) = \frac{1}{n}\sum_i \left[1 - \min\left(1, \frac{x_{i1}}{z_1}, \frac{x_{i2}}{z_2}\right)\right]^{\alpha}. \tag{2}$$

In this case, the isopoverty contours are of rectangular shape—the two attributes are perfect complements. Note that the index in (2) requires information only on relative shortfalls of different persons and a poverty aversion parameter.

An alternative of interest arises from the specification

$$P^n(X;z) = \sum_{j=1}^{2}\sum_{i=1}^{n} f_j\left(\frac{x_{ij}}{z_j}\right), \tag{3}$$

where the real-valued function $f_j$ defined on $[0, \infty)$ is nonincreasing, convex and $f_j(t) = 0$ for all $t \geq 1$. As an illustration, we may choose $f_j(t) = -\alpha_j \log t$, where $\alpha_j > 0$ is a constant and $t \in (0, 1]$. We may interpret $\alpha_j$ as the weight given to

[7] Under SUD, attributes are substitutes or complements depending on whether the cross derivative of the individual poverty function $p(x_1, x_2; z_1, z_2)$ with respect to $x_1$ and $x_2$ is positive or negative.

attribute $j$ in the overall poverty index. Then the resulting index is

$$P^n(x; z) = \sum_{j=1}^{2} \sum_{i=1}^{n} \alpha_j \log\left(\frac{z_j}{\hat{x}_{ij}}\right), \quad (4)$$

where $\hat{x}_{ij} = \min(x_{ij}, z_j) > 0$. This is a simple multidimensional extension of the well-known Watts index.[8] Note that because of additivity the index in (3) [hence in (4)] is not sensitive to correlation increasing switch.

## 3 Multidimensional Poverty Orderings

The concern of this section is the ranking of attribute matrices by a chosen set of poverty measures assuming that the threshold limits are common. It is assumed at the outset that the poverty index satisfies the following set (**S**) of properties among the ones listed above: **FOC**, **SYM**, **POP**, **SUD** and **twice differentiability**. The last property replaces **CON**. Also, the exposition will be simplified by consideration of a continuous representation of the bivariate distribution, rather than the discrete formulation used until now. The analysis that follows relies on stochastic dominance results originally established by Hadar and Russel (1974) and Levy and Paroush (1974), and extended to multidimensional inequality by Atkinson and Bourguignon (1982). [9]

As this section is formulated in terms of a continuum of population, the suffix $i$ in the vector $x_i$ is dropped, and the distribution of attributes $x = (x_1, x_2)$ in the population is represented by the cumulative distribution function $H(x_1, x_2)$, defined on the $[0, a_1] \times [0, a_2]$ range. The objective is to compare two distributions represented by the distribution functions $H$ and $H^*$, the difference of which will be denoted by $\Delta H(x_1, x_2)\ (= H(x_1, x_2) - H^*(x_1, x_2))$.

In view of the **SUD** property, poverty associated to distribution $H$, may be written as:

$$P(H, z) = \int_0^{a_1} \int_0^{a_2} p(x_1, x_2; z_1, z_2)\, \mathrm{d}H,$$

where $p(x_1, x_2; z_1, z_2)$ is the level of poverty associated with a person whose attributes are $(x_1, x_2)$. To simplify notation, the individual poverty functions $p(x_1, x_2; z_1, z_2)$

[8] A characterization of this index was developed by Chakravarty and Silber (2007).

[9] Kosvevoy (1998) demonstrated equivalence between cone Lorenz majorization and cone directional majorization, where a distribution is said to be cone directional majorized by another if at any set of prices in a cone the expenditure distribution in the former is less dispersed than that in the latter (see also Koshevoy 1995 and Koshevoy and Mosler 1996). This is equivalent to using linear poverty functions. In contrast, we use all possible functions satisfying the desirable axioms.

will be written as $\pi_z(x_1, x_2)$ in what follows. The difference in poverty between distributions $H$ and $H^*$ is then defined as:

$$\Delta P(z) = \int_0^{a_2}\int_0^{a_2} \pi_z(x_1, x_2)\,\mathrm{d}\Delta H. \tag{5}$$

The distribution $H$ is then said to (weakly) dominate $H^*$ in the sense of $P^c$ when $\Delta P(z)$ is (nonpositive) negative for all individual poverty functions $\pi_z(x_1, x_2)$ belonging to the class $P^c$.

Note that **FOC**, **NOM**, and **MON** imply the following properties (**T**) for the function $\pi_z(x_1, x_2)$:

$$\pi_z(x_1, x_2) = 0 \quad \text{for } x_1 \geq z_1 \text{ and } x_2 \geq z_2;$$
$$\pi_{z1}(x_1, x_2) \leq 0 \text{ and } \pi_{z2}(x_1, x_2) \leq 0 \quad \text{for } x_1 < z_1 \text{ and } x_2 < z_2;$$
$$\pi_{z12}(x_1, x_2) = 0 \quad \text{for } x_1 \geq z_1 \text{ or } x_2 \geq z_2;$$

where $\pi_{zi}(x_1, x_2)$ is the derivative of $\pi_z(x_1, x_2)$ with respect to $x_i$ and $\pi_{z12}(x_1, x_2)$ is the second cross derivative. As stated in footnote 7, **NDP** requires $\pi_{z12}(x_1, x_2) \geq 0$ in the *TDPS* $(z_1, z_2)$, whereas **NIP** requires $\pi_{z12}(x_1, x_2) \leq 0$.

Following the discussion on the importance of the **NIP/NDP** properties in the preceding section, three classes of poverty indices will be considered in what follows:

*Class* $P^+$: Properties (**S**), **MON** and **NDP**,
*Class* $P^-$: Properties (**S**), **MON** and **NIP**,
*Class* $P^0$: Properties (**S**), **MON** and $\pi_{z12}(x_1, x_2) = 0$ in *TDPS*,

Clearly, $P^0$, which corresponds to additive individual poverty function, may be considered as an intermediate case between classes $P^+$ and $P^-$.

Following the stochastic dominance literature, integrating (5) by parts and taking into account properties (**T**) above, we get the following decomposition formula—see Appendix:

$$\Delta P(H, H^*, z) = -\int_0^{z1} \pi_{z1}(x_1, z_2)\Delta H_1(x_1)\mathrm{d}x_1 - \int_0^{z2} \pi_{z2}(x_1, z_2)\Delta H_2(x_2)\mathrm{d}x_2$$
$$+ \int_0^{z1}\int_0^{z2} \pi_{z12}(x_1, x_2)\Delta H(x_1, x_2)\mathrm{d}x_1\mathrm{d}x_2, \tag{6}$$

where $\Delta H_1(x_1)$ stands for the difference in the marginal distribution of attribute 1, i.e., $\Delta H(x_1, a_2)$ and $\Delta H_2(x_2)$ is the analogous notation for attribute 2.

On the basis of (6), the following proposition follows—see Appendix for proof.

**Proposition 1**
*Let H and $H^*$ be two bivariate distribution functions on the same range* $[0,\ a_1] \times [0,\ a_2]$. *Then the following conditions are equivalent*:

(i) $\Delta P(H, H^*, z) \leq 0$ for all poverty indices belonging to $P^+$.
(ii) (a) $\Delta H_i(x_i) \leq 0$ for all $x_i < z_i$ and for $i = 1,\ 2$; (b) $\Delta H(x_1, x_2) \leq 0$ for all $x_1 < z_1$ and $x_2 < z_2$.

In other words, poverty dominance under properties (**S**), **MON** and **NDP** requires: (a) the poverty headcount to be lower in each dimension for all poverty thresholds below the thresholds $z_i$, that is, one dimensional dominance in the sense of Atkinson (1987) and Foster and Shorrocks (1988a, b), the poverty headcount to be lower in the TDPS $(x_1, x_2)$ defined by any combination of poverty lines below the thresholds $z_i$. Overall dominance thus requires single dimensional dominance in each dimension plus two-dimensional dominance over the set of persons who are poor simultaneously in all dimensions.

It is also shown in the Appendix that:

$$\begin{aligned}\Delta P(H, H^*, z) = &-\int_0^{z1} \pi_{z1}(x_1, 0)\Delta H_1(x_1)\mathrm{d}x_1\\ &-\int_0^{z2} \pi_{z2}(0, x_1)\Delta H_2(x_2)\mathrm{d}x_2\\ &+\int_0^{z1}\int_0^{z2} \pi_{z12}(x_1, x_2)[\Delta H(x_1, x_2) - \Delta H_1(x_1) - \Delta H_2(x_2)]\mathrm{d}x_1\mathrm{d}x_2.\end{aligned} \tag{7}$$

The decomposition formula (7) leads to a slightly different proposition—see Appendix for proof.

**Proposition 2**
*Let H and $H^*$ be two bivariate distribution functions on the same range* $[0,\ a_1] \times [0,\ a_2]$. *Then the following conditions are equivalent*:

(i) $\Delta P(H, H^*, z) \leq 0$ for all poverty indices belonging to $P^-$.
(ii) $\Delta H_1(x_1) + \Delta H_2(x_2) - \Delta H(x_1, x_2) \leq 0$ for all $x_1 < z_1$ and/or $x_2 < z_2$.

Note that condition (ii) implies single dimensional poverty dominance, as in Proposition 1 (ii.a), when the condition is evaluated at $x_1 = 0$ or $x_2 = 0$. Dominance in two dimensions thus requires single dimensional dominance, irrespective of whether **NDP** or **NIP** holds. The two-dimensional dominance condition for **NIP** differs from the one obtained under **NDP**. In the **NIP** case, dominance requires the poverty headcount not to be higher in the *union*, rather than in the *intersection* of *SDPS* defined by all possible combinations of poverty lines below the original thresholds.

The difference between the two dominance criteria obtained under **NDP** and **NIP** is illustrated in Fig. 3. Consider any point A in the original TDPS $(z_1, z_2)$. **NDP** dominance requires the poverty headcount corresponding to the area (II) South-West of A not to be greater with distribution *H*. Clearly, (II) is the *TDPS* corresponding to A, that is, corresponding to poverty lines $x_1$ and $x_2$. This region may thus be denoted by TDPS $(x_1, x_2)$. Thus, with **NDP**, the poverty headcount must not higher with *H* than with $H^*$ for all possible TDPS $(x_1, x_2)$ defined within the original TDPS $(z_1, z_2)$. With **NIP**, the headcount must not be greater in the region consisting of the three areas (I), (II), and (III). This rectangular region actually corresponds to the union of *SDPS* $(x_1)$ and *SDPS* $(x_2)$—I + (II) and (II) + (III). Interestingly enough, **NDP** thus appears to be associated with the *TDPS* definition of poverty, whereas **NIP** is associated with a definition of poverty based on the union on *SDPS*.

The intuition behind the preceding proposition is as follows. Consider the two alternative definitions of poverty shown in Fig. 1 and an increasing correlation switch as in Fig. 2. Then consider all combinations of poverty lines $x_1$ and $x_2$ below the original threshold levels $z_1$ and $z_2$. In Fig. 4, these combinations are represented by a point like B. The **NDP** property requires that poverty should not be decreasing with a correlation increasing switch. If the poverty headcount is required not to decrease for all possible combinations of $x_1$ and $x_2$, then the headcount ratio must be defined on the area *TDPS* $(x_1, x_2)$, which lies South-West of point B. In fact, it can

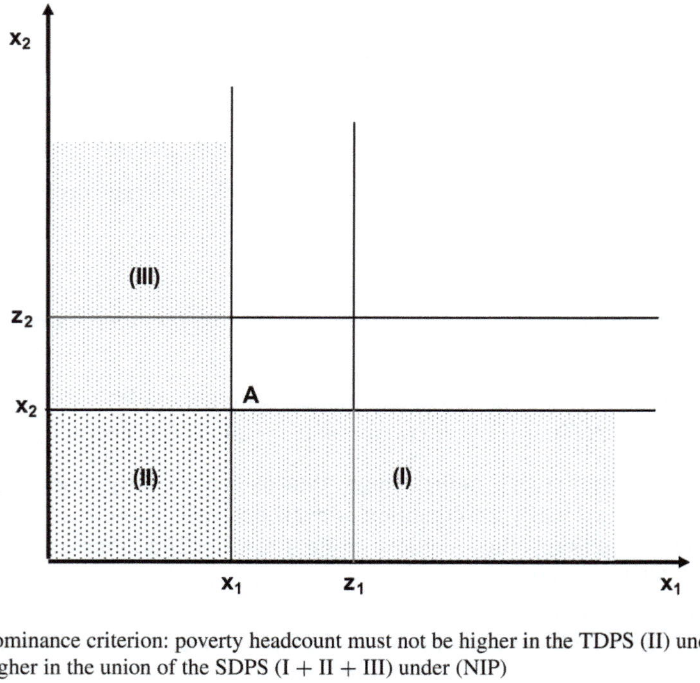


**Fig. 3** Dominance criterion: poverty headcount must not be higher in the TDPS (II) under (NDP) and not higher in the union of the SDPS (I + II + III) under (NIP)

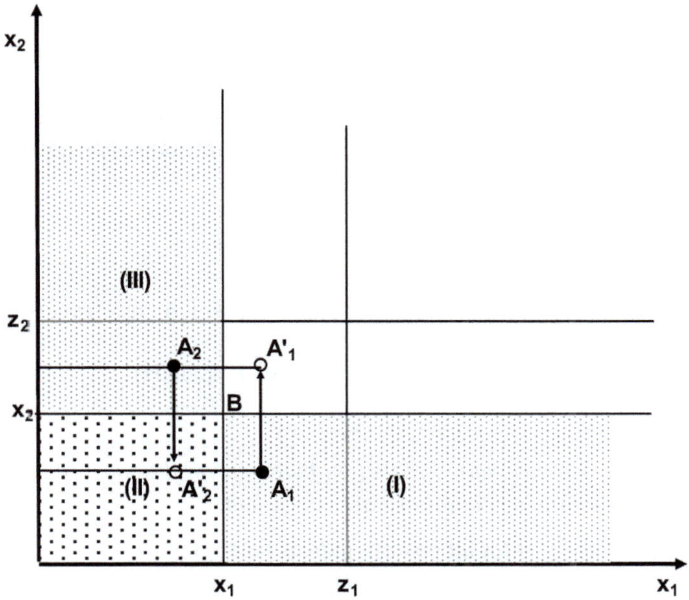


**Fig. 4** A correlation increasing switch does not reduce the poverty headcount in the TDPS regions (II) but does not increase it in the union of the SDPS regions

be seen in Fig. 4 that the correlation increasing switch does not modify the poverty headcount in *TDPS* $(x_1, x_2)$ as long as point B is outside the rectangle $A_2A_2'A_1A_1'$ and it necessarily increases it if it lies inside that rectangle. (To see this, consider a leftward horizontal movement of the point B so that it lies on the left-hand side of the line $A_2A_2'$. Given that the poverty thresholds are set at $(x_1, x_2)$, the correlation increasing switch changes the positions of the persons in the sense that person 2 who was rich at B becomes poor and the reverse happens for person 1. The switch thus keeps the headcount index unaltered. The other cases can be proven similarly.) The opposite occurs when we take the union of *SDPS* $(x_1)$ and *SDPS* $(x_2)$. The headcount would not change for all B outside the rectangle but the headcount in the region (I) + (II) + (III) goes down if B is inside the rectangle. The latter result violates the **NDP** property, but fulfills **NIP**.

Coming back to the issue of the definition of two-dimensional poverty discussed earlier, the preceding propositions would seem to imply that overall poverty should be measured over TDPS $(z_1, z_2)$ if the two attributes are taken as substitutes and over the union of SDPS $(z_1)$ and SDPS $(z_2)$ if they are complements. This would be pushing the argument too far, however. The distinction between defining poverty on the *TDPS* or the union of the two *SDPS* arises when considering dominance conditions of one distribution over another. Consideration of headcount ratios in the union or the intersection of areas SDPS $(x_1)$ and SDPS $(x_2)$ arises only within the basic rectangle $[0, z_1] \times [0, z_2]$. Outside that rectangle only one dimension of poverty matters and dominance is taken care of there by the marginal dominance conditions on $\Delta H_1(x_1)$ and $\Delta H_2(x_2)$, as shown in the preceding propositions. This point is further strengthened and analyzed by Atkinson (2003).

The relevance of the two one dimensional dominance conditions appears still more clearly in the limit case where the two attributes are neither complements nor substitutes. In that case, the second cross derivative of the individual poverty function $\pi_z(x_1, x_2)$ is nil, so that the function is additive:

$$\pi_z\,(x_1, x_2) = p(x_1, x_2; z_1, z_2) = f_1(x_1; z_1) + f_2(x_2; z_2). \tag{8}$$

One such example is the poverty gap function, which corresponds to the case $b = 1$, $\alpha = 1$ and $\beta = 1$ in Eq. (1).

The following proposition is then proved in the Appendix.

**Proposition 3**

*Let H and H* be two bivariate distribution functions on the same range* $[0,\ a_1] \times [0,\ a_2]$. *Then the following conditions are equivalent*:

(i) $\Delta P\,(H, H^*, z) \leq 0$ for all poverty indices belonging to $P^0$.
(ii) $\Delta H_1(x_1) \leq 0$ for all $x_1 < z_1$ and $\Delta H_2(x_2) \leq 0$ for all $x_2 < z_2$.

The preceding propositions give a neat interpretation of the multivariate first order stochastic dominance results when applied to multidimensional poverty ordering. It is not clear whether second-order stochastic dominance can be employed analogously. The reason behind this is that the second order dominance criterion involves restrictions on the signs of third and fourth order derivatives of the poverty function. The interpretation of these restrictions is not obvious in poverty context. However, if $\pi_z(x_1, x_2)$ is additive across components, then we have an unambiguous comparability result. Note that under additivity the attributes are treated independently and our result reduces to single dimensional ordering.

**Proposition 4**

*Let H and H* be two bivariate distributions on the common domain* $[0,\ a_1] \times [0,\ a_2]$. *Then the following conditions are equivalent*:

(i) $\Delta P\,(H, H^*, z) \leq 0$ for all poverty indices belonging to $P^0$ and satisfying *TRP*.
(ii) $\int_0^{x1} \Delta H_1(u)\,du \leq 0$ for all $x_1 < z_1$ and $\int_0^{x2} \Delta H_2(u)\,du \leq 0$ for all $x_2 < z_2$.

Note that this proposition makes use of the transfer principle. Given additivity of the poverty index *P*, *TRP* simply means that $f_1'' \geq 0$ and $f_2'' \geq 0$, that is, each $p_{ii} \geq 0$. A well-known equivalent condition of the criteria, stated in the second part of proposition 4, is that poverty gaps must not be higher under distribution *H* than under $H^*$ for all poverty lines $x_i$ below the threshold level $z_i$, where $i = 1,\ 2$.

# 4 A Numerical Illustration

To illustrate the preceding propositions and see how they can be applied, consider the very simple example portrayed in Figs. 5, 6, 7 and 8. The two dimensions of poverty are income and education. The income poverty line is set at $ 35 per month whereas education poor are those people with less than 6 years of schooling. To simplify, these two dimensions are further 'discretized' into two categories of equal magnitude: from $0 to $17.5 and from $17.5 to $35 on the one hand, and below 3 years of education and from 3 to 5 on the other hand. Differences in education and income within these categories are simply ignored, but it would be a simple matter to generalize this example to a finer grid.

The initial distribution of a population of 12 individuals is represented by squares. The new distribution is represented by diamonds. Except for one or two cases, diamonds are close to squares and should be considered essentially as identical observations.

The application of the dominance criteria consists of counting the number of observations in the intersection or union of the *SDPS* areas at the vertices of the grid ($A_1$, $A_2$, $B_1$, $B_2$) within the overall poverty rectangle [0, 35] × [0, 6]. The bottom pair of numbers corresponds to the *TDPS* headcounts in the initial and in the new distribution. The top pair corresponds to the headcounts in the union of the *SDPS*.

Figure 5 depicts the effects of a dominant single shift. The solid arrow shows a drop in income poverty for one individual in the population. Poverty unambiguously

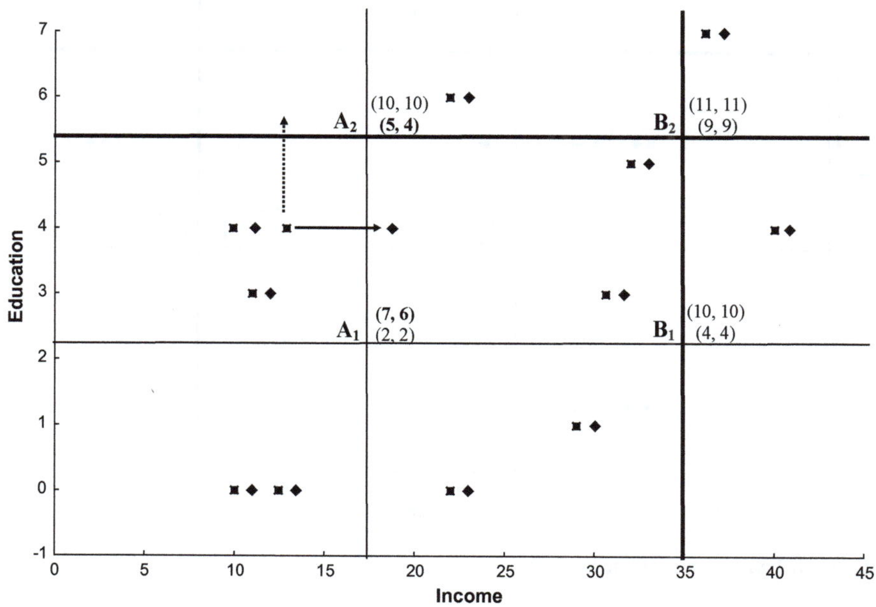


**Fig. 5** Overall dominant single shift

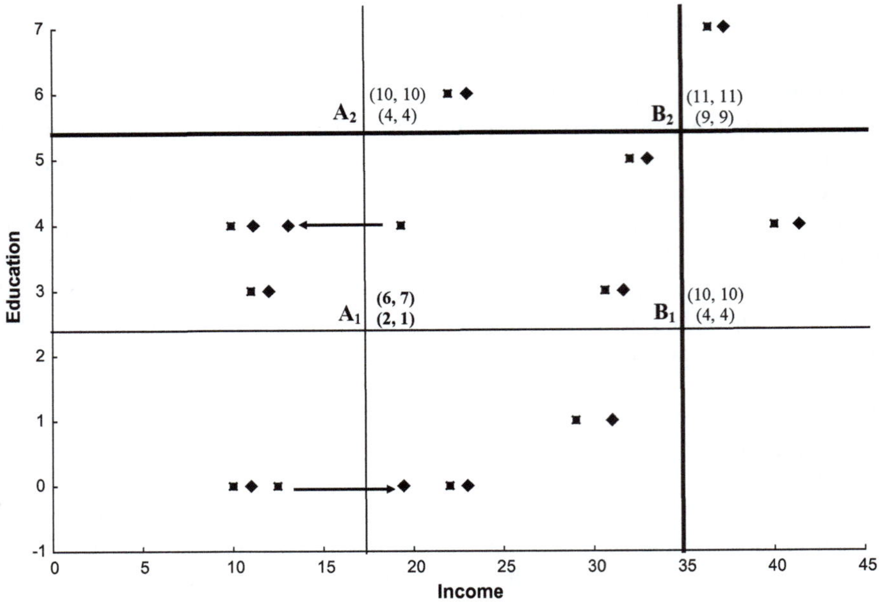


**Fig. 6** NDP type dominant double shift

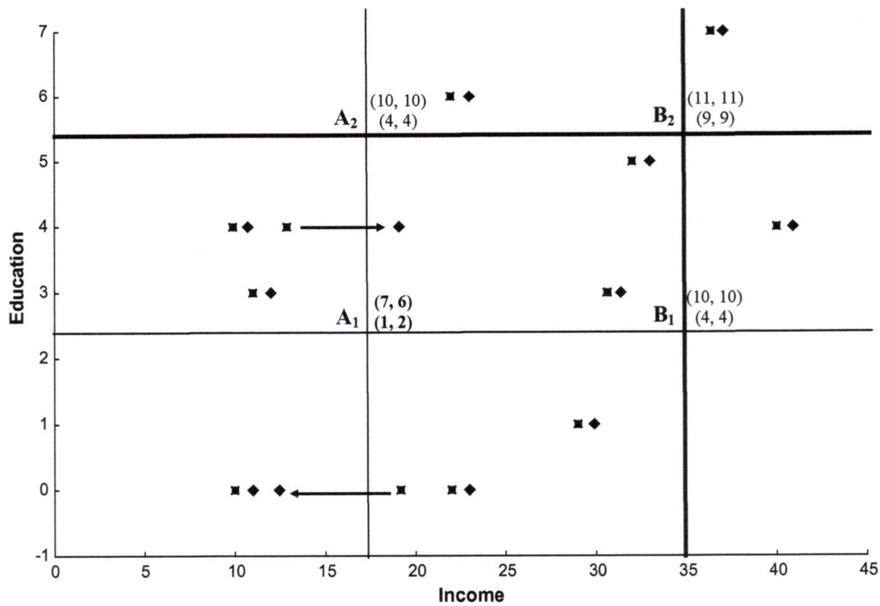


**Fig. 7** NIP type dominant double shift

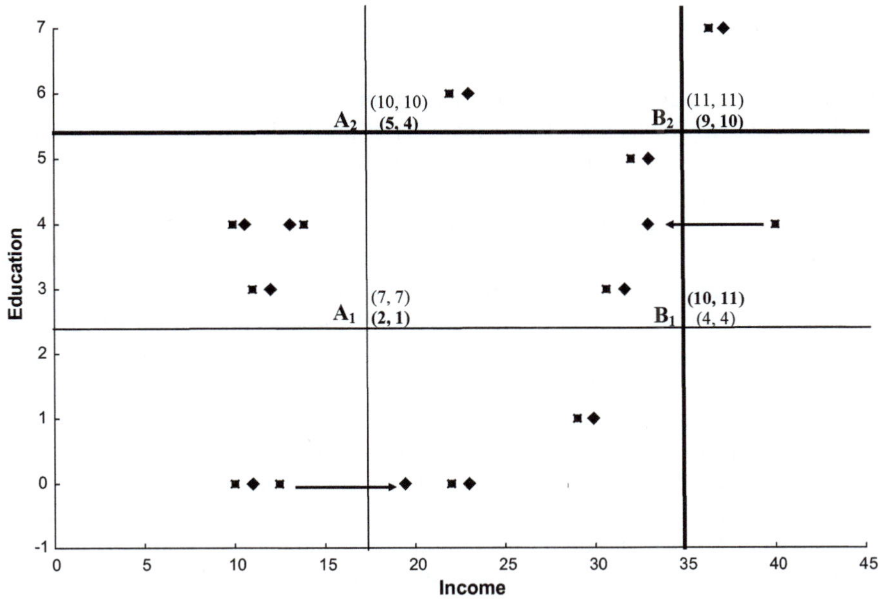


**Fig. 8** Non-dominant double shift

declines as can be seen from the headcount pairs at $A_1$, $A_2$. Note that all dominance criteria are satisfied, whether one considers the intersection or the union of the two *SDPS*. The same result would be obtained with the dotted arrow and also if the shift originated above one of the two poverty lines.

Figure 6 shows the effect of a 'correlation decreasing' switch. The income of one individual goes up whereas that of another, more educated goes down. In agreement with the NDP property, there is dominance at $A_1$ when we consider the *TDPS* area, but the dominance criterion is violated at the same point when considering the union of *SDPS* criterion. Figure 7 shows the opposite case of a correlation increasing switch that violates the former dominance condition and satisfies the latter.

Finally, Fig. 8 shows the same type of double and opposite shift but at very different levels of income, with an individual moving from above to below the income poverty line. There cannot be dominance in that case since marginal dominance does not hold in the income dimension. One can check that the pairs of headcounts in the grid confirm this result. There is an improvement in the bottom pair at $A_1$ and $A_2$, but there is a worsening at $B_2$. Likewise, there is no change in the top pair except a worsening at $B_1$.

This simple example is useful in showing how the dominance criteria derived in this paper can be practically applied. It is indeed a simple matter to extend it to more complex case, more numerous populations and a finer grid of sub-poverty lines.

## 5 Conclusion

In income-based poverty measurement it is assumed that individuals in a society are distinguished only by income. But in many cases in addition to low income a person may have insufficient levels of other attributes of well-being e.g., literacy, health care, etc. Therefore, a genuine measure of poverty should be based on monetary as well as nonmonetary attributes of well-being. A particular measure of poverty will completely rank alternative distributions of attributes of well-being. But two different measures satisfying the same set of postulates may order two distributions in different directions. Therefore, it seems worthwhile to investigate whether one distribution can be unambiguously regarded as displaying not more poverty than another for certain class of poverty indices. This paper may be regarded as a step toward this direction.

A simple generalization of the existing results for first order income poverty dominance has been provided. First, two-dimensional dominance of a distribution over another requires one-dimensional dominance for the marginal distribution of each attribute. Second, it requires the multidimensional poverty headcount not to be higher with the first distribution than with the second for all combinations of poverty lines below the original threshold levels. However, the sets on which the headcount is evaluated differs depending on whether the two attributes may be taken as substitutes or complements. This second requirement is irrelevant in the case where the two attributes are neither complements nor substitutes. In this case, two-dimensional poverty dominance is simply equivalent to one-dimensional poverty dominance for each attribute. It may be noted that our results can be generalized to the $n$-dimensional case, but for expositional ease we have considered the two-attribute case only.

## Appendix

**Derivation of formula** (6). Integrate by parts the definition of the dominance condition (5) with respect to $x_2$. This yields:

$$\begin{aligned}\Delta P(H, H^*, z) &= \int_0^{a1}\int_0^{a2} \pi_z(x_1, x_2)\mathrm{d}\Delta H \\ &= \int_0^{a1}\left[\pi_z(x_1, x_2)\int_0^{x2} \mathrm{d}\Delta H(x_1, u_2)\right]_{x_2=0}^{x_2=a_2} \\ &\quad - \int_0^{a1}\int_0^{a2} \pi_{z2}(x_1, x_2)\left[\int_0^{x2} \mathrm{d}\Delta H(x_1, u_2)\right]\mathrm{d}x_2. \end{aligned} \tag{9}$$

After evaluating the first square bracketed term, we get:

$$\Delta P(H, H^*, z) = \int_0^{a1} \pi_z(x_1, a_2) \mathrm{d}\Delta H(x_1, a_2) - \int_0^{a1}\int_0^{a2} \pi_{z2}(x_1, x_2) \left[ \int_0^{x2} \mathrm{d}\Delta H(x_1, u_2) \right] \mathrm{d}x_2. \tag{10}$$

Integrating the first term by parts yields:

$$\int_0^{a1} \pi_z(x_1, a_2) \mathrm{d}\Delta H(x_1, a_2) = [\pi_z(x_1, a_2)\Delta H_1(x_1)]_{x_1=0}^{x_1=a_1} - \int_0^{a1} \pi_{z1}(x_1, a_2)\Delta H_1(x_1)\mathrm{d}x_1, \tag{11}$$

where $H_1(x_1) = H(x_1, a_2)$ is the marginal distribution of $x_1$ and we have the symmetric notion for $x_2$.

Integration of the second term of (10) by parts with respect to $x_1$ leads to:

$$\begin{aligned}\int_0^{a1}\int_0^{a2} \pi_{z2}(x_1, x_2) \left[ \int_0^{x2} \mathrm{d}\Delta H(x_1, u_2) \right] \mathrm{d}x_2 &= \int_0^{a2} \left[ \pi_{z2}(x_1, x_2) \int_0^{x1}\int_0^{x2} \mathrm{d}\Delta H(u_1, u_2) \right]_{x_1=0}^{x_1=a_1} \mathrm{d}x_2 \\ &- \int_0^{a1}\int_0^{a_2} \pi_{z12}(x_1, x_2)\Delta H(x_1, x_2)\mathrm{d}x_1\mathrm{d}x_2. \end{aligned}\tag{12}$$

Finally putting together (11) and (12), and after evaluating the various functions at the bounds of integration intervals, we get:

$$\Delta P(H, H^*, z) = \int_0^{a1} \pi_{z1}(x_1, a_2)\Delta H_1(x_1) - \int_0^{a2} \pi_{z2}(a_1, x_2)\Delta H_2(x_2)$$

$$+\int_0^{a1}\int_0^{a_2}\pi_{z12}(x_1,x_2)\Delta H(x_1,x_2)\mathrm{d}x_1\mathrm{d}x_2. \qquad (13)$$

Let us now take into account the following properties implied by (**T**):

$$\pi_{zi}(x_1,x_2)=0 \quad \text{for } i=1,2, x_1\in[z_1,a_1] \text{ and } x_2\in[z_2,a_2]$$
$$\pi_{z12}(x_1,x_2)=0 \quad \text{for } x\in[z_1,a_1] \text{ or } x_2\in[z_2,a_2].$$

These conditions are sufficient to replace the bounds $a_1$ and $a_2$ in (13) by the poverty thresholds $z_1$ and $z_2$. This leads to decomposition (6) of the text:

$$\Delta P(H,H^*,z)=-\int_0^{z1}\pi_{z1}(x_1,z_2)\Delta H_1(x_1)\mathrm{d}x_1-\int_0^{z2}\pi_{z2}(x_1,z_2)\Delta H_2(x_2)\mathrm{d}x_2$$
$$+\int_0^{z1}\int_0^{z_2}\pi_{z12}(x_1,x_2)\Delta H(x_1,x_2)\mathrm{d}x_1\mathrm{d}x_2.$$

**Proof of Proposition 1**

The sufficiency part of Proposition 1 is obtained by the following argument. Since the sign of the first derivatives of $\pi_z(x_1,x_2)$ is implied by properties **T** and the sign of the second cross derivative is implied by **NDP**, the conditions $\Delta H_1(x_1)\leq 0$, $\Delta H_2(x_2)\leq 0$, $\Delta H(x_1,x_2)\leq 0$ for all $(x_1,x_2)\in[0,z_1]\times[0,z_2]$ make $\Delta P(H,H^*,z)$ nonpositive. Necessity is obtained by exhibiting a particular function $\pi_z(x_1,x_2)$ satisfying properties (**S**) and **NDP** and leading to $\Delta P(H,H^*,z)>0$ whenever one of the three conditions $\Delta H_1(x_1)\leq 0$, $\Delta H_2(x_2)\leq 0$, $\Delta H(x_1,x_2)\leq 0$ is not satisfied on some subset of $[0,z_1]\times[0,z_2]$. The proof of this is not given here.[10]

**Derivation of formula** (7): Some modification must be made in the preceding argument. Note first that

$$\pi_{z1}(x_1,z_2)=\pi_{z1}(x_1,0)+\int^{z2}\pi_{z12}(x_1,x_2)\mathrm{d}x_2,$$

and, symmetrically:

$$\pi_{z2}(z_1,x_2)=\pi_{z2}(0,x_2)+\int_0^{z1}\pi_{z12}(x_1,x_2)\mathrm{d}x_1.$$

Substituting these two expressions into (6) we get (7) of the text:

[10] See Atkinson and Bourguignon (1982) for a similar proof.

$$\Delta P(H, H^*, z) = -\int_0^{z1} \pi_{z1}(x_1, 0)\Delta H_1(x_1)\mathrm{d}x_1 - \int_0^{z2} \pi_{z2}(0, x_2)\Delta H_2(x_2)\mathrm{d}x_2$$
$$+ \int_0^{z1}\int_0^{z2} \pi_{z12}(x_1, x_2)[\Delta H(x_1, x_2) - \Delta H_1(x_1) - \Delta H_2(x_2)]\mathrm{d}x_1\mathrm{d}x_2.$$

Proposition 2 then follows from the same arguments as employed for Proposition 1.

**Proposition 3** Whether one chooses decomposition (6) or (7), additivity of the individual poverty function implies that $\pi_{z12}(x_1, x_2) = 0$. Then, Proposition 3 follows from the negative sign of the derivatives of the poverty function with respect to its arguments.

## References


Atkinson, A. B. (1987). On the measurement of poverty. *Econometrica, 5,* 244–263.

Atkinson, A. B. (1992). Measuring poverty and difference in family composition. *Economica, 59,* 1–16.

Atkinson, A. B. (2003). Multidimensional deprivation: Contrasting social welfare and counting approaches. *Journal of Economic Inequality, 1,* 51–65.

Atkinson, A. B. & Bourguignon, F. (1982). The comparison of multidimensioned distributions of economic status. *Review of Economic Studies, 49,* 183–201.

Bourguignon, F. & Chakravarty, S. R. (1999). A family of multidimensional poverty measures. In D. J. Slottjee (Ed.), *Advances in Econometrics, Income Distribution and Methodology of Science, Essays in Honor of C. Dagum*. New York: Springer–Verlag.

Bourguignon, F., & Chakravarty, S. R. (2003). Measurement of multidimensional poverty. *Journal of Economic Inequality, 1,* 25–49.

Bourguignon, F., & Fields, G. (1997). Discontinuous losses from poverty, generalized measures and optimal transfers to the poor. *Journal of Public Economics, 63,* 155–175.

Chakravarty, S. R. (1990). *Ethical social index numbers*. New York: Springer-Verlag.

Chakravarty, S. R. (2006). An axiomatic approach to multidimensional poverty measurement via fuzzy sets. In A. Lemmi & G. Betti (Eds.), *Fuzzy set approach to multidimensional poverty measurement*. New York: Springer-Verlag.

Chakravarty, S. R., Mukherjee, D., & Ranade, R. (1998). The family of subgroup and factor decomposable measures of multidimensional poverty. *Research on Economic Inequality, 8,* 175–194.

Chakravarty, S. R., & Silber, J. (2007). Measuring multidimensional poverty: The axiomatic approach. In N. Kakwani & J. Silber (Eds.), *Quantitative approaches to multidimensional poverty*. New York Palgrave Macmillan.

Donaldson, D., & Weymark, J. A. (1986). Properties of fixed population poverty indices. *International Economic Review, 27,* 667–688.

Duclos, J.-Y., Shan, D., & Younger, S. (2002). Robust multidimensional poverty comparisons. *Mimeo*. University of Laval.

Foster, J. E. (1984). On economic poverty: A survey of aggregate measures. In: R.L. Basman and G.F. Rhodes (Eds.), *Advances in Econometrics*, Vol. 3. Connecticut: JAI Press.

Foster, J. E., & Jin, Y. (1996). Poverty orderings for the dalton utility-gap measures. In S. Jenkins, A. Keptyn, & B. van Praag (Eds.), *The distributions of welfare and household production: International perspective*. Cambridge: Cambridge University Press.
Foster, J. E., Greer, J., & Thorbecke, E. (1984). A class of decomposable poverty measures. *Econometrica, 52,* 761–766.
Foster, J. E., & Sen, A. K. (1997). *On economic equality after a quarter century, annexe to enlarged edition of "on economic inequality" by A. K. Sen.* Oxford: Clarendon Press.
Foster, J. E., & Shorrocks, A. F. (1988a). Poverty orderings. *Econometrica, 56,* 173–177.
Foster, J. E., & Shorrocks, A. F. (1988b). Poverty orderings and welfare dominance. *Social choice and welfare, 5,* 175–198.
Foster, J. E., & Shorrocks, A. F. (1991). Subgroup consistent poverty indices. *Econometrica, 59,* 687–709.
Hadar, J., & Russell, R. R. (1974). Stochastic dominance in choice under uncertainty. In M. S. Balch, D. L. McFadden, & S. Y. Wu (Eds.), *Essays on economic behavior under uncertainty.* Amsterdam: North Holland.
Jenkins, S., & Lambert, P. J. (1993). Ranking income distributions when needs differ. *Review of Income and Wealth, 39,* 337–356.
Jenkins, S. & Lambert P. J. (1997). Three 'I's of poverty curves, with an analysis of UK poverty trends. *Oxford Economic Papers, 49,* 317–327.
Jenkins, S., & Lambert, P. J. (1998a). Three 'I's of poverty curves and poverty dominance: TIP for poverty analysis. *Research on Economic Inequality, 8,* 39–56.
Jenkins, S., & Lambert, P. J. (1998b). Ranking poverty gap distributions: Further TIPs for poverty analysis. *Research on Economic Inequality, 8,* 31–38.
Kolm, S. C. (1977). Multidimensional egalitarianism. *Quarterly Journal of Economics, 91,* 1–13.
Koshevoy, G. (1995). Multivariate Lorenz majorization. *Social Choice and Welfare, 12,* 93–102.
Koshevoy, G. (1998). The Lorenz Zonotope and multivariate majorizations. *Social Choice and Welfare, 15,* 1–14.
Koshevoy, G., & Mosler, K. (1996). The Lorenz Zonoid of a multivariate distribution. *Journal of the American Statistical Association, 60,* 252–276.
Levy, H., & Paroush, J. (1974). Toward multivariate efficiency criteria. *Journal of Economic Theory, 7,* 129–142.
Ravallion, M. (1996). Issues in measuring and modeling poverty. *Economic Journal, 106,* 1328–1343.
Seidl, C. (1988). Poverty measurement: A survey. In D. Bos, M. Rose, & C. Seidl (Eds.), *Welfare and Efficiency in Public Economics*. New York: Springer–Verlag.
Sen, A. K. (1976). Poverty: An ordinal approach to measurement. *Econometrica, 44,* 219–231.
Sen, A. K. (1985). *Commodities and capabilities*. Amsterdam: North–Holland.
Sen, A. K. (1992). *Inequality reexamined.* Cambridge: Harvard University Press.
Shorrocks, A. F. (1998). Deprivation profiles and deprivation indices. In S. Jenkins, A. Keptyn, & B. van Praag (Eds.), *The distributions of welfare and household production: International perspective*. Cambridge: Cambridge University Press.
Spencer, B., & Fisher, S. (1992). On comparing distributions of poverty gaps. *Sankhya, The Indian Journal of Statistics B, 54,* 114–126.
Tsui, K. Y. (2002). Multidimensional poverty indices. *Social Choice and Welfare, 19,* 69–93.
UNDP. (1997). *Human development report.* New York: Oxford University Press.
Zheng, B. (1997). Aggregate poverty measures. *Journal of Economic Surveys, 11,* 123–163.
Zheng, B. (1999). On the power of poverty orderings. *Social Choice and Welfare, 16,* 349–371.

# The Measurement of Social Exclusion

**Satya R. Chakravarty and Conchita D'Ambrosio**

**Abstract** This paper develops an axiomatic approach to the measurement of social exclusion. At the individual level, social exclusion is viewed in terms of deprivation of the person concerned with respect to different functionings in the society. At the aggregate level we treat social exclusion as a function of individual exclusions. The class of subgroup decomposable social exclusion measures using a set of independent axioms is identified. We then look at the problem of ranking exclusion profiles by the exclusion dominance principle under certain restrictions. Finally, applications of decomposable and nondecomposable measures suggested in the paper using European Union and Italian data are also considered.

## 1 Introduction

The subject of this paper is the measurement of social exclusion. The broad questions that we try to address in this paper are: (i) When do we say that an individual is socially excluded? (ii) What is the level of social exclusion in a country? (iii) Can we say that social exclusion in country A is less than that in country B? (iv) Given the level of social exclusion in a society, which subgroups of the population, partitioned according to ethnic, geographic, or any other socioeconomic characteristic, contribute more to aggregate social exclusion? (v) When can we say that one society dominates another with respect to social exclusion and what are the consequences of such a dominance relationship?

This article published in Review of Income and Wealth, Volume 52, 2006, is being reprinted with a generous approval of John Wiley & Sons. The publisher's consent is profoundly acknowledged.

S. R. Chakravarty
Indian Statistical Institute, Kolkata 700108, India
e-mail: styarchakravarty@gmail.com

C. D'Ambrosio (✉)
Maison des Sciences Humaines, Université du Luxembourg, 11, Porte des Sciences, 4366 Esch-sur-Alzette, Luxembourg
e-mail: conchita.dambrosio@uni.lu

 
S. R. Chakravarty (ed.), *Poverty, Social Exclusion and Stochastic Dominance*, Themes in Economics, https://doi.org/10.1007/978-981-13-3432-0_11

Broadly speaking, a person is said to be socially excluded if he is unable to "participate in the basic economic and social activities of the society in which he lives." In the European Commission's Programme specification for "targeted socioeconomic research," social exclusion is described as "disintegration and fragmentation of social relations and hence a loss of social cohesion. For individuals in particular groups, social exclusion represents a progressive process of marginalization leading to economic deprivation and various forms of social and cultural disadvantage."

As Atkinson (1998) said, social exclusion is not just a consequence of unemployment. It is true that an unemployed person may not have income to maintain a subsistence standard of living and hence becomes socially excluded. But many employed persons may not be integrated fully in the society they live in. Expansion of employment may increase the income gap between low-paid and high-paid workers and hence it may not reduce or end social exclusion. Social exclusion may arise from the operations of the market and supplies of key goods and services. For instance, people may not be able to participate in the customary consumption activities because profit maximizing prices may exclude them from the markets. A person may not be allowed to have an account in a bank if he does not fulfill certain constraints. It can as well emanate from operations of the State if the State's social security benefit programmes are targeted towards some particular groups or persons.

As social exclusion includes economic, social and political aspects of life, it is a multidimensional phenomenon. Since fundamental to achieving human choices is building human capabilities, we can also interpret the issue in terms of (i) functionings, the various things a person value doing or being and (ii) capability, the ability to achieve (Sen 1985). The valued functionings may vary from such elementary ones as adequate nourishment and literacy, to complex activities like participation in social gatherings and having self-respect. The standard of living in this framework is determined by the opportunity set of basic capabilities to function. The freedom of choice, that is, the extent of opportunities available rather than merely the point chosen becomes an important component of living standard. Now, if social exclusion is viewed as the inability to meet needs valuable to the individual, then regarding it as capability failure makes considerable sense. We regard the concept of capability failure as a notion of deprivation because people feel deprived when they lack such opportunities.[1] Hence social exclusion implies deprivation in a wide range of indicators or functionings of living standards, which can be of quantitative or qualitative type.[2]

Social exclusion is related to both inequality and poverty, but should not be equated with either of them (Atkinson 1998). According to Sen (1998), social exclusion is wider than poverty. Multidimensional inequality is a measure of the dispersion of the multidimensional distribution of quantities of consumption of the functionings for different individuals (Tsui 1999). Multidimensional poverty measurement, on the other hand, specifies a poverty threshold for each functioning, looks at the shortfalls

[1] See Runciman (1966) for a general treatment of deprivation.

[2] See Atkinson et al. (2002) for a list of functionings that can be used for the measurement of social exclusion.

of the functioning quantities of different individuals from the threshold levels, and aggregates these shortfalls into an overall magnitude of poverty (Bourguignon and Chakravarty 2003). Thus, both multidimensional poverty and social exclusion deal with capability failures, while in the former we view it in terms of the shortfalls from thresholds in a given point in time, in the latter the problem is one of inability to participate.[3] Note further that in the case of both multidimensional inequality and poverty the functionings have to be of quantitative type, whereas social exclusion considers qualitative type functionings as well. Social exclusion can be regarded as a state and as a process leading to deprivation in the form of non-participation. More explicit differences may be noted. A country with low deprivation (in terms of non-participation) but high degree of dispersion among attribute quantities and high levels of shortfalls of meagre attribute sizes from respective thresholds will be characterized with high inequality and high poverty but low exclusion. Similarly, there may be situations with high exclusion but low inequality and poverty.

Atkinson (1998) argued further that it is a relative concept, we cannot say whether a person is socially excluded or not by looking at his position alone. The positions of the others in the society have to be taken into account for a proper implementation of any criterion for exclusion. It has, furthermore, a dynamic character because an individual is socially excluded if his deprivation continues or worsens over time.

Three types of implicit conceptualization of social exclusion is currently available in the literature. In the first, it is interpreted as the lack of participation in social institutions (Duffy 1995; Rowntree Foundation 1998; U.K. House of Commons 1999; Paugam and Russell 2000); whereas the second regards the problem as the denial or non-realization of rights of citizenship (Room 1995; Klasen 2002). Finally, the third views social exclusion in terms of increase in distance among population groups (Akerlof 1997; Bossert, D'Ambrosio and Peragine (BDP) 2004). Some researchers attempted to suggest measures of social exclusion building on these approaches (see, among others, Bradshaw et al. 2000; Tsakloglou and Papadopoulos 2002). However, the theoretical foundations of these measures are often unclear.

In this paper, we adopt an axiomatic approach to the measurement of social exclusion. An alternative approach has been proposed by BDP. To the best of our knowledge, theirs is the only other axiom-based paper. The two contributions exhibit substantial differences in how different aspects of social exclusion are taken into consideration (see Sect. 2 for details).

Since in order to be socially integrated a person needs to have access to some social functionings, we first look at the capability failure, that is, the number of functionings from which the person is excluded over time. This number may be regarded as the deprivation score of the person under consideration. However, some

[3]Tsakloglou and Papadopoulos (2002) proposed an index of social exclusion based on the distribution of an individual welfare indicator. Imposing a threshold, they identified a person at high risk of deprivation if his indicator falls below the threshold. The dynamic aspect of social exclusion is included by considering the number of years during which the deprivation takes place. Evidently, specification of such a threshold involves some degree of arbitrariness. Since our approach does not rely on a threshold of this type, it has an advantage over that of Tsakloglou and Papadodopoulos (2002).

of the functionings may be more important than others. Therefore, a more general way is to assign an integer weight to each failure depending on the importance of the functioning and the deprivation score of a person is the sum of these integers.

The social exclusion measure that we propose is a real-valued function of the deprivation scores of different individuals in the society. In a sense our approach is similar to the view that considers social exclusion as lack of participation in social institutions, where lack of participation is treated as capability failures. We first characterize the family of exclusion measures whose members satisfy *normalization, monotonicity, subgroup decomposability, and have non-decreasing marginals.*

Normalization means that social exclusion is zero if nobody is socially excluded. Monotonicity requires the measure to increase if the deprivation score of a person increases. According to subgroup decomposability, for any partitioning of the population with respect to some socioeconomic or demographic characteristic, the overall social exclusion is the population share weighted average of subgroup exclusion levels. This property enables us to calculate a particular subgroup's contribution to aggregate exclusion and hence to identify the subgroups that are more afflicted by exclusion and to implement anti-exclusion policy. Clearly, according to this notion of policy recommendation, an assessment of overall exclusion becomes contingent on the implicit valuation of the exclusion measure. However, an exercise of this type may be useful for two reasons. First, following Sen (1985), the non-welfarist approach to policy analysis is becoming quite popular. Second, in many situations policy is evaluated using specific forms of measures. So it seems worthwhile to see what type of policy would be implied by the use of a specific exclusion measure.

Marginal social exclusion is defined as the change in social exclusion when we increase the deprivation score of a person by one. Non-decreasingness of marginal social exclusion ensures that in aggregating individual deprivation scores into an overall indicator of exclusion, a higher deprivation score does not get a lower weight than a lower score.

The characterized family of measures is shown to possess some additional interesting properties. It is also shown that the properties employed in the characterization exercise are independent, that is, none of these properties implies or is implied by another.

In subgroup decomposability we calculate each subgroup's exclusion independently of exclusions of other subgroups. Thus, one subgroup's exclusion does not affect exclusions of other subgroups. We, therefore, have to use weights for different functionings that do not violate this condition. Hence the weights should be independent of the overall population size. However, an alternative assumption, which appears to be quite realistic, is dependence of weights on the population size (see Sect. 5 for one such approach). Consequently, it may also be worthwhile to study non-subgroup decomposable measures. We therefore consider two measures of this type, the symmetric mean exclusion of order $\nu > 1$ and the Gini exclusion measure, and use population size dependent weights to calculate them. These measures satisfy all the axioms except subgroup decomposability.

Next, we consider the problem of ranking two societies by the social exclusion dominance criterion. We demonstrate that for two societies with a common population size and the same total deprivation score, if one dominates the other by the exclusion dominance criterion, then the former becomes at least as socially excluded as the latter by all additive social exclusion measures that satisfy anonymity and have non-decreasing marginals. This result parallels the if part of the well-known Atkinson (1970) result on Lorenz Domination which says that if $u$ and $v$ are two income distributions of a given total over a fixed population size, and if $u$ Lorenz dominates $v$, then all symmetric utilitarian social welfare functions regard u at least as good as v, where the identical individual utility function is concave.

Finally, we apply different measures to the EU member states and to the Italian regions in the 1990s and consider some policy implications.

The paper is organized as follows. The next section introduces the formal framework for measuring social exclusion and presents the properties for an exclusion measure. In Sect. 3, we characterize the family of exclusion measures and discuss its properties. Section 4 deals with social exclusion dominance relation. The application is contained in Sect. 5. Section 6 concludes.

## 2 Properties for a Measure of Social Exclusion

Let $N$ ($N_0$) be the set of all positive (nonnegative) integers and $\mathbf{R}$ be the set of real numbers. For all $n \in N$, $D^n$ is the $n$-fold Cartesian product of $N_0$ and $1^n$ is the $n$-coordinated vector of ones. For any society with a population of size $n \in N$, there is a finite nonempty set of functionings $F$ relevant for social integration. Throughout this paper, we assume that $F$ is fixed so that cross-population comparisons of social exclusion can be made in terms of elements of $F$.[4] An individual in an $n$-person society can be excluded from any subset of $F$, where $n \in N$, is arbitrary. The degree of exclusion or deprivation of a person can be captured using the number of functionings from which he is excluded. For each functioning, we define a characteristic function which takes on the value 1 or 0 according as the person is excluded or not from the functioning. Since some functionings may be more important than others, the characteristic function of each functioning is weighted by an integer, where the integer weights are determined in terms of importance of the functionings.[5] The deprivation score of the person concerned is then given by the sum of integer weighted characteristic functions. More precisely, let $F_i \subseteq F$ be the set of functionings from which person i is excluded. Denote the weight attached to attribute $j$ by $w_j$, then $x_i = \sum_{j \in F_i} w_j$. Note that this particular method of calculating deprivation is applicable to both qualitative and quantitative attributes.

This procedure of calculating the individual deprivation scores is quite similar to the Basu and Foster (1998) way of determining a household literacy profile. They assumed that individual literacy is a 0–1 variable and an adult member of a household is identified by the number 0 or 1 according to whether he is illiterate or literate. The

[4] See Atkinson et al. (2002) for common elements of $F$ for the EU as a whole.

[5] See Sect. 5 for one approach to the calculation of weights.

total number of literates in the household is then simply the sum of the 1's in the household. This procedure can also be extended to the situation when literacy is assumed to be multidimensional.

We assume that the calculation of the deprivation score of person $i$, $x_i$, involves a dynamic or longitudinal aspect and depends on the rest of the society.[6] If $x_i$ is positive, a trade-off between excluded and non-excluded functionings is not allowed. For instance, a person's high income cannot compensate the dissatisfaction associated with his job.

An exclusion profile in a society of $n$ persons is a vector $x = (x_1, \ldots, x_n)$, where $x_i \in N_0$ is the deprivation score of person $i$. The set of exclusion profiles for an n-person population is $D^n, n \geq 1$. Thus, $x \in D^n$ for some $x_i \in N$. The set of all possible exclusion profiles is $D = U_{n \in N} D^n$.

A measure of social exclusion is a function $E : D \to R$. For any $x \in N$, the restriction of $E$ on $D^n$ is given by $E^n$. For any $x \in N, x \in D^n, E^n(x)$ is a measure of the extent to which different individuals are excluded from the activities taking place in the society, that is, the degree of exclusion suffered by all individuals in the society as a whole. For all $x \in N, x \in D^n$, let $S(x)$ be the set of persons with positive deprivation scores, that is $S(x) = \{i, 1 \leq i \leq n | x_i > 0\}$. For any $x \in N$, $x \in D^n$, let $q$ be the cardinality of $S(x)$, that is the number of persons in $S(x)$. For any $x \in N, x \in D^n$, we write $\bar{x}$ for non increasingly ordered permutation of $x$, that is $\bar{x}_1 \geq \bar{x}_2 \geq \cdots \geq \bar{x}_n$.

We assume that an arbitrary exclusion measure $E : D \to R$ should satisfy the following postulates.

*Axiom 1*: *Normalization* (*NOM*). For all $n \in N$, $E^n(0.1^n) = 0$.
*Axiom 2*: *Monotonicity* (*MON*). For any $x \in N, x \in D^n$ and for any $i$, $1 \leq i \leq n$.

$$E^n(x) < E^n(x_1, \ldots, x_{i-1}, x_i + c, x_{i+1}, \ldots, x_n),$$

where $c \in N$.
*Axiom 3*: *Nondecreasingness of Marginal Social Exclusion* (*NMS*). For any $x \in N$, $x \in D^n$, and for any $i, j$, $1 \leq i, j \leq n$, if $x_i \geq x_j$ then:

$$E^n\big(x_1, \ldots, x_{t-1}, x_i + 1, x_{i+1}, \ldots, x_{j-1}, x_j, x_{j+1}, \ldots, x_n\big) - E^n(x) \geq$$
$$E^n\big(x_1, \ldots, x_i, x_{i+1}, \ldots, x_{j-1}, x_j + 1, x_{j+1}, \ldots, x_n\big) - E^n(x).$$

*Axiom 4*: *Subgroup Decomposability* (*SUD*). For any $x^i \in D^n, i = 1, \ldots, k, E^n(x) = \sum_{i=1}^{k} \frac{n_i}{n} E^n(x')$, where $x = (x^1, x^2, \ldots, x^k)$.
*Axiom 5*: *Anonymity (ANY)*. For all $x \in N, x \in D^n, E^n(x) = E^n(x.P)$, where $P$ is any $n \times n$ permutation matrix.[7]

---

[6]See Sect. 5 for one example of the inclusion of dynamic considerations.

[7]An $n \times n$ matrix is a permutation matrix if each of its entries is either zero or one, and each of its rows and columns sums to one.

Normalization is a miniminality principle. It says that if nobody is excluded from any functioning in the society, then the value of the social exclusion measure is zero. NOM has a relative flavor because it is based on an identical position of all persons in the society. Monotonicity says that if the deprivation score of an individual increases, then social exclusion should increase. This axiom has a flavor similar to Sen's (1976) monotonicity axiom, which requires poverty to increase if the income deprivation of a poor person goes up (see Bourguignon and Chakravarty 2003, for a multidimensional analogue to Sen's axiom). Now, in terms of capability failure curtailment of freedom of choice or opportunity of some persons can certainly make them worse off given that the positions of all other persons remain unaffected. For instance, the lack of proper medical care for some persons and for all persons are possibly two situations of exclusion, the latter being more severe than the former (see Sen 1985; Xu 2002). The axiom MON tries to capture this idea. Evidently, social exclusion is a multifaceted phenomenon and we try to look at the problem as one of capability failure. But there can also be other views concerning its measurement and in such cases MON may not be a relevant postulate (see, for example, BDP). If a social exclusion measure satisfies NOM and MON, then it will take a positive value if at least one individual has a positive deprivation score.

Sen (1976) argued that in income poverty measurement the poverty line can be taken as the reference point for all poor persons and the poverty gap of a poor person, his income shortfall from the poverty line, is a measure of deprivation suffered by him. In order to attach higher weight to higher deprivation, Sen assumed that the weight on individual $i$'s poverty gap is equal to his rank in the income distribution of the poor. This guarantees that an increase in poverty due to a reduction in the income (increase in deprivation) of the poor will be higher the lower (higher) is the income (deprivation) of the poor. Conversely, in order that an increase in poverty due to reduction in the income of the poor is higher the lower the income of the poor is, a necessary condition is to attach higher weight lower down the income scale. Our NMS postulate has a similar spirit. We consider two persons where the deprivation score of the first is not lower than that of the second. Then the change in social exclusion, if the deprivation score of the former increases by one, is at least as large as the corresponding change when the deprivation score of the latter increases by the same amount. Since NMS affects deprivations of two persons directly, it also reflects that social exclusion is a relative phenomenon.

SUD, which expresses aggregate exclusion in a society as a weighted average of subgroup exclusion levels, where the weights are population shares of the subgroups, is very important from policy point of view. $\frac{n_i}{n}E^{n_i}(x^i)$ is the contribution of subgroup $i$ to total exclusion, i.e. the amount by which social exclusion will decrease if exclusion in subgroup $i$ is eliminated. $\left(\frac{n_i E^{ni}(x^i)}{nE^n(x)}\right)$ 100 is the percentage contribution of subgroup $i$ to total exclusion. Each of these figures is useful to planners and analysts to formulate anti-exclusion policies. It may be important to note that if $x_i's$ are dependent on the population size, SUD may be violated. Finally, ANY means that the exclusion measure is symmetric, i.e. any reordering of the deprivation scores leaves the exclusion level unchanged. ANY is unavoidable as long as the individuals are not distinguished by anything other than deprivation scores.

An interesting implication of SUD and ANY is the principle of population, which requires social exclusion to remain unaltered under any $m\ (\geq 2)$-fold replication of population (see Chakravarty and Majumder 2006). This principle allows us to make cross-population comparisons of social exclusion.

Since to the best of our knowledge, the only other axiom-based paper in this area is by BDP, it seems worthwhile to compare our approach with the alternative approach of BDP who argued that social exclusion can be interpreted as persistence in the state of deprivation. At the outset BDP characterized measures of individual deprivation, which have been sequentially transformed into measures of social exclusion. While in the present paper it is assumed that minimal level of social exclusion is achieved when nobody is excluded from any functioning, in the BDP framework minimal value of individual deprivation is reached if everybody has the same number of capability failures, however small or large it may be. Further, their measures are homogeneous of degree one and satisfy translation invariance, where translation invariance of a measure requires it to remain unchanged under equal absolute changes in all failures. Two "proportionality properties" defined in terms of replications of the population, a conditional "anonymity" principle, which is different from ours, and a "focus axiom" which says that a person's deprivation depends on his capability failures and on those of individuals who have fewer failures, have also been used in the characterization exercise. Their measures of social exclusion are not subgroup decomposable. In view of this discussion, it is clear that the two approaches are quite different.

## 3 The Family of Subgroup Decomposable Social Exclusion Measures

In this section we derive the class of social exclusion measures whose members satisfy *NOM*, *MON*, *NMS*, in addition to *SUD*. Let $\Phi$ be the class of all functions $f : N_0 \rightarrow R$ such that $f(0) = 0$, $f$ is increasing, and $f$ has a non-decreasing marginal, that is:

$$f(x_i + 1) - f(x_i) \geq f\left(x_j + 1\right) - f\left(x_j\right), \tag{1}$$

where $x_i \geq x_j$.

For Theorems 1 and 2 of this section we assume that the weights attached to different functionings are independent of the population size.

We then have:

**Theorem 1** *A social exclusion measure E: D → R satisfies NOM, MON, NMS, and SUD if and only if for all* $n \in N$, $x \in D^n$,

$$E^n(x) = \frac{1}{n}\sum_{i\in S(x)} f(x_i), \tag{2}$$

where $f$ is a member of $\Phi$.

*Proof* Let $n \in N$ and $x \in D^n$ be arbitrary. Then by repeated applications of SUD:

$$E^n(x) = \frac{1}{n}\sum_{i=1}^{n} E^1(x_i). \tag{3}$$

We can rewrite $E^n$ in (3) as:

$$E^n(x) = \frac{1}{n}\sum_{i=1}^{n} f(x_i), \tag{4}$$

where $f = E^1$. Clearly, $f : N_0 \to R$. MON demands increasingness of $f$. Now, suppose $x_i \geq x_j$. The inequality:

$$\begin{aligned} &E^n(x_1, \ldots, x_{t-1}, x_i, x_i + 1, x_{i+1}, \ldots, x_{j-1}, x_j, x_{j+1}, \ldots, x_n) - E^n(x) \geq \\ &E^n(x_1, \ldots, x_{t-1}, x_i, x_{i+1}, \ldots, x_{j-1}, x_j + 1, x_{j+1}, \ldots, x_n) - E^n(x). \end{aligned},$$

on simplification, reduce to:

$$f(x_i + 1) - f(x_i) \geq f(x_j + 1) - f(x_j),$$

which is nondecreasingness of marginal of $f$. Clearly, if $x_i = 0$ for all $i$, then *NOM* requires that $f(0) = 0$.

Obviously, $f(0) = 0$ enables us to rewrite $\frac{1}{n}\sum_{i=1}^{n} f(x_i)$ as $\frac{1}{n}\sum_{i\in S(x_i)} f(x_i)$. This establishes the necessity part of the theorem on $D^n$ for a given $n \in N$.

The sufficiency is easy to verify. Since $n \in N$ was chosen arbitrarily, our result holds for all $n \in N$. ■

Note that the general measure in (2) satisfies ANY although we did not use this property in its derivation. We can interpret $f$ in (2) as the individual exclusion function. An alternative way of writing the formula (2) is:

$$E^n(x) = \frac{H}{q}\sum_{i\in S(x)} f(x_i), \tag{5}$$

where $H = \frac{q}{n}$ is the head-count measure of social exclusion, the proportion of persons that is socially excluded in the population. For a fixed $n$, on social exclusion profiles with a given $q$, $H$ is a constant function. Thus $H$ is violator of *MON* although it meets *NOM*, *SUD*, *ANY*, and NMS.

The head-count measure of social exclusion is quite analogous to the multidimensional poverty head-count ratio. Multidimensional poverty measurement considers for each person a poverty indicator variable that takes on the value of 1 if his consumption of some attribute(s) falls below the corresponding threshold(s). Otherwise the indicator variable assumes the value zero. The total number of multidimensional poor is then given by the sum of indicator variables across persons (see Bourguignon and Chakravarty 2003).

In order to illustrate the general formula in (2), let $f \in \Phi$ be of the form $f(t) = t^{\delta}, \delta \geq 1$. Then the corresponding measure is:

$$E_{\delta}^{n}(x) = \frac{H}{q} \sum_{i \in S(x)} x_i^{\delta}. \tag{6}$$

For any $\delta \geq 1$, $E_{\delta}^{n}$ satisfies all the postulates. For $0 < \delta < 1$, $E_{\delta}^{n}$ is a violator of NMS but not of others. As $\delta \to 0$, $E_{\delta}^{n} \to H$. The single parameter in (6) is a value judgement parameter. $E_{\delta}^{n}$ becomes more sensitive to the higher deprivation scores as $\delta$ increases from 1 to plus infinity. For a given $x \in D^n$, an increase in the value of $\delta$ does not decrease $E_{\delta}^{n}$. For $\delta = 1$, $E_{\delta}^{n}$ becomes the average deprivation score of the society, that is, $A = \frac{1}{n} \sum_{i \in S(x)} x_i$. For $\delta = 2$, we can rewrite $E_{\delta}^{n}$ as:

$$E_{\delta}^{n}(x) = \sigma^2(x) + A^2(x), \tag{7}$$

where $\sigma^2$ is the variance of the society deprivation scores. Given $A$, a reduction in $\sigma^2$ reduces the measure in (7). Such a situation may arise if a higher deprivation score decreases and a lower deprivation score increases by the same amount. Over social exclusion profiles with the same population size and the same average deprivation score, the ranking of the profiles generated by $E_{\delta}^{n}$ (for $\delta = 2$) is the same as that generated by $\sigma^2$.

An alternative of interest arises from the specification $f(t) = e^{\alpha x} - 1$, where $\alpha > 0$. The resulting measure is:

$$E_{\alpha}^{n}(x) = \frac{H}{q} \sum_{i \in S(x)} \left(e^{\alpha x_i} - 1\right). \tag{8}$$

For a given $x \in D^n$,$E_{a}^{n}$ is nondecreasing in $\alpha$. $E_{\alpha}^{n}$ satisfies all the properties for all positive $\alpha$. As $\alpha$ increases, the underlying evaluation attaches more weight to the higher deprivation scores.

We will now show that the postulates *NOM*, *MON*, *NMS*, and *SUD* are independent. Independence means that none of the postulates implies or is implied by another, that is, none of them is redundant. It is thus a minimal condition. Therefore, if one of the postulates is dropped, there will be measures that will satisfy the remaining postulates but not the dropped one.

**Theorem 2** *The properties NOM, MON, NMS, and SUD are independent.*

*Proof*

(a) Evidently the measure $\overset{\smile n}{E}(x) = \frac{1}{n}\sum_{i\in S(s)} e^{x_i}$ is not normalized, but it will fulfil the other properties.
(b) Since the measure $\overset{\frown n}{E}(x) = -\frac{1}{n}\sum_{i\in S(s)} \frac{x_i}{1+x_i}$ is decreasing in $x_i$, it is a violator of MON, but not of the remaining postulates.
(c) The measure $\tilde{E}^n(x) = \frac{1}{n}\sum_{i\in S(s)} x_i^{\theta}$, $0 < \theta < 1$, has a decreasing marginal and hence it fails to satisfy NMS, but it verifies the other properties.
(d) Since the measures $\bar{E}^n(x) = \left(\frac{1}{n}\sum_{i\in S(s)} x_i^{\nu}\right)^{\frac{1}{\nu}}$, $\nu > 1$, and $\hat{E}^n(x) = \frac{1}{n}\sum_{i\in S(s)} \bar{x}_i(2(n-i)+1))$ are not additive across components, they are not subgroup decomposable. However, they are normalized, monotonic, and have increasing marginals. ■

The measure $\bar{E}^n(x)$ is the symmetric mean exclusion of order $\nu(> 1)$. We can refer to $\hat{E}^n(x)$ as the Gini exclusion measure since it involves a Gini type averaging.[8] One of our main objectives is certainly to calculate the additive measures, which demand weights to be independent of the overall population size. Alternatively, when dependence of weights on the population size is preferred, the two measures, $\bar{E}^n(x)$ and $\hat{E}^n(x)$, which satisfy all properties except SUD, could be used. In the empirical applications we will, therefore, show results for $E_{\delta}^n(x)$ in (6), $\bar{E}^n(x)$, and $\hat{E}^n(x)$.

It is clear that for every individual exclusion function $f \in \Phi$, there corresponds a different social exclusion measure of the form (2). They will differ only in the manner how a person's individual exclusion is specified as a function of his deprivation score. However, there is no guarantee that these social exclusion measures will rank exclusion profiles in the same way. We consider the problem of ranking exclusion profiles in the next section.

## 4 The Social Exclusion Dominance Relation

We begin this section by defining the social exclusion dominance criterion and look at its implications for exclusion profiles with a fixed total over a given population size.

For $x, y \in D^n$, we say that $x$ dominates $y$ by the social exclusion relation, which we write $x \geq_{SE} y$, if:

$$\sum_{j=1}^{k} \bar{x}_j \geq \sum_{j=1}^{k} \bar{y}_j \tag{9}$$

for all $k = 1, 2, \ldots, n$.

---

[8] Strictly speaking, when incomes are arranged in non-increasing order, the Gini index of inequality can be written as a linear function with weights being the odd natural numbers in increasing order. Since the averaging in $\hat{E}^n$ is quite similar in nature, we call it the Gini social exclusion measure.

Given that the exclusion profiles $\bar{x}$ and $\bar{y}$ are ranked in nonincreasing order of capability failures of the individuals, $x \geq_{SE} y$ demands that the cumulative deprivation score of the first $k$ persons in $\bar{x}$ is at least as large as that in $\bar{y}$, where $k = 1, 2, \ldots, n$.

In order to study implications of the relation $x \geq_{SE}$ in terms of exclusion measures, we now have the following:

**Definition 1** For any $x \in D^n$ we say that $\bar{y}$ is obtained from $\bar{x}$ by a favorable composite change (FCC) if:

$$\begin{aligned} \bar{y}_i &= \bar{x}_i - 1 \\ \bar{y}_j &= \bar{x}_j + 1 \\ \bar{y}_k &= \bar{x}_k \quad \text{for all } k \neq i, j, \end{aligned} \tag{10}$$

where $\bar{x}_i > \bar{x}_j$.

In FCC the degree of exclusion of a more deprived person (i) is reduced by 1, whereas that of a less deprived person ($j$) is increased by 1, so that the total scores in the two profiles are the same. However, the variance of the new profile ($\bar{y}$) is less than that of the original one ($\bar{x}$). Note that the rank preserving transformation in (10) does not alter the relative positions of the affected individuals and it reduces the deprivation score of the worse off person ($i$). This is the reason why we call it an FCC.

Marshall and Olkin (1979) defined a special kind of linear transformation, called a $T$-transformation, of a vector that leaves all but two components of the vector unchanged, and replaces these two components by averages. An FCC is a $T$-transformation, which is used extensively for studying dominance conditions, since:

$$\begin{aligned} \bar{y}_i &= \lambda \bar{x}_i + (1-\lambda)\bar{x}_j \\ \bar{y}_j &= (1-\lambda)\bar{x}_i + \lambda \bar{x}_j \\ \bar{y}_k &= \bar{x}_k \quad \text{for all } k \neq i, j, \end{aligned} \tag{11}$$

where $\lambda = \frac{(\bar{x}_i - \bar{x}_j - 1)}{(\bar{x}_i - \bar{x}_j)}$.

The following theorem gives an interesting consequence of the relation $\geq_{SE}$ for additive exclusion measures that satisfy anonymity and have non decreasing marginals.

**Theorem 3** *Let $x, y \in D^n$, where $\sum_{l=1}^n x_l = \sum_{l=1}^n y_l$. Then $x \geq_{SE} y$ implies that $\sum_{l=1}^n h(x_l) \geq \sum_{l=1}^n h(y_l)$ for all individual exclusion measures $h : N_0 \to R$ whose marginals are nondecreasing.*

*Proof* Muirhead (1903) showed that given $x, y \in D^n$ along with $\sum_{l=1}^n x_l = \sum_{l=1}^n y_l$, if $x \geq_{SE} y$ holds, then $\bar{y}$ can be derived from $\bar{x}$ by successive applications of a finite number of FCCs. Assume, without loss of generality, that only one FCC affecting individuals $i$ and $j$, where $\bar{x}_i > \bar{x}_j$, takes us from $\bar{x}$ to $\bar{y}$.

Given $\bar{x}_i > \bar{x}_j$, let $\theta = \bar{x}_i - \bar{x}_j - 1$. Note that $\theta \in N_0$. Since the marginal of the individual exclusion function $h$ is nondecreasing, we have:

$$h(\bar{x}_j + 1) - h(\bar{x}_j) \leq h(\bar{x}_j + \theta + 1) - h(\bar{x}_j + \theta), \tag{12}$$

which we can rewrite as

$$h(\bar{x}_j + 1) - h(\bar{x}_j) \leq h(\bar{x}_i) - h(\bar{x}_i - 1). \tag{13}$$

Inequality (13) on rearrangement gives:

$$h(\bar{x}_j + 1) + h(\bar{x}_i - 1) \leq h(\bar{x}_i) + h(\bar{x}_j). \tag{14}$$

Substituting the value of $\bar{x}_j + 1$ and $\bar{x}_i - 1$ in (14), we get

$$h(\bar{y}_j) + h(\bar{y}_i) \leq h(\bar{x}_i) + h(\bar{x}_j). \tag{15}$$

Inequality (15) along with the information that $\bar{y}_k = \bar{x}_k$ for all $k \neq i, j$ gives us:

$$\sum_{l=1}^{n} h(\bar{y}_l) \leq \sum_{l=1}^{n} h(\bar{x}_l), \tag{16}$$

Since the social exclusion measure $\Sigma h(\cdot)$ satisfies anonymity, we can rewrite (16) as

$$\sum_{l=1}^{n} h(y_l) \leq \sum_{l=1}^{n} h(x_l), \tag{17}$$

which is the desired result. ■

Theorem 3 is very valuable. It shows how an FCC becomes helpful in ranking two exclusion profiles. It also provides a justification for using NMS as a postulate for a social exclusion measure.

In an FCC the deprivation scores of the two affected persons change in opposite directions. But often unidirectional changes in the scores of the two or more persons may take place. The following result, whose proof can be found in Fulkerson and Ryser (1962), states that under certain conditions the relation $x \geq_{SE} y$, where the total scores in $x$ and $y$ are the same, is preserved.

**Theorem 4** *Let $x, y \in D^n$, where $\sum_{l=1}^{n} x_l = \sum_{l=1}^{n} y_l$ be arbitrary. Then $x \geq_{SE} y$ implies that $(\bar{x} - e_j) \geq_{SE} (\bar{y} - e_i)$, where $i \leq j$* and *$e_k$ is the n-coordinated vector with 1 in the* $k$th *position and zeros elsewhere.*

The intuitive appeal of Theorem 4 is quite clear. Given that $x$ dominates $y$ if we reduce the degree of exclusion of one person in $\bar{x}$ and one person in $\bar{y}$, where the latter is relatively worse off than the former, the exclusion dominance remains preserved.

The following result, whose formal proof can be found in Fulkerson and Ryser (1962), is a generalization of Theorem 4.

**Theorem 5** *Let $x, y \in D^n$, where $\sum_{l=1}^{n} x_l = \sum_{l=1}^{n} y_l$ be arbitrary. Let u be obtained from $\bar{x}$ be reducing deprivation scores of persons in position $i_1, i_2, \ldots, i_k$ by 1. Similarly, suppose v is obtained from $\bar{y}$ by reducing deprivation scores of persons in positions $j_1, j_2, \ldots, j_k$. If $i_1 \leq j_1, i_2 \leq j_2, \ldots, i_k \leq j_k$* and *$x \leq_{SE} y$, then $u \leq_{SE} v$.*

## 5 An Empirical Illustration

The purpose of this section is to illustrate the social exclusion measures proposed in this paper, namely: $E_\delta$ in (6), $\bar{E}$, the symmetric mean exclusion of order $\nu$, and $\hat{E}$, the Gini exclusion measure using the European Community Household Panel (ECHP) data.[9] Note that the 14 non-monetary indicators defined below are based on subjective evaluations. Therefore, any definitional change or a change in the composition of a group will affect the analysis. Since this section can be regarded as an example of application of our indices, we take for granted the variables that Eurostat (2000) deemed appropriate to measure social exclusion. Since $\bar{E}$ and $\hat{E}$ are calculated to illustrate non-subgroup decomposability, we calculate them using population size dependent weights for different functionings. We base our analysis on the first six waves of ECHP, which cover the period from 1994 to 1999. The surveys are conducted nationally. The ECHP is an ambitious effort at collecting information on the living standards of the households of the EU member-states using common definitions, information collection methods and editing procedures. It contains detailed information on incomes, socio-economic characteristics, housing amenities, consumer durables, social relations, employment conditions, health status, subjective evaluation of well-being, etc. Of the 15 EU member-states, we could not consider Austria, Finland, Luxembourg, and Sweden since the data for these countries were not available for all the waves. For similar reasons we had to exclude Germany and the U.K. In particular, the ECHP surveys of these countries were substituted by national surveys, SOEP and BHPS respectively, that did not collect information on all the variables considered in our application.

Information were collected at the individual or the household level depending on the variable, but the unit of our analysis is the individual. The calculation uses required sample weights. In ECHP a person's quality of life has been measured along the following domains: financial difficulties, basic needs and consumption, housing conditions, durables, health, social contacts and participation, and life satisfaction. The 14 non-monetary indicators[10] suggested by Eurostat (2000) as best candidates to meet the following requirements are included in the analysis: (1) reflecting a negative

[9]Since our illustration involves cross-population comparisons, we drop the superscript $n$ from $E_\delta$, $\bar{E}^n$ and $\hat{E}^n$.

[10]In fact, the non-monetary indicators recommended in Eurostat (2000) are 15. We decided to drop the one belonging to the health domain, namely the proportion of people that were severely hampered in their daily activity by long-lasting health problems, since there was a considerable discontinuity between the ECHP waves for this indicator.

aspect of a life pattern common to a majority of the population in the EU; (2) allowing international and intertemporal comparisons; and (3) expressing a link with income poverty. These are the following:

- Financial difficulties: (1) Persons living in households that have great difficulties in making ends meet. (2) Persons living in households that are in arrears with (re)payment of housing and/or utility bills.
- Basic necessities: (3) Persons living in households which cannot afford meat, fish or chicken every second day. (4) Persons living in households which cannot afford to buy new clothes. (5) Persons living in households which cannot afford a week's holiday away from home.
- Housing conditions: (6) Persons living in the accommodation without a bath or shower. (7) Persons living in dwellings with damp walls, floors, foundations, etc. (8) Persons living in households which have a shortage of space.
- Durables: (9) Persons not having access to a car due to lack of financial resources in the household. (10) Persons not having access to a telephone due to lack of financial resources in the household. (11) Persons not having access to a color TV due to lack of financial resources in the household.
- Health: (12) Persons (over 16) reporting bad or very bad health.
- Social contact: (13) Persons (over 16) who meet their friends or relatives less often than once a month (or never).
- Dissatisfaction: (14) Persons (over 16) being dissatisfied with their work or main activity.

While it is true that with a high income a person may be able to increase his purchasing power in several dimensions of well-being, low income should not be mixed up with falling short of minimum standards unambiguously in all dimensions. For instance, there is a debate about the importance of low income as a determinant of undernutrition (Lipton and Ravallion 1995). In their illustration of the generalized human poverty index, Chakravarty and Majumder (2005) used the deprivations in three basic dimensions of life considered by UNDP (namely, failures in longevity, knowledge and decent living standard) and the anthropometric indicators, for example, "children with low birth weight," "undernourished people" and "children with low height for age." These dimensions of human life may not be mutually exclusive. Therefore, they carried a principal component analysis and the leading eigen value (which explains 69% of the total variance) puts weights ranging between 0.56 and 0.93 to the variables, thus justifying inclusion of all the variables in measuring the underlying latent construction of poverty. This parallels UNDP's arguments for including "adult literacy rate," "per capita real GDP" and "life expectancy at birth" in the construction of the human development index. That is why in this paper we include both financial difficulties and failures in other dimensions.

We first calculate $E_\delta$ for $\delta = 0, 1$, and 2 separately for two sets of indicators $V_1$ and $V_2$, where $V_1$ includes the indicators in the domains of financial difficulties, basic necessities, housing conditions, and durables, and $V_2$ includes the remaining indicators. The reason for separate calculations is that for indicators covered under $V_1$ we have household level information, whereas for the indicators in $V_2$ the available information is at the individual level, with the additional constraint that the minimum age of the reporter is 16. We prefer to keep the analysis separate and not to restrict the sample to $V_2$ since we do not want to exclude children from our data, who are considered in $V_1$ but not in $V_2$.

We call a person socially excluded with respect to a variable in a given domain if he has been deprived of the variable for at least four years out of the six years that we observe. In addition, exclusion for a functioning occurs if the person concerned is deprived for the last three years. Thus, our calculation of the individual exclusion score explicitly takes into account the dynamic or longitudinal aspect of social exclusion. A person's exclusion in a given domain has been obtained by adding up his exclusions over the concerned variables, that is, here the deprivation score is calculated under the assumption that $w_j = 1$ for all $j$.

Since in this calculation $x_i$ is independent of the population size, SUD holds. Calculation of non-additive measures $\bar{E}$ and $\hat{E}$ involving $x_i's$ which are dependent on the population size is presented later in the section. As an example of the construction of the individual exclusion scores, let's consider the variables in $V_2$: we assign value 0 to the individuals who had access to all the functionings in the relevant time period, 1 to those who had failure only in one dimension over the period, for instance, to those who met their friends or relatives less often than once a month (or never) or to those who were never satisfied with their main work or activity, and so on.

Numerical estimates of social exclusion for the EU member states are reported in Table 1. The upper part of the table presents the estimates for $V_1$ while its lower part gives the analogous values for $V_2$. The first column of the table gives the names of the countries for which required information were available. In column 2 we report the population shares of different countries in the total of EU sample population considered for our analysis. In columns 3–5 we present, for each country, the values of $E_\delta$ for $\delta = 0$, 1 and 2 respectively.[11] The country-wise social exclusion levels are then weighted by the corresponding population shares to determine the contributions of different countries to total exclusion, which are given as percentages of total exclusion in columns 6–8. From a policy perspective, complete elimination of exclusion within a country would lower aggregate exclusion precisely by the percentage by which it contributes to total exclusion.

Several interesting features emerge from Table 1. We note that the values of measures as well as percentage contributions are sensitive to the values of $\delta$. We first analyze the upper part of the table. Portugal turns out to be the country with the highest level of social exclusion, followed by Greece. But there is no unanimous agreement about the country with minimum exclusion. The Netherlands is the country with minimum $H$, whereas $E_1$ and $E_2$ regard Denmark as the country with the lowest level of social exclusion.

The maximum percentage contribution to total exclusion comes from Italy due to high exclusion scores and high population share, whereas Denmark is the least contributing country. Ireland and Belgium occupy respectively the second and third

[11] Recall that for $\delta = 0$ and 1, $E_\delta$ becomes respectively the head-count ratio, $H$, and the average deprivation score of the society, A.

**Table 1** Social Exclusion in EU Member States (1993–1998)

| Values of $E_\alpha$ | | | | | Percentage contributions based on: | | |
|---|---|---|---|---|---|---|---|
| | Population shares | $E_0$ (head-count ratio, H) | $E_1$ (average deprivation score, A) | $E_2$ | $E_0$ (head-count ratio, H) | $E_1$ (average deprivation score, A) | $E_2$ |
| $V_1$ | | | | | | | |
| Belgium | 4.86 | 0.224 | 0.375 | 0.985 | 2.76 | 2.45 | 2.27 |
| Denmark | 2.54 | 0.195 | 0.273 | 0.495 | 1.26 | 0.93 | 0.60 |
| Greece | 4.98 | 0.952 | 1.605 | 6.235 | 7.47 | 10.75 | 14.71 |
| Spain | 18.91 | 0.510 | 0.897 | 2.202 | 24.45 | 22.83 | 19.74 |
| France | 27.35 | 0.332 | 0.549 | 1.317 | 23.00 | 20.21 | 17.08 |
| Ireland | 1.72 | 0.359 | 0.749 | 2.336 | 1.56 | 1.73 | 1.90 |
| Italy | 27.46 | 0.397 | 0.668 | 1.627 | 27.65 | 24.69 | 21.18 |
| Netherlands | 7.35 | 0.177 | 0.301 | 0.734 | 3.29 | 2.98 | 2.56 |
| Portugal | 4.82 | 0.700 | 2.067 | 8.731 | 8.56 | 13.42 | 19.97 |
| Total | 100 | 0.394 | 0.743 | 2.110 | 100 | 100 | 100 |
| $V_2$ | | | | | | | |
| Belgium | 4.82 | 0.061 | 0.063 | 0.068 | 2.90 | 2.67 | 2.31 |
| Denmark | 2.56 | 0.034 | 0.035 | 0.037 | 0.85 | 0.78 | 0.67 |
| Greece | 5.09 | 0.074 | 0.078 | 0.087 | 3.72 | 3.48 | 3.10 |
| Spain | 18.70 | 0.087 | 0.088 | 0.091 | 15.95 | 14.38 | 11.90 |
| France | 26.84 | 0.082 | 0.092 | 0.115 | 21.55 | 21.58 | 21.51 |
| Ireland | 1.55 | 0.022 | 0.023 | 0.025 | 0.34 | 0.31 | 0.27 |
| Italy | 28.25 | 0.146 | 0.172 | 0.23 | 40.52 | 42.33 | 45.51 |
| Netherlands | 7.42 | 0.032 | 0.034 | 0.039 | 2.31 | 2.21 | 2.04 |
| Portugal | 4.76 | 0.254 | 0.295 | 0.381 | 11.86 | 12.25 | 12.69 |
| Total | 100 | 0.102 | 0.115 | 0.143 | 100 | 100 | 100 |

*Notes* $V_1$ considers jointly the variables included in the domains of financial difficulties, basic necessities, housing conditions, durables; $V_2$ considers jointly the variables included in the domains of health, social contact and dissatisfaction

Estimates derived using distributions of persons, with the additional constraint of age being at least 16 for $V_2$

position in terms of low percentage contributions. The sixth column of this part of the table shows that Portugal, Italy, Spain, and Greece, the Southern European countries, report 68.13% of social exclusion as judged by the headcount index. Their contribution to overall exclusion rises to 71.69% (75.60%) if one uses $A(E_2)$.

The higher contributions of these four countries is partly due to their almost average or more than average social exclusions. Spain and France come next after Italy in the ranking by percentage contributions. A comparison between Italy and Ireland is worth noting here. Although the latter has a better position than the former with respect to $H$ and $A$, for the other measure it becomes worse off. The reason is that the variance of the deprivation scores is much higher in Ireland than in Italy. By percentage contributions, Ireland shows a much better picture than Italy. This is because the country has a very low population share among the member states.

In $V_2$ as well, Portugal is the member state with the highest level of social exclusion and Italy by percentage contribution. Ireland performs the best by showing the lowest values with respect to both the factors. Belgium, Denmark, and the Netherlands also show low values for both factors. But Denmark has a better position than the other two countries by percentage contributions, and Denmark and the Netherlands perform better than Belgium by the other factor. France and Spain do not have unambiguous ranking between themselves with respect to index values, but by percentage contributions France is regarded as worse than Spain. These two countries perform worse than Greece by both the factors. Portugal, Italy, Spain and France jointly contribute more than 87% to total exclusion by any measure. Finally, except for Portugal, the ranking of countries by any measure in $V_2$ is different from that in $V_1$.

From a policy point of view, the breakdown of the variables into two subgroups enables us to identify the countries separately in each subset that are most susceptible to exclusion.

In Table 2 we carry out a similar analysis for Italy. The country has been divided into 11 geographic areas.[12] In $V_1$, the South is the area with the highest level of social exclusion by $E_1$ and $E_2$, while Sardegna occupies this position for $H$. Similarly, there is no unanimous agreement about the area with the lowest level of social exclusion. It is worth noting that South is only a part of the south of the country. If we add to South the remaining southern area, namely Campania, we can conclude that the southern areas contribute between 33 and 46% to total exclusion observed in Italy, depending on the measure. We note the difference with the northern regions, namely North–West, North–East, Lombardia, and Emilia–Romagna, whose total percentage contribution ranges between 14 and 25%. The other two areas with high levels of exclusion are the two islands, Sicilia and Sardegna, while only the former presents high percentage contributions. In the same way in $V_2$, South is the geographic area with the highest level of social exclusion and unanimous agreement about the area with minimum exclusion is not reached. However, the northern areas occupy low

[12]The information on the geographic areas of the Italian households are available in ECHP at the Nuts 1 level.

**Table 2** Social exclusion in Italy by geographic areas(1993–98)

| Values of $E_\delta$ | | | | | Percentage contributions based on: | | |
|---|---|---|---|---|---|---|---|
| | Population shares | $E_0$ (head-count ratio, H) | $E_1$ (average deprivation score, A) | $E_2$ | $E_0$ (head-count ratio, H) | $E_1$ (average deprivation score, A) | $E_2$ |
| $V_1$ | | | | | | | |
| North West | 10.65 | 0.210 | 0.318 | 0.626 | 5.64 | 5.07 | 4.10 |
| Lombardia | 15.39 | 0.236 | 0.317 | 0.551 | 9.13 | 7.31 | 5.21 |
| North East | 11.33 | 0.227 | 0.313 | 0.543 | 6.48 | 5.30 | 3.78 |
| Emilia-Romagna | 7.06 | 0.223 | 0.249 | 0.317 | 3.96 | 2.63 | 1.38 |
| Centre | 10.39 | 0.402 | 0.591 | 1.192 | 10.51 | 9.19 | 7.61 |
| Lazio | 9.02 | 0.390 | 0.620 | 1.409 | 8.85 | 8.37 | 7.80 |
| Abruzzo-Molise | 2.84 | 0.434 | 0.580 | 0.961 | 3.10 | 2.47 | 1.68 |
| Campania | 9.88 | 0.541 | 0.947 | 2.347 | 13.45 | 14.00 | 14.24 |
| South | 11.84 | 0.666 | 1.460 | 4.454 | 19.86 | 25.86 | 32.40 |
| Sicilia | 8.68 | 0.644 | 1.108 | 3.054 | 14.08 | 14.40 | 16.30 |
| Sardegna | 2.92 | 0.670 | 1.239 | 3.071 | 4.93 | 5.42 | 5.51 |
| Total | 100 | 0.397 | 0.668 | 1.627 | 100 | 100 | 100 |
| $V_2$ | | | | | | | |
| North West | 11.06 | 0.105 | 0.125 | 0.178 | 7.96 | 8.06 | 8.56 |
| Lombardia | 15.75 | 0.090 | 0.107 | 0.150 | 9.65 | 9.85 | 10.24 |
| North East | 11.38 | 0.098 | 0.112 | 0.143 | 7.65 | 7.44 | 7.07 |
| Emilia-Romagna | 7.29 | 0.122 | 0.130 | 0.146 | 6.05 | 5.50 | 4.63 |
| Centre | 10.46 | 0.164 | 0.188 | 0.241 | 11.70 | 11.42 | 10.95 |
| Lazio | 8.76 | 0.139 | 0.166 | 0.227 | 8.31 | 8.48 | 8.63 |
| Abruzzo-Molise | 2.79 | 0.140 | 0.167 | 0.220 | 2.68 | 2.71 | 2.67 |
| Campania | 9.31 | 0.212 | 0.248 | 0.329 | 13.49 | 13.44 | 13.28 |
| South | 11.60 | 0.242 | 0.293 | 0.407 | 19.22 | 19.78 | 20.50 |

(continued)

**Table 2** (continued)

| Values of $E_\delta$ | | | | | Percentage contributions based on: | | |
|---|---|---|---|---|---|---|---|
| | Population shares | $E_0$ (head-count ratio, H) | $E_1$ (average deprivation score, A) | $E_2$ | $E_0$ (head-count ratio, H) | $E_1$ (average deprivation score, A) | $E_2$ |
| Sicilia | 8.56 | 0.155 | 0.187 | 0.263 | 9.07 | 9.32 | 9.78 |
| Sardegna | 3.03 | 0.204 | 0.227 | 0.280 | 4.22 | 4.00 | 3.68 |
| Total | 100 | 0.146 | 0.172 | 0.230 | 100 | 100 | 100 |

*Notes* $V_1$ considers jointly the variables included in the domains of financial difficulties, basic necessities, housing conditions, durables; $V_2$D considers jointly the variables included in the domains of health, social contact and dissatisfaction
Estimates derived using distributions of persons, with the additional constraint of age being at least 16 for $V_2$

exclusion positions without showing unambiguous ranking among themselves. More generally, ranking of areas by any measure is different in $V_1$ from that in $V_2$.

The high contributing areas require attention from a policy perspective for reduction of their contributions so that a higher living standard can be achieved.

In Table 3 we present results of deprivation scores using population size dependent weights.

The measures that we apply are $\bar{E}$, the symmetric mean exclusion of order $v$, and $\hat{E}$, the Gini exclusion measure. Here we take into account the local dimension of the concept, i.e. people compare themselves with their reference society, and following Runciman (1966), we define the degree of deprivation inherent in not having access to an item as an increasing function of the proportion of persons in the society who have access to the item. Hence the weight attached to attribute $j$, $w_j$, reflects the percentage of the population in the country of residence of the individual that is not deprived from that specific attribute. More precisely, we assume that, if the percentage of the population not deprived of functioning $j$ lies in the interval $(10\,(i-1),\ 10\,i]$, where $i = 1, 2, \ldots, 10$, then $w_j = i$. If nobody is excluded from $j$, then the definition of the characteristic function ensures that deprivation with respect to $j$ is zero.

The upper part of the table presents the estimates for $V_1$ while its lower part gives the analogous values for $V_2$. In columns 2–4 we present, for each country, the values of $\bar{E}$, for $\upsilon = 0.5$, 1 and 2 respectively. The parameter $\upsilon$ is the sensitivity parameter; the more positive it is, the more sensitive the index will be to the capability failures of the more deprived. In column 5 the values of the Gini exclusion measure, $\hat{E}$, are reported.

The results are strikingly different from the analysis of Table 1 in the case of both $V_1$ and $V_2$. The reason behind this is that in the case of Table 1 for all countries we use constant weights in order to calculate deprivation scores of a person, whatever the proportions of population that are better off than him in the relevant dimensions.

**Table 3** Social Exclusion in EU Member States (1993–1998)

| Values of $E_i$ | | | | |
|---|---|---|---|---|
| | $\bar{E}(v = 0.5)$ | $\bar{E}(v = 1)$ | $\bar{E}(v = 2)$ | $\hat{E}$ |
| $V_1$ | | | | |
| Belgium | 14.072 | 15.598 | 19.826 | 34.283 |
| Denmark | 12.460 | 13.192 | 15.155 | 19.056 |
| Greece | 17.486 | 19.829 | 24.607 | 36.615 |
| Spain | 12.000 | 13.519 | 13.936 | 27.222 |
| France | 13.485 | 14.780 | 18.199 | 25.966 |
| Ireland | 16.907 | 19.059 | 23.830 | 61.128 |
| Italy | 11.266 | 16.295 | 12.677 | 35.034 |
| Netherlands | 15.729 | 17.050 | 20.386 | 43.573 |
| Portugal | 17.084 | 19.834 | 25.327 | 74.395 |
| $V_2$ | | | | |
| Belgium | 10.293 | 10.361 | 10.568 | 13.333 |
| Denmark | 10.282 | 10.338 | 10.495 | 12.488 |
| Greece | 10.435 | 10.530 | 10.809 | 12.449 |
| Spain | 9.261 | 9.293 | 9.391 | 11.777 |
| France | 11.056 | 11.267 | 11.833 | 13.398 |
| Ireland | 10.295 | 10.353 | 10.516 | 16.781 |
| Italy | 10.471 | 10.758 | 11.526 | 18.312 |
| Netherlands | 10.623 | 10.756 | 11.136 | 14.098 |
| Portugal | 9.734 | 10.015 | 10.724 | 28.515 |

*Notes* $V_1$ considers jointly the variables included in the domains of financial difficulties, basic necessities, housing conditions, durables; $V_2$D considers jointly the variables included in the domains of health, social contact and dissatisfaction
Estimates derived using distributions of persons, with the additional constraint of age being at least 16 for $V_2$

In contrast, Table 3 is based on Runciman-type weights for deprivation scores that explicitly take into account the population size of a country, that is, the weights are country-wise population size-specific. South European countries are split into two groups located at the opposite side of the ranking with respect to $\hat{E}$, due to the weighting scheme reflecting on an average higher percentage of the population deprived in Portugal and Greece than in Spain and Italy. On the one hand, Portugal and Greece are still the most deprived countries, while Spain and Italy now with Denmark are the countries where social exclusion is lowest. The latter is also the country with minimum exclusion according to the Gini measure. When we consider relatively high exclusion values (more than 35), starting with Italy the ranking of countries from low to high exclusion by the Gini measure is Italy, Greece, the Netherlands, Ireland and Portugal. Another notable difference with the previous unweighted case is that of the Netherlands. It is now a member state with a relatively high level of social exclusion according to all the measures. In the Netherlands the percentage of the population deprived in all dimensions is low, reflecting high weights assigned to those who are deprived; in addition there is more cumulation of disadvantage since the excluded individuals are more likely to be so in more dimensions at the same time.

For $V_2$, the domains of health, social contact, and dissatisfaction, the values of $\bar{E}$ are quite similar among all the countries, while we observe more variance for $\hat{E}$. The lowest excluded country by $\bar{E}$ is always Spain, followed by Portugal when $v = 0.5$ and 1, and Denmark when $v = 2$. On the contrary, Portugal is the most excluded country when disadvantage is evaluated with the Gini measure, while France is the country with the highest level of exclusion by $\bar{E}$.

## 6 Conclusions

Social exclusion refers to inability of a person to participate in basic day to day economic and social activities of life.

In this paper, we have developed an axiomatic approach to the measurement of social exclusion and characterized the class of subgroup decomposable measures of exclusion. We have also proposed non-decomposable measures that could be applied to take into account the local dimension of the concept. A dominance criterion for ranking two societies by symmetric additive exclusion measures under constancy of population size and total deprivation score was suggested. An application of the-decomposable and nondecomposable measures considered in the paper has been made using European Union data.

Several extensions of our analysis are possible. First, a characterization of some class of measures, for example of $E_\delta$, will be quite interesting. Second, extension of our dominance criterion to the cases of non-additive measures, variable total and variable population size, and a rigorous discussion on the converse of Theorems 3 and 4 will be worthwhile. Finally, we have considered only decomposability according to population subgroups. We can as well consider decomposition of population exclusion by attributes and study the impact of each of them on the aggregate exclusion. This will enable us to identify the attributes that are more/less susceptible to social exclusion.

**Acknowledgements** Chakravarty wishes to thank Università Bocconi, Milano, for financial support and hospitality. D'Ambrosio acknowledges financial support from the European Commission-DG Research Sixth Framework Programme (Polarization and Conflict Project CIT-2-CT-2004-506084) and the Università Bocconi, ricerca di base "Social Exclusion and Social Distance." We are grateful to Panos Tsakloglou for useful suggestions. We also thank Joan Esteban, James Foster, Patrick Moyes, Debraj Ray, Tony Shorrocks, Jacques Silber, Claudio Zoli, two referees, seminar participants at Università di Bari, Bocconi, di Lecce, di Parma, and the participants at the "Polarization and Conflict" meeting 2002, at the 2nd Journées d'Economie Publique LAGV, at the WIDER conference "Inequality, Poverty and Human Well-being," and at the ESPE 17th annual meeting, for useful comments.

## References

Akerlof, G. A. (1997). Social distance and social decision. *Econometrica, 65,* 1005–1027.
Atkinson, A. B. (1970). On the measurement of inequality. *Journal of Economic Theory, 2,* 244–263.
Atkinson, A. B. (1998). *Social exclusion, poverty and unemployment.* CASE/4, Centre for Analysis of Social Exclusion, London School of Economics, pp. 1–20.
Atkinson, A. B., Cantillon, B., Marlier, E., & Nolan, B. (2002). *Social indicators: The EU and social inclusion.* Oxford.
Basu, K., & Foster, J. E. (1998). On measuring literacy. *Economic Journal, 108,* 1733–1749.
Bossert, W., D'Ambrosio, C., & Peragine, V. (2004). Deprivation and social exclusion. CIREQ Working Paper, No. 2-2004. *Economica,* forthcoming.
Bourguignon, F., & Chakravarty, S. R. (2003). The measurement of multidimensional poverty. *Journal of Economic Inequality, 1,* 25–49.
Bradshaw, J., Williams, J., Levitas, R., Pantazis, C., Patsios, D., Townsend P., Gordon, D., & Middleton, S. (2000). *The relationship between poverty and social exclusion in Britain.* Paper presented at the 26th General Conference of the International Association for Research in Income and Wealth, Cracow, Poland.
Chakravarty, S. R., & Majumder, A. (2005). Measuring human poverty: A generalized index and an application using basic dimensions of life and some anthropometric indicators. *Journal of Human Development, 6,* 275–299.
Chakravarty, S. R., & Majumder, A. (2006). Intersociety literacy comparisons. In M. McGillivray (Ed.), *Inequality, poverty and well-being.* Palgrave, Macmillan, London.
Duffy, K. (1995). *Social exclusion and human dignity in Europe.* Strasbourg: Council of Europe.
Eurostat. (2000). European social statistics. income, poverty and social exclusion. In *THEME 3, population and social conditions.* Luxembourg.
Fulkerson, D. R., & Ryser, H. J. (1962). Multiplicities and minimal widths for (0–1) matrices. *Canadian Journal of Mathematics, 14,* 498–508.
Klasen, S. (2002). Social exclusion and children in OECD countries: Some conceptual issues. *The School Field, 13,* 9–25.
Lipton, M., & Ravallion, M. (1995). Poverty and policy. In J. Behrman & T. N. Sinivasan (Eds.), *Handbook of development economics* (Vol. 3). Amsterdam: North Holland.
Marshall, A. W., & Olkin, I. (1979). *Inequalities: Theory of majorization and its applications.* Academic Press.
Muirhead, R. F. (1903). Some methods applicable to identities and inequalities of symmetric algebraic functions of n letters. *Proceedings of Edimburgh Mathematical Society, 21,* 144–157.
Paugam, S., & Russell, H. (2000). The effects of employment precarity and unemployment on social isolation. In D. Gallie & S. Paugam (Eds.), *Welfare regimes and the experience of unemployment in Europe.* Oxford: Oxford University Press.
Room, G. (1995). *Beyond the threshold: The measurement and analysis of social exclusion.* Bristol: Policy Press.
Rowntree Foundation. (1998). *The report of key indicators of poverty and social exclusion.* www.parliament.the-stationeryoffice.co.uk/pa/cm199798/cmselect/777/8060303.htm.
Runciman, W. G. (1966). *Relative deprivation and social justice.* London: Routledge.
Sen, A. K. (1976). Poverty: An ordinal approach to measurement. *Econometrica, 44,* 219–231.
Sen, A. K. (1985). *Commodities and capabilities.* Amsterdam: North Holland.
Sen, A. K. (1998). *Social exclusion and economic measurement.* Paper presented at the 25th General Conference of the International Association for Research in Income and Wealth, Cambridge, UK.
Tsakloglou, P., & Papadopoulos, F. (2002). Identifying population groups at high risk of social exclusion. In R. Muffels & P. Tsaklogou (Eds.), *Social exclusion in European welfare states.* Cheltenham: Edward Elgar.
Tsui, K.-Y. (1999). Multidimensional inequality and multidimensional generalized entropy measures: An axiomatic derivation. *Social Choice and Welfare, 16,* 145–57.
U.K. House of Commons. (1999). Poverty and social exclusion (national strategy) bill. www.parliament.the-stationeryoffice.co.uk/pa/cm199899/cmbills/045/1999045.htm.
Xu, Y. (2002). Functioning, capability and the standard of living. *Economic Theory, 20,* 387–399.

# Multidimensional Poverty and Material Deprivation with Discrete Data

**Walter Bossert, Satya R. Chakravarty and Conchita D'Ambrosio**

**Abstract** We propose a characterization of a popular index of multidimensional poverty which, as a special case, generates a measure of material deprivation. This index is the weighted sum of the functioning failures. The important feature of the variables that may be relevant for poverty assessments is that they are discrete in nature. Thus, poverty measures based on continuous variables are not suitable in this setting and the assumption of a discrete domain is mandatory. We apply the measure to European Union member states where the concept of material deprivation was initiated and illustrate how its recommendations differ from those obtained from poverty measures based exclusively on income considerations.

**Keywords** Counting approach · Material deprivation · Multidimensional poverty measurement

**JEL Code** D63

This chapter is a reprint of an article published in Review of Income and Wealth, volume 59, 2013. Generous consent of John Wiley & Sons is acknowledged wholeheartedly.

W. Bossert (✉)
Department of Economics, University of Montreal, PO Box 3128, Station Downtown, Montreal, QC H3C 3J7, Canada
e-mail: walter.bossert@umontreal.ca

S. R. Chakravarty
Indian Statistical Institute, Kolkata 700108, India
e-mail: satyarchakravarty@gmail.com

C. D'Ambrosio
Maison des Sciences Humaines, Université du Luxembourg, 11, Porte des Sciences, 4366 Esch-sur-Alzette, Luxembourg
e-mail: conchita.dambrosio@uni.lu

 
S. R. Chakravarty (ed.), *Poverty, Social Exclusion and Stochastic Dominance*, Themes in Economics, https://doi.org/10.1007/978-981-13-3432-0_12

# 1 Introduction

An important development in the study of inequality and poverty in the recent past is the shift of emphasis from a single dimension, such as income, to a multidimensional framework. There are several reasons for this phenomenon.

First, contributions such as those of Townsend (1979), Streeten (1981), and Sen (1992) highlighted that the well-being of an individual, and hence the inequality and poverty in a population, is dependent on many dimensions of human life such as housing, education, and life expectancy; income is but one of these dimensions. Thus, poverty may be better defined as a situation that reflects failures in different dimensions of human well-being. The multidimensionality of an individual's well-being has also been emphasized by the Commission on the Measurement of Economic Performance and Social Progress (see Stiglitz et al. 2009, p. 14).

Second, in the income distribution literature, income is not important per se but is supposed to be an indicator of an individual's command over economic resources. But income may not always be suitable for this purpose because it neglects command over resources out of wealth, non-cash transfers from the government, and support from family and friends (see also, for instance, Ringen 1988). Thus, to measure command over economic resources, aspects other than income should be included. In doing so, it is necessary to distinguish the absence of consumption due to individual preferences from the absence of consumption due to inability to afford. Obviously, the former should not be considered in measuring poverty. In addition, for policy purposes, it is necessary to identify the fragment of the population who is *currently* poor. In a typical dataset, the information on income received refers to the previous calendar year (and is more likely to be misreported—particularly, underreported) while items of consumption are reported contemporaneously.

The third reason is of great importance for the European Union, where a shift in policy focus from pure income poverty toward a wider multidimensional framework has been particularly pronounced. Changes in public policies implemented by the member states were initiated at the March 2000 Lisbon European Council. At this Council, the member states agreed to adopt the Open Method of Coordination, which involves the definition of a set of common objectives on poverty and social exclusion for the EU as a whole. The successor of the Lisbon Agenda is the Europe 2020 strategy of growth: the EU has set five objectives—on employment, innovation, education, social inclusion, and climate/energy—to be reached by 2020. The EU distinguishes itself from other political entities in that it clearly endorses the use of relative poverty lines. The measures of income poverty adopted are based on member-specific poverty lines, that is, for each member state, the income threshold depends on the income distribution of the specific country and does not take into account inequality between member states. This practice has become more problematic with the enlargement of the Union and the substantial differences that can be observed between the income distributions of old and new members. Someone poor in one of the old member states is likely to be located well above average in the income distribution of a new member state. Should the poor member states be taxed and the rich countries receive a transfer in response? This clearly would be an absurd recommendation. It appears evident that the development of other indicators of an individual's command over economic resources is desirable. For a discussion of this point in the EU context, see, among others, Fahey (2007) and Whelan et al. (2008).

The distinction between multidimensional poverty and material deprivation we use is that endorsed by the EU. In particular, a multidimensional poverty measure takes into consideration all dimensions of well-being that may be of relevance (including non-material attributes such as health status and political participation), whereas an index of *material deprivation* restricts attention to functioning failures regarding material living conditions (see, among others, Guio 2005). According to EU policy, indices of material deprivation are to be combined with income-based poverty measures and indicators of low employment. This paper constitutes an attempt to contribute to this objective.

The purpose of this paper is to characterize a popular measure of multidimensional poverty and use it to evaluate material deprivation in the EU. This index is the weighted sum of the functioning failures. An important feature of the variables that may be relevant for poverty assessments is that they are *discrete* in nature, that is, what is considered relevant for a person (and what appears in the data) is whether or not a functioning failure with respect to the dimension under consideration obtains. Thus, poverty measures based on continuous variables are not suitable in this setting and the assumption of a discrete domain is mandatory. This distinction is usually referred to as qualitative/ordinal versus *quantitative/cardinal* variables; however, because we identify a functioning failure with a value of one and the absence of a functioning failure with a value of zero for the requisite variable, we prefer to use the terms *discrete* and *continuous* instead.

The importance of the ability to deal with discrete data is that, usually, only very few of a survey's variables on individual well-being are continuous in nature. This situation is common to many surveys; see, for example, the European Community Household Panel or the more recent EU Statistics on Income and Living Conditions (EU-SILC) for EU countries, and the United States' Current Population Survey, where most of the variables that may be used to measure multidimensional poverty are discrete. Hence, most of the indices proposed in the literature dealing with continuous variables cannot be applied. An alternative is what Atkinson (2003) refers to as the counting approach. The counting measure of individual poverty consists of the number of dimensions in which a person is poor, that is, the number of individual functioning failures. But this measure treats all dimensions symmetrically in the sense that in the aggregation of an individual's functioning failures, the same weight is assigned to each dimension. Since some of the dimensions may be more important than others, a more appropriate counting measure can be obtained by assigning different weights to different dimensions and then adding these weights for the dimensions in which functioning failure is observed. These weights may be assumed to reflect the importance a policy-maker attaches to alternative dimensions in a poverty-alleviation proposal. For instance, for evaluating multidimensional poverty in Mexico, Foster (2007) assumed a weight structure which first splits weights between income and non-income dimensions equally and then uses equal weights for non-income dimensions.

Alternatively, the weights may reflect views of the society under analysis, which is the approach followed in the present contribution. This weighting scheme is known in the EU political debate as *consensus* weighting. As opposed to the prevalence or frequency-based weighting, it has the advantage of better reflecting the minimum acceptable standard of living, which is what material deprivation indicators aim to capture. For a discussion of weighting schemes in EU indicators, see Guio et al. (2009). A survey on the use of weights in multidimensional indices of well-being can be found in Decancq and Lugo (2012).

The shift of emphasis toward multidimensionality has raised many challenges for social scientists interested in measuring poverty in well-being. The two-stage procedure suggested by Sen (1976)—consisting of first identifying the poor and then aggregating the information available on this segment of the population into an index of poverty for the entire society—has to be extended.

In the multidimensional framework, each person is assigned a vector of several attributes that represent different dimensions of well-being. For measuring multidimensional poverty, it then becomes necessary to check whether a person has "minimally acceptable levels" of these attributes (see Sen 1992, p. 139). These minimally acceptable quantities of the attributes represent their threshold limits or cut-offs that are necessary for an adequate standard of living. Therefore, a person is treated as deprived or poor in a dimension if the requisite observed level falls below this cut-off. In this case, we say that the individual is experiencing a functioning failure. Poverty at the individual level is an increasing function of these failures.

The first stage, consisting of the identification of the poor in a multivariate framework, is still an issue subject to debate. One possible way of regarding a person as poor is if the individual experiences a functioning failure in every dimension, which identifies the poor as those who are poor in all dimensions. This is known as the *intersection* method of identification of the poor. But if a person is poor in one dimension and non-poor in another, then trading off between the two dimensions may not be possible. Lack of access to essential durables, say, cannot be compensated by housing. In view of this, a person may be treated as poor if she is poor in at least one dimension. This is the union method of identifying the poor (see Tsui 2002; Bourguignon and Chakravarty 2003). In between these two extremes lies the *intermediate* identification method which regards a person as poor if she is deprived in at least $m \in \{1, \ldots, K\}$ dimensions, where $K$ is the number of dimensions on which human well-being depends (see Mack and Lindsay 1985; Gordon et al. 2003; Alkire and Foster 2011). Evidently, the intermediate method contains the union and the intersection methods as special cases for $m = 1$ and $m = K$, respectively. Our approach to identification follows the union method: a person is considered poor if she is poor in at least one dimension.

The axiomatic literature on the subject has proposed some measures of multidimensional poverty and explored the properties that are at the basis of these indices (see, for example, Chakravarty et al. 1998; Tsui 2002; Bourguignon and Chakravarty 2003; Diez et al. 2008; Alkire and Foster 2011). However, with the exception of Alkire and Foster (2011), the functionings considered in these contributions are expressed by means of continuous variables. Alkire and Foster's (2011) index is for discrete data but no characterization has been provided by the authors. Hence, to the best of our knowledge, our approach is novel in this respect. Another important contribution on multidimensional poverty with discrete variables is that of Lasso de la Vega (2010), where counting poverty orderings and deprivation curves are proposed.

The remainder of the paper proceeds as follows. We characterize the index of multidimensional poverty that allows for the assignment of different weights to the considered dimensions in Sect. 2, and we apply this measure to illustrate its use in assessing material deprivation in the European Union using the EU-SILC dataset in Sect. 3. Section 4 provides some brief concluding remarks.

## 2 The Index of Multidimensional Poverty

Suppose there are $K \in \Gamma \setminus \{1\}$ dimensions that may be relevant for the degree of well-being of an individual, such as housing conditions, where $\Gamma$ is the set of positive integers. These dimensions are the same across societies and they are represented by binary variables: a value of one indicates that the individual is poor with respect to this dimension; a value of zero identifies an attribute with respect to which the individual is not poor. Throughout, the number of relevant dimensions is assumed to be fixed. We adopt the union method of identifying the poor in the sense that a person is considered poor if she is poor in at least one of the relevant dimensions.

In order to be applied to different societies or to different time periods, a suitable measure of poverty must be capable of accommodating different population sizes. Thus, we consider all possible population sizes $N \in \Gamma$ when defining a measure of multidimensional poverty. Let $N \in \Gamma$ and $K \in \Gamma \setminus \{1\}$. A *dichotomous* $N \times K$ *matrix* is a matrix

$$M = \left(m_n^k\right)_{\substack{n \in \{1,\ldots,N\} \\ k \in \{1,\ldots,K\}}}$$

such that $m_n^k \in \{0, 1\}$ for all $n \in \{1, \ldots, N\}$ and for all $k \in \{1, \ldots, K\}$. The rows of $M$ correspond to the members of society, the columns represent the attributes considered relevant for poverty measurement. If $m_n^k = 1$, individual $n \in \{1, \ldots, N\}$ is poor with respect to attribute $k \in \{1, \ldots, K\}$ and if $m_n^k = 0$, the person is not poor with respect to this dimension. For $N \in \Gamma$, let $M_N$ be the set of all dichotomous $N \times K$ matrices. The number of attributes $K$ is suppressed in this definition because it is assumed to be fixed. For $N \in \Gamma$, $n \in \{1, \ldots, N\}$ and $k \in \{1, \ldots, K\}$, we write $m_n$ for the $1 \times K$ matrix consisting of the $n$th row and $m^k$ for the $N \times 1$ matrix consisting of the $k$th column of $M \in \boldsymbol{M}_N$.

Define $\boldsymbol{M} = \cup_{N \in \Gamma} \boldsymbol{M}_N$. An anonymous multidimensional poverty measure is a function $P : \boldsymbol{M} \rightarrow R$ such that, for all $M \in \boldsymbol{M}$, $P$ is invariant with respect to row permutations of $M$—that is, $P$ is anonymous in the sense that $P$ treats individuals symmetrically, paying no attention to the labels that we may assign to them.

We now formulate the properties that we require $P$ to possess. To do so, we introduce some more notation. For $N \in \Gamma$, let $0_N$ be the $N \times K$ matrix, all of whose entries are equal to zero. For $k \in \{1, \ldots, K\}$, let $1^k$ be the $1 \times K$ matrix with $m_1^k = 1$ and $m_1^j = 0$ for all $j \in \{1, \ldots, K\} \setminus \{k\}$. In order to keep our exposition simple, we adopt the convention

$$\sum_{k \in \phi} \alpha^k = 0.$$

The first two axioms are limited in scope because they apply to one-person societies only.

**Zero normalization**. For all $M \in \boldsymbol{M_1} \setminus \{0_1\}$,

$$P(M) > P(0_1) = 0$$

This normalization assumption is standard: if the individual in a one-person society is not poor in any attribute, we require the value of the index to be zero and if she is poor in at least one dimension, the index assumes a positive value. Note that this property is based on a union identification of the poor.

**Additive decomposability in attributes**. For all $M, M' \in \boldsymbol{M}_1$ such that $(M + M') \in \boldsymbol{M}_1$,

$$P(M + M') = P(M) + P(M')$$

Additive decomposability in attributes is straightforward as well and has been employed in numerous contributions in the field of social index numbers. Sometimes a non-additive formulation may generate problems which do not arise with additively decomposable measures. For instance, in the (non-additive) human development index, if attainment in one of the dimensions approaches its minimum value, this index approaches zero no matter what values are assumed in the other dimensions. This problem can be avoided under an additively decomposable structure (see Ravallion 2011, 2012).

Additive decomposability in attributes entails a separability property: the contribution of any variable to the overall index value can be examined in isolation, without having to know the values of the other variables. Thus, additive decomposability properties are often linked to independence conditions of various forms. Note that, because of the discrete domain considered here, an independence condition is not sufficient unless there are at most four dimensions to poverty; this can be seen by adapting the corresponding result in Kraft et al. (1959) to our setting. Because we work with a general number of poverty attributes and, moreover, the dataset used in our application covers more than four attributes, the full force of additive decomposability in attributes is required in our characterization.

We are well aware that additive decomposability is a strong property and that it is no surprise that the resulting index is additive. However, given that our objective is the characterization of a known additive measure, an additivity property cannot but appear in the list of requisite axioms. Given the prominent role played by this measure and the absence of a characterization on a discrete domain in the existing literature, it seems to us that this is an appropriate way to proceed. It may be worthwhile to note that variants of the continuous counterpart to the additive decomposability postulate were used earlier in the literature. Chakravarty et al. (1998) used one form of this axiom along with subgroup decomposability to characterize the multidimensional poverty indices that are both factor and subgroup decomposable. Alkire and Foster (2011) noted that given the identification step, total poverty according to their index can be regarded as a weighted average of dimensional values. For a characterization of an additive measure of social exclusion on a discrete domain, see Chakravarty and D'Ambrosio (2006). Jayaraj and Subramanian (2010) apply this index to measure deprivation in India.

As a preliminary result, we identify the class of measures that satisfy the above axioms. Clearly, due to the restriction to one-person societies in these properties, all that can be deduced at this stage is the structure of $P$ on the subdomain of dichotomous matrices with a single row only.

**Lemma 1** *If an anonymous multidimensional poverty measure P satisfies zero normalization and additive decomposability in attributes, then there exists a vector of parameters* $\alpha = (\alpha^1, \ldots, \alpha^K) \in R^K_{++}$, *such that, for all* $M \in \boldsymbol{M}_1$.

$$P(M) = \sum_{\substack{k \in \{1,2,..,K\}: \\ m_1^k = 1}} \alpha^k.$$

*Proof* Suppose P satisfies zero normalization and additive decomposability in attributes. That $P(0_1) = 0$ follows immediately from the equality in zero normalization. Now suppose $M \in \boldsymbol{M_1} \backslash \{0_1\}$. Define, for all $k \in \{1, \ldots, K\}$, $\alpha^k = P(1^k)$. By the inequality in the definition of zero normalization, it follows that $\alpha^k > 0$ for all $k \in \{1, \ldots, K\}$. Writing $M$ as

$$M = \sum_{\substack{k \in \{1,2,..,K\}: \\ m_1^k = 1}} 1^k,$$

additive decomposability in attributes requires

$$P(M) = \sum_{\substack{k \in \{1,2,..,K\}: \\ m_1^k = 1}} P(1^k) = \sum_{\substack{k \in \{1,2,\ldots,K\}: \\ m_1^k = 1}} \alpha^k,$$

which completes the proof. ■

The real number $\alpha^j$ is an indicator of the importance that we assign to dimension $j$ when a person is found to be deprived in this dimension. It can as well be interpreted as the priority assigned by the government to remove deprivation in dimension $j$. The index $P(M)$ is simply the total of such indicators across dimensions.

The last axiom used in our characterization parallels the above additive decomposability property with respect to attributes. We require that $P$ be additively decomposable in individuals as well, with suitable weights applied so as to take proper account of population size. Clearly, as is the case for unidimensional poverty measures, the total number of individuals matters. Consider a society $A$ in which one hundred out of a thousand people are poor. Furthermore, suppose a society $B$ is such that, again, one hundred people are poor (to the same degree as the poor in $A$) but total population size is one million in $B$. All poverty measures usually employed assign a higher level of poverty to $A$ than to $B$, which reflects the view that poverty is a per-capita notion. Thus, we formulate our third axiom as follows.

**Population-weighted additive decomposability in individuals**. For all $N \in \Gamma$, for all $M' \in \boldsymbol{M}_N$, for all $M'' \in \boldsymbol{M}_1$ and for all $M \in \boldsymbol{M}_{N+1}$, if $m_n = m'_n$ for all $n \in \{1, \ldots, N\}$ and $m_{N+1} = m''_1$, then

$$P(M) = \frac{N}{N+1} P(M') + \frac{1}{N+1} P(M'')$$

See our earlier discussion of additive decomposability in attributes for a motivation of this decomposability property. Again, a property of this nature is required given that we aim at characterizing a measure with an additive structure on a discrete domain.

We obtain:

**Theorem 1** *An anonymous multidimensional poverty measure P satisfies zero normalization, additive decomposability in attributes and population-weighted additive decomposability in individuals if and only if there exists a vector of parameters* $\alpha = (\alpha^1, \ldots, \alpha^K) \in R^K_{++}$ *such that, for all* $N \in N$ *and for all* $M \in \boldsymbol{M}_N$,

$$P(M) = \frac{1}{N} \sum_{n=1}^{N} \sum_{\substack{k \in \{1, 2, .., K\} : \\ m_1^k = 1}} \alpha^k. \quad (1)$$

*Proof* The "if" part of the theorem statement is straightforward to verify. To prove the "only if" part, we proceed by induction on the population size. Suppose that P satisfies the required axioms. Lemma1establishes the claim for all $M \in \boldsymbol{M}_1$. Now suppose (1) is true for all population sizes from one to $N \in \Gamma$. Let

$$M \in \boldsymbol{M}_{N+1}$$

$$M' = \left(m_n^k\right)_{\substack{n \in \{1,\ldots,N\} \\ k \in \{1,\ldots,K\}}}$$

$$M'' = m_{N+1},$$

By population-weighted additive decomposability in individuals and our induction hypothesis, it follows that

$$\begin{aligned} P(M) &= \frac{N}{N+1}P(M') + \frac{1}{N+1}P(M'') \\ &= \left(\frac{N}{N+1}\right)\frac{1}{N}\sum_{n=1}^{N}\sum_{\substack{k \in \{1,2,\ldots,K\}: \\ m_1^k = 1}} \alpha^k + \frac{1}{N+1}\sum_{\substack{k \in \{1,2,..,K\}: \\ m_1^k = 1}} \alpha^k \\ &= \frac{1}{N+1}\sum_{n=1}^{N+1}\sum_{\substack{k \in \{1,2,..,K\}: \\ m_1^k = 1}} \alpha^k \end{aligned}$$

where we used the anonymity assumption on $P$ to deduce that the parameters $\alpha^k$ do not depend on the labels of the individuals under consideration. ■

It may be noted that while Bourguignon and Chakravarty (2003) used the deprivation count, the number of dimensions of well-being from which a person is deprived in the union/intersection framework for identification of the poor, the Alkire and Foster (2011) identification method relies on the counting formula using unequal weighting for dimensions in the intermediate set-up. Lasso de la Vega (2010) examined dominance conditions for poverty orderings using the counting approach based on this identification method. Aaberge and Peluso (2011) compared deprivation counts of distributions using rank dependent social evaluation criteria. This clearly indicates that Theorem 1 has different objectives than the counting based results reported in the above papers.

Note that we do not employ a focus axiom analogous to that familiar from unidimensional poverty measurement. This is the case because our (union) identification of the poor is implicit in our axioms—the poor are those who experience a functioning failure in at least one dimension, and the characteristics of the non-poor (those who do not experience any functioning failure) do not influence the value of the index.

## 3 Material Deprivation Within the EU

In this section, we illustrate the index defined in (1) by employing it to the problem of measuring material deprivation in the EU. Recall that, in assessing material deprivation as opposed to multidimensional poverty in general, we focus on dimensions that represent access to material economic resources. The dataset we use is EU-SILC, which is employed by European Union member states and the Commission to monitor national and EU progress toward key objectives for the social inclusion process and Europe 2020 growth strategy. Our analysis covers the years from 2005 to 2008. The variables that may be used in the measurement of material deprivation are available mainly at the household level. We follow a conservative approach in the sense that we treat the households reporting a missing value like those reporting not to experience the functioning failure. As a result, we may be underestimating material deprivation since we are attributing a functioning failure exclusively to households who explicitly claim to have the failure. We also perform a sensitivity analysis by excluding the missing values from the sample. The results do not change, hence they are omitted but are available upon request. The unit of our analysis is the individual, that is, the household failure is attributed to each household member and we analyze the distribution of functioning failures among individuals.

In line with the Europe 2020 framework, the variables we consider are the following:

1. The household has been in arrears at any time in the last 12 months on mortgage or rent payments.
2. The household has been in arrears at any time in the last 12 months on utility bills.
3. The household lacks the ability to keep the home adequately warm.
4. The household lacks the capacity to face unexpected required expenses.
5. The household cannot afford a meal with meat, chicken, fish (or a vegetarian protein equivalent) every second day.
6. The household cannot afford to pay for a one-week annual holiday away from home.
7. The household cannot afford to have a car.
8. The household cannot afford a washing machine.
9. The household cannot afford a color TV.
10. The household cannot afford a telephone.

The weights are constructed from the views of EU citizens as surveyed in 2007 in the special Eurobarometer 279 on poverty and social exclusion (see TNS Opinion & Social 2007). This weighting method was first proposed by Guio et al. (2009). For each variable, we use as weight the percentage of the EU27 citizens answering "absolutely necessary, no one should have to do without" to the requisite question as expressed by these instructions: "In the following questions, we would like to understand better what, in your view, is necessary for people to have what can be considered as an acceptable or decent standard of living in [OUR COUNTRY]. For a person to have a decent standard of living in [OUR COUNTRY], please tell me how necessary do you think it is...(if one wants to)." The possible answers also included "necessary," "desirable but not necessary" and "not at all necessary." The answers given by citizens living in EU27 are reported in Table 1. The weights we use constitute the entries in column 2. They range from 68% for the absolutely necessity of not being in arrears on utility bills to 17% for the absolutely necessity of affordability of a car. We compare our results (using the ten discrete variables introduced above) with those obtained by weighting all functioning failures equally, and with those according to the (solely income-based) headcount ratio with the 60-percent-of-the-median-equivalent income country-specific poverty lines.

The results of our analysis are summarized in Table 2. The first column lists the official abbreviation of country names, whereas the second set of columns contains the rankings for the four years obtained according to the headcount ratio on household equivalent income. The remaining two sets of columns include the values of the material deprivation index defined in (1) for the various years, the first four with the Eurobarometer weights, the other four when equal weight is given to each dimension. The performance of the countries over time is more stable for material deprivation than for income poverty as measured by the headcount ratio. The results are sensitive to the choice of the weights for some of the countries such as Austria, Estonia, Iceland, and Spain. Iceland's position improves by five when equal weighting is given to all dimensions in 2005, three in the next two years, and two positions in 2008. Estonia moves down in the rankings by four positions in 2005 and 2008 and by three in the two other years.

In Figs. 1and 2 we plot, for each year, the rankings of material deprivation with respect to the headcount ratio. A very different picture emerges when comparing the performance of the countries depending on whether we look at income poverty (measured by the headcount ratio) or at material deprivation, confirming that these two phenomena differ considerably among European countries. For similar findings, see, among others, Guio et al. (2009) and Whelan and Maître (2009). We observe a decrease in the rankings of old EU member states, where a substantial level of material living conditions has been reached, and a worsening of the position of new member states, with few exceptions. Ireland, Luxembourg, the UK, and Spain are the countries which considerably improve their position in all of the years, whereas for the Republic of Cyprus, the Czech Republic, Hungary, and Slovakia, we observe the reverse phenomenon. Slovenia belongs to the latter group only for the first three

**Table 1** Answers in percentances to "in the following questions, we would like to understand better what, in your view, in necessary for people to have what can be considered as an acceptable or decent standard of living in [our country]. For a person to have a decent standard of living in [our country], please tell me how necessary do you think it is … (if one wants to)"

| EU 27 | Absolutely necessary no one should have to do without (%) | Necessary (%) | Desirable but not necessary (%) | Not at all necessary (%) |
|---|---|---|---|---|
| A place to live without a leaking roof, damp walls, floors, foundation | 68 | 28 | 3 | 1 |
| To be able to keep one's home adequately warm | 62 | 35 | 3 | 0 |
| A place to live with its own bath or shower | 63 | 31 | 6 | 0 |
| An indoor flushing toilet for sole use of the household | 69 | 27 | 4 | 0 |
| To be able to pay rent or mortgage payments on time | 62 | 34 | 3 | 0 |
| To be able to pay utility bills (electricity, water, gas, etc.,) on time | 68 | 30 | 2 | 0 |
| To be able to repay loans (such as loans to buy electrical appliances, furniture, a car or student loan etc.,) on time | 48 | 40 | 9 | 2 |
| Paying for one week annual holiday away from home | 15 | 29 | 43 | 13 |
| A meal with meat, chicken, or fish at least once every two days | 43 | 37 | 17 | 3 |

(continued)

**Table 1** (continued)

| EU 27 | Absolutely necessary no one should have to do without (%) | Necessary (%) | Desirable but not necessary (%) | Not at all necessary (%) |
|---|---|---|---|---|
| To be able to cope with an unexpected financial expense of X (national currency) | 32 | 43 | 21 | 2 |
| A fixed telephone, landline | 18 | 37 | 32 | 13 |
| A mobile phone | 12 | 26 | 37 | 25 |
| A color TV | 19 | 36 | 35 | 10 |
| A computer | 9 | 21 | 41 | 28 |
| A washing machine | 48 | 41 | 10 | 1 |
| A car | 17 | 34 | 36 | 13 |
| A place to live without too much noise from neighbors or noise from the street (traffic, businesses, factories, etc.) | 28 | 43 | 27 | 2 |
| A place to live without too much pollution or other environmental problems (such as air pollution, grime, or rubbish) | 42 | 44 | 13 | 1 |
| A place to live without crime, violence, or vandalism in the area | 49 | 38 | 12 | 1 |

**Table 2** Material, deprivation (MD) and income poverty (H) ranks among EU Member States in the years 2005–2008, without Eurobarometer weights (EU) and with unitary (EQ) weights

| Country | H05 | H06 | H07 | H08 | MD_EU05 | MD_EU06 | MD_EU07 | MD_EU08 | MD_EQ05 | MD_EQ06 | MD_EQ07 | MD_E Q08 |
|---|---|---|---|---|---|---|---|---|---|---|---|---|
| AT | 9 | 9 | 7 | 8 | 3 | 5 | 5 | 11 | 5 | 6 | 8 | 10 |
| BE | 14 | 13 | 13 | 12 | 11 | 11 | 10 | 7 | 11 | 9 | 9 | 7 |
| BG | | | | 24 | | | | 26 | | | | 25 |
| CY | 15 | 14 | 15 | 15 | 20 | 20 | 22 | 18 | 19 | 20 | 20 | 18 |
| CZ | 3 | 2 | 1 | 1 | 17 | 17 | 15 | 14 | 16 | 16 | 16 | 15 |
| DE | 8 | 10 | 14 | 13 | 6 | 13 | 12 | 13 | 7 | 13 | 12 | 11 |
| DK | 6 | 6 | 6 | 5 | 4 | 4 | 4 | 3 | 3 | 4 | 4 | 5 |
| EE | 16 | 16 | 21 | 20 | 16 | 14 | 14 | 8 | 20 | 17 | 17 | 12 |
| ES | 23 | 22 | 22 | 21 | 10 | 9 | 9 | 10 | 13 | 11 | 10 | 9 |
| FI | 5 | 8 | 10 | 11 | 8 | 6 | 6 | 6 | 9 | 7 | 7 | 6 |
| FR | 10 | 11 | 11 | | 12 | 12 | 13 | | 12 | 12 | 13 | |
| GR | 12 | 24 | 24 | 23 | 19 | 19 | 18 | 15 | 18 | 18 | 18 | 16 |
| HU | 21 | 15 | 8 | 9 | 22 | 22 | 23 | 24 | 22 | 22 | 24 | 24 |
| IE | 22 | 18 | 17 | 14 | 7 | 10 | 11 | 16 | 6 | 10 | 11 | 14 |
| IS | 2 | 1 | 2 | 2 | 13 | 8 | 8 | 5 | 8 | 5 | 5 | 3 |
| IT | 17 | 21 | 23 | 18 | 14 | 15 | 17 | 17 | 14 | 14 | 15 | 17 |
| LT | 24 | 23 | 20 | 22 | 24 | 23 | 21 | 21 | 24 | 23 | 22 | 21 |
| LU | 13 | 12 | 12 | 10 | 1 | 1 | 1 | 2 | 1 | 1 | 2 | 2 |

(continued)

**Table 2** (continued)

| Country | H05 | H06 | H07 | H08 | MD_EU05 | MD_EU06 | MD_EU07 | MD_EU08 | MD_EQ05 | MD_EQ06 | MD_EQ07 | MD_E Q08 |
|---|---|---|---|---|---|---|---|---|---|---|---|---|
| LV | 19 | 25 | 25 | 26 | 25 | 25 | 25 | 23 | 25 | 25 | 25 | 23 |
| NO | 4 | 3 | 9 | 4 | 5 | 3 | 2 | 1 | 4 | 3 | 1 | 1 |
| PL | 25 | 19 | 16 | 16 | 23 | 24 | 24 | 22 | 23 | 24 | 23 | 22 |
| PT | 20 | 17 | 18 | 17 | 18 | 18 | 20 | 20 | 17 | 19 | 19 | 19 |
| RO | | | | 25 | | | | 25 | | | | 26 |
| SE | 1 | 7 | 4 | 6 | 2 | 2 | 3 | 4 | 2 | 2 | 3 | 4 |
| SI | 7 | 5 | 5 | 7 | 15 | 16 | 16 | 12 | 15 | 15 | 14 | 13 |
| SK | 11 | 4 | 3 | 3 | 21 | 21 | 19 | 19 | 21 | 21 | 21 | 20 |
| UK | 18 | 20 | 19 | 19 | 9 | 7 | 7 | 9 | 10 | 8 | 6 | 8 |

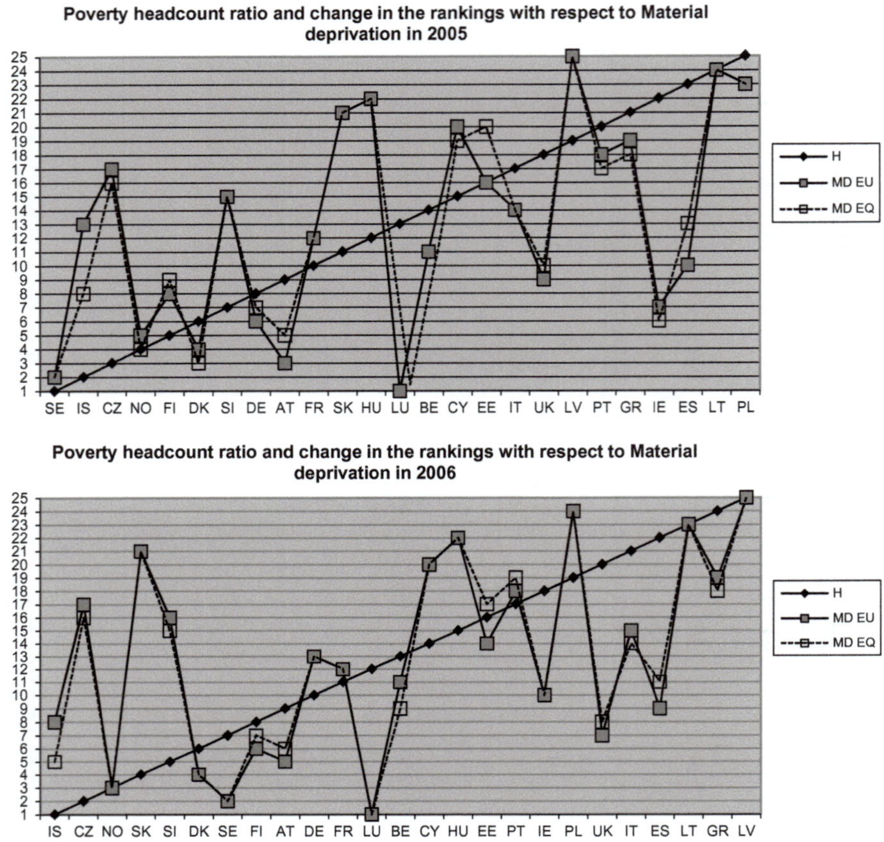


**Fig. 1** Changes in the ranks in material deprivation (MD) with respect to income poverty (H) among EU Member States in 2005 and 2006, with Eurobarometer weights (EU) and with Unitary (EQ) weights

years of the analysis. The highest material deprivation rates are exhibited by the new EU member states, where income poverty is low due to a narrow income distribution.

These basic findings suggest that European social policy aiming at assisting citizens with low well-being may be better performed by combining information on income poverty and material deprivation: indicators based solely on income poverty do not appear to be sufficient to capture living conditions adequately. Since the EU endorses the use of relative poverty lines, the absolute component of well-being is considered with measures of material deprivation.

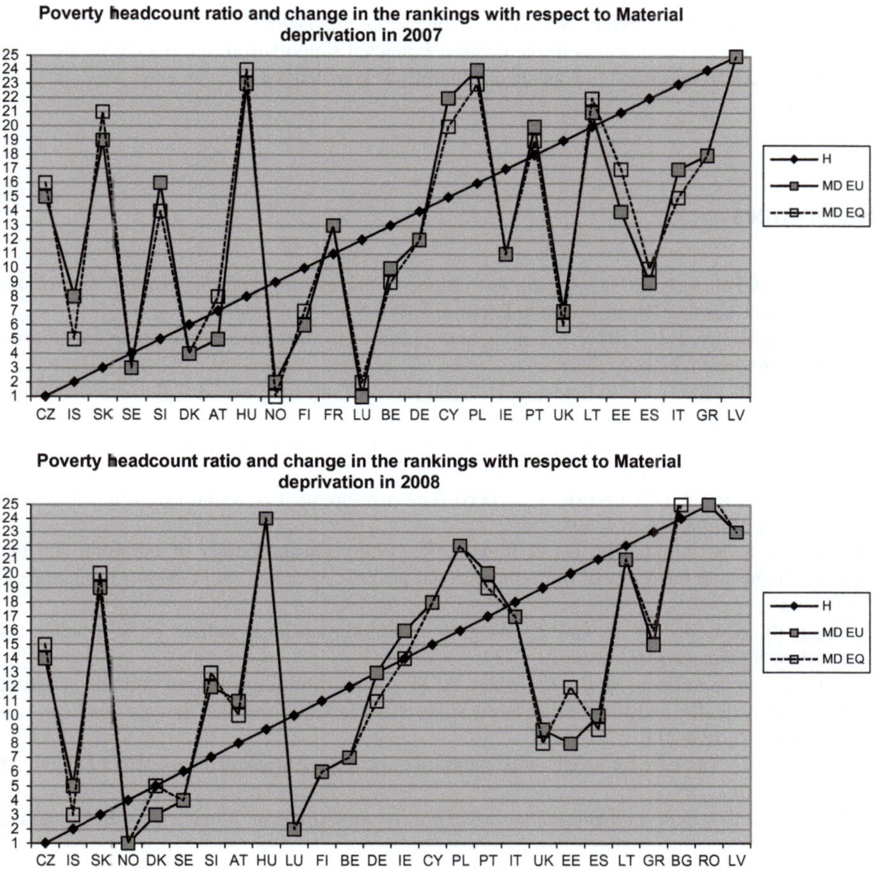


**Fig. 2** Changes in the ranks in material deprivation (MD) with respect to income poverty (H) among EU Member States in 2007 and 2007, with Eurobarometer weights (EU) and with Unitary (EQ) weights

## 4 Concluding Remarks

In this paper, we provide an axiomatic characterization of a popular index of multidimensional poverty, the weighted sum of the functioning failures, and apply it to assess material deprivation in the EU. The novelty of the theoretical approach is that the characterization applies to a discrete domain where standard techniques used on a continuum cannot be applied. The measure resembles Bourguignon and Chakravarty's (2003) index for measuring multidimensional poverty in the case of continuous variables. An interesting possibility for future research is to provide a characterization of an index based on both continuous and discrete data. This index may also consider the degree of dependence between attributes, an issue that has attracted increasing attention in the study of multidimensional well-being.

**Acknowledgements** We thank two referees for useful suggestions as well as the Fondazione Debenedetti for providing access to the dataset. Financial support from the Social Sciences and Humanities Research Council of Canada is gratefully acknowledged.

## References


Aaberge, R., & Peluso, E. (2011). *A counting approach for measuring multidimensional deprivation*. Università di Verona, Dipartimento di Economia, WP No. 7.

Alkire, S., & Foster, J. E. (2011). Counting and multidimensional poverty measurement. *Journal of Public Economics, 95*, 476–87.

Atkinson, A. B. (2003). Multidimensional deprivation: Contrasting social welfare and counting approaches. *Journal of Economic Inequality, 1,* 51–65.

Bourguignon, F., & Chakravarty, S. R. (2003). The measurement of multidimensional poverty. *Journal of Economic Inequality, 1,* 25–49.

Chakravarty, S. R., & D'Ambrosio, C. (2006). The measurement of social exclusion. *Review of Income and Wealth, 52,* 377–398.

Chakravarty, S. R., Mukherjee, D., & Ranade, R. (1998). On the family of subgroup and factor decomposable measures of multidimensional poverty. *Research on Economic Inequality, 8,* 175–194.

Decancq, K., & Lugo, M. A. (2012). Weights in multidimensional indices of well-being: An overview. *Econometric Reviews, 32,* 7–34.

Diez, H., Lasso de la Vega, M. C., & Urrutia, A. M. (2008). Multidimensional unit and subgroup consistent inequality and poverty measures: Some characterization results. *Research on Economic Inequality, 16*, 189–211.

Fahey, T. (2007). The case for an EU-wide measure of poverty. *European Sociological Review, 23,* 35–47.

Foster, J. E. (2007). *Report on multidimensional poverty measurement*. Mexico City: El Colegio de Mexico.

Gordon, G., Nandy, S., Pantazis, C., Pemberton, S., & Townsend, P. (2003). *Child poverty in the developing world*. Bristol: The Policy Press.

Guio, A.-C. (2005). Material deprivation in the EU. Statistics in focus, population and social conditions, living conditions and welfare, 21/2005, Eurostat, Luxembourg.

Guio, A.-C., Fusco, A., Marlier, E. (2009). *An EU approach to material deprivation using EU-SILC and eurobarometer data*. IRISS Working Paper 2009–19.

Jayaraj, D., & Subramanian, S. (2010). A Chakravarty–D'Ambrosio view of multidimensional deprivation: Some estimates for India. *Economic and Political Weekly, 45,* 53–65.

Kraft, C. H., Pratt, J. W., & Seidenberg, A. (1959). Intuitive probability on finite sets. *Annals of Mathematical Statistics, 30,* 408–419.

Lasso de la Vega, M. C. (2010). Counting poverty orderings and deprivation curves. *Research on Economic Inequality, 18*, 153–72.

Mack, J., & Lindsay, S. (1985). *Poor Britain*. London: George Allen and Unwin.

Ravallion, M. (2011). The human development index: A comment on Klugman, Rodriguez and Choi. *Journal of Economic Inequality, 9,* 475–478.

Ravallion, M. (2012). Troubling tradeoffs in the human development index. *Journal of Development Economics, 99,* 201–209.

Ringen, S. (1988). Direct and indirect measures of poverty. *Journal of Social Policy, 17,* 351–365.

Sen, A. (1976). Poverty: An ordinal approach to measurement. *Econometrica, 44,* 219–231.

Sen, A. (1992). *Inequality re-examined*. Cambridge, MA: Harvard University Press.

Stiglitz, J. E., Sen, A., & Fitoussi, J.-P. (2009). *Report by the commission on the measurement of economic performance and social progress*. Paris: CMEPSP.

Streeten, P. (1981). *First things first: Meeting basic human needs in developing countries*. New York: Oxford University Press.
TNS Opinion &Social. (2007). Poverty and exclusion. Report on the Special Eurobarometer No.279/Wave 67.1. Available at: http://ec.europa.eu/public_opinion/archives/ebs/ebs_279.pdf.
Townsend, P. (1979). *Poverty in the United Kingdom*. Harmondsworth: Penguin.
Tsui, K.-Y. (2002). Multidimensional poverty indices. *Social Choice and Welfare, 19*, 69–93.
Whelan, C. T., & Maître, B. (2009). Europeanization of inequality and European reference groups. *Journal of European Social Policy, 19*, 117–130.
Whelan, C. T., Nolan, B., Maître, B. (2008). *Measuring material deprivation in the enlarged EU*. ESRI Working Paper No. 249.

# Stochastic Dominance Relations for Integer Variables

**Satya R. Chakravarty and Claudio Zoli**

**Abstract** The objective of this paper is to derive some integer-majorization results for variable-sum comparisons. We use an axiomatic framework to establish equivalence between several intuitively reasonable conditions. © 2011 Elsevier Inc. All rights reserved.

**Keywords** Stochastic dominance · Generalized Lorenz curve · Grids · Integers · Measures · Majorization

**JEL classification** D63 · D81

## 1 Introduction

Stochastic dominance analysis is frequently employed for ranking alternative social states: see, for instance, the surveys by Levy (2006) and Shaked and Shanthikumar (2006). Traditionally, the variables of interest are defined on the continuum. However, in many applications, variables can only take non-negative integer values. Consider, for instance, the problem of comparing social exclusion, health conditions, or literacy levels across different countries or over time. In the evaluation of social exclusion we may measure the exclusion or deprivation score of a person by the number of

Elsevier has been kind enough to allow reprinting of this article published in Journal of Economic Theory, Volume, 147, 2012. Elsevier's permission in this context is acknowledged with sincere gratitude.

S. R. Chakravarty
Indian Statistical Institute, Kolkata 700108, India
e-mail: satyarchakravarty@gmail.com

C. Zoli (✉)
Dipartimento di Scienze Economiche, Università degli Studi di Verona, Via dell'Artigliere n. 19, 37129 Verona, Italy
e-mail: claudio.zoli@univr.it

 
S. R. Chakravarty (ed.), *Poverty, Social Exclusion and Stochastic Dominance*, Themes in Economics, https://doi.org/10.1007/978-981-13-3432-0_13

functionings or dimensions of well-being from which he is excluded.[1] Equivalently, the functioning score of an individual can be defined as the number of dimensions of well-being possessed by the person. Self-reported health status data typically consider five health categories ('poor', 'fair', 'good', 'very good' and 'excellent'), to which positive integer values are assigned in increasing order (see Allison and Foster 2004). Levels of literacy are usually measured in a similar way.

In all of these applications, the objects to be compared are vectors of non-negative integers. A few papers have used the stochastic dominance approach to compare vectors of integer-valued variables. Fishburn and Lavalle (1995) considered stochastic dominance analysis for probability distributions on a finite grid. By a grid, we mean a finite set of evenly spaced points. Their first and second order stochastic dominance results can be regarded as unidimensional grid counterparts to the traditional ones. The central idea underlying the Fishburn–Lavalle analysis goes back to the Muirhead (1903) integer-majorization result with a constant total.

In a recent contribution, Savaglio and Vannucci (2007) considered a finite set of basic alternatives/opportunities with a minimum opportunity threshold and developed a preordering of opportunity profiles involving the height function of an opportunity set. The height of an opportunity set is the number of opportunity sets which stand below it according to the preorder. Savaglio and Vannucci refer to this result, which holds for a fixed sum of heights, as 'an opportunity-profile counterpart' to the Hardy–Littewood–Pólya (1934) theorem in the measurement of inequality.

In each of the above contributions, the vectors under comparison have a fixed sum. Moreover, Fishburn and Lavalle (1995) compared probability distributions so that the sums are always equal to one. Milne and Neave (1994) considered stochastic dominance relations between discrete random variables on a common integer domain and showed that the dominated variable equals, in distribution, the dominating variable plus perturbation terms. While for first order dominance, perturbations are downward shift terms, for second-order dominance, all but two of such terms are disturbance terms with zero mean (See also Aboudi and Thon 1995).

In the applications mentioned above, and in many others, the sum of the scores need not be constant. The objective of this paper is to extend the integer-majorization analysis to the case of variable-sum vectors. For concreteness, the dominance relations are interpreted in terms of ranking of profiles of functioning scores. Our theorem can be interpreted as an integer-majorization counterpart to the Shorrocks (1983)–Marshall and Olkin (1979 A.2. Proposition, p. 108) result on generalized Lorenz ordering.

The most innovative feature of our article is the demonstration that if one profile of functioning scores integer-generalized Lorenz dominates another, then the former can be obtained from the latter by a sequence of transformations satisfying monotonicity and non-increasingness of marginal social evaluations, where monotonicity demands that if the functioning score of a person increases by one, then the resulting profile of scores cannot have a lower social evaluation than the original one. On the other hand,

[1] See Akerlof (1997), Atkinson (1998) and Chakravarty and D'Ambrosio (2006), among others, for alternative approaches to the measurement of social exclusion.

non-increasingness of marginal social evaluations indicates that an increase in the functioning score of a person by one has higher impact on the social evaluation the lower is the person's functioning score. Another innovative aspect of our result is that we determine the minimal number of transformations that are necessary to move from one distribution to another, where the latter integer-generalized Lorenz dominates the former. In order to derive this result, we make use of a restricted set of transformations satisfying monotonicity and non-increasingness of marginal social evaluations that are rank-preserving and 'distance-minimizing', where distance-minimization means that the transformations do not increase the gap between achievements of individuals with the same position in the initial and final distribution. Milne and Neave (1994) did not develop any result of this type. For a fixed total, our theorem is similar to Theorem 2 in Savaglio and Vannucci (2007),with the exception that our result is obtained by applying rank-preserving and 'distance-minimizing' transformations, and gives an integer version of the demonstration that of two income distributions with a given total, if one Lorenz dominates the other, then the former can be obtained from the latter by a sequence of progressive transfers and vice versa (see Atkinson 1970; Dasgupta et al. 1973; Kolm 1969; Rothschild and Stiglitz 1970, 1973).

## 2 Preliminaries and Notation

For any society with a given population size of $n \geq 2$, there is a finite non-empty set of $m \in N$ [where $N$ denotes the set of natural numbers] attributes or functionings of well-being, where $m \geq 1$ is given exogenously. Let $x_i$ be the functioning score of person $i$, that is, the number of functionings in which person $i$ is able to participate (see Chakravarty and D'Ambrosio 2006). Thus, $x_i$ takes on integer values from 0 to $m$. The whole population score profile is the vector $x = (x_1, x_2, \ldots, x_i, \ldots, x_n)$. Let $D^n = \otimes_{i=1}^{n}\{0, 1, \ldots, m\}$ be the set of attainment profiles for this $n$-person society.[2]

A measure of functioning evaluation is a function $E^n : D^n \rightarrow R$, where $R$ represents the real line. For any $x \in D^n$, $E^n(x)$ is an indicator of the degree of functioning attainment enjoyed by the persons in the society.

We write $\hat{x}$ to denote the non-decreasingly ordered permutation of $x$, that is, $\hat{x}_1 \leq \hat{x}_2 \leq \ldots \leq \hat{x}_i \leq \ldots \leq \hat{x}_{n-1} \leq \hat{x}_n$.

The following properties specify the behavior of the functioning evaluation indicators $E^n(\cdot)$.

**Axiom 1** (*Anonymity* [*ANY*]). For all $n \in N, x \in D^{n}$, $E^n(x) = E^n(xP)$, where $P$ is an $x \times n$ permutation matrix.

**Axiom 2** (*Monotonicity* [*MON*]). For all $n \in N, x \in D^{n}$, all $i \in \{1, 2, \ldots, n\}$ such that $x_i < m$

[2]For simplicity, we restrict attention to a fixed population set up. But our results can be extended easily to the variable population case under the assumption of replication invariance of the evaluation function in the spirit of Dasgupta et al. (1973).

$$E^n(x_1, x_2, \ldots, x_i + 1, \ldots, x_n) \geq E^n(x_1, x_2, \ldots, x_i, \ldots, x_n).$$

**Axiom 3** (*Non-increasingness of marginal evaluations* [*NIME*]). For all $n \in N$, $x \in D^{n,\cdot}$, all $i, j \in \{1, 2, \ldots, n\}$, if $m > x_i > x_j$ then

$$E^n(x_1, x_2, \ldots, x_j + 1, \ldots, x_i, \ldots, x_n) \geq E^n(x_1, x_2, \ldots, x_j, \ldots, x_i + 1, \ldots, x_n).$$

This set of axioms identifies the impact on the functioning evaluation of some transformations of the vectors $x$. We now make these transformations explicit.

Axiom ANY requires that the social evaluation does not depend on the identities of the individuals but only on their attainment profiles. Therefore, permuting the identities of the individuals does not affect the functioning evaluation. We introduce first the following transformation.

**Definition 1** (*$T_A$ transformation*). For all $x, y \in D^{n,\cdot}$, $x$ is obtained from $y$ through a "$T_A$ transformation", denoted $x = T_A(y)$, if and only if there exists a permutation function $\pi\colon \{1, 2, \ldots, n\} \to \{1, 2, \ldots, n\}$ such that $x_{\pi(i)} = y_i$ for all $i \in \{1, 2, \ldots, n\}$.

Let $\Psi$ denote the set of all $T_A$ transformations associated with all permutation functions $\pi$. Therefore, ANY is equivalent to stating that for all $T_A \in \Psi$, if $x = T_A(y)$, then $E^n(x) = E^n(y)$.

The following transformation is associated with the MON axiom, it requires that $x$ is obtained from $y$ through a unit increase in functioning score of one individual.

**Definition 2** (*$T_M$ transformation*). For all $x, y \in D^{n,\cdot}$, $x$ is obtained from $y$ through a "$T_M$ transformation", denoted $x = T_M(y)$, if and only if there exists $i \in \{1, 2, \ldots, n\}$ such that $x_\pi = y_i + 1 \leq m$ and $x_h = y_h$ for all $i \in \{1, 2, \ldots, n\} \backslash \{i\}$.

MON says that under a $T_M$ transformation, the final distribution cannot exhibit a lower level of functioning evaluation than the original one. Let $\Lambda$ denote the set of all $T_M$ transformations. Then, MON is equivalent to stating that for all $T_M \in \Lambda$, if $x = T_M(y)$, then $E^n(x) \geq E^n(y)$.

The next transformation is associated with the NIME axiom, which says that an increase in an individual's functioning attainment score has a higher impact on the social evaluation the lower is the individual's functioning score.

**Definition 3** (*$T_{\mathrm{NIME}}$ transformation*). For all $x, y \in D^{n,\cdot}$, $x$ is obtained from $y$ through a "$T_{\mathrm{NIME}}$ transformation", denoted $x = T_{\mathrm{NIIME}}(y)$, if and only if there exists $i \in \{1, 2, \ldots, n\}$ such that $m > y_i - 1 > y_j$, $x_h = y_h$ for all $h \neq i.j$, $x_i = y_i - 1$ and $x_i = y_j + 1$.

Let $\Gamma$ denote the set of all $T_{\mathrm{NIME}}$ transformations. Axiom NIME is, therefore, equivalent to stating that for all $T_{\mathrm{NIME}} \in \Gamma$, if $x = T_{\mathrm{NIME}}(y)$, then $E^n(x) \geq E^n(y)$.[3]

[3]This implication can be obtained as follows: note that the NIME axiom posits that

$$E^n(x_1, \ldots, x_j + 1, \ldots, x_i, \ldots, x_n) - E^n(x_1, \ldots, x_j, \ldots, x_i, \ldots, x_n)$$

$$\geq E^n(x_1, \ldots, x_j, \ldots, x_i + 1, \ldots, x_n) - E^n(x_1, \ldots, x_j, \ldots, x_i, \ldots x_n)$$

In order to investigate the minimal number of $T_M$ and $T_{\text{NIME}}$ transformations linking two ordered distributions $\hat{z}$ and $\hat{y}$ such that $\hat{z}$ can be obtained from $\hat{y}$ through a finite sequence of $T_M$ and $T_{\text{NIME}}$ transformations, we will introduce the following two sets of transformations that are respectively included in $\Lambda$ and $\Gamma$. Both definitions are based on ranked distributions and require that the transformations are rank-preserving and do not increase the absolute distance $\left|\hat{z}_i - \hat{x}_i\right|$ between $\hat{z}$ and $\hat{x}$ evaluated at each position $i \in \{1, 2, \ldots, n\}$. Here we have restricted attention to ordered distributions to strengthen the normative requirement of the $T_M$ and $T_{\text{NIME}}$ transformations and formalize the notion of distance-minimizing transformation that is based on comparisons between the attainments of individuals at the same rank in $\hat{z}$, $\hat{y}$ and $\hat{x}$. Because of the rank-preserving nature of the transformations, these comparisons involve only individuals whose attainments are affected by the transformations.

**Definition 4** ($T_{M|\hat{Z}}$ *transformation*). For all $x, y \in D^{n,}, x$ is obtained from $y$ through a "$T_{M|\hat{Z}}$ transformation", denoted $x = T_{M|\hat{z}}(y)$, if and only if there exists $i \in \{1, 2, \ldots, n\}$ such that $\hat{x}_i = \hat{y}_i + 1 \leq m$, and $\hat{x}_h = \hat{y}_h$ for all $h \in \{1, 2, \ldots, n\} \backslash \{i\}$, where (a) $\hat{y}_i < \hat{y}_{1+1}$ [with $\hat{y}_{1+1} := m$] and (b) $\hat{y}_i < \hat{z}_i$.

Condition (a) in the previous definition requires that the transformation is rank-preserving while condition (b) requires that $\left|\hat{z}_i - \hat{y}_i\right| > \left|\hat{z}_i - \hat{x}_i\right|$.

**Definition 5** ($T_{\text{NIME}|\hat{Z}}$ *transformation*). For all $x, y \in D^{n,}$, $x$ is obtained from $y$ through a "$T_{\text{NIME}|\hat{Z}}$ transformation", denoted $x = T_{\text{NIME}|\hat{z}}(y)$, if and only if there exists $i \in \{1, 2, \ldots, n\}$ such that $m > \hat{y}_i - 1 > \hat{y}_j, \hat{x}_h = \hat{y}_h$ for all $h \neq i, j, \hat{x}_i = \hat{y}_i - 1, \hat{x}_j = \hat{y}_j + 1$ (a.1) $\hat{y}_i > \hat{y}_{i-1}$, (a.2) $\hat{y}_j < \hat{y}_{j+1}$ and (b.1) $\hat{y}_i > \hat{z}_i$ (b.2) $\hat{y}_j < \hat{z}_j$.

Conditions (a.1) and (a.2) in the previous definition impose the restriction that the transformation is rank preserving, while conditions (b.1) and (b.2) require that $\left|\hat{z}_k - \hat{y}_k\right| > \left|\hat{z}_k - \hat{x}_k\right|$ for $k \in \{i, j\}$.

## 3 The Results

The following theorem identifies the set of partial orderings defined over distributions in $D^n$ consistent with the measures satisfying the previous axioms. A rank-dependent class of linear social evaluation indices is also presented (see Weymark 1981; Yaari 1987). It can be considered equivalent to the generalized Gini social evaluation function for profiles of opportunity sets characterized in Weymark (2003) for a domain analogous to $D^n$.

**Theorem 1** *Let* $x, y \in D^{n,}$. *The following statements are equivalent*:

---

while if $x = T_{\text{MIME}}(y)$, then the conditions $E^n(x) \geq E^n(y)$ is

$$E^n(y_1, \ldots, y_j + 1, \ldots, y_{i-1}, \ldots, y_n) \geq E^n(y_1, \ldots, y_j, \ldots, y_i, \ldots, y_n)$$

Subtracting $E^n(y_1, \ldots, y_j, \ldots, y_i - 1 \ldots, y_n)$ from both sides of the second inequality, we obtain the NIME axiom requirement if $y_i - 1 = x_i$ and $y_k = x_k$ for all $k \neq i$.

(1) $\sum_{i=1}^{n} \upsilon_i^n \cdot \hat{x}_i \geq \sum_{i=1}^{n} \upsilon_i^n \cdot \hat{y}_i$ *for all* $\upsilon_i^n \geq \upsilon_{i+1}^n \geq 0$
(2) $\sum_{i=1}^{k} \hat{x}_i \geq \sum_{i=1}^{k} \hat{y}_i$ *for all* $k = 1, 2, \ldots, n$.
(3) *Either* $\hat{x} = \hat{y}$ *or* $\hat{x}$ *can be obtained from* $\hat{y}$ *through a finite sequence of* $T_{T|\hat{x}}$ *and* $T_{\text{NIME}|\hat{x}}$ *transformation.*
(4) $x$ *can be obtained from* $y$ *through a finite sequence of* $T_A$, $T_M$ *and* $T_{\text{NIME}}$ *transformations.*
(5) $E^n(x) \geq E^n(y)$ *for all indices* $E^n(\cdot)$ *satisfying ANY, MON and NIME.*

According to condition (1) of Theorem 1, the weighted sum of individual functionings levels in profile $\hat{x}$ is at least as high as that in the profile $\hat{y}$, where the non-negative weights are arranged non-increasingly. Given that $\hat{x}$ and $\hat{y}$ are arranged in non-decreasing order, condition (2) says that the cumulative sum of the functioning scores of the first $k$ persons in $\hat{x}$ is at least as large as that in $\hat{y}$, where $k = 1, 2, \ldots, n$, that is, $x$ integer-generalized Lorenz dominates $y$. Condition (5) of the theorem shows that these two conditions are equivalent to the requirement that y does not have a larger social functioning evaluation than $x$ for all social evaluation indices that fulfill ANY, MON and NIME. Condition (4) identifies the corresponding set of transformations leading from $y$ to $x$. More interestingly, condition (3) shows that it is possible to move from $\hat{y}$ to $\hat{x}$ through a finite set of $T_{M|\hat{x}}$ and $T_{\text{NIME}|\hat{x}}$ transformations. Because of their construction, these sequences will also be minimal in terms of the number of steps leading from $\hat{y}$ to $\hat{x}$.

*Proof of Theorem 1* If $\hat{x} = \hat{y}$ the implications are immediate. We consider the case $\hat{x} \neq \hat{y}$.

(1) $\Rightarrow$ (2): Le $\delta_i := \hat{x}_i - \hat{y}_i$. We prove that $\sum_{i=1}^{n} \upsilon_i^n \cdot \delta_i \geq 0$ for all $\upsilon_i^n \geq \upsilon_{i+1}^n \geq 0$ implies $\sum_{i=1}^{k} \delta_i \geq 0$ for all $k = 1, 2, \ldots, n$. Without loss of generality, we define $\upsilon_i^n = \sum_{k=i}^{n} \alpha_k^n$. If $\alpha_k^n \geq 0$ for all $k = 1, 2, \ldots, n$ then $\upsilon_i^n \geq \upsilon_{i+1}^n \geq 0$. As a result, we can rewrite

$$\sum_{i=1}^{n} \upsilon_i^n \cdot \delta_i = \sum_{i=1}^{n} \sum_{k=i}^{n} \alpha_k^n \cdot \delta_i = \sum_{k=1}^{n} \alpha_k^n \sum_{i=1}^{k} \delta_i$$

Condition (1) is, therefore, equivalent to $\sum_{k=1}^{n} \alpha_n^k \sum_{i=1}^{k} (\hat{x}_i - \hat{y}_i) \geq 0$ for all $\alpha_k^n \geq 0$. Condition (2) follows by letting $\alpha_{k^*}^n = 0$ for all $k^* \neq k$ and $\alpha_k^n > 0$.

(2) $\Rightarrow$ (3): We show that if (2) is satisfied, then it is possible to decompose the vector of elements $\delta_i$ into a finite sequence of changes associated with $T_{M|\hat{x}}$ and/or $T_{\text{NIME}|\hat{x}}$ transformations. The decomposition process is divided into two parts. The first part only applies if $\sum_{i=1}^{n} \hat{x}_i \neq \sum_{i=1}^{n} \hat{y}_i$. (A) First, we identify the $T_{M|\hat{x}}$ transformations $\delta_i^*$ such that $\sum_{i=1}^{n} \hat{x}_i = \sum_{i=1}^{n} \left(\hat{y}_i + \delta_i^*\right)$, that is, starting from $\hat{y}$ we get a distribution with the same total functioning score as $\hat{x}$. (B) Then we compare the two distributions $\hat{x}$ and $\hat{y} + \delta^*$ with same total scores identifying the set of $T_{\text{NIME}|\hat{x}}$ transformations leading to $\hat{x}$ starting from $\hat{y} + \delta^*$, where $\delta^*$ is the vector of $\delta_i^*$'s.

Part (A)

Let $\delta_i : \hat{x}_i - \hat{y}_i$ and $\Delta_i := \hat{y}_{t+1} - \hat{y}_i \geq 0$ for $i \in \{1, 2, \ldots, n\}$, where $\hat{y}_{n+1} : m$. Let $X_k = \sum_{i=1}^{k} \hat{x}_i$ and $X = \sum_{i=1}^{n} \hat{x}_i$ with analogous notation $Y_k$ and $Y$ for distribution $y$.

Suppose that $X > Y$. Because $X > Y$, there must be some $k \in \{1, ..., n\}$ such that $y_k < m$. Because $y_{n+1} = m$, it then follows that there is some $i \in \{1, ..., n\}$for which $\Delta_i > 0$. Let $i^* := \max\{i : \delta_i > 0, \Delta_i > 0\}$. Then we identify the sequence of $T_{M|\hat{x}}$ transformations making use of a sequence of increases $\delta_i^{(t)} \in \{1, \ldots, m\}$, where $t$ denotes the index of the element in the sequence and $i$ is the position of the individual experiencing the increase in the functioning score. Each of these increases corresponds to $\delta_i^{(t)}$ many $T_{M|\hat{x}}$-type transformations and will lead to a sequence of distributions $\hat{y}^{(t)}$ starting from $\hat{y}^{(0)} : \hat{y}$.

Let $\delta_{i^*}^{(1)} := \min\{\delta_{i^*}, \Delta_{i^*}, X - Y\}$ be the first element of the sequence. By construction, the new distribution $\hat{y}^{(1)}$ is obtained by letting $\hat{y}^{(1)} : \hat{y}$ for all $i \neq i^*$ and $\hat{y}_{i^*}^{(1)} : \hat{y}_{i^*} + \delta_{i^*}^{(1)}$. According to the definition of $\delta_{i^*}^{(1)}$, the ranking in $\hat{y}^{(1)}$ is preserved (because $\Delta_{i^*} > 0$ is considered in the definition of $\delta_{i^*}^{(1)}$). Furthermore, $\hat{y}_{i^*} < \hat{y}_{i^*}^{(1)} \leq \hat{x}_{i^*}$ (given that $\delta_{i^*} > 0$ is considered in the definition of $\delta_{i^*}^{(1)}$) and $X \geq Y^{(1)} > Y$ (because $X - Y > 0$ is considered in the definition of $\delta_{i^*}^{(1)}$.

We prove that:

**Claim (i)** *If $\hat{x} \neq \hat{y}$ then $i^*$ exists.*

**Claim (ii)** $\sum_{i=1}^{k} \hat{x}_i \geq \sum_{i=1}^{k} \hat{y}_i^{(1)} \geq \sum_{i=1}^{k} \hat{y}_i$ for all $k \in= \{1, 2, \ldots, n\}$.

*Proof of Claim (i)* Consider $\hat{x} \neq \hat{y}$ and suppose that $i^*$ does not exist. Then, recalling that, by dentition, $\Delta_i \geq 0$, it follows that for any $i \in \{1, 2, \ldots, n\}$ either $\delta_i \leq 0$ or $\Delta_i = 0$. Recalling again that $\sum_{i=1}^{k} \delta_i \geq 0$ for all $i$ and $\hat{x} \neq \hat{y}$, it follows that there exists some position $i_0$ such that $\delta_{i0} = \hat{x}_{i0} - \hat{y}_{i0} > 0$. Thus, we necessarily have $\Delta i_0 = 0$, implying $\hat{y}_{i0} = \hat{y}_{i0+1}$. Suppose that $i_0 \neq n$, then, since the vector $\hat{x}$ is ranked in non-decreasing order, we also have $\hat{x}_{i0+1} \geq \hat{x}_{i0}$ leading to $\hat{x}_{i0+1} \geq \hat{x}_{i0} > \hat{y}_{i0} = \hat{y}_{i0+1}$. Therefore, $\hat{x}_{i0+1} - \hat{y}_{i0+1} > 0$, thereby contradicting our initial assumption unless $\Delta_{i0+1} = 0$. By repeating the same argument, we get to the case where $i_0 + 1 = n$. In view of the initial assumption, then $\hat{x}_n - \hat{y}_n > 0$ and $\Delta_n = 0$ have to hold. However, by construction $\Delta_n = 0 \leftrightarrow m = \hat{y}_{n+1} = \hat{y}_n$ . Thus, since $\hat{y}_n = m$ is the maximum functioning score, it is impossible that $\delta_n = \hat{x}_n - \hat{y}_n > 0$. This final consideration contradicts the initial hypothesis that $i^*$ does not exist, thereby, proving Claim (i).

*Proof of Claim (ii)* By construction $\sum_{i=1}^{k} \hat{y}_i^{(1)} \geq \sum_{i=1}^{k} \hat{y}_i$ for all $k$. We need to prove that $X_k = \sum_{i=1}^{k} \hat{x}_i \geq \sum_{i=1}^{k} \hat{y}_i^{(1)} = Y_k^{(1)}$ for all $k \in \{1, 2, \ldots, n\}$.

Condition $X_k \geq Y_k^{(1)}$ holds by construction for $k \in \{1, 2, \ldots, i^*\}$ because $Y_k^{(1)} = Y_k$ for $k \in \{1, 2, \ldots, i^* - 1\}$ and consequently, since $\delta_{i^*} \geq \delta_{i^*}^{(1)} > 0$ we have also $X_{i^*} - Y_{i^*}^{(1)} = X_{i^*-1} - Y_{i^*-1}^{(1)} + (\delta_{i^*} - \delta_{i^*}^{(1)})$. Recalling that $X_{i^*-1} - Y_{i^*-1}^{(1)} = X_{i^*-1} - Y_{i^*-1} \geq 0$ and that $\delta_{i^*} - \delta_{i^*}^{(1)} \geq 0$, we obtain $X_* \geq Y_{i^*}^{(1)}$.

We now consider the case where $k \in \{i^*+1, \ldots n\}$. Let $\Im := \arg\min\{X_k - Y_k : k \in \{i^* + 1, \ldots, n\}\}$. The condition $X_k \geq Y_k^{(1)}$ does not hold if there exist $k_0 \in \Im$ (not necessarily unique) such that $X_{k0} - Y_{k0} < \delta_{i^*}^{(1)}$ .

If $n \notin \Im$, then for any $k_0 \in \Im$, there exists an $i' > k_0$ such that $\delta_{i'} > 0$. If $\Delta_{i'} > 0$, let $i_0 = i'$. If $\Delta_{i'} = 0$, reasoning as in the proof of Claim (i), there must exist an $i_0 > i'$ such that both $\delta_{i0} > 0$ and $\Delta_{i0} > 0$. Because $i_0 > k_0 > i^*$, we have a contradiction with the definition of $i^*$.

If $n \in \Im$, then $X_n - Y_n = X - Y > 0$. In this case, by construction we have argued that $X - Y \geq \delta_{i^*}^{(1)}$, thereby, establishing the final contradiction that proves Claim (ii).

Having derived the first stage of the algorithm, we can move to its general specification. The decomposition algorithm can be constructed letting $\hat{y}_i^{(t)} := \hat{y}_i^{(t-1)}$ for all $i \neq i^*$ and $\hat{y}_{i^*}^{(t)} := \hat{y}_{i^*}^{(t-1)} + \delta_{i^*}^{(t)}$, where $\hat{y}^{(0)} := \hat{y}$. We then let $\delta_{i,t} := \hat{x}_i - \hat{y}_i^{(t-1)}$ and $\Delta_{i,t} := \hat{y}_{i+1}^{(t-1)} - \hat{y}_i^{(t-1)}$ for $i \in \{1, 2, \ldots, n\}$, where $\hat{y}_{n+1,t} := m$ and $Y^{(t)} = \sum_{i=1}^n \hat{y}_i^{(t)}$.

The algorithm is obtained by identifying at each stage $t$

$$i^* := \max\{i : \delta_{i,t} > 0, \Delta_{i,t} > 0\} \tag{1}$$

and

$$\delta_{i^*}^{(t)} := \min\{\delta_{i^*,t}; \Delta_{i^*,t}; X - Y^{(t-1)}\} \tag{2}$$

The procedure followed by the algorithm stops after $T$ stages when $\delta_{i^*}^{(T)} = X - Y^{(T-1)}$. Given that the difference $X - Y^{(T-1)}$ is reduced by at least one unit after each stage, $T$ equals at most $X - Y$, which is finite. As a result, the final distribution $\hat{y}^{(T)}$ is obtained as $\hat{y} + \delta^*$, where the vector $\delta^*$ is such that $\delta_i^* = \sum_{t=1}^T \delta_i^{(t)}$ for all $i$ associated with at least one positive $\delta_i^{(i)}$ and 0 for all the other elements of $\delta^*$.

Part (B)

We consider now the case $X = Y$, where the distribution $\hat{y}$ can also be considered as obtained through the set of transformations in Part (A). We then apply a sequence of $T_{\text{NIME}|\hat{x}}$ transformations to $\hat{y}$ in order to obtain $\hat{x}$. Recall that by construction $\hat{y}^{(t)}$ is obtained from $\hat{y}^{(t-1)}$ through a $T_{\text{NIME}|\hat{x}}$ transformation if $\hat{y}_j^{(t)} - \hat{y}_j^{(t-1)} = 1$ and $\hat{y}_i^{(t)} - \hat{y}_i^{(t-1)} = -1$, where $j < i$ and $\hat{y}_h^{(t)} - \hat{y}_h^{(t-1)} = 0$ for all $h \neq i, j$, where these transformations do not affect the ranking of the agents involved. Moreover, it is required that $\hat{x}_j - \hat{y}_j^{(t-1)} > 0$ and $\hat{x}_i - \hat{y}_j^{(t-1)} < 0$.

We now introduce the algorithm that decomposes the transition from $\hat{y}$ to $\hat{x}$ applying $T_{\text{NIME}|\hat{x}}$ transformation. We define $\delta_{i,t}$ and $\Delta_{i,t}$ as in Part (A). Let

$$i^- := \max\{i : \delta_{i,t} < 0, \Delta_{i-1,t} > 0\} \tag{3}$$

and letting

$$i^+ := \max\{i : \delta_{i,t} > 0, \Delta_{i,t} > 0\} \tag{4}$$

The algorithm is constructed by letting $\hat{y}_i^{(t)} := \hat{y}_i^{(t-1)}$ for all $i \neq i^-$, $i^+$, $\hat{y}_h^{(t)} := \hat{y}_h^{(t-1)} + \delta_h^{(t)}$ for $h = i^-$ and $h = i^+$, where $\hat{y}^{(0)} : \hat{y}$.

**Claim (iii)** *If $\hat{x} \neq \hat{y}$, then $i^-$ and $i^+$ exist. Moreover, $i^- > i^+$.*

*Proof of Claim (iii)* For expositional purposes, without loss of generality, we let $t = 1$ and suppress the subscript $t$ in the notation of this proof. The claim of existence of $i^+$ is thus analogous to Claim (i) in Part (A) concerning $i^*$.

In order to prove that $i^-$ exists and $i^- > i^+$, we note that $X_k \geq Y_k$ for all $k$ with $X = Y$, or equivalently, $\sum_{i=1}^{k} \delta_i \geq 0$ for all $k$ and $\sum_{i=1}^{n} \delta_i = 0$, which imply that $\sum_{i=k}^{n} \delta_i \leq 0$ for all $k \in \{1, 2, \ldots, n-1\}$. Thus, the last $\delta_i$ element which is different from 0 is negative. Because $\hat{x} \neq \hat{y}$, such an element exists. Suppose that $i^-$ does not exist. Then there exists $j$ such that $\delta_j < 0$ and $\delta_i = 0$ for $i \in \{j+1, 2, \ldots, n\}$ with $\Delta_{j-1} = 0$. Note that $\delta_j < 0 \leftrightarrow \hat{x}_j < \hat{y}_j$ and $\Delta_{j-1} = 0 \leftrightarrow \hat{y}_j = \hat{y}_{j-1}$. Recalling that $\hat{x}_{j-1} \leq \hat{x}_j$, it follows that, $\hat{x}_{j-1} \leq \hat{x}_j < \hat{y}_j = \hat{y}_{j-1}$, and thus, $\delta_{j-1} < 0$. Then if $\Delta_{j-2} > 0$ it follows that $i^-$ exists and $i^- > i^+$. Otherwise, if $\Delta_{j-2} = 0$, we can repeat the previous argument. However, notice that in order to guarantee that $X_k \geq Y_k$ for all $k$, because $\hat{x} \neq \hat{y}$, there must exist $i$ such that $\delta_i > 0$ and, therefore, there is at least one $\ell > n$ such that $\delta_\ell \geq 0$ while $\delta_{\ell+1} < 0$. Hence, it is necessarily true that $\Delta_\ell > 0$, otherwise, if $\Delta_\ell = 0$, we obtain $\hat{x}_\ell \geq \hat{y}_\ell = \hat{y}_{\ell+1} > \hat{x}_{\ell+1}$, which contradicts $\hat{x}_\ell \leq \hat{x}_{\ell+1}$. Combining $\Delta_\ell > 0$ with $\delta_{\ell+1} < 0$, we obtain that $i^- = \ell + 1$. Moreover, $i^+ \leq \ell$ and thus $i^- > i^+$, which completes the proof of Claim (iii).

We now let

$$-\delta_{i^-}^{(t)} = \delta_{i^+}^{(t)} := \min\{\delta_{i^+,t} - \delta_{i^-,t};\ \Delta_{i^+,t};\ \Delta_{i^--1,t}\},$$

which completes the algorithm for deriving the set of $T_{\mathrm{NIME}|\hat{x}}$ transformations. Note that the transformations $-\delta_{i^-}^{(t)} = \delta_{i^+}^{(t)} > 0$, where $i^+ < i^-$, coincides with $\delta_{i^+}^{(t)}$ many $T_{\mathrm{NIME}|\hat{x}}$ transformations. Furthermore, these transformations are rank-preserving given that by construction $\delta_{i^+}^{(t)} \leq \Delta_{i^+,t}$ and $\delta_{i^-}^{(t)} \geq \Delta_{i^--1,t}$. They are also distance-minimizing since $\delta_{i^+}^{(t)} > 0$ and $\delta_{i^-}^{(t)} < 0$.

Note also that, by construction, after each transformation we reduce $\sum_{i=1}^{n} |\delta_i|$ by 2 units. Thus, $T = \sum_{i=1}^{n} |\delta_i|/2$ is the (finite) number of $T_{\mathrm{NIME}|\hat{x}}$ transformations implementing $\hat{x}$ from $\hat{y}$.

In order to complete the proof we show that:

**Claim (iv)** $\sum_{i=1}^{k} \hat{x}_i \geq \sum_{i=1}^{k} \hat{y}_i^{(t)} \geq \sum_{i=1}^{k} \hat{y}_i^{(t-1)} \geq \sum_{i=1}^{k} \hat{y}_i$ for all $k \in \{1, 2, \ldots, n\}$, $t \in \{1, 2, \ldots, T\}$.

*Proof of Claim (iv)* Each $T_{\mathrm{NIME}|\hat{x}}$ transformation implies that $\sum_{i=1}^{k} \hat{y}_i^{(t)} \geq \sum_{i=1}^{k} \hat{y}_i^{(t-1)}$ for all $k \in \{1, 2, \ldots, n\}$, where $t \in \{1, 2, \ldots, T\}$. For $t = 1$ we have $\sum_{i=1}^{k} \hat{y}_i^{(1)} \geq \sum_{i=1}^{k} \hat{y}_i^{(0)} = \sum_{i=1}^{k} \hat{y}_i$, while for $t = T$ we have $\sum_{i=1}^{k} \hat{x}_i = \sum_{i=1}^{k} \hat{y}_i^{(T)} \geq \sum_{i=1}^{k} \hat{y}_i^{(T-1)}$. Because of transitivity of the dominance relation, it is always guaranteed that $\sum_{i=1}^{k} \hat{x}_i \geq \sum_{i=1}^{k} \hat{y}_i^{(t)}$ for $t \in \{1, 2, \ldots, T-1\}$.Thus, dominance holds at each stage of the algorithm.

(3) $\Rightarrow$ (4): Note that the sets of $T_{M|\hat{x}}$ and $T_{\mathrm{NIME}|\hat{x}}$ transformations are respectively subsets of the sets of $T_M$ and $T_{\mathrm{NIME}}$ transformations. Moreover, because of $T_A$ transformations we can move attention from $\hat{x}$ and $\hat{y}$ to $x$ and $y$.

(4) ⇒ (5): By definition.

(5) ⇒ (1): We prove that the class of social evaluation measures in (1) is a special case of those in (5). Let $E_v^n(x) := \sum_{i=1}^n v_i^n \cdot \hat{x}_i$. The index $E_v^n$ satisfies ANY since it is defined in terms of ranked vectors $\hat{x}$. $E_v^n$ satisfies MON if and only if $E_v^n(x') - E_v^n(x) = \sum_{j=1}^n v_j^n \cdot (\hat{x}_j' - \hat{x}_j) \geq 0$ if $x' = T_M(x)$. Letting $\hat{x}_j - \hat{x}_j' = 0$ for all $j \neq i$ and $\hat{x}_i' - \hat{x}_i' = 1$, then $E_v^n(x') - E_v^n(x) \geq 0$ implies that $v_i^n \geq 0$. Given that we can choose any $i \in \{1, 2, \ldots, n\}$, it follows that a necessary condition for $E_v^n$ to satisfy MON is $v_i^n \geq 0$ for all $i$. This condition is also sufficient.

$E_v^n$ satisfies NIME if and only if $E_v^n(x') - E_v^n(x) \geq 0$, where $x' = T_{\text{NIME}(x)}$. Suppose that $x$ is obtained from $x'$ through a $T_{\text{NIME}}$ transformation involving individuals in positions $i$ and $i+1$ for $i \leq n-1$. Then $E_v^n(x') - E_v^n(x) = v_i^n - v_{i+1}^n$. Thus, $v_i^n \geq v_{i+1}^n$ for all $i \in \{1, 2, \ldots, n-1\}$ is necessary for $E_v^n$ to satisfy NIME. It is also sufficient.

Of interest is the algorithm adopted for the decomposition of the integer-generalized Lorenz dominance condition into two sequences of $T_M$ and $T_{\text{NIME}}$ transformations. Both sequences of transformations $T_{M|\hat{x}}$ and $T_{\text{NIME}|\hat{x}}$ are rank-preserving and distance-minimizing. In this respect, the algorithm in Part (B) of our proof differs from the one used to prove integer majorization in Muirhead (1903) (and also the one in Marshall and Olkin 1979, Lemma B.B.1, p. 21). It also differs from those in Bossert and Fleurbaey (2002) and Aboudi and Thon (2006) that are defined for real variables which are distance-minimizing but not rank-preserving. Moreover, our algorithm in Part (A) differs from the one adopted in Shorrocks (1983) for the same purposes because the latter does not necessarily guarantee that $\hat{y}_i^{(t)} \leq \hat{x}_i$ at each stage $t$ if individual $i$ is affected by a $T_M$ transformation.

Our algorithm and the integer nature of the variables considered allows us to derive the minimal $T_M$ and $T_{TIME}$ transformations leading from $\hat{y}$ to $\hat{x}$ (see also Deineko et al. 2009). The following remark is a direct consequence of the fact that condition (2) implies condition (3) in Theorem 1.

*Remark 1* For any $x, y \in D^n$ such that $\sum_{i=1}^k \hat{x}_i \geq \sum_{i=1}^k \hat{y}$ for all $k = 1, 2, \ldots, n$, the minimal numbers of $T_M$ and $T_{\text{TIME}}$ transformations leading from $\hat{y}$ to $\hat{x}$, denoted respectively by $\#T_M^n(y, x)$ and $\#T_{\text{NIME}}^n(y, x)$ are

$$\#T_M^n(y, x) = X - Y; \quad \#T_{\text{NIME}}^n(y, x) = \frac{\sum_{i=1}^n |\hat{x}_i - \hat{y}_i| - (X - Y)}{2}; \tag{5}$$

These indices can be considered as bidimensional measures of "distance" between the two distributions ranked according to integer-generalized Lorenz dominance.

When $X > Y$ the algorithm in Part (A) of the proof of Theorem 1, that makes use of $T_{M|\hat{x}}$ transformations, allows us to obtain a distribution which is "as close as possible" to $\hat{x}$ in the metric of the number of $T_{\text{TIME}}$ transformations as illustrated in the following example.

*Example 1* Let $\hat{x} = (2, 2), \hat{y} = (1, 2)$, and $\hat{z} = (0, 3)$ with $m = 4$. Note $\sum_{i=1}^k \hat{x}_i \geq \sum_{i=1}^k \hat{y}_i \geq \sum_{i=1}^k \hat{z}$ for all $k \in \{1, 2\}$, and $X - Y = X - Z = 1$. Moreover, $\hat{x}$ rank dominates $\hat{y}$, that is, $\hat{x}_i \geq \hat{y}_i$ for $i \in \{1, 2\}$ . If we modify $\hat{y}$, with a $T_M$ transformation that increases the higher functioning score leading to $\hat{y}' = (1, 3)$, the integer-generalized Lorenz dominance condition for $\hat{x}$ over $\hat{y}'$ is satisfied. However, one more $T_{\text{NIME}}$ transformation is then necessary to lead to $\hat{x}$ starting from $\hat{y}'$. If instead we use the unique $T_{M|\hat{x}}$ admissible transformation that increases the lower functioning score in $\hat{y}$, we obtain immediately $\hat{x}$. Similar considerations apply in moving from $\hat{z}$ to $\hat{x}$. If we use a $T_M$ transformation that is not distance-minimizing from $\hat{z}$ to obtain $\hat{z}' = (0, 4)$, then two more $T_{\text{NIME}}$ transformations are necessary to lead to $\hat{x}$ starting from $\hat{z}'$. If instead we apply the unique $T_{M|\hat{x}}$ admissible transformation to $\hat{z}'$, we obtain $\hat{z}'' = (1, 3)$ that requires only one $T_{\text{NIME}}$ transformation to lead to $\hat{x}$.

If $\hat{x}$ rank dominates $\hat{y}$, only $T_{M|\hat{x}}$ transformations are necessary to move from $\hat{y}$ to $\hat{x}$. In general, if $\hat{x}$ integer-generalized Lorenz dominates $\hat{y}$, then by using $T_M$ transformations that are not distance-minimizing with respect to $\hat{x}$, we increase the minimal number of $T_{\text{NIME}}$ transformations that are required to lead to $\hat{x}$.

## 4 Conclusion

Often it becomes necessary to rank social states where each component of a state is represented by an integer. In this paper, we have developed some majorization results for ranking states of this type under the quite general assumption of variability of the total. Our characterizations can be treated as generalizations of the existing results in the literature.

**Acknowledgements** For comments and suggestions, we are grateful to two referees, an associate editor of this journal, Vincenzo Denicolò and participants of the JET Symposium on "Inequality and Risk", Paris, June 25–26, 2010. Chakravarty thanks the Bocconi University, Milan, Italy, for support. Financial support from the Italian Ministero dell'Istruzione, dell'Università e della Ricerca (Prin 2007) is gratefully acknowledged by Claudio Zoli.

## References

Aboudi, R., & Thon, D. (1995). *The duality approach to stochastic dominance with standardized random variables*. Mimeo.

Aboudi, R., & Thon, D. (2006). Refinements of Muirhead's lemma and income inequality. *Mathematical Social Sciences, 51,* 201–216.

Akerlof, G. A. (1997). Social distance and social decision. *Econometrica, 65,* 1005–1027.

Allison, R. A., & Foster, J. E. (2004). Measuring health inequality using qualitative data. *Journal of Health Economics, 23,* 505–524.

Atkinson, A. B. (1970). On the measurement of inequality. *Journal of Economic Theory, 2,* 244–263.

Atkinson, A. B. (1998). *Social exclusion, poverty and unemployment* (pp. 1–20). CASE/4, Centre for Analysis of Social Exclusion, London School of Economics.

Bossert, W., & Fleurbaey, M. (2002). Equitable insurance premium schemes. *Social Choice and Welfare, 19,* 113–125.

Chakravarty, S. R., & D'Ambrosio, C. (2006). The measurement of social exclusion. *Review of Income and Wealth, 52,* 377–398.

Dasgupta, P., Sen, A. K., & Starrett, D. (1973). Notes on the measurement of inequality. *Journal of Economic Theory, 6,* 180–187.

Deineko, V. G., Klinz, B., & Woeginger, G. J. (2009). The complexity of computing the Muirhead-–Dalton distance. *Mathematical Social Sciences, 57,* 282–284.

Fishburn, P., & Lavalle, I. H. (1995). Stochastic dominance on unidimensional grids. *Mathematical Operations Research, 20*(3), 513–525.

Hardy, G. H., Littlewood, J. E., & Pólya, G. (1934). *Inequalities*. Cambridge: Cambridge University Press.

Kolm, S. C. (1969). The optimal production of social justice. In J. Margolis & H. Guitton (Eds.), *Public economics* (pp. 145–200). London: Macmillan.

Levy, H. (2006). *Stochastic dominance. Investment decision making under uncertainty* (2nd ed.). New York: Springer.

Marshall, A. W., & Olkin, I. (1979). *Inequalities: Theory of majorization and its applications*. New York: Academic Press.

Milne, F., & Neave, E. (1994). Dominance relations among standardized variables. *Management Science, 40*(10), 1343–1352.

Muirhead, R. F. (1903). Some methods applicable to identities and inequalities of symmetric algebraic functions of letters. *Proceedings of the Edinburgh Mathematical Society, 21,* 144–167.

Rothschild, M., & Stiglitz, J. E. (1970). Increasing risk: I. A definition. *Journal of Economic Theory, 3,* 225–243.

Rothschild, M., & Stiglitz, J. E. (1973). Some further results on the measurement of inequality. *Journal of Economic Theory, 6,* 188–204.

Savaglio, E., & Vannucci, S. (2007). Filtral preorders and opportunity inequality. *Journal of Economic Theory, 132,* 474–492.

Shaked, M., & Shanthikumar, G. (2006). *Stochastic orders*. New York: Springer.

Shorrocks, A. F. (1983). Ranking income distributions. *Economica, 50*(2), 3–17.

Weymark, J. A. (1981). Generalized Gini inequality indices. *Mathematical Social Sciences, 1,* 409–430.

Weymark, J. A. (2003). Generalized Gini indices of equality of opportunity. *The Journal of Economic Inequality, 1,* 5–24.

Yaari, M. E. (1987). The dual theory of choice under risk. *Econometrica, 55,* 95–115.

# Multidimensional Indicators of Inequality and Poverty

**Satya R. Chakravarty and Maria Ana Lugo**

**Abstract** This chapter reviews the main features of multidimensional indices of inequality and poverty. For each of these cases, the discussion is divided into two approaches: a direct approach, where desirable properties are specified and a measure of inequality or poverty obtained; and the inclusive measure of well-being approach, where an index of individual well-being is defined in a first step, and the measure of inequality or poverty obtained in a second step. The emphasis will be on the properties that different measures satisfy and on the main justifications put forward when properties disagree.

**Keywords** Multidimensional indicators · Inequality · Poverty · Well-being

*Prepared for Handbook on Well-Being and Public Policy, edited by Matthew Adler and Marc Fleurbaey, Oxford University Press (OUP), Oxford.*

## 1 Introduction

The traditional focus for the assessment of the well-being or destitution of individuals has been on the income distribution. It is indeed true that a person's income often determines how much of different goods he or she can consume; higher income allows a person to consume more of some of the goods and/or shift consumption to higher quality variants. But income as the only attribute of well-being is often inappropriate. A sub-optimal supply of a public good in a community might not be sufficient for

The kind consent of Oxford University Press to reprint this article from its volume 'Oxford Handbook of Well-Being and Public Policy', 2016 is acknowledged with utmost gratitude.

S. R. Chakravarty
Indian Statistical Institute, Kolkata 700108, India
e-mail: satyarchakravarty@gmail.com

M. A. Lugo (✉)
World Bank, 1850 I Street NW (I4-405), Washington, DC 20433, United States of America
e-mail: mlugo1@worldbank.org

 
S. R. Chakravarty (ed.), *Poverty, Social Exclusion and Stochastic Dominance*, Themes in Economics, https://doi.org/10.1007/978-981-13-3432-0_14

the residents. For example, many people in developing countries suffer or even die from malaria because the malaria prevention program, a local public good, is not well organized or available at any price. Thus, it may not be possible to trade-off income for a better position in a non-income attribute which is non-tradable in a market. Likewise, a healthy porter who just earns hand-to-mouth daily by loading and unloading of cargos in a dockyard cannot tradeoff his good health for any additional income. These illustrations indicate that non-income dimensions of well-being contribute significantly to quality of life. Examples of such dimensions are literacy, housing, life expectancy, public goods, social cohesion, human security and so on. This supports the view that traditional economic indices of well-being should be supplemented with alternative indicators that capture non-economic or non-material dimensions of human life. In fact, it is now commonly accepted that human well-being should be regarded as a multidimensional phenomenon along the lines advocated by Rawls (1971), Kolm (1977), Townsend (1979), Streeten (1981), Atkinson and Bourguignon (1982), Sen (1985, 1993), Stewart (1985), Doyal and Gough (1991), Ramsay (1992), Cummins (1996), Ravallion (1996), Nussbaum (2000) and Thorbecke (2008).[1]

Consequently, in recent years a very important development in the research on the measurement of well-being of a population is the shift of emphasis from a single monetary dimension to a multidimensional framework that incorporates non-monetary aspects as well. One of the most influential formalization of this is the capability approach—discussed in more detail in Alkire chapter 21, the OUP Handbook. For nearly two decades now, Sen (1985, 1993) has emphasized the need to move away from the space of incomes or resources for assessing individuals' well-being in favor of a focus on the spaces of functionings and capabilities. Functionings are "parts of the state of a person in particular the things that he or she manages to do or be in leading a life" (Sen 1993, 31) (e.g., being healthy, riding a bicycle), whereas the capability set is the set of potential functionings vectors available to the person. The key idea behind the capabilities approach is that individuals differ in their ability to transform resources into well-being or "flourishing". Even for those goods for which markets exist, there is no reason to believe that relative market prices between the particular goods included as proxies for certain functionings is an appropriate approximation for the well-being trade-off between the functionings themselves since the rate of transformation of goods into functionings may differ and also vary across individuals.

The recognition that well-being and deprivation are multi-faceted does not necessarily lead to a multidimensional indicator—a single number summarizing society's overall condition, the degree of inequality, or the degree of poverty as a function of

[1]The World Development Report 2000–2001 stressed the view that traditional view of poverty should be supplemented with low achievements in health and education. The multidimensional nature of well-being is implicitly recognized by the set of dimensions considered by the European Union to judge the performance of its member countries (Atkinson et al. 2002). European Union policy recommends that for measuring failure in material living conditions income-based poverty should be combined with low employment and material deprivation (Bossert et al. 2013). The Commission on the Measurement of Economic Performance and Social Progress has also insisted on looking at well-being of a population from a multidimensional perspective (Stiglitz et al. 2009).

the pattern of individuals' achievements along the multiple well-being dimensions. Some have argued that a portfolio of indicators (Atkinson et al. 2002; Ravallion 2011), whereby each dimension is assessed separately, is to be preferred so that the efforts are focused on the "best possible distinct measures of the various dimensions of poverty [...] rather than a single 'multidimensional index'" (Ravallion 2011, 13). This approach also avoids requiring agreement on the relative importance of each dimension. On the other hand, the often called 'dashboard approach', while looking at the distribution of each of the components, will overlook the dependency structure in the joint distribution of these achievements, which may represent an important aspect in the comparison of distributions (Tsui 1999; Pogge 2002; Stiglitz et al. 2009). Others have favoured an intermediate approach which combines a dimension-wise assessment with a description of the dependency structure (Atkinson et al. 2010; Decancq 2014; Ferreira and Lugo 2013). A third and influential approach is through the use of a multivariate version of stochastic dominance (for instance, Atkinson and Bourguignon 1982, 1987; Duclos et al. 2006; Muller and Trannoy 2011, 2012). The multivariate stochastic dominance approach is more readily applied when the number of dimensions is limited; for a discussion, see Duclos and Tiberti, chapter 23, the OUP Handbook.

However, multidimensional indicators of social welfare (overall social condition), inequality and deprivation have been embraced by both among academics and policy makers. Since 1990 the United Nations Development Program has been using the Human Development Index, which combines income with life expectancy at birth and educational achievement, instead of the per capita GDP, to rank countries.[2] Recently, the Multidimensional Poverty Index developed by Alkire and Santos (2010)[3] has been incorporated into the UNDP's core indicators. The OECD launched the Better Life Index website where the user can build her own index assigning weights to eleven dimensions of well-being that have been found to be essential in many countries and cultures (OECD 2011). Countries are also proposing their own measures of multidimensional poverty.[4] The National Council for the Evaluation of Social Policy (CONEVAL) in Mexico adopted a multidimensional index of poverty as the country's official poverty measure (CONEVAL 2010). A similar multidimensional measure is used in Colombia and Bhutan and various other countries (such as El Salvador, Pakistan, and Malaysia) are considering following these examples.

Undoubtedly, multidimensional indices are appealing in that they provide unique rankings, and thus are seen as useful tools for governments and analysts to readily obtain a picture of the distribution of well-being of a society.

---

[2] Alkire and Foster (2010) consider an inequality adjusted HDI, which uses an Atkinson-type aggregation for each dimension.

[3] See Alkire, chapter 21, the OUP Handbook, for a discussion of the Multidimensional Poverty Index.

[4] While the interest in developing a multidimensional poverty measure in Latin America and Europe has gained force in recent years, there is a long tradition of using the counting approach to consider the existence of multiple deprivations at the same time—for instance, the Basic Needs Approach widely used in Latin American countries since the 1980s and still relevant nowadays. See Atkinson (2003).

Several normative issues are involved in the selection of a multidimensional indicator—of overall social condition, poverty or inequality. Of critical importance, one must decide on a functional form to aggregate attributes and on the relative weights to be assigned to each of these attributes.[5] The rest of the chapter will concentrate on alternative functional forms proposed for measuring multidimensional inequality and poverty.[6] But weights also play a crucial role in determining the set of dimensions to be included in the analysis (a dimension with zero weight is excluded) and the trade-offs between the selected dimensions. See Decancq and Lugo (2013).

The literature suggests a variety of approaches for specifying multidimensional indices of inequality and poverty. These include the axiomatic approach, which starts with desirable properties of the indicator and derives a family of indices that satisfies these principles; the fuzzy set approach; information theory; and the statistical approach. Often there may be insufficient information concerning achievements of different attributes. In a situation of this type where indefiniteness arises from ambiguity, the fuzzy set approach is quite sensible (Chakravarty 2006). The statistical approach relies on multivariate statistical techniques such as principal components or latent variable models to aggregate dimensions (Klasen 2000; Krishnakumar and Nadar 2008). In the information theory-based approach aggregation of achievements relies on the Shannon entropy formula (Maasoumi 1986; Maasoumi and Lugo 2008). In this chapter, our focus will be on the axiomatic approach. For ease of exposition, the emphasis will be on the properties that different measures satisfy (rather than on the set of axioms that characterize them) and on the main justifications put forward when properties disagree.

The next section introduces the notation and framework that will be used throughout the chapter. Sections 3 and 4 discuss the properties and provide some examples of indicators of multidimensional inequality and poverty, respectively. Functional forms of indicators when dimensions are measured on different scales, e.g. ratio or ordinal, are discussed. Section 5 concludes.

## 2 Preliminaries

For simplicity of exposition we refer to the population under consideration as a society and the unit of analysis in the society as a person (see Chiappori, chapter 27, the OUP Handbook, for inferring individual achievements from household data). Since some

---

[5]Other key decisions include: choosing the (set of) indicators for each dimension and the transformation function where the variables are not measured in the same measurement units and made comparable. On transformation functions see Jacobs et al. (2004) and Nardo et al. (2005).

[6]Weymark (2006) discusses indicators of overall social condition defined directly on multidimensional matrices. Of course, a traditional social welfare function (SWF) is also such an indicator. SWFs are discussed in Weymark, chapter 5, the OUP Handbook, and in this chapter with reference to the inclusive-measure of well-being approach (IMWB) to multidimensional inequality and poverty metrics.

concepts relevant to our exposition, such as inequality, become meaningless for a single-person society, it is assumed that each society contains at least two persons.

We denote the number of persons in the society by $n$ (with $n \in N$), where $N$ is the set of positive integers. Let $d$ be the number of such dimensions, where $d \geq 2$ is an integer. We assume that the number of dimensions $d$ is fixed—and exogenously given—in order to make meaningful comparisons of well-being across populations.

Let $x_{ij} \geq 0$ be the achievement of person $i$ in attribute or dimension $j$, where achievement indicates the performance of a person in a given dimension such as income or education. Person $i$'s achievements in different dimensions are summarized in a $d$-dimensional vector $x_{i.} = (x_{i1}, x_{i2}, \ldots, x_{id})$. The row vector $x_{i.}$ is the $i$th row of an $n \times d$ distribution matrix $X$. The column vector $x_{.j}$, which summarizes the distribution of achievements in dimension $j$ $(j = 1, 2, \ldots, d)$ among $n$ persons, is the $j$th column of $X$ and we denote the mean of this vector by $\mu(x_{.j})$.

In a four-person society with three dimensions of well-being (say, years of education, a six-point health score, and income), an example of a distribution matrix $X$ is

$$X = \begin{bmatrix} 9 & 5 & 1200 \\ 6 & 3 & 900 \\ 8 & 6 & 1000 \\ 1 & 4 & 400 \end{bmatrix}.$$

The entry in the third row and first column of the above matrix show that persons 3's achievement in dimension 1 (education) is 8. Other entries of the matrix can be similarly explained. If the set all $n \times d$ matrices with non-negative entries is represented by $M$, then $X \in M$.

Finally, we define a $d$-dimensional vector $z = (z_1, z_2, \ldots, z_d)$, where each element $z_j$ is the poverty threshold for dimension $d$. An individual $i$ is considered deprived (or poor) in dimension $d$ if her achievement $x_{id} < z_d$. For instance, a relevant poverty lines vector for the matrix $X$ above could be,

$$z = \begin{bmatrix} 9 & 5 & 500 \end{bmatrix}.$$

In this example, person 1 will be rich in all three dimensions, since her achievements lie always above or at the respective threshold, whereas person 2 is deprived in education and health but his income level (900) is above the minimum required to be considered deprived.

## 3 Multidimensional Inequality

We divide our discussion into two subsections. Section 3.1 describes the direct approach, whereby axioms and indicators are specified directly in terms of distribution matrices. Section 3.2 describes the derivation of multidimensional inequality metrics from an inclusive measure of well-being (IWMB).

## 3.1 The Direct Approach

The distribution of well-being has been the concern of social scientists since at least Smith's (1776) *An Inquiry into the Nature and Causes of the Wealth of Nations.*[7] In the last 50 years, as household data became more easily available, economists attempted to define ways of measuring the extent to which the observed distributions differ from some ideal one. In the beginning of the 1970s, almost simultaneously, Atkinson (1970), Kolm (1969), and Sen (1973) proposed a normative view to measuring inequality as the loss in social welfare due to the fact that income (seen here as the measure of each individual's well-being) is not distributed equally among all individuals. This approach is univariate (unidimensional) because $d = 1$; no dimension of individual achievement other than income is included.

At this point several important families of univariate inequality indices have been characterized using Aktinson–Kolm–Sen's normative approach. Among the relative inequality indices, these include the Gini coefficient, Atkinson index, Theil 0 and Theil 1 (belonging to the General Entropy class of measures), and the Dalton Index. Within the absolute measures, the Kolm index, the variance, and the absolute Gini coefficient are the most widely used ones. All of these measures have been characterized axiomatically, from a set of desirable properties that either the underlying social welfare function or the inequality index itself is required to satisfy (Ebert 1988). By setting the desiderata upfront, all values are made explicit. The family of measures derived is the one that satisfies these postulates simultaneously. (Detailed discussions along this line are available in Cowell's chapter of the OUP Handbook.)

In the last 20 years, various authors have presented generalizations of the most salient univariate inequality measures along with their extensions in the multidimensional context. In this chapter, the focus will be on the discussion on the postulates behind multidimensional indicators where the extension is less straightforward.[8] In particular, we will discuss invariance, distributional, and decomposability properties (formal definitions of axioms are relegated to the appendix). We will also present a selection of multidimensional indices to illustrate how these properties are applied.

A multidimensional inequality indicator $I$ is a real-valued continuous function defined on set of well-being matrices $M$. More precisely, $I : M \to \Re^1$, where $\Re^1$ is the set of real numbers. For any $X \in M$, $I(X)$ determines the extent of inequality that exists in the distribution matrix $X$.

We divide this subsection in three parts, based on the nature of the properties.

---

[7]See also Rousseau's (1754) *Discourse on the Origin and Basis of Inequality Among Men.*

[8]We do not discuss here Normalization, Symmetry, Population Replication Invariance, and Continuity which are presented in the appendix with formal notation.

### 3.1.1 Invariance Properties

Relative inequality indices are those that satisfy a property known as ratio scale invariance. In the unidimensional context, this property ensures that the measurement of inequality does not vary when each person's achievement is multiplied by the same positive constant, such as when incomes are expressed in a different currency unit or when everyone's incomes are increased by the same proportion. The extension to the multidimensional context requires more careful attention, since often the achievements in different dimensions are measured in different units of measurement.

- **Ratio Scale Invariance (RSI)** says that inequality is invariant to proportional changes in the achievements in different dimensions. If, for instance, the duration of education is measured in months instead of years, the evaluation of inequality should not change. The RSI property allows for the rescaling factor to differ across the different dimensions. This is particularly attractive when the variables are expressed in different measurement units, such as income in dollars and schooling in years. Importantly, this property permits the standardization of each vector by an entry-specific rescaling such as division by their respective mean or range. For instance, if distribution $X^*$ expressed each attribute as a proportion of its respective median, a multidimensional inequality index satisfying RSI will consider that,

$$I(X) = I(X^*), \quad \text{where } X = \begin{bmatrix} 9 & 5 & 1200 \\ 6 & 3 & 900 \\ 8 & 6 & 1000 \\ 1 & 4 & 400 \end{bmatrix} \text{ and } X^* = \begin{bmatrix} 1.3 & 1.1 & 1.3 \\ 0.9 & 0.7 & 0.9 \\ 1.1 & 1.3 & 1.1 \\ 0.1 & 0.9 & 0.4 \end{bmatrix}$$

  Note that $X^*$ is obtained by dividing each of the elements in matrix $X$ by the median of each of the attributes (columns).[9] For instance, the median of the first attribute (years of education) equals 7, thus the first element in matrix $X^* = 9/7 = 1.3$. Similar calculation holds for other entries in $X^*$.
  An inequality indicator satisfying RSI is called *relative.*
  On the other hand, RSI can be disputed because it implies that proportional changes in one dimension (say, doubling of incomes) have no impact on overall inequality, ignoring possible interactions across dimensions. A stronger version of this property (strong RSI) requires instead that the inequality index should remain constant only when all attributes are rescaled *by the same factor*. That is, when all attributes are doubled, then the measurement of multidimensional inequality should not change. This property is particularly appealing when all attributes are measured in the same scale.
- **Unit Consistency (UCO)** is a weaker form of ratio scale invariance which demands that the inequality ordering[10] of two distribution matrices should remain unaltered

[9]The median of an odd number of observations that are non-decreasingly ordered is the middle-most observation. For the first column of $X$, the non-decreasingly ordered rearrangement is (1, 6, 8, 9) and the median of these numbers is 7, the average of the two middle numbers.

[10]By inequality ordering, we mean the ranking of matrices by the inequality index.

under changes in the scales of dimensions (Zheng 2007a, b; Diez et al. 2008; Chakravarty and D'Ambrosio 2012). To illustrate this, suppose of two countries, I and II, country I has lower multidimensional inequality than country II. Assume that in both the countries incomes are expressed in the currency of country I and the unit of educational attainment is one year. Now, let incomes in the two countries be converted into the currency of country II and educational attainments be measured in months, while the units of measurement of all other dimensions are assumed to remain unaltered. Unit consistency demands that the ranking of the two countries by the multidimensional inequality index should remain unchanged under this alteration of units of measurement of two dimensions. As we will observe, all ratio scale invariant multidimensional inequality indices are unit consistent, but there exist unit consistent indices which do not satisfy ratio scale invariance.

- **Translation Scale Invariance** (**TSI**), suggested by Kolm (1976), requires that the addition of a constant to the quantities of different attributes does not alter the level of inequality. If everyone's health scores move up two points, then overall inequality will not change. The implication is that from a normative perspective, it does not matter where the zero is set. An inequality indicator satisfying this property is called *absolute*.

Ratio scale invariance and translation scale invariance represent two different value judgments concerning inequality invariance. These two axioms cannot be satisfied simultaneously by a multidimensional inequality indicator—except for a trivial indicator that assigns the same number to all distribution matrices.

### 3.1.2 Distributional Properties

Distributional axioms specify when a redistribution of achievements *between* individuals increases or decreases inequality. In the unidimensional framework, distributional concerns are generally introduced through the Pigou–Dalton transfers principle (Pigou 1912; Dalton 1920). This postulate demands that a progressive transfer, a transfer of income from a person to a poorer one, should decrease inequality, provided that the donor does not become poorer than the recipient as a result of the transfer and all other incomes remain unaffected. There are a number of ways in which this principle has been extended to the multivariate framework. In the present review, we will include three of the most widely used ones.

Formally, a Pigou–Dalton transfer can be expressed in terms of a $T$-transformation. The formulation can be motivated by an example. Let $y = (3, 6, 7)$ and $x = (4, 5, 7)$ be two income distributions so that $x$ is obtained from $y$ by a Pigou–Dalton transfer of 1 unit of income from the second person to the first person. This transfer can also be expressed in the following way: $(4, 5, 7) = (3, 6, 7)\left(\frac{2}{3}\begin{pmatrix} 1 & 0 & 0 \\ 0 & 1 & 0 \\ 0 & 0 & 1 \end{pmatrix} + \frac{1}{3}\begin{pmatrix} 0 & 1 & 0 \\ 1 & 0 & 0 \\ 0 & 0 & 1 \end{pmatrix}\right)$.
The first matrix within the first bracketed term on the right-hand side is a $3 \times 3$ identity matrix each of whose diagonal elements is one and off-diagonal elements is zero. The

second matrix is a $3 \times 3$ permutation matrix, a matrix with entries 0 and 1, and each of whose rows and columns sums to one. This matrix is obtained by exchanging the first two rows of the identity matrix. The remaining row corresponds to the person unaffected by the transfer. A weighted average of these two $3 \times 3$ matrices, where the weights are respectively $\frac{2}{3}$ and $\frac{1}{3}$, after matrix-multiplication with (3, 6, 7), gives us the distribution (4, 5, 7). The weighted average $\left(\frac{2}{3}\begin{pmatrix}1&0&0\\0&1&0\\0&0&1\end{pmatrix}+\frac{1}{3}\begin{pmatrix}0&1&0\\1&0&0\\0&0&1\end{pmatrix}\right)$ is known as a $T$-transformation (for more on this, see Marshall et al. 2011; Weymark 2006; Chakravarty 2009).

The unidimensional Pigou–Dalton transfer principle can be extended straightforwardly to the multidimensional case by applying the same sequence of $T$-transformations to all the dimensions, as per the following postulate:

- **Uniform Pigou–Dalton Transfers Principle (UPD)** says that for any two distribution matrices $X$ and $Y$ if $X$ is obtained from $Y$ by multiplying by a finite number of $T$-transformations, then $X$ has less inequality than $Y$.

However, the justifiability of UPD can be disputed. The complexity of extending the Pigou–Dalton principle to multiple dimensions arises because of, precisely, the existence of the other dimensions. Consider a case in which a Pigou–Dalton transfer is implemented for each dimension between two individuals. If the donor has more achievements than the recipient in some dimension (say, income) but less in others (say, health and education), then it is not clear whether an income transfer from the donor to the recipient reduces multidimensional inequality. Fleurbaey and Trannoy (2003) offer a restricted version of the above, confining the relevant transfers to be among individuals where the giver is at least as well-off as the recipient in every dimension:

- **Pigou–Dalton Bundle Transfers Principle (PBT)** represents the idea that if, between two individuals, one has at least as much achievement in every dimension as the other and strictly more in at last one dimension, then dimension-wise Pigou–Dalton transfers from the former to the latter in one or more dimensions reduces multidimensional inequality, given that achievements of all other individuals remain unaffected.

Unfortunately PBT comes into conflict with efficiency. Fleurbaey and Trannoy (2003) formally demonstrated that under certain very mild conditions a social ranking of distribution matrices cannot simultaneously satisfy PBT and the Weak Pareto Principle, which demands that if each individual prefers her vector of achievements in ne matrix to a second, then the first is socially better than the latter.[11] See also Fleurbaey and Maniquet (2011), Weymark (2013) and Bourguignon and Chakravarty (2003) for a variant of PBT, referred to as Multidimensional Transfer Principle.

[11] It may be worthwhile to mention that, following the literature, our formulation in this chapter uses directly individual achievements. Therefore, our presentation has ignored individual preferences.

A third alternative for extending the unidimensional Pigou–Dalton transfer principle to the multidimensional context is presented by Kolm (1976)—for discussions, see also Marshall et al. (2011), Duclos et al. (2006, 2007), Weymark (2006) and Chakravarty (2009). In this case, the series of transfers are the same (in percentage terms) in all dimensions. Specifically, the following is noteworthy.

- **Uniform Majorization Principle (UM)** requires that if there is a similar smoothing of achievements in all the dimensions, multidimensional inequality should decrease. For example, consider a matrix $Y$ which is obtained from $X$ after a sequence of (mean-preserving) equalizing transfers across individuals for each dimension.[12]

$$X = \begin{bmatrix} 9 & 5 & 1200 \\ 6 & 3 & 900 \\ 8 & 6 & 1000 \\ 1 & 4 & 400 \end{bmatrix} \text{ and } Y = \begin{bmatrix} 6.2 & 4.5 & 890 \\ 6.7 & 3.9 & 970 \\ 7.6 & 5.5 & 1000 \\ 3.5 & 4.1 & 640 \end{bmatrix}.$$

We note that the sum of all entries in each column of the two matrices $X$ and $Y$ is the same. Under this operation there is a smoothing of the distribution of achievements in each dimension and all the dimensions are considered simultaneously. UM says that $Y$ should have lower inequality than $X$.

Lasso de la Vega et al. (2010) made a systematic comparison between PBT and UM. Under UM one distribution matrix is obtained from another by transferring achievements in all dimensions in the same proportions. This notion of transfer is not valid if some of dimensions are ordinally measurable (see Sect. 4.3 for a discussion on ordinal measurability of dimensions). In addition, and crucially, if transfers are made between two persons in all dimensions where one is not unambiguously richer than the other, then there is ambiguity regarding treatment of the new distributions as more equitable. PBT takes care of all these difficulties. By definition, the transfer is performed between two persons, one richer than the other. Also, the transfers in different dimensions need not be made in the same proportions, or even at all in some dimensions. The distinction between these two principles is particularly important since, as Lasso de la Vega et al. (2010) noted, not all inequality indices, including those satisfying UM, will satisfy PBT.

While the different versions of the Pigou–Dalton principle focus on the redistribution of attributes among the persons, there is a second important form of inequality that arises only in the multidimensional context. Atkinson and Bourguignon (1982)

[12]Formally, uniform mean-preserving averaging (smoothing) can be obtained by multiplying the distribution matrix $X$ by a bistochastic matrix, which is a square nonnegative matrix of appropriate order where all the rows and columns add up to 1. UM says that $BX$ should have lower inequality than $X$. The $B$ matrix in this case is

$$B = \begin{bmatrix} 0.2 & 0.3 & 0.3 & 0.2 \\ 0.4 & 0.5 & 0 & 0.1 \\ 0.3 & 0 & 0.6 & 0.1 \\ 0.1 & 0.2 & 0.1 & 0.6 \end{bmatrix}.$$

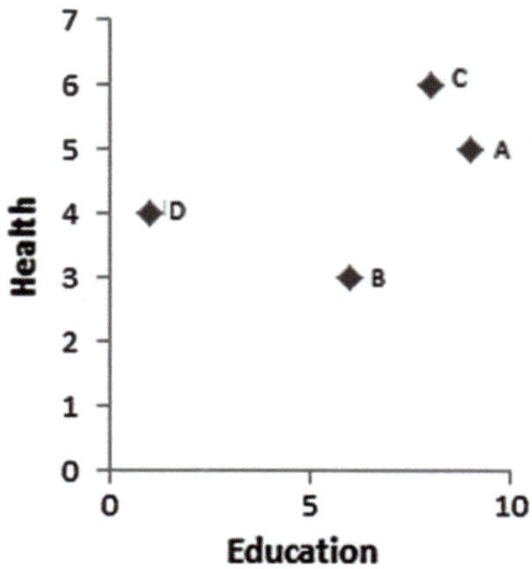


**Fig. 1** Example: Distribution matrix $X$ of health and education in a four-person society

argued that a multidimensional inequality indicator should capture the association (more precisely, rank correlation) between distributions of achievements. Following Epstein and Tanny (1980) and Tchen (1980), the authors introduced the concept of a *correlation increasing switch* between two individuals, whereby one individual receives at least as much of every attribute as the other and more of at least one attribute (see also Boland and Prochan 1988; Decancq 2012). To understand this, suppose that in the original distribution $X$ presented above $x_{11} > x_{21}$ but $x_{22} > x_{12}$. That is, the second person (person B) has six years of education (while person D has only one), and scores three points in health (whereas person D scores 4). This situation is represented in Fig. 1, with diamond-shaped dots—for simplicity of exposition income is ignored in this figure.

If we make a switch of the second attribute, say health, between the two individuals, then their achievements after the switch are given by $y_{11} = x_{11}$, $y_{12} = x_{22}$, $y_{21} = x_{21}$ and $y_{22} = x_{12}$ (positions B* and D* in Fig. 2 for persons B and D, respectively). Person B, who had higher achievement in education, has higher achievement in health as well after the switch. Consequently, the correlation between the attributes has gone up. Note that a correlation increasing switch keeps the mean of each attribute constant, like UPD, PBT and UM.

Tsui (1999) formally introduced this idea to the literature on multidimensional inequality indices via an axiom know as Correlation Increasing Majorization:

- **Correlation Increasing Majorization (CIM)** states that if a distribution $Y$ is obtained from another distribution $X$ by a switch in attributes such that the correlation across these attributes is increased, then $Y$ is more unequal than $X$.

**Fig. 2** Example: Distribution matrix $X$ of health and education after a correlation increasing switch

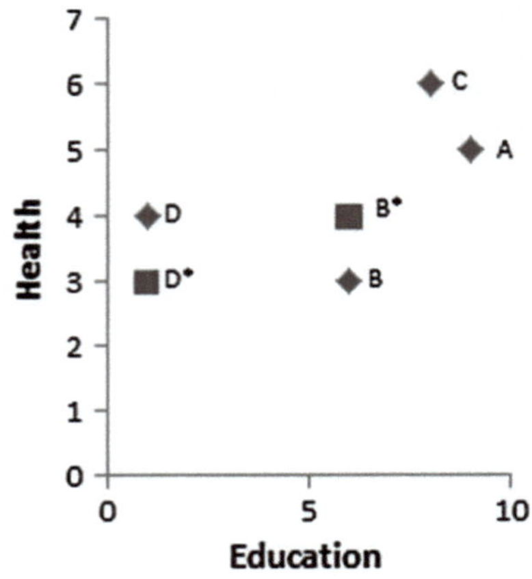


In the example, consider the distributions $X = \begin{bmatrix} 9 & 5 & 1200 \\ 6 & 3 & 900 \\ 8 & 6 & 1000 \\ 1 & 4 & 400 \end{bmatrix}$ and $Y = \begin{bmatrix} 9 & 5 & 1200 \\ 6 & 4 & 900 \\ 8 & 6 & 1000 \\ 1 & 3 & 400 \end{bmatrix}$.

In all of the dimensions, except in dimension 2 (say, health), the achievements of the second person (B) in the distribution $X$ are more than the corresponding achievements of the fourth person (D). The distribution matrix $Y$ obtained from $X$ by a switch in achievements in health between these two individuals is such that the second person has now higher achievements than the fourth one in all three dimensions. This transfer has increased the correlation between dimensions which implies that the situation of the person who was better off in some dimensions is now also better off in the other dimension. CIM will assess this new distribution as being less equal (not preferable) to the original one.

Tsui (1999) showed that UM and CIM are independent axioms. That is, there exist indicators that satisfy both UM and CIM; and also there are indicators that satisfy UM but are violators of CIM and vice versa. Weymark (2006) and Chakravarty (2009) provide further discussion along this line.

A weaker version of CIM has been proposed by Dardanoni (1996) as follows:

- **Unfair Rearrangement Principle (UR)** requires that the initial distribution matrix is preferred to one in which the distributional profiles in all dimensions are unaltered but where the dimensions are perfectly rank-correlated.

To understand this property, let us assume a new distribution $Z$ where one person is ranked first in all dimensions, another one is ranked second in all dimensions and so on. For instance, consider

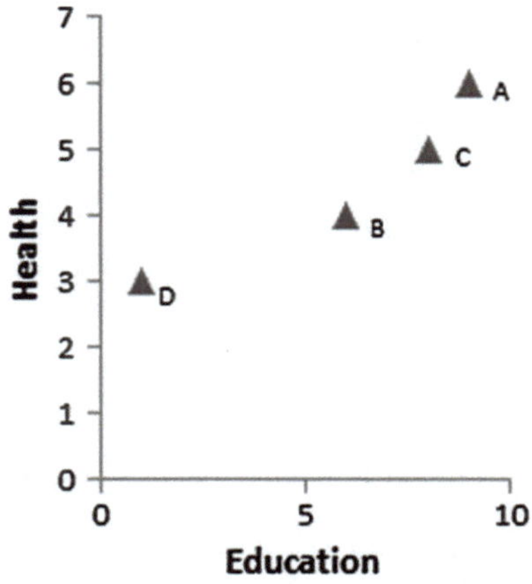


**Fig. 3** Example: Distribution matrix $\bar{X}$ of health and education after a switch that makes dimensions perfectly correlated

$Z = \begin{bmatrix} 9 & 6 & 1200 \\ 6 & 4 & 900 \\ 8 & 5 & 1000 \\ 1 & 3 & 400 \end{bmatrix}$, depicted in Fig. 3 [once again, for clarity of exposition the figure only depicts education and health, but income also follows the same rule]. UR implies that distributions $X$ and $Y$ will be preferred to distribution $Z$, but does not determine the ranking of $X$ versus $Y$. Thus, UR is indeed a weak property and can be seen as a minimum requirement to be imposed when correlation across dimension is deemed undesirable.

### 3.1.3 Decomposability Properties

Since the mid-1980s, many multidimensional inequality indicators have been proposed in the literature that can be seen as extensions of the most widely used measures on inequality in the unidimensional framework, including Gini, Atkinson, Generalized Entropy (Theils), and Kolm indices. Table 1 presents a selection of extension of these indices, and the properties that they satisfy. Only for exposition purposes, we consider at least one measure for each family of unidimensional indices, but recognize that the literature contains many more measures that are not discussed here.

Tsui developed a characterization of the multidimensional Atkinson inequality indicator (Tsui 1995), as well as an extension of the Generalized Entropy inequality index (Tsui 1999). These indices have the advantage of being able to satisfy a convenient property related to the decomposability of the measures. One such property is the following:

- **Subgroup Decomposability (SDE)**: For any partitioning of the population into subgroups such as race, religion, sex, ethnic groups, age etc., overall inequality can be expressed in terms of inequality levels of subgroups, vectors of means

**Table 1** Inequality

| Authors | Family | Measure | Properties | | | | | |
|---|---|---|---|---|---|---|---|---|
| | | | RSI | UCO | TSI | UM | CIM | UR |
| Tsui (1995) | Atkinson | $I_{AM}(X) = 1 - \left[\frac{1}{n}\sum_{i=1}^{n}\prod_{j=1}^{d}\left(\frac{x_{ij}}{\mu(x_j)}\right)^{c_j}\right]^{\frac{1}{\sum_{j-1}^{d} c_j}}$ <br> $I_{AM}(X) = 1 - \left[\frac{1}{n}\prod_{i=1}^{n}\prod_{j=1}^{d}\left(\frac{x_{ij}}{\mu(x_{.j})}\right)^{\frac{c_j}{\sum_{j-1}^{d} c_j}}\right]^{\frac{1}{n}}$ | Yes | Yes | | ucc | ucc | |
| Gajdos and Weymark (2005) | Generalized Gini | $I_{GWR}(X) = 1 - \frac{\left[\sum_{j=1}^{d} a_j\left(\sum_{i=1}^{n} b_{ik}x_{ij}^0\right)^{\omega}\right]^{\frac{1}{\omega}}}{\sum_{j=i}^{d} a_j\mu(x_{.j})}$ <br> $I_{GWR}(X) = 1 - \frac{\prod_{j=1}^{d}\left(\sum_{i=1}^{n} b_{ij}x_{ij}^0\right)^{a_j}}{\prod_{j=1}^{d}\mu(x_{.j})^{a_j}}$ | Yes | Yes | | ucc | | |
| Decancq and Lugo (2012) | Generalized Gini | $I_{DL}(X) = 1 - \frac{\sum_{i=1}^{n} b_i\left(\sum_{j=1}^{d} a_j(x_{ij})^{\omega}\right)^{\frac{1}{\omega}}}{\left(\sum_{j=1}^{d} a_j(\mu(x_j))^{\omega}\right)^{\frac{1}{\omega}}}$ <br> $where\ \ b_i = \left(\frac{r^i}{n}\right)^{\delta} - \left(\frac{r^i-1}{n}\right)^{\delta}$ | Yes | Yes | | ucc | | ucc |

(continued)

**Table 1** (continued)

| Authors | Family | Measure | Properties | | | | | |
|---|---|---|---|---|---|---|---|---|
| | | | RSI | UCO | TSI | UM | CIM | UR |
| Bosmans, Decancq and Ooghe (2013) | CES | $BDO^{(X)} = \left[\frac{1}{n}\sum_{i=1}^{n}\left(\frac{\sum_{i=j}^{d}\left(a_j x_{ij}^{1-\beta}\right)}{\sum_{j=1}^{d}\left(a_j \mu(x_{.j})^{1-\beta}\right)}\right)^{\frac{1-\alpha}{1-\beta}}\right]^{\frac{1}{1-\alpha}}$ | Yes | Yes | | Yes | ucc | |
| Tsui (1999) | Generalized Entropy | $I_{TME} = \frac{e}{n}\sum_{i=1}^{n}\left(\prod_{j=1}^{d}\left(\frac{x_{ij}}{\mu(x_{.j})}\right)^{c_j} - 1\right)$ | Yes | Yes | | ucc | ucc | |
| Maasoumi (1986) | Generalized Entropy | $I_{MM}(X) = \begin{cases} \frac{1}{nc(c-1)}\sum_{i=1}^{n}\left[\left(\frac{x_i}{\mu(x)}\right)^{c} - 1\right], c \neq 0, 1, \\ \frac{1}{n}\sum_{i=1}^{n}\left[\log\left(\frac{\mu(x)}{x_i}\right)\right], c = 0, \\ \frac{1}{n}\sum_{i=1}^{n}\left[\left(\frac{x_i}{\mu(x)}\right)\log\left(\frac{x_i}{\mu(x)}\right)\right], c = 1, \end{cases}$ | Yes | Yes | | | | |
| Bourguignon (1999) | Dalton | $I_{BDM}(X) = 1 - \frac{\sum_{i=1}^{n}\left(a_2 x_{i1}^{-\delta} + a_2 x_{x2}^{-\delta}\right)^{\frac{-(1+c)}{\delta}}}{n\left(a_1(\mu(x_{.1}))^{-\delta} + (a_2\mu(x_{.2}))^{-\delta}\right)^{\frac{-(1+c)}{\delta}}}$ | | Yes | | Yes | | ucc |
| Tsui (1995) | Kolm | $I_{KPM}(X) = \frac{1}{\sum_{j=1}^{d}\beta_j}\log\left[\frac{1}{n}\sum_{i=1}^{n}\exp\left(\sum_{j=1}^{d}\beta_j\left(\mu(x_{.j}) - x_{ij}\right)\right)\right]$ | | | Yes | ucc | | |

Note: "ucc" refers to "under certain conditions" and means that the measures could satisfy the property by setting restrictions to the parameters. RSI: Ratio scale invariance, UCO: Unit consistency, TSI: Translation scale invariance, UM: uniform majorization, CIM: correlation increasing majorization, UR: unfair rearrangement principle of attributes corresponding to different subgroups and population sizes of the subgroups.

Such decompositions become particularly useful for policy makers interested in determining the significance of variations of attributes corresponding to these various characteristics.

A second well-known family of measures is associated with the widely used Gini inequality index. This index has several multivariate extensions (see for example, Koshevoy and Mosler 1996; List 1999; Gajdos and Weymark 2005; Banerjee 2010; Decancq and Lugo 2012). In this chapter, we consider two that are explicitly normative, as characterized by Gajdos and Weymark (2005) and by Decancq and Lugo (2012), respectively. The two indices differ mainly in the order of aggregation of dimensions and individuals; the former aggregates first across individuals and then across dimensions whereas the latter does the reverse. As in the univariate case, these multidimensional extensions of the Gini index are not subgroup decomposable. Yet, the measure proposed by Gajdos and Weymark is separable across dimensions of well-being (that is, overall inequality can be calculated as a function of the inequality in each of the separate dimensions). Formally, this measure satisfies a restricted form of attribute separability proposed by Shorrocks (1982).

- **Factor Decomposability** (**FDE**): Overall inequality is the sum of attribute-wise indicators. FDE becomes helpful for assessment of inequality contribution of different dimensions of well-being.

The Gajdos and Weymark generalized Gini index satisfies FD for $\alpha = \theta = 1$ (see Table 1). Nonetheless, the cost of satisfying FDE is that Gajdos and Weymark's measure (as any two-step measure that first aggregate across dimensions and then across attributes) is insensitive to changes in the correlation across the different attributes. Instead, Decancq and Lugo's Gini measure is able to satisfy UR for specific choices of parameter values at the expense of a weaker separability axiom, that is, the axiom of rank-dependent separability which states that the comparison of two distributions is not affected by the magnitude of the common attributes as long as the initial ranking is maintained (formal definition in the appendix).

## 3.2 *The Inclusive—Measure-of Well-Being Approach*

This section considers the inclusive measure of well-being approach (IMWB), which assigns a well-being number to each person $i$ as a function of the person's achievements in all $d$ dimensions. These indices of individual well-being can be then aggregated across persons to arrive at an evaluation of "social welfare" (overall social condition), inequality or poverty. Formally, person $i$'s IMWB is denoted by $U(x_{i.}) = U(x_{i1}, x_{i2}, \ldots, x_{id})$, where $U : Q \rightarrow \Re^1$ is the individual well-being function, $Q \subset \Re^d$ being the set of all achievements that individuals can possess in the $d$ dimensions. A social policy evaluation metric $W$ ranks outcomes by incorporating the associated well-being numbers. In other words, the distribution of achievements $(x_{1..}, x_{2.}, \ldots, x_{.n.})'$ is at least as good as the distribution $(y_{1..}, y_{2..}, \ldots, y_{n..})'$ if and only if $W$ ranks $(U(x_{1..}), U(x_{2...}), \ldots, U(x_{n..}))$ at least as good as $(U(y_{1..}), U(y_{2...}), \ldots, U(y_{n..}))$.

There are two distinct ways in which the IMWB approach can be used to derive a multidimensional inequality indicator. In the first variation, $W$ is a social welfare function (SWF), which is then used to construct a multidimensional inequality indicator. In the second variation, $W$ is a unidimensional inequality index, which is applied directly to the vector of individual well-being levels (as in Maasoumi 1986).

In the first alternative, a SWF ranks vectors of individual well-being numbers, or "utilities." See Weymark, chapter 5, the OUP Handbook. In the literature on income inequality, individual income is often seen as a proxy for individual welfare, and thus a SWF is used to rank vectors of individual incomes. See Cowell, chapter 4, the OUP Handbook. The Atkinson-Kolm-Sen (AKS) approach, used to deriving an income inequality metric from an SWF applied to incomes, is as follows. The AKS representative income $x_e$ corresponding to the distribution $x$ is the level of income which, if enjoyed by everybody, would make the distribution $x$ ethically indifferent, that is, $W(x_{e.}, x_e, \ldots, x_e) = W(x)$. The AKS relative inequality index $I_{\text{AKS}}$ is thus defined as the proportionate gap between $x_e$ and the mean income $\mu(x)$. When efficiency considerations are absent, that is, when the mean income is fixed, an increase in social welfare is equivalent to a reduction in inequality and vice versa. From a policy perspective, this inequality index determines the fraction of total income that could be saved if the society distributed incomes equally without any loss of social welfare or, in other words, the fractional social welfare loss resulting from the existence of inequality.

We can now describe the first variation of the IMWB approach. Kolm (1977) extends the AKS approach to the multidimensional context—showing how to derive a multidimensional inequality indicator from a social ranking of matrices, such as the ranking defined by an SWF.

Let us define $X_\lambda$ as the distribution matrix in which each person enjoys the average level of achievements in each dimension $\mu(x_{.j})$ so that $X_\mu$ represents the perfectly equal situation. Now, define $\Lambda(X)$ implicitly by $W(X_\mu \Lambda(X)) = W(X)$, that is, as a positive scalar which, when multiplied by the ideal distribution matrix $X_\mu$, is socially or ethically indifferent to the existing distribution matrix $X$ (according to $W$). $\Lambda(X)$ is the multidimensional counterpart to the Atkinson-Kolm-Sen representative income. Given appropriate assumptions about $W$, $\Lambda(X)$ is well-defined and $0 < X_\mu < 1$ if $X \neq X_\mu$ and takes on the maximal value 1 when each attribute is equally distributed among the individuals (Weymark 2006).

The multidimensional Kolm (1977) inequality indicator $I_{\text{KM}} : M \to \Re^1$ is defined as $I_{\text{KM}}(X) = 1 - \Lambda(X)$, where $X \in M$ is arbitrary. $I_{\text{KM}}$ determines the fraction of welfare loss incurred by moving from the ideal distribution $X_\mu$ to the actual distribution $X$. If there is only one dimension, say income, $I_{\text{KM}}$ coincides with the Atkinson–Kolm–Sen inequality index. Assume that the $W$ fulfils the strong Pareto principle, is continuous and increasing under a smoothing of the distribution of achievements. Given these assumptions, the continuous indicator $I_{\text{KM}}$ satisfies symmetry (SYM) and UM.[13] For an unequal distribution matrix $X$, $I_{\text{KM}}$ is positive and bounded above by one. $I_{\text{KM}}$ takes on the minimum value zero if $X = X_\mu$. The behaviour of $I_{\text{KM}}$ under a correlation increasing switch depends on the form of the utility function.

The procedure may be illustrated using some examples. Tsui's (1995) characterization of the multidimensional Atkinson inequality index can be accommodated within the IMWB approach. Tsui characterized the symmetric utilitarian social welfare function $W(X) = \sum_{i=1}^{n} U(x_{i.})$, where the identical individual multi-attribute utility function is either of the product type or of the logarithmic type.[14] For this form of the utility function, the resulting Kolm (1977) inequality index becomes the multidimensional Atkinson inequality index. If there is only one dimension, the formula coincides with the single dimensional Atkinson (1970) index.

Another example of the first variation of the IMWB-based approach is the double-CES multi-attribute inequality indicator suggested by Bosmans et al. (2013). The individual utility function aggregates individual achievements (assumed to be always positive) using a CES-type aggregator. Next, the social welfare function uses a CES function to aggregate utilities at the social level. The corresponding Kolm (1977) multi-attribute inequality indicator is the Bosmans–Decancq–Ooghe (2013) multidimensional inequality index. This symmetric index satisfies UM for all permissible values of the parameters. It is unambiguously increasing under a correlation increasing switch if the parameter associated with the CES utility function is higher than the corresponding parameter in the welfare function.[15]

These two examples clearly demonstrate that there are multi-attribute inequality indices that relate to social welfare functions applied to some measure of individual well-being. They show that the two-stage approach can be justified by a solid theoretical background within the normative framework. But there also exists inequality indices that cannot be supported by the IMWB structure. The Gajdos–Weymark generalized Gini index is an example of an inequality indicator that cannot be supported by the IMWB structure because in this case aggregation is first done across individuals and then the obtained values are aggregated across dimensions. It is in fact the Kolm index $I_{\text{KM}}$ where the underlying multidimensional generalized Gini social evaluation function is defined directly on the set of distribution matrices, rather than being a social welfare function operating on vectors of individual utilities. The social evaluation function is assumed to satisfy continuity, strong Pareto principle and increasingness under a smoothing of the distribution of achievements (see Weymark 2006).

[13]SYM demands that any reordering of the individuals does not change inequality. That is, any characteristic other than the achievement levels, for example, the names of the individuals, is irrelevant to the measurement of inequality.

[14]Formally, the individual utility function is defined as a strictly increasing concave function assuming the forms: $a + b \prod_{j=1}^{d} x_{ij}^{c_j}$ or $a + b \sum_{j=1}^{d} c_j \log x_{ij}$, where $a$ is an arbitrary constant, and the parameters $b$ and $c_j$ should be appropriately restricted to ensure that $U(.)$ is increasing and strictly concave.

[15]For a characterization of a multidimensional social welfare function where the individual well-being function is linear, see Bosmans et al. (2009).

The second variation of the IMWB approach is suggested by Maasoumi (1986). The author developed the first extension of the Generalized Entropy index to the multidimensional set up using a CES-type utility function in the first step to aggregate dimensional achievements of an individual, and a Generalized Entropy-type aggregation of individual utilities in the second step. In other words, Maasoumi employs a uni-dimensional inequality metric, instead of a welfare function, to aggregate individual well-beings. Unfortunately, Maasoumi's index has the weakness that it may not satisfy UM or other multivariate formulations of the Pigou–Dalton principle. The Pigou–Dalton principle is satisfied, however, in the (unidimensional) well-being space.[16]

# 4 Multidimensional Poverty

Even in the early twenty-first century, poverty alleviation remains one of the major economic policies in many countries of the world. In order to understand the depth and threat of poverty, it is helpful to quantify poverty and measure its change over time. The objective of this section is to briefly outline different poverty measurement methodologies that have been suggested in the literature and that adopt an explicitly multidimensional structure, as adopted, among others, by Tsui (2002), Bourguignon and Chakravarty (2003) and Alkire and Foster (2011). As in Sect. 3, we first discuss the direct approach—the main approach in the literature—whereby axioms and poverty measures are defined directly on multidimensional matrices. See also Duclos and Tiberti's chapter 23 in the OUP Handbook for a similar discussion. We then turn to the IMWB perspective on poverty measurement.

## *4.1 The Direct Approach*

We divide the discussion in this subsection into several parts.

### 4.1.1 Properties

Since well-being of a population is a multidimensional phenomenon, poverty, which arises because of insufficiency of achievements in one or more dimensions, is as well a multidimensional aspect of human life. As Sen (1976) argued, in income poverty measurement two exercises are involved: (i) the identification of the poor and (ii)

[16]Tsui (1999) also proposes a multidimensional extension of the Generalized Entropy index but he does it in one stage, and thus it is not directly based on individual well-being levels—i.e. is based on a direct approach. The literature contains many more indices that do not use such a two-step aggregation method (for further discussion see Chakravarty 2009, Chap. 5).

aggregation of the characteristics of the poor into an overall indicator of poverty in society. The former problem requires the specification of a poverty line, the income necessary for a subsistence standard of living. A person is regarded as income poor if his income falls below the poverty line. The second problem requires aggregation of income shortfalls of the poor from the poverty line. See Cowell, chapter 4, the OUP Handbook, discussing univariate (income) poverty measures.

Following Sen (1976), various authors have suggested extensions of the standard properties associated with each of these two steps for the multivariate setting and derived multidimensional poverty measures. The introduction of multiple dimensions requires an additional step in the derivation of the poverty measure, which is the aggregation across dimensions. The dimension-wise aggregation is done before the aggregation across individuals (step ii above) but can be done either before or after the specification of the poverty threshold (step i). The decision on the sequence of these steps will have implications in terms of the substitutability assumed across dimensions. In fact, most of the proposals in the literature opt to set the poverty thresholds for each dimension and then aggregate each individual's dimension-specific achievements into a single indicator of each individual's poverty.[17] The argument is that each attribute is considered essential so no substitution across dimension should be permitted above and below the "minimum acceptable levels" (Sen 1992, 139). See, for instance, Tsui (2002), Bourguignon and Chakravarty (2003), Chakravarty and Silber (2008) and Alkire and Foster (2011). These exogenously given "minimally acceptable levels" are the threshold limits for different dimensions for a person to be non-deprived in the dimensions.

Formally, we can define a vector of poverty thresholds $z = (z_1, \ldots, z_d) \in Z \subset \Re^d_{++}$, where $\Re^d_{++}$ is the strictly positive part of the $d$-dimensional Euclidean space. Person $i$ is said to be deprived or non-deprived in dimension $j$ according as $x_{ij} < z_j$ or $x_{ij} \geq z_j$ and he is called non-deprived if $x_{ij} \geq z_j$ for all $j$. A multidimensional poverty index $P$ is a non-constant real-valued continuous function defined on $M \times Z$, that is, $P : M \times Z \to \Re^1$. For any $n \in N$, $X \in M$ and $z \in Z$, $P(X; z)$ gives the level of poverty associated with $X$ and the threshold limit vector $z$.

When thresholds are imposed before the aggregation across dimensions, the identification of who is to be considered poor presents the additional challenge of defining the number of dimensions in which a person needs to be deprived in order to consider her multidimensionally poor. One extreme is known as the *union* method of identification which says that a person is poor if she is deprived in at least one dimension. On the other hand, the *intersection* criterion identifies a person as poor if she is deprived in all $d$ dimensions (see Tsui 2002; Atkinson 2003; Bourguignon and Chakravarty 2003). The Alkire–Foster (2011)'s counting approach, in turn, propose an *intermediate* option that contains these two extremes as special cases. According to these

[17]The alternative method, of aggregating first across dimensions and then setting a poverty threshold, will be discussed in Sect. 4.1 below.

authors a person is identified as multidimensionally poor if she is deprived in at least $k$ dimensions, where $1 \leq k \leq d$, whenever dimensions are weighted equally.[18]

To illustrate the concepts better, suppose threshold vector is $z = (9,\ 5, 500)$ and consider the matrix $X$ presented above, which we repeat here for ease of exposition.

$$X = \begin{bmatrix} 9 & 5 & 1200 \\ 6 & 3 & 900 \\ 8 & 6 & 1000 \\ 1 & 4 & 400 \end{bmatrix}$$

According to the union rule the second, third, and fourth persons are multidimensionally poor since each of them is deprived in at least one attribute. Person two is deprived in dimensions 1 and 2, person three is only deprived in dimension 1, whereas person four is deprived in all the dimensions. The intersection approach instead would only identify the fourth person as poor. Finally, if a person is considered multidimensionally poor if she is deprived in at least two dimensions ($k = 2$), then the intermediate approach will identify persons two and four as poor, while person three will be considered non-poor.

As in the case of inequality indices presented in Sect. 3, multidimensional poverty measures can be obtained by defining a set of desirable properties (axioms) that the index should satisfy. Most of the postulates we consider below are immediate generalizations of different axioms proposed for an income poverty index.[19] Unless stated otherwise, all the axioms and indicators presented in this section follow the union rule of identification.[20]

One of the most important postulates in poverty measurement is the requirement of focus on the poor, that is, those whose well-being fall below the poverty threshold. Extending this principle to the multivariate setting has two main variations:

- **Weak Focus (WFC)**: Poverty does not change under an improvement in the achievement of a non-poor person (Bourguignon and Chakravarty 2003).

In the example presented above, since person 1 in distribution $X$ is non-deprived in all three attributes, an increase in this person's achievement in any dimension should not affect poverty. A stronger version of this axiom has also been put forward.

- **Strong Focus (SFC)**: If a person is non-deprived in a dimension, then an increase in his/her achievement in the dimension does not change poverty. This holds irrespective of whether the person is deprived or not in any other dimension. Strong Focus rules out the possibility of reducing poverty by subsidizing a poor per-

[18] When dimensions are not weighted equally, the condition for a person to be considered multidimensionally poor is when the *minimum dimension weight* $\leq k \leq d$.

[19] For discussion on properties of an income poverty index, see Sen (1976), Foster et al. (1984), Donaldson and Weymark (1986), Chakravarty (1983, 2009), Foster and Shorrocks (1991), and Zheng (1997).

[20] We can as well state these axioms for other rules of identifying the poor.

son in a non-deprived dimension but leaving unaffected her achievements in the dimensions where she is deprived.[21]

For example, if the achievement in dimension 3 (income) of the second person reduces to 750, then the distribution matrix becomes $Y = \begin{bmatrix} 9 & 5 & 1200 \\ 6 & 3 & 750 \\ 8 & 6 & 1000 \\ 1 & 4 & 400 \end{bmatrix}$. SFC demands that poverty remains unchanged because this person, while deprived in dimensions 1 and 2, is not deprived in dimension 3.

If instead of affecting the attainments of dimensions for which the person is not deprived, one modifies the achievement in the deprived dimension, poverty measurement should be impacted. For instance, if we reduce achievement in second dimension of person 4 from 4 to 3, poverty should increase. This is required by **monotonicity**.

- **Monotonicity** (**MON**): A reduction in the achievement of a deprived dimension of a poor person increases poverty.

A second type of monotonicity, relevant for the multidimensional setting, has been introduced by Alkire and Foster (2011).

- **Dimensional Monotonicity** (**DIM**): Poverty should not decrease if a poor person who is non-deprived in a dimension becomes deprived in the dimension.

For instance, if person 3 who is not deprived in dimension 2 in $X$ sees her attainment reduced from 6 to 4, and the distribution becomes $Y = \begin{bmatrix} 9 & 5 & 1200 \\ 6 & 3 & 900 \\ 8 & 4 & 1000 \\ 1 & 4 & 400 \end{bmatrix}$, then DIM requires that $P(X; z) \leq P(Y; z)$. While this property is consistent with both the union and intersection approaches, it is particularly important for the intermediate option proposed by Alkire and Foster, where the number of deprivations suffered by individuals plays a crucial role in the measurement of poverty.

As in the case of inequality indices reviewed in Sect. 3, multidimensional poverty indicators are desired to satisfy three postulates related to decomposition, distribution sensitivity within dimensions and correlation sensitivity across dimensions, in addition to invariance and normalization axioms stated in the Appendix.

Two decomposability postulates are used in the poverty measurement context; the first relates to decomposing the measure across population groups and the second across attributes.

- **Subgroup Decomposability** (**SUD**) says that for any partitioning of the population into subgroups with respect to individuals' exogenous characteristic, like age, sex,

[21] Alkire and Foster (2011) refer to strong focus axiom as poverty focus and weak focus as deprivation focus.

region etc., the overall poverty becomes the population share weighted average of poverty levels of individual subgroups.

SUD shows that the percentage contribution made by subgroup $i$ to the overall poverty is $\frac{n_i P(X^i;z)}{nP(X;z)} * 100$, where $n_i$ is the population size of group $i$. Such contributions become helpful in isolating subgroups of the population that are more affected by poverty and hence to formulate anti-poverty policy (see Anand 1997; Chakravarty 1983, 2009; Foster et al. 1984; Foster and Shorrocks 1991). Assuming that $P(X; z)$ satisfies SUD, repeated application of the axiom shows that we can write the poverty indicator as

$$P(X; z) = \frac{1}{n} \sum_{i=1}^{n} P(x_{i.}; z).$$

Given that $P(x_{i.}; z)$ depends only on person $i$'s achievements, we call it 'individual poverty function'. Thus, under SUD, the overall poverty is a simple average of individual poverty levels.

- **Factor Decomposability (FAD)** says that the overall poverty is a weighted average of dimensional poverty levels, such that $P(X; z) = \sum_{j=1}^{d} b_j P(x_{.j}, z_j)$, where $b_j \geq 0$ is the weight assigned to the poverty in dimension $j$ and $\sum_{j=1}^{d} b_j = 1$.

The contribution of dimension $j$ to overall poverty is given by $\frac{b_j P(x_{.j}; z_j)}{P(X;z)}$. FAD was introduced by Chakravarty et al. (1998) and adopted by Alkire and Foster (2011), and is stated under the assumption that only the deprivations of the poor are taken into account and the deprivations of the non-poor are ignored. The coefficient $b_j$ may be interpreted as the importance that a policy maker assigns to eliminating poverty from dimension $j$. Being able to decompose poverty into the different dimensions is particularly attractive in structuring government policy to reduce poverty—by indicating the attributes where deprivations are the largest. But, as in the case of FDE for inequality measures, the cost of imposing this property is that it makes the measure insensitive to changes in the degree of dependence across attributes.

Regarding distributional properties, we consider the poverty counterpart to UM. Discussions for other variants are similar.

- **Multidimensional Transfers Principle (MT)** requires that if a new distribution is obtained by an averaging of achievements among the deprived dimensions of the poor, then poverty should decrease.

In addition, it is often thought to be appropriate that poverty indicators reflect the dependency structure across dimensions. Formally, we consider the following, which is the stronger version of a Bourguignon and Chakravarty (2003) axiom:

- **Increasing Poverty under Correlation Increasing Switch (IPC)** requires that poverty should go up after a switch such that the correlation across dimensions is increased. This property is the equivalent of CIM presented above, where attributes are seen as substitutes.

The intuitive reasoning of this property is that among dimensions that fall below their respective poverty thresholds, one can compensate the insufficiency in one attribute (say, education) with additional quantities of another attribute (say, income). If a switch in the quantities of one of the dimensions is performed across two poor individuals such that the person who is more deprived on a second dimension (income) becomes worse off in the first (education) after the switch and poor person who was richer in income has now higher education, poverty should increase. The corresponding property when the attributes are seen as complements requires poverty to decrease under such a switch (DPC). If a poverty indicator remains insensitive to a correlation—increasing switch, then the attributes are regarded as 'independents'. It is evident that a poverty indicator satisfying FAD cannot satisfy at the same time IPC or DPC. In other words, multidimensional poverty measures that are required to be able to be decomposable by dimension, need to assume that deficiencies in one attribute cannot be compensated or complemented with additions of the other attributes.

### 4.1.2 Indicators

Table 2 presents some examples of multidimensional poverty measures presented in the literature. Chakravarty et al. (1998) (CMR) were among the first to suggest axiomatic multidimensional poverty indicators. One of the most attractive features of this measure is that the function $f(.)$ can be defined such that it becomes generalizations of three well-known one-dimensional poverty indices: the Foster–Greer–Thorbecke (1984), the Chakravarty (1983), and the Watts (1968) unidimensional poverty indices. Tsui (2002) presented a slightly different version of this index that has as special cases both the Charkravarty and the Watts indices.

The CMR indicator satisfies the axioms introduced above, as well as ratio-scale invariance (RSI), except for being sensitive to changes in correlation across attributes. As explained, this is due to the fact that the indicator satisfies FAD which is incompatible with IPC/DPC. In contrast, Tsui's measure is a violator of FAD but satisfies all other axioms including IPC. Tsui also presented a translation invariant poverty index that includes a generalization of the Zheng (2000) single dimensional index and the multidimensional extension of the absolute poverty gap, as special cases.

A highly influential paper in this literature is by Bourguignon and Chakravarty (2003). The measure proposed aggregates a weighted average of individual deprivations across dimensions by taking a power function type transformation over the set of poor persons. The dimension weight $a_j$ may be interpreted as the importance that a policy maker assigns to dimension $j$. The measure $P_{\alpha,\theta}$ is a single-parameter generalization of the Foster–Greer–Thorbecke (1984) single dimensional index.[22] Since $P_{\alpha,\theta}$ is, in general, not additive across dimensions it does not satisfy FAD; however it fulfills all other axioms for all positive values of parameters and MT for a

[22]Bourguignon and Chakravarty (2003) suggested an alternative generalization of this family using the transformation $f(t) = t^{\alpha_j}$, where $\alpha_j > 1$ is a parameter, in CMR indicator.

**Table 2** Poverty

| Authors | Measure | Properties | | | | | | |
|---|---|---|---|---|---|---|---|---|
| | | SFC | WFC | DIM | SUD | FAD | MTP | IPC/DPC |
| Chakravarty, Mukherjee and Ranade (1998) | $P_{CMR}(X;z) = \frac{1}{n}\sum_{i=1}^{n}\sum_{j=1}^{d} b_j\, f\left(\frac{\hat{x}_{ij}}{z_j}\right)$<br>where *f:[0,1] -> R*$^{1}$ is continuous, decreasing, strictly convex, *f(0)* = 1 and *f(1)*=0 | yes | yes | yes | yes | yes | yes | |
| Tsui (2002) | $P_{TCM}(X;z) = \frac{1}{n}\sum_{j=1}^{n}\left[\prod_{j=1}^{d}\left(\frac{z_j}{\hat{x}_{ij}}\right)^{ej} - 1\right]$ | yes | yes | yes | | yes | yes | yes |
| Bourguignon and Chakravarty (2003) | $P_{BC}(X;z) = \frac{1}{n}\sum_{i\in\pi(X;z)}\left[\sum_{j=1}^{d} a_j\left(1-\frac{\hat{x}_{ij}}{z_j}\right)^{\theta}\right]^{\frac{\alpha}{\theta}}$<br>where $\alpha$, $\theta$>0 are parameters, and $a_i$ >0 for all $j = 1, 2, \ldots, d$ with | yes | yes | yes | yes | | ucc | ucc |
| Alkire and Foster (2011) | $P_{AFM}(X;z) = \frac{1}{nd}\sum_{i\in\pi(X;z)}\sum_{j=1}^{d} d_{ij}^{\alpha}(k)$ | yes | yes | yes | yes | yes | ucc | |

(continued)

**Table 2** (continued)

| Authors | Measure | Properties | | | | | | |
|---|---|---|---|---|---|---|---|---|
| | | SFC | WFC | DIM | SUD | FAD | MTP | IPC/DPC |
| Diez, lasso de la Vega and Urrutia (2008) and Chakravarty and D'Ambrosio (2012) | $P_U(X;z) = \frac{\rho}{n \prod_{j=1}^{d} z_j^{\mu_j - \varepsilon}} \sum_{i \in \pi(X;z)} \left[ \prod_{j=1}^{d} z_j^{\mu_j} - \prod_{j=1}^{d} \hat{x}_{ij}^{\mu_j} \right]$ | yes | | yes | yes | | ucc | ucc |
| Maasoumi and Lugo (2008) | $P_{LMM}(X;z) = \left( \begin{array}{l} \frac{1}{n} \sum_{i=1}^{n} \left( 1 - \frac{\left( \sum_{j==1}^{d} c_j (\hat{x}_{ij})^{-\delta} \right)^{\frac{-1}{\delta}}}{\left( \sum_{j==1}^{d} c_j (z_j)^{-\delta} \right)^{\frac{-1}{\delta}}} \right)^{\alpha}, \delta \neq 0, \\ \frac{1}{n} \sum_{i=1}^{n} \left( 1 - \frac{\prod_{j=1}^{d} (\hat{x}_i)^{c_j}}{\prod_{j=1}^{d} (z_j)^{c_j}} \right)^{\alpha}, \delta = 0, \end{array} \right.$ | | yes | yes | yes | | yes | yes |
| Decancq, Fleurbaey, and Maniquet (2013) | $P\_DFM(X; \Re\_((n))) =$ $[1/n \sum 24\_(i=1)^\wedge n \quad \phi(1 - \min\{1, \eta(x\_i, \Re\_i)\})]$ where $\Re\_((n))$ is the vector of preference of individual $n$ | yes | yes | yes | yes | | yes | ucc |

Note: "ucc" refers to "under certain conditions", meaning that the measures could satisfy the property by setting restrictions to the parameters subset of these. $P_{\alpha,\theta}$ satisfies IPC or DPC (and even independence) under alternative assumptions about the parameters.

Alkire and Foster (2011) adopted an intermediate identification method, where people are identified as multidimensionally poor if they are deprived in at least $k$ dimensions, where $1 \leq k \leq d$, when dimensions are equally weighted or in at least minimum weight dimensions, where this is $\leq k \leq d$. $P_{\mathrm{AFM}}$ is the sum of $\alpha$th powers of the normalized achievement gaps of the poor divided by the maximal value that this sum can assume. This measure is subgroup decomposable, and meets MTP for values of the parameter $\alpha > 1$. However, the Alkire–Foster measure is non-decreasing under a correlation increasing switch for all $\alpha > 0$, even if transformations of such measure can permit IPC to be satisfied (see Silber and Yalonetzky 2013, for a recent discussion).

Diez et al. (2008) and Chakravarty and D'Ambrosio (2012) axiomatically characterized the family of unit consistent multidimensional poverty indicator. This family of indices satisfies IPC/DPC under certain conditions, allowing for attributes to be considered substitutes or complement, but does not comply with FAD. In addition, if there are only two dimensions MTP holds for a subset of parameter values.

## *4.2 IMWB-Based Approach to Poverty*

In this subsection we briefly analyze the possibility of accommodating multidimensional poverty indices within the IMWB-based approach to poverty measurement. First, we ask whether standard multidimensional poverty indicators, which use a series of dimension-specific poverty thresholds, correspond to a univariate poverty metric applied to a vector of individual well-being numbers.

The issue can be illustrated using some examples. The first example we consider is Tsui's (2002) generalization of the Chakravarty index. From the formulation (in Table 2) it appears that at the first stage for each individual, a product-type well-being function is used to aggregate allocation of the $d$ dimensions into a measure of personal well-being and then at the second stage a simple averaging is applied to aggregate a transformation of these well-being levels. (All achievement quantities are assumed to be positive.) But this well-being function is implausible in the sense that it is not uniformly sensitive to the given person's achievements below and above poverty thresholds for different dimensions. All achievements above any threshold, however small or large they may be, are replaced by the threshold itself. Therefore, the Tsui (2002) index cannot be regarded as an IMWB-based index. The same remark applies to the Chakravarty–Mukherjee–Ranade (1998), Bourguignon–Chakravarty (2003), and Alkire–Foster (2011) indices.

Different from all these previous proposals, Maasoumi and Lugo (2008) (ML) suggested an indicator of multidimensional poverty that inverts the sequence of steps to derive the measure. Relying on an information theory-based approach, the authors in a first stage aggregate attributes of well-being—as done in Maasoumi (1986)—to obtain an individual well-being function. Dimension-specific poverty thresholds are aggregated using the same criterion defining a poverty frontier. Thus, in the second stage, a person's poverty levels are obtained as the shortfall of the ratio between the aggregated achievements and the aggregated poverty thresholds. The third step involves applying a Foster–Greer–Thorbecke (1984) type transformation over the individual poverty functions across persons to arrive at the overall poverty indicator. By construction, the indicator allows for some degree of substitution across attributes even between those that fall above the dimension-specific poverty threshold. This implies, for instance, that if a person does not have the "minimum acceptable level" of one dimension, say education, but she is, say, extremely income rich, she might be considered non poor. Essentiality of attributes is relaxed, at least to a certain degree, depending on the parameter defining the degree of substitution allowed. Therefore, in terms of postulates, the ML measure satisfies the weak version of the focus axiom, but not the strong one—SFC. In addition, the measure meets MT unambiguously and is subgroup decomposable. However, it satisfies only IPC, that is, all the dimensions are implicitly assumed to be substitutes and compensation across dimensions is allowed.

By construction an IMWB-based index is a violator of the strong focus axioms. One way to resolve this issue is to adopt Decancq et al. (2013) suggestion to look to individual preferences in order to identify the poor and aggregate dimensional achievements. Under these authors' approach, the strong Pareto principle is satisfied among the poor. Furthermore, the assessment of complementarity or substitutability between dimensions is left to the individuals themselves. This contrasts with the direct approach where the complementarity-substitutability issue is resolved by imposing parameter restrictions in the form of composite indicator, which may or may not respect individual preferences.

Specifically, Decancq et al. (2013) have characterized a poverty indicator based on the idea that there is a single poverty threshold vector $z$ and a person is treated as poor if and only if he/she prefers $z$ over his/her current consumption bundle. Thus, this contribution offers a two-fold suggestion: endogenizing the poverty thresholds and using individual preferences in the context of identification of the poor.

## 4.3 Measurement of Multidimensional Poverty for Ordinally Measurable Dimensions

While some of the typical dimensions of well-being and deprivation correspond to ratio scale variables (for instance, income and wealth), others such as health and literacy are generally represented by ordinal variables. (See Alkire's chapter 21 in the OUP Handbook for a similar discussion.) Ordinal variables like gender, ethnicity, and religion have one or more categories or types and their categories have a well-defined ordering rule. For instance, self-reported health is often presented in the following six categories 'very poor', 'poor', 'fair', 'good', 'very good' and 'excellent'. To each of these categories, one can assign positive integral values in an increasing order. This assignment of integral values is arbitrary; the only restriction is that to preserve the ordering a higher number should be assigned to a better category—so that 'very good' should get a higher number than 'good' (see Allison and Foster 2004). A second example can be ordering of educational achievement levels of individuals in a society starting from illiteracy to university education by assigning numbers in an increasing way (see Chakravarty and Zoli 2012). Several indicators of multidimensional poverty have been proposed in the literature to incorporate ordinal characteristic of the dimensions. Ordinal measurability information invariance for a multidimensional poverty indicator requires that the poverty level based on $x_{ij}$ and $z_j$ values should be same as that based on any arbitrary increasing transformation applied to these values, where the transformations need not be the same across dimensions.

The headcount ratio, while a violator of DIM, is an appropriate indicator of multidimensional poverty if some of the dimensions are measurable on ordinal scale and the other dimensions have ratio scale significance. The Alkire–Foster (2011) dimension adjusted headcount ratio also survives this requirement. It is defined as the ratio between the deprivation score of the poor in the Alkire–Foster (intermediate) sense and $nd$, which is the society deprivation count when all the persons become deprived in all the dimensions.[23] (This is a limiting case of $P_{\text{AFM}}$ as $\alpha \rightarrow 0$ and it satisfies DIM (see Table 2)).

Chakravarty and D'Ambrosio (2006) suggested an indicator of multidimensional social exclusion when the dimensions have ordinal significance. This normalized indicator verifies SFC, SUD, DIM but not FAD. It is non-decreasing under a correlation increasing switch, but not increasing.[24] A related indicator is proposed by Bossert et al. (2013) who characterize a multidimensional indicator where the dimensions are discrete in nature and used it for evaluating material deprivation in the European Union. They have defined a person as materially deprived if his deprivation score is at least one. The measure satisfies similar properties as the previous index.

## 5 Conclusions

The increasing interest among both academics and policy makers in alternative conceptualizations of well-being and deprivation that take into account multiple dimensions has spawned the development of a wide range of measures of multidimensional inequality and poverty. The present chapter attempted to summarize, in a structured way, the main relevant considerations in developing these measures. Within both inequality and poverty, the discussion has been divided into two lines: the direct approach—where a set of desirable properties or postulates in terms of multidimensional matrices are first identified and then measures satisfying these properties

[23]For a recent discussion on the counting approach to multidimensioned deprivation, see Dutta and Yalonetzky (2014).

[24]Jayaraj and Subramanian (2009) employed this indicator to determine multidimensional poverty in India.

are obtained; and the inclusive measure of well-being approach, where a multidimensional indicator of inequality or poverty is derived by applying a social welfare function, univariate inequality measure, or univariate poverty measure to a vector of individual well-being numbers that take account of each individual's multidimensional achievements.

Irrespective of the approach and set of properties chosen, selecting any scalar indicator to summarize the complete distribution of well-being or deprivation attributes across individuals involves imposing important value judgments. There is no escape from that, and thus, there will be always grounds to object to any given multidimensional indicator. However, it is vitally important that policy makers be aware of the full range of normatively plausible options. It may be worthwhile to mention that, following the literature, our formulation in this chapter uses directly individual achievements. Therefore, our presentation has ignored individual preferences. Research on multidimensional poverty and inequality metrics continues to be extremely fertile; alternative new postulates and indicators are proposed on a regular basis. Although there has been tremendous progress in this area, reviewed in this chapter, there is much still to learn.

**Acknowledgements** We are grateful to the editors for their comments and suggestions. We also thank Koen Decancq and Sabina Alkire who went through an earlier draft of the chapter and offered many helpful suggestions.

## Appendix

Let $x_{ij} \geq 0$ be the achievement of person $i$ in attribute or dimension $j$. An achievement indicates the performance of a person in a dimension, for instance, how much is his or her income. Person $i$'s achievements in different dimensions are summarized by a $d$-dimensional vector $x_{i.} = (x_{i1}, x_{i2}, \ldots, x_{id})$. The row vector $x_{i.}$ is the $i$th row of an $n \times d$ distribution matrix $X$. The column vector $x_{.j}$, which summarizes the distribution of achievements in dimension $j$ ($j = 1, 2, \ldots, d$) among $n$ persons, is the $j$th column of $X$ and we denote the mean of this vector by $\mu(x_{.j})$. If we denote the set all $n \times d$ matrices whose entries are non-negative real numbers by $M_1^n$, then $X \in M_1^n$. Similarly, $M_2^n$ stands for the set of all distribution matrices such that $x_{ij} \geq 0$ for all pairs $(i, j) \in \{1, 2, \ldots, n\} \times \{1, 2, \ldots, d\}$ and $\mu(x_{.j}) > 0$ for all $1 \leq j \leq d$. Finally, $M_3^n$ denotes the set of all distribution matrices such that $x_{ij} > 0$ for all pairs $(i, j) \in \{1, 2, \ldots, n\} \times \{1, 2, \ldots, d\}$. Thus, for matrices in the sets $M_2^n$ and $M_3^n$ the mean of each attribute is positive. Since our analysis will often involve different-sized populations, it will be necessary to consider the set $M_1 = \cup_{n \in N} M_1^n$ of all distribution matrices with $d$ columns. Let $M_2$ and $M_3$ be the corresponding sets associated with $M_2^n$ and $M_3^n$ and $\boldsymbol{M} = \{M_1, M_2, M_3\}$. We denote an arbitrary element of the set $\boldsymbol{M}$ by $M$, that is, the set $M$ can be anyone of the three $M_i$ sets.

An $n \times n$ matrix $B$ with non-negative entries is called a bistochastic matrix of order $n$ if each of its columns and rows sums to unity. Any permutation matrix is a bistochastic matrix, but the converse is not true.

An $n \times n$ matrix is called a diagonal matrix of order $n$ if its off-diagonal elements are equal to zero, but diagonal elements may or may not be equal to zero. Throughout this chapter we will consider diagonal matrices with positive diagonal entries. We will denote a diagonal matrix $\Omega$ of order $n$ by $\Omega = \text{diag}(\omega_1, \omega_2, \ldots, \omega_d)$, where $\omega_i > 0$ for all $i$.

For any $n \in N$, $X, Y \in M^n$, $X$ is said to be obtained from $Y$ by a simple increment if $x_{ij} = y_{ij} + \delta$ for some pair $(i, j) \in \{1, 2, \ldots, n\} \times \{1, 2, \ldots, d\}$, where $\delta > 0$ is a scalar and $x_{lk} = y_{lk}$ for all pairs $(l, k) \in \{1, 2, \ldots, n\} \times \{1, 2, \ldots, d\}$ such that $(l, k) \neq (i, j)$.

*Axioms for multidimensional inequality indices*

- **Ratio Scale Invariance (RSI)**: An inequality indicator $I : M \to \Re^1$ is a ratio scale invariant or relative indicator if for all $n \in N$, $X \in M^n$,

$$I(X\Omega) = I(X), \tag{1}$$

where $\Omega = \text{diag}(\omega_1, \omega_2, \ldots, \omega_d)$, $\omega_i > 0$ for all $i$.

- **Unit Consistency (UCO)**: For any $n \in N$, $X^1, X^2 \in M^n$, $I(X^1) < I(X^2)$ implies that $I(X^1\Omega) < I(X^2\Omega)$ for all $\Omega = \text{diag}(\omega_1, \omega_2, \ldots \omega_d)$, $\omega_i > 0$ for all $i$.
- **Translation Scale Invariance (TSI)**: An inequality indicator $I : M \to \Re^1$ is a translation scale invariant or an absolute indicator if for all $n \in N$, $X \in M^n$,

$$I(X + A) = I(X), \tag{2}$$

where $A$ is any $n \times d$ matrix with identical rows such that $X + A \in M$.

- **Symmetry (SYM)**: For all $n \in N$, $X \in M^n$, $I(\Pi X) = I(X)$, where $\Pi$ is any $n \times n$ permutation matrix.
- **Population Replication Invariance (PRI)**: For all $n \in N$, $X \in M^n$, $I(X) = I(X^{(l)})$, where $X^{(l)}$ is the $l$-fold replication $X$, that is, $X^{(l)} = \begin{pmatrix} X^1 \\ X^2 \\ \vdots \\ X^l \end{pmatrix}$ with each $X^i = X$, and $l \geq 2$ is any integer.
- **Normalization (NOM)**: For all $n \in N$, $X \in M^n$, if $X$ has identical rows, then $I(X) = 0$.
- **Continuity (CON)**: For all $n \in N$, $I(X)$ is a continuous function.
- **Uniform Pigou–Dalton Transfers Principle (UPD)**: For all $n \in N$, $X, Y \in M^n$ if $X$ is obtained by pre-multiplying $Y$ by a $T$-transformation, then $I(X) < I(Y)$,

where a $T$-transformation is a linear transformation defined by an $n \times n$ matrix $T$ of the form $T = tIM_n + (1-t)\Pi_{ij}$, for some $t \in (0, 1)$, $IM_n$ is the $n \times n$ identity matrix, and $\Pi_{ij}$ is the $n \times n$ permutation matrix that interchanges the $i$ and $j$ coordinates for some $i, j \in \{1, 2, \ldots, n\}$.

*Definition*: Let $X, Y \in M^n$. Distribution $Y$ is derived from $X$ by a *PDB transfer* if there exist two individuals $p$, $q$ such that: (i) $x_q > x_p$; (ii) $y_m = x_m \forall m \neq p, q$; (iii) $y_q = x_q - \delta$ and $y_p = x_p + \delta$ where $\delta = (\delta_1, \ldots, \delta_d) \in \Re^d_+$ with at least one $\delta_j > 0$; (iv) $y_q \geq y_p$.

- **Pigou–Dalton Bundle Transfer Principle** (**PBT**): For all $n \in N$, $X, Y \in M^n$ if $Y$ is obtained from $X$ by a finite sequence of PBD transfers, then $I(Y) \leq I(X)$.
- **Uniform Majorization Principle** (**UM**): For all $n \in N$, $X, Y \in M^n$, if $X = BY$ for some $n \times n$ bistochastic matrix $B$ that is not a permutation matrix, then $I(X) < I(Y)$.

*Definition*: For $a, b \in R^d$, define $a \vee b = (\max\{a_1, b_1\}, \ldots, \max\{a_d, b_d\})$ and $a \wedge b = (\min\{a_1, b_1\}, \ldots, \min\{a_d, b_d\})$. For $X, Y \in M^n$, we say that $X$ is obtained from $Y$ by a *correlation increasing switch* if $X \neq Y$ and there exist $1 \leq i, l \leq n$ such that (i) $x_{i.} = y_{i.} \wedge y_{l.}$, (ii) $x_{l.} = y_{i.} \vee y_{l.}$, (iii) $x_{i_1.} = y_{i_1.}$ for all $i_1 \notin \{i, l\}$. That is, a correlation increasing switch between two individuals means a rearrangement of their achievements such that one of them ($l$) receives at least as much of every attribute as the other ($i$) and more of at least one attribute.

- **Correlation Increasing Majorization** (**CIM**): For all $n \in N$, $X, Y \in M^n$, if $Y$ is obtained from $X$ by a correlation increasing switch, then $I(X) < I(Y)$.
- **Unfair Rearrangement** (**UR**): For all $n \in N$, $X, Y \in M^n$, if $Y$ is obtained from $X$ by a sequence of dimension-wise permutations which make one individual in $Y$ top-ranked in all dimensions, another individual second-ranked in all dimensions as so forth, and $Y \neq X$, then $I(X) < I(Y)$.
- **Subgroup Decomposability** (**SDE**): For all $n_1, n_2 \in N$, $X \in M^{n_1}$, $Y \in M^{n_2}$, $I(X, Y)^{/} = A\Big(I(X), I(Y); \underline{\mu}(X), \underline{\mu}(Y); n_1, n_2\Big)$, where the aggregative function $A$ is continuous and increasing in first two arguments, $\underline{\mu}(X)$ and $\underline{\mu}(Y)$ are the vectors of means of attributes corresponding to the distribution matrices $X$ and $Y$ respectively and / denotes transpose.
- **Factor Decomposability** (**FDE**): For all $n \in N$, $X \in M^n$, $I(X) = \sum_{j=1}^{d} I\big(x_{.j}\big)$.

*Axioms for multidimensional poverty indices*

- **Normalization** (**NOM**): For any $(X; z) \in M^n \times Z$ if $x_{ij} \geq z_j$ for all $i$ and $j$, then $P(X; z) = 0$.
- **Symmetry** (**SYM**): For any $(X; z) \in M^n \times Z$, $P(X; z) = P(\Pi X; z)$, where $\Pi$ is any $n \times n$ permutation matrix.
- **Population Replication Principle** (**PRI**): For any $(X; z) \in M^n \times Z$, $P(X; z) = P\big(X^{(l)}; z\big)$, where $X^{(l)}$ is the $l$-fold replication of $X$.
- **Ratio Scale Invariance** (**RSI**): For all $(X; z) \in M^n \times Z$, $P(X; z) = P(X\Omega; z\Omega)$, where $\Omega = \mathrm{diag}(\omega_1, \omega_2, \ldots \omega_d)$, $\omega_i > 0$ for all i.

- **Weak Focus (WFC)**: For $X, Y \in M^n$ if for some $i$, $x_{ij} \geq z_j$ for all $j$ and for some $j \in \{1, 2, \ldots, d\}$, $y_{ij} = x_{ij} + \eta$, where $\eta > 0$, and $x_{hk} = y_{hk}$ for all $(h, k) \neq (i, j) \in \{1, 2, \ldots, n\} \times \{1, 2, \ldots, d\}$, then $P(Y; z) = P(X; z)$.
- **Strong Focus (SFC)**: Suppose $Y \in M^n$ is obtained from $X \in M^n$ such that for some pair $(i, j) \in \{1, 2, \ldots, n\} \times \{1, 2, \ldots, d\}$, $y_{ij} = x_{ij} + \eta$, where $x_{ij} \geq z_j$, $\eta > 0$, and $x_{hk} = y_{hk}$ for all $(h, k) \neq (i, j) \in \{1, 2, \ldots, n\} \times \{1, 2, \ldots, d\}$. Then $P(Y; z) = P(X; z)$.
- **Monotonicity (MON)**: Suppose $Y \in M^n$ is obtained from $X \in M^n$ such that for some pair $(i, j) \in \{1, 2, \ldots, n\} \times \{1, 2, \ldots, d\}$, $y_{ij} = x_{ij} - c$, where $i \in \pi(X)$, $x_{ij} < z_j$, $c > 0$, and $x_{hk} = y_{hk}$ for all $(h, k) \neq (i, j) \in \{1, 2, \ldots, n\} \times \{1, 2, \ldots, d\}$. Then, $P(Y; z) > P(X; z)$.
- **Dimensional Monotonicity (DIM)**: Suppose $Y \in M^n$ is obtained from $X \in M^n$ such that for some pair $(i, j) \in \{1, 2, \ldots, n\} \times \{1, 2, \ldots, d\}$, $y_{ij} = x_{ij} - c < z_j$, where $i \in \pi(X)$, where $\pi(X)$ is the set of poor persons in $X$, $x_{ij} \geq z_j$, $c > 0$, and $x_{hk} = y_{hk}$ for all $(h, k) \neq (i, j) \in \{1, 2, \ldots, n\} \times \{1, 2, \ldots, d\}$. Then, $P(Y; z) > P(X; z)$.
- **Subgroup Decomposability (SUD)**: For any $X^1, X^2, \ldots, X^l \in M$ and $z \in Z$, $P(X; z) = \sum_{i=1}^{l} \frac{n_i}{n} P\left(X^i; z\right)$, where $X = (X^1, \ldots, X^l)^/ \in M^n$, / denotes transpose, $n_i$ is the population size associated with $X^i$ and $\sum_{i=1}^{l} n_i = n$.
- **Factor Decomposability (FAD)**: For any $(X; z) \in M^n \times Z$, $P(X; z) = \sum_{j=1}^{d} b_j P\left(x_{.j}, z_j\right)$, where $b_j \geq 0$ is the weight assigned to the poverty in dimension $j$ and $\sum_{j=1}^{d} b_j = 1$.
- **Multidimensional Transfers Principle (MT)**: For any $X, Y \in M^n$ if $X$ is obtained from $Y$ by an averaging of achievements among the deprived dimensions of the poor, then $P(X; z) < P(Y; z)$.
- **Increasing Poverty under Correlation Increasing Switch (IPC)**: Under SUD, for any $X \in M^n$, if $Y \in M^n$ is obtained from $X$ by a correlation-increasing switch between two poor persons, then $P(X; z) < P(Y; z)$, given that the two attributes are substitutes.

# References


Alkire, S., & Foster, J. E. (2010). *Designing the inequality-adjusted Human Development Index (IHDI)*. Human Development Research Papers (2009 to Present) HDRP-2010-28, Human Development Report Office (HDRO), United Nations Development Programme.

Alkire, S., & Foster, J. E. (2011). Counting and multidimensional poverty measurement. *Journal of Public Economics, 95,* 476–487.

Alkire, S., & Santos, M. E. (2010). *Acute multidimensional poverty: A new index for developing countries*. OPHI Working Paper Series #38. Oxford, UK: Oxford University, Oxford Poverty and Human Development Initiative.

Allison, R. A., & Foster, J. E. (2004). Measuring health inequality using qualitative data. *Journal of Health Economics, 23*(3), 505–524.

Anand, S. (1997). Aspects of poverty in Malaysia. *Review of Income and Wealth, 23,* 1–16.

Atkinson, A. B. (1970). On the measurement of inequality. *Journal of Economic Theory, 2,* 244–263.

Atkinson, A. B. (2003). Multidimensional deprivation: Contrasting social welfare and counting approaches. *Journal of Economic Inequality, 1,* 51–65.
Atkinson, A. B., & Bourguignon, F. (1982). The comparison of multidimensioned distributions of economic status. *Review of Economic Studies, 49,* 183–201.
Atkinson, A. B., & Bourguignon, F. (1987). Income distribution and differences in needs. In G. F. Feiwel (Ed.), *Arrow and the foundation of the theory of economic policy* (pp. 350–370). London: Macmillan.
Atkinson, A. B., Cantillion, B., Marlier, E., & Nolan, B. (2002). *Social indicators. The EU and social inclusion.* Oxford: Oxford University Press.
Atkinson, A. B., Marlier, E., Monatigne, F., & Reinstadler, A. (2010). Income poverty and income inequality. In A. B. Atkinson & E. Marlier (Eds.), *Income and living conditions in Europe*. Luxemburg: Eurostat.
Banerjee, A. K. (2010). A multidimensional Gini index. *Mathematical Social Sciences, 60*(2), 87–93.
Boland, P. J., & Prochan, F. (1988). Multivariate arrangement increasing functions with applications in probability and statistics. *Journal of Multivariate Analysis, 25,* 286–298.
Bosmans, K., Decancq, K., & Ooghe, E. (2013). What do normative indices of multidimensional inequality really measures? CORE DP 2013/35.
Bosmans, K., Lauwers, L., & Ooghe. E. (2009). A consistent multidimensional Pigou–Dalton transfer principle. *Journal of Economic Theory, 144*, 1358–1371.
Bossert, W., Chakravarty, S. R., & D'Ambrosio, C. (2013). Multidimensional poverty and material deprivation with discrete data. *Review of Income and Wealth, 59,* 29–43.
Bourguignon, F. (1999). Comment on multidimensioned approaches to welfare analysis by E. Maasoumi. In J. Silber (Ed.), *Handbook of income inequality measurement* (pp. 477–484). London: Kluwer Academic.
Bourguignon, F., & Chakravarty, S. R. (2003). The measurement of multidimensional poverty. *Journal of Economic Inequality, 1,* 25–49.
Chakravarty, S. R. (1983). A new index of poverty. *Mathematical Social Sciences, 6,* 307–313.
Chakravarty, S. R. (2006). An axiomatic approach to multidimensional poverty measurement via fuzzy sets. In G. Betti & A. Lemmi (Eds.), *Fuzzy set approach to multidimensional poverty measurement* (pp. 49–92). New York: Springer.
Chakravarty, S. R. (2009). *Inequality, polarization and poverty: Advances in distributional analysis*. New York: Springer.
Chakravarty, S. R., & D'Ambrosio, C. (2006). The measurement of social exclusion. *Review of Income and Wealth, 52,* 377–398.
Chakravarty, S. R., & D'Ambrosio, C. (2012). A family of unit consistent multidimensional poverty indices. In V. Berenger & F. Bresson (Eds.), *Monetary poverty and social exclusion around the mediterranean sea*. New York: Springer.
Chakravarty, S. R., Mukherjee, D., & Ranade, R. (1998). On the family of subgroup and factor decomposable measures of multidimensional poverty. *Research on Economic Inequality, 8,* 175–194.
Chakravarty, S. R., & Silber, J. (2008). Measuring multidimensional poverty: The axiomatic approach. In N. Kakwani & J. Silber (Eds.), *Quantitative approaches to multidimensional poverty measurement*. New York: Palgrave Macmillan.
Chakravarty, S. R., & Zoli, C. (2012). Stochastic dominance relations for integer variables. *Journal of Economic Theory, 147*(4), 1331–1341.
CONEVAL. (2010). Methodology for Multidimensional Poverty Measurement in Mexico. Consejo Nacional de Evaluación de la Política de Desarrollo Social.
Cummins, R. A. (1996). Domains of life satisfaction: An attempt to order chaos. *Social Indicators Research, 38*(3), 303–328.
Dalton, H. (1920). The measurement of the inequality of incomes. *Economic Journal, 30,* 348–461.
Dardanoni, V. (1996). On multidimensional inequality measurement. In C. Dagum & A. Lemmi (Eds.), *Research on economic inequality* (Vol. 6, pp. 201–205). London: JAI Press.

Decancq, K. (2012). Elementary multivariate rearrangements and stochastic dominance on a Fréchet class. *Journal of Economic Theory, 147*(4), 1450–1459.
Decancq, K. (2014). Copula-based measurement of dependence between dimensions of well-being. *Oxford Economic Papers, 66*(3), 681–701.
Decancq, K., Fleurbaey, M., & Maniquet, F. (2013). *Multidimensional poverty measurement: Shouldn't we take preferences into account*? Mimeographed. Brussels: CORE.
Decancq, K., & Lugo, M. A. (2012). Inequality of well-being: A multidimensional approach. *Economica, 79,* 721–746.
Decancq, K., & Lugo, M. A. (2013). Weights in multidimensional indices of well-being: An overview. *Econometric Reviews, 32,* 7–34.
Diez, H., Lasso de la Vega, M. C., & Urrutia, A. M. (2008). Multidimensional unit- and subgroup consistent inequality and poverty measures: Some characterization results. *Research on Economic Inequality, 16,* 189–211.
Donaldson, D., & Weymark, J. A. (1986). Properties of fixed-population poverty indices. *International Economic Review, 27,* 667–688.
Doyal, L., & Gough, I. (1991). *A theory of human need.* Basinkstoke: Macmillan.
Duclos, J. Y., Sahn, D. E., & Younger, S. D. (2006). Robust multidimensional poverty comparisons. *Economic Journal, 116,* 943–968.
Duclos, J. Y., Sahn, D. E., & Younger, S. D. (2007). Robust multidimensional poverty comparisons with discrete indicators of well-being. In S. P. Jenkins & J. Micklewright (Eds.), *Poverty inequality re-examined.* Oxford: Oxford University Press.
Dutta, I., & Yalonetzky, G. (2014). *The 'Counting' approach to multidimensional deprivation.* Mimeo.
Ebert, U. (1988). Measurement of inequality: An attempt at unification and generalization. *Social Choice and Welfare, 5,* 147–169.
Epstein, L. G., & Tanny, S. M. (1980). Increasing generalized correlation: A definition and some economic consequences. *Canadian Journal of Economics, 13*(1), 16–34.
Ferreira, F., & Lugo, M. A. (2013). Multidimensional poverty analysis: Looking for a middle ground. *The World Bank Research Observer, 28,* 220–235.
Fleurbaey, M., & Maniquet, F. (2011). Compensation and responsibility. In K. J. Arrow, A. K. Sen, & K. Suzumura (Eds.), *Handbook of social choice and welfare* (Vol. 2). Amsterdam: North-Holland.
Fleurbaey, M., & Trannoy, A. (2003). The impossibility of a Paretian egalitarian. *Social Choice and Welfare, 21,* 243–264.
Foster, J. E., Greer, J., & Thorbecke, E. (1984). A class of decomposable poverty measures. *Econometrica, 42,* 761–766.
Foster, J. E., & Shorrocks, A. F. (1991). Subgroup consistent poverty indices. *Econometrica, 59,* 687–709.
Gajdos, T., & Weymark, J. A. (2005). Multidimensional generalized Gini indices. *Economic Theory, 26,* 471–496.
Jacobs, R., Smith, P., & Goddard, M. (2004). *Measuring performance: An examination of composite performance indicators.* CHE Technical Paper Series 29, Centre for Health Economics, University of York.
Jayaraj, D., & Subramanian, S. (2009). A Chakravarty-D'Ambrosio view of multidimensional deprivation: Some estimates for India. *Economic and Political Weekly, 45*(6), 53–65.
Klasen, S. (2000). Measuring poverty and deprivation in South Africa. *Review of Income and Wealth, 46*(1), 33–58.
Kolm, S.-C. (1969). The optimal production of social justice. In J. Margolis & H. Guitton (Eds.), *Public economics* (pp. 145–200). London: Macmillan.
Kolm, S. C. (1976). Unequal inequalities I. *Journal of Economic Theory, 12,* 416–442.
Kolm, S. C. (1977). Multidimensional egalitarianism. *Quarterly Journal of Economics, 91,* 1–13.
Koshevoy, G., & Mosler, K. (1996). The Lorenz zonoid of a multivariate distribution. *Journal of the American Statistical Association, 91*(434), 873–882.

Krishnakumar, J., & Nadar, A. (2008). On exact statistical properties of multidimensional indices based on principal components, factor analysis, MIMIC and structural equation models. *Social Indicators Research, 86*(3), 481–496.
Lasso de la Vega, C., Urrutia, A., & Sarachu, A. (2010). Characterizing multidimensional inequality measures which fulfil the Pigou-Dalton bundle principle. *Social Choice and Welfare, 35*(2), 319–329.
List, C. (1999). *Multidimensional inequality measurement: A proposal*. Economics Series Working Papers 1999-W27, University of Oxford, Department of Economics.
Maasoumi, E. (1986). The measurement and decomposition of multi-dimensional inequality. *Econometrica, 54,* 991–997.
Maasoumi, E., & Lugo, M. A. (2008). The information basis of multivariate poverty assessments. In N. Kakwani & J. Silber (Eds.), *Quantitative approaches to multidimensional poverty measurement*. New York: Palgrave Macmillan.
Marshall, A. W., Olkin, I., & Arnold, B. (2011). *Inequalities: Theory of majorization and its applications*. New York: Springer.
Muller, C., & Trannoy, A. (2011). A dominance approach to the appraisal of the distribution of well-being across countries. *Journal of Public Economics, 95*(3–4), 239–246.
Muller, C., & Trannoy, A. (2012). Multidimensional inequality comparisons: A compensation perspective. *Journal of Economic Theory, 147*(4), 1427–1449.
Nardo, M., Saisana, M., Saltelli, A., & Taranto, S. (2005). *Tools for composite indicators building.* EUR 21682 EN, European Communities.
Nussbaum, M. C. (2000). *Women and human development: The capabilities approach*. Cambridge: Cambridge University Press.
OECD. (2011). *How is life? Measuring well-being*. Paris: OECD Publishing. http://dx.doi.org/10.1787/9789264121164-en.
Pigou, A. C. (1912). *Wealth and welfare*. London: Macmillan.
Pogge, T. (2002). *World poverty and human rights: Cosmopolitan responsibilities and reforms*. Cambridge: Polity Press.
Ramsay, M. (1992). *Human needs and the market*. Aldershot: Avebury.
Ravallion, M. (1996). Issues in measuring and modeling poverty. *Economic Journal, 106,* 1328–1343.
Ravallion, M. (2011). On multidimensional indices of poverty. *Journal of Economic Inequality, 9,* 235–248.
Rawls, J. (1971). *A theory of justice*. Cambridge: Harvard University Press.
Rousseau, J. J. (1754). *Discourse on the origin and basis of inequality among men*. Paris.
Sen, A. K. (1973). *On economic inequality*. New York: Norton.
Sen, A. K. (1976). Poverty: On ordinal approach to measurement. *Econometrica, 44,* 219–231.
Sen, A. K. (1985). *Commodities and capabilities*. Amsterdam: North-Holland.
Sen, A. K. (1992). *Inequality re-examined*. Cambridge, MA: Harvard University Press.
Sen, A. K. (1993). In M. Nussbaum (Ed.), *The quality of life*. Oxford: Clarendon Press.
Shorrocks, A. F. (1982). Inequality decomposition by factor components. *Econometrica, 50*(1), 193–211.
Silber, J., & Yalonetzky, G. (2013). Measuring multidimensional deprivation with dichotomized and ordinal variables. In G. Betti & A. Lemmi (Eds.), *Poverty and social exclusion: New methods of analysis*. Abingdon: Routledge.
Smith, A. (1776). *An inquiry into the nature and causes of the wealth of the nations* (1 ed.). London: W. Strahan.
Stewart, F. (1985). *Basic needs in developing countries*. Baltimore, MD: Johns Hopkins University Press.
Stiglitz, J., Sen, A. K., & Fitoussi, J. P. (2009). *Report by the Commission on the Measurement of Economic Performance and Social Progress*. www.stiglitz-sen-fitoussi.fr.
Streeten, P. (1981). *First things first: Meeting basic human needs in developing countries*. New York, Oxford: Oxford University Press.

Tchen, A. (1980). Inequalities for distributions with given margins. *The Annals of Probability, 8*, 814–827.

Thorbecke, E. (2008). Multidimensional poverty: Conceptual and measurement issue. In N. Kakwani & J. Silber (Eds.), *The many dimensions of poverty* (pp. 3–20). New York: Palgrave Macmillan.

Townsend, P. (1979). *Poverty in the United Kingdom: A survey of household resources and standards of living*. Harmondsworth: Penguin Books.

Tsui, K.-Y. (1995). Multidimensional generalizations of the relative and absolute inequality indices: The Atkinson-Kolm-Sen approach. *Journal of Economic Theory, 67*, 251–265.

Tsui, K.-Y. (1999). Multidimensional inequality and multidimensional generalized entropy measures: An axiomatic derivation. *Social Choice and Welfare, 16*.

Tsui, K.-Y. (2002). Multidimensional poverty indices. *Social Choice and Welfare, 19*, 69–93.

Watts, H. (1968). An economic definition of poverty. In D. P. Moynihan (Ed.), *On understanding poverty*. New York: Basic Books.

Weymark, J. A. (2006). The normative approach to the measurement of multidimensional inequality. In F. Farina & E. Savaglio (Eds.), *Inequality and economic integration*. London: Routledge.

Weymark, J. A. (2013). *Conundrums for nonconsequentialists*. Vanderbilt University Department of Economics Working Papers 13-00010, Vanderbilt University Department of Economics.

Zheng, B. (1997). Aggregate poverty measures. *Journal of Economic Surveys, 11*, 123–162.

Zheng, B. (2000). Minimum distribution-sensitivity, poverty aversion and poverty orderings. *Journal of Economic Theory, 95*.

Zheng, B. (2007a). Unit-consistent decomposable inequality measures. *Economica, 74*, 97–111.

Zheng, B. (2007b). Unit-consistent poverty indices. *Economic Theory, 31*, 113–142.

MIX
Papier aus verantwortungsvollen Quellen
Paper from responsible sources
FSC® C105338

If you have any concerns about our products,
you can contact us on
**ProductSafety@springernature.com**

In case Publisher is established outside the EU,
the EU authorized representative is:
**Springer Nature Customer Service Center GmbH**
**Europaplatz 3, 69115 Heidelberg, Germany**

Printed by Libri Plureos GmbH
in Hamburg, Germany